Spirit of God

EDITED BY
Susan Mader Brown, Mark E. Ginter,
and Joseph G. Mueller, SJ

TRANSLATED BY
Susan Mader Brown, Mark E. Ginter,
Joseph G. Mueller, SJ, and
Catherine E. Clifford

Yves Congar, OP

Spirit of God

SHORT WRITINGS ON
THE HOLY SPIRIT

THE CATHOLIC UNIVERSITY
OF AMERICA PRESS
Washington, D.C.

Part 1: The Human Spirit and the Spirit of God
originally published as *Esprit de l'homme, Esprit de Dieu*,
Foi Vivante 206 by Editions du Cerf, Paris. Copyright © 1983
Editions du Cerf, Paris.
Part 2: A Theology of the Holy Spirit originally published as
"Pneumatologie dogmatique," in *Initiation à la pratique de la
théologie*, tome 2, Dogmatique 2, éd. Bernard Lauret and
François Réfoulé by Editions du Cerf, Paris.
Copyright © 1982 Editions du Cerf
(Paris: Cerf), 483–516.
English translation and editing (including selection, introduction,
notes, and bibliography) Copyright © 2018
The Catholic University of America Press
All rights reserved

Library of Congress Cataloging-in-Publication Data
Names: Congar, Yves, 1904–1995, author.
Title: Spirit of God : short writings on the Holy Spirit /
Yves Congar, OP ; edited by Susan Mader Brown, Mark E. Ginter,
and Joseph G. Mueller, SJ ; translated by Susan Mader Brown,
Mark E. Ginter, Joseph G. Mueller, SJ, and Catherine E. Clifford.
Description: Washington, D.C. : The Catholic University of America
Press, 2018. | Includes bibliographical references and index.
Identifiers: LCCN 2017042301 | ISBN 9780813237077
(pbk)
Subjects: LCSH: Holy Spirit. | Catholic Church—Doctrines.
Classification: LCC BT122 .C65513 2018 | DDC 231/.3—dc23
LC record available at https://lccn.loc.gov/2017042301

Dedicated to our much-loved families—
natural, religious, and academic

Contents

Abbreviations ix

General Introduction 1
by Mark E. Ginter with Susan Mader Brown
and Joseph G. Mueller, SJ

A Word about the Translation 10

Part One: The Human Spirit and the Spirit of God, 15

1. Evidence of the "Holy Spirit" in the Past and Today 19
2. Difficulties: Critical Objections 23
3. The Spirit Is the Source of Life in Us Personally and in the Church 36
4. A Theology of the Third Person 52

Conclusion 68

Part Two: A Theology of the Holy Spirit, 71

1. Testimony about the Holy Spirit 75
2. The Spirit in the Personal Prayer and in the Personal Lives of Christians 83
3. An Ecclesiological Pneumatology 87
4. The Spirit Is the Breath *of the Word* and the Spirit *of the Son* 102

5. The Spirit, the Eschatological Gift, Brings the "Redemption" to Fulfillment	114
Bibliography	121

Part Three: The Promise of the Father (Acts 1:4), 125

Article 1. Theology of the Holy Spirit and Theology of History	131
Article 2. The Holy Spirit in the Thomistic Theology of Moral Action	145
Article 3. Pneumatology or "Christomonism" in the Latin Tradition?	162

Part Four: Pneumatological Ecclesiology, 197

Article 4. Pneumatology Today	203
Article 5. Christological and Pneumatological Implications of Vatican II's Ecclesiology	225
Article 6. The Third Article of the Creed: The Impact of Pneumatology on the Life of the Church	243

Selected Bibliography (in addition to sources listed in Bibliography at the end of Part Two)	265
Index of Biblical References	285
General Index	289

Abbreviations

Editions of the Collected Works of St. Thomas Aquinas

LC   *Sancti Thomae Aquinatis doctoris angelici opera omnia iussu impensaque/Leonis XIII.P.M. edita* (some volumes have the general title: *Opera omnia iussu edita Leonis XIII. P.M.*). Edited by the members of the Leonine Commission. Rome: Sta. Sabina, 1882–.

Parma   *Sancti Thomae Aquinatis doctoris angelici ordinis praedicatorum opera omnia ad fidem optimarum editionum accurate recognita*. 25 vols. Parmae: Tipis Petri Fiaccadori, 1852–73; reprinted New York: Musurgia, 1950.

Vivès   *Doctoris angelici divi Thomæ Aquinatis Opera omnia*. Ed. Stanislas Édouard Fretté and Paul Maré. 34 vols. Parisiis: Apud Ludovicum Vivès, 1871–80.

Individual Works of St. Thomas Aquinas

1, 2, 3, 4 Sent.   *Commentum in primum/secundum/tertium/quartum librum sententiarum magistri Petri Lombardi* (Vivès) or *Scriptum super libros sententiarum magistri Petri Lombardi episcopi Parisiensis*, I–IV. Parisiis: Lethielleux, 1929–47.

ST   *Summa theologica* (Vivès) or *Summa theologiæ* (LC).

Writings of Yves M.-J. Congar

ES   *Je crois en l'Esprit Saint*. 3 vols. Paris: Cerf, 1979–80.

HS   *I Believe in the Holy Spirit*. 3 vols. Trans. David Smith. London: Geoffrey Chapman / New York: Seabury, 1983; reprinted as part of the Milestones in Catholic Theology Series. New York: Crossroad Herder, 1997. ET of *ES*.

Documents of the Second Vatican Council

AA *Apostolicam Actuositatem*, Decree on the Apostolate of the Laity

AG *Ad Gentes Divinitus*, Decree on the Missionary Activity of the Church

CD *Christus Dominus*, Decree on the Pastoral Office of Bishops in the Church

DH *Dignitatis Humanae*, Declaration on Religious Freedom

DV *Dei Verbum*, Dogmatic Constitution on Divine Revelation

GS *Gaudium et Spes*, Pastoral Constitution on the Church in the Modern World

LG *Lumen Gentium*, Dogmatic Constitution on the Church

OE *Orientalium Ecclesiarum*, Decree on Eastern Catholic Churches

OT *Optatam Totius*, Decree on Priestly Formation

PO *Presbyterorum Ordinis*, Decree on the Ministry and Life of Priests

SC *Sacrosanctum Concilium*, Constitution on the Sacred Liturgy

UR *Unitatis Redintegratio*, Decree on Ecumenism

Other Abbreviations

AAS *Acta Apostolicae Sedis.* Vatican City: Typis Polyglottis Vaticanis, 1909–.

ANF The Ante-Nicene Fathers. 10 vols. Ed. Alexander Roberts and James Donaldson with A. Cleveland Coxe. New York: Charles Scribner's Sons, 1903–17.

CSEL Corpus scriptorum ecclesiasticorum latinorum.

D Henricus Denzinger et Clemens Bannwart, Iohannes Bapt. Umberg, et Carolus Rahner, *Enchiridion symbolorum, definitionum et declarationum de rebus fidei et morum*. Friburgi Brisg.–Barcinone, 1953.

DS Denzinger, Henry and Aldofus Schönmetzer. *Enchiridion symbolorum, definitionum et declarationum de rebus fidei et morum*. 33d ed. Freiburg im Breisgau: Herder, 1965. ET: J. Neuner and J. Dupuis, eds. *The Christian Faith in the Doctrinal Documents of the Catholic Church*, 7th ed., rev. and enlarged. New York: Alba House, 2001.

DictSpir	*Dictionnaire de spiritualité: Ascétique et mystique, doctrine et histoire*. 17 vols. Edited by Marcel Viller et al. Paris: Beauchesne, 1937–95.
DTC	*Dictionnaire de théologie catholique*. 15 vols. Edited by Jean Michel Alfred Vacant and E. Mangenot et al. Paris: Letouzey et Ané, 1899–1950.
Harvey	*Sancti Irenaei episcopi Lugdunensis libros quinque adversus haereses*. Ed. W. W. Harvey. Cambridge: Cambridge University Press, 1857.
Mansi	Mansi, J. D. *Sacrorum conciliorum nova et amplissima collectio*, 54 vols. Paris: H. Welter, 1901–27.
NPNF	Select Library of Nicene and Post-Nicene Fathers of the Christian Church. 1st series, 14 vols. 2d series, 14 vols. H. Wace and P. Schaff, eds. New York: Christian, 1887–1900.
PG	Migne, J.-P. Patrologiae cursus completus, Series graeca, 161 vols. Paris: Lutetiae Parisiorum-Montrouge, 1857–66.
PL	Migne, J.-P. Patrologiae cursus completus, Series latina, 221 vols. Paris: Migne-Montrouge, 1844–64.
SChr	Sources chrétiennes. Collection edited by H. de Lubac and J. Daniélou, later, C. Mondésert. Paris: Cerf, 1942–.
TDNT	*Theological Dictionary of the New Testament*. Trans. G. W. Bromiley. 10 vols. Grand Rapids, Mich. and London: Eerdmans, 1964–76. ET of *TWNT*.
TWNT	*Theologisches Wörterbuch zum Neuen Testament*. Gerhard Kittel and Gerhard Friedrich, eds., 10 vols. Stuttgart: W. Kohlhammer, 1933–79.

Spirit of God

General Introduction

Mark E. Ginter with Susan Mader Brown
and Joseph G. Mueller, SJ

Spirit of God brings together eight significant apologetic and scholarly writings on the Holy Spirit by Yves Cardinal Congar, OP (1904–95), previously untranslated into English. These publications also touch upon the fields of patristic and medieval theology, fundamental and sacramental theology, Christology and ecclesiology, spirituality and ecumenism. They show Congar's familiarity not only with the Catholic tradition but also with Orthodox and Protestant perspectives. One of the most influential theologians at Vatican II, Congar is widely regarded as the most significant voice in Catholic pneumatology in the twentieth century. The nearly 1800 articles and books in Congar's bibliography treat a broad range of theological topics,[1] but pneumatology became the focus of his last works,

---

1. Joseph Famerée and Gilles Routhier, *Yves Congar*, Initiations aux théologiens (Paris: Cerf, 2008), 55. Sources of Congar's bibliography are: Pietro Quattrochi, "General Bibliography of Fr. Yves M-J. Congar," in Jean-Pierre Jossua, OP, *Yves Congar: Theology in the Service of God's People*, trans. Sr. Mary Jocelyn, OP (Chicago: The Priory Press, 1968), 185–241; Aidan Nichols, "An Yves Congar Bibliography 1967–1987," *Angelicum* 66 (1989): 422–66; Gabriel Flynn, "Appendix: An Yves Congar Bibliography 1987–1995, with Addenda: 1996–2002," in Gabriel Flynn, *Yves Congar's Vision of the Church in a World of Unbelief* (Aldershot, Hampshire; Burlington, Vt.: Ashgate, 2004), 229–33; "Select Bibliography," in *Yves Congar: Theologian of the Church*, ed. Gabriel Flynn, Louvain Theological & Pastoral Monographs 32 (Peeters Press / W. B. Eerdmans: Louvain, 2005), 465–68; and Jean-Marie Vezin, "Une présentation raisonnée de

especially his trilogy, *Je crois en l'Esprit Saint* [*I Believe in the Holy Spirit*], which appeared in 1979–80[2] and his short work *La Parole et le Souffle* [*The Word and the Spirit*], published in 1984.[3]

Chronologically, the eight writings in this volume originally appeared in the following order:

1969   "Pneumatologie ou 'christomonisme' dans la tradition latine?" ("Pneumatology or 'Christomonism' in the Latin Tradition?")

1971   "Pneumatologie et théologie de l'Histoire" ("Theology of the Holy Spirit and Theology of History")

1974   "Le Saint-Esprit dans la théologie thomiste de l'agir moral" ("The Holy Spirit in the Thomistic Theology of Moral Action")

1981   "Les implications christologiques et pneumatologiques de l'ecclésiologie de Vatican II ("Christological and Pneumatological Implications of Vatican II's Ecclesiology")

1982   "Pneumatologie dogmatique" ("A Theology of the Holy Spirit")

1983   *Esprit de l'homme, Esprit de Dieu* (*The Human Spirit and the Spirit of God*) originally published as *Geist und Heiliger Geist* in *Christlicher Glaube in moderner Gesellschaft: Eine enzyklopädische Bibliothek in 30 Teilbänden* (Freiburg: Herder, 1982), 22:59–116.

1983   "Actualité de la pneumatologie" ("Pneumatology Today")

---

la bibliographie d'Yves Congar," *Transversalités: Revue de l'Institut catholique de Paris* 98 (2006): 37–59.

2. *Je crois en l'Esprit Saint*, 3 vols. (Paris: Cerf, 1979–1980); ET: *I Believe in the Holy Spirit*, 3 vols., trans. David Smith (London: Geoffrey Chapman / New York: Seabury, 1983). Hereafter, the three volumes are cited as *ES* 1, 2, 3 (French) or *HS* 1, 2, 3 (ET).

3. *La Parole et le Souffle*, Jésus et Jésus-Christ 20 (Paris: Desclée, 1984); ET: *The Word and the Spirit*, trans. David Smith (London: Geoffrey Chapman, 1986).

1985   "Le troisième article du symbole: L'impact de la pneumatologie dans la vie de l'Église" ("The Third Article of the Creed: The Impact of Pneumatology on the Life of the Church.")

We decided to arrange these short works thematically in four parts so they could be more easily understood. Parts One and Two are brief presentations of the pneumatology outlined in *I Believe in the Holy Spirit*. Intended for different audiences, they cover correspondingly different but somewhat overlapping material. Part One, originally an article written for a theological reference book published in German, was intended for nonspecialists and was published in the next year as a separate French monograph directed to a popular audience. It is more apologetic in character than the chapter, included as our Part Two, taken from a multivolume introduction to theology whose intended audience was those preparing for ordination or some other ecclesial ministry. In this piece, Congar takes for granted his audience's interest in the Holy Spirit, and his focus is to explain rather than to defend Catholic teaching. Part Three considers specific theological topics—theology of history, the moral life, sacramental theology, and ecclesiology—to which pneumatology makes an important contribution. Part Four summarizes modern developments in pneumatology and shows how those developments influenced both the ecclesiology of the Second Vatican Council and the Church in the post-conciliar period.

From his first full-time teaching assignment in 1932 at the Dominican House of Studies for the French province in exile in Belgium, Le Saulchoir, until his later years at Couvent Saint-Jacques in Paris, Congar was keenly interested in the credible articulation of the Catholic tradition. He never lost sight of his pastoral role as a priest and always retained a sense of obligation to present the Catholic faith accurately but effectively to those who did not yet appreciate what it offered. Having experienced the effect upon religious practice of two world wars and the drastic social changes of the twentieth century, he was aware of how one's context can affect how one hears the gospel message, and he was anxious to present the faith in such a way that its truth could be heard by people today. Furthermore, as a scholar with a vast knowledge of the history of the tradition, he knew that the essentials of the Catholic tradition had been presented over the centuries in different manners and with different degrees of effectiveness. Congar was not inclined simply to repeat familiar formulae. His approach was more creative, because he wanted to renew the face that the Church turned toward the world.

In the short works included in this collection, Congar's originality is apparent in several ways: (1) he continually connects his theological work to experience—human experience in general and the experience of living out the Gospel as a person of faith; (2) he explains the enduring importance for the whole Church of the Charismatic Renewal, while warning against the dangers of "pneumatocentrism" (this is connected with his concern to relate theology to the lived faith experience of believers); (3) Congar demonstrates such a thorough ecumenical consciousness that he will not discuss any controverted issue concerning the Holy Spirit without considering the implications of that issue for dialogue with ecumenical partners; (4) Congar's direct focus upon pneumatology, at a time when the Holy Spirit was usually discussed only as part of the treatises on the Trinity or Soteriology or Grace or Sacraments, argued (and argues) for a revision of Catholic dogmatics that puts pneumatology on par with Christology, with its own distinctive slot in the core seminary curriculum;[4] (5) Congar's sustained investigation of the mission of

---

4. See the United States Conference of Catholic Bishops, *Program for Priestly Formation*, 5th ed. (Washington, D.C.: USCCB, 2006), #202: "In dogmatic theology, the core must include theology of God, One and Three, Christology, Creation, the Fall and the nature of sin, redemption, grace and the human person, ecclesiology, sacraments, eschatology, Mariology, and missiology." Bernard Lauret and François Refoulé were breaking new ground with their five-volume *Initiation à la pratique de la théologie* (Paris: Cerf) when it first appeared in 1982, but the seeds they sowed have yet to mature fully.

the Holy Spirit in the life of Christ, his disciples, and the Church recovered biblical, patristic, and medieval perspectives to develop a "new-yet-old" pneumatological Christology,[5] pneumatological sacramental theology,[6] pneumatological anthropology and pneumatological ecclesiology;[7] (6) his balanced work in pneumatological ecclesiology contributed to, and continues to influence, the post-conciliar attempt to revision the Church, once presented as *societas perfecta*, as a communion of persons analogous to the Holy Trinity.[8]

---

5. Philip Caldwell, *Liturgy as Revelation: Re-Sourcing a Theme in Catholic Theology*, Renewal: Conversations in Catholic Theology (Minneapolis: Fortress, 2014); Vincent Holzer, "Karl Rahner, Hans Urs von Balthasar, and Twentieth-Century Catholic Currents on the Trinity," trans. Francesca A. Murphy, in *The Oxford Handbook of the Trinity*, ed. Gilles Emery and Matthew Levering (Oxford: Oxford University Press, 2012); Peter D. Neumann, *Pentecostal Experience: An Ecumenical Encounter*, Princeton Theological Monograph Series 187 (Eugene, Ore.: Pickwick, 2012); Jaroslav Z. Skira, "Breathing with Two Lungs: The Church in Yves Congar & John Zizioulas," in *In God's Hands: Essays on the Church and Ecumenism in Honor of Michael A. Fahey, S.J.*, ed. Jaroslav Z. Skira and Michael S. Attridge, Bibliotheca ephemeridum theologicarum Lovaniensium 199 (Leuven: Peeters and Leuven University Press, 2006), 283–306.

6. Yves Congar, "The *Ecclesia* or Christian Community as a Whole Celebrates the Liturgy," in *At the Heart of Christian Worship: Liturgical Essays of Yves Congar*, trans. and ed. Paul Philibert (Collegeville, Minn.: Liturgical Press / A Pueblo Book, 2010). On p. 15, Philibert describes this article as "a work of synthesis of the highest order." In his view, "nothing quite like it exists, and it has never been surpassed." See also Douglas M. Koskela, *Ecclesiality and Ecumenism: Yves Congar and the Road to Unity* (Milwaukee, Wisc.: Marquette University Press, 2008) and Isaac Kizhakkeparampil, *The Invocation of the Holy Spirit as Constitutive of the Sacraments according to Cardinal Yves Congar* (Rome: Gregorian University Press, 1995).

7. Elizabeth Groppe writes: "Yves Congar's distinctive contribution to a contemporary Roman Catholic theology of the Holy Spirit is his insight into the pressing need to reunite spiritual anthropology and ecclesiology. He himself advanced this reunion through his elaboration of both a pneumatological anthropology and a pneumatological ecclesiology." *Yves Congar's Theology of the Holy Spirit* (New York: Oxford University Press, 2004), 138.

8. The references here could be multiplied quickly. A recent, widely disseminated example is Pope Benedict XVI's encyclical letter *Caritas in Veritate* (*Love in Truth*), June 29, 2009. See especially no. 54, which speaks about the Church as God's sign and instrument of communion for all of humanity. Anthony Oelrich also acknowledges a shift in Congar's understanding of Church authority as a result of this developing pneumatology. See *A Church Fully Engaged: Yves Congar's Vision of Ecclesial Authority* (Collegeville, Minn.: Liturgical Press / A Michael Glazier Book, 2011).

While Congar did not ignore or undervalue the pneumatological work of Protestant theologians, it was the Orthodox critique of Roman Catholic pneumatology that most strongly influenced his thinking in the post-conciliar period. Even though he had written about the Holy Spirit before Vatican II, a pivotal event in the development of Congar's pneumatology came from what appeared at the time to be a rather minor luncheon meeting on Oct. 17, 1963, with two Orthodox Christian observers of the Council, with whom Congar had been meeting regularly to solicit their comments upon the proposed documents. One was the Russian Orthodox theologian, Fr. Alexander Schmemann, and the other was the Greek Orthodox theologian, Dr. Nikos A. Nissiotis. While Congar's private journal of the Council narrates this meeting in an unremarkable way,[9] Congar's writings on the Holy Spirit from that time forward manifest his efforts to reply to Nissiotis's claim that Catholic ecclesiology lacks a real pneumatology and that this results in a deficient anthropology. Nissiotis's comments really drove Congar to think more deeply about the Holy Spirit and about the impact of pneumatology upon Roman Catholic theology.[10]

Looking back upon Congar's writings, one can see that a cou-

9. Yves Congar, OP, *My Journal of the Council*, translated by Mary John Ronayne, OP, and Mary Cecily Boulding, OP, edited by Denis Minns, OP (Collegeville, Minn.: Liturgical Press / Michael Glazier, 2012), 382–83.

10. He mentions the meeting with Nissiotis in several publications, including "Pneumatology Today," *The American Ecclesiastical Review* 167 (1973): 435, and "The Spirit in Action," in *Called to Life*, trans. William Burridge (Slough: St. Paul Publications / New York: Crossroad, 1987), 60. The longest narration of the meeting is in *HS* 2:66. The longest reply to that conversation is the entire second volume of *HS*, a fact that Congar acknowledges later in *The Word and the Spirit*, 121, n. 48. In this same footnote Congar also lists as his reply to that conversation our Part Three, Article 3 below. In "Pneumatologie ou 'christomonisme' dans la tradition latine?" *Ephemerides theologicae Lovanienses* 45 (1969): 395, n. 5, Congar cites Nissiotis thus: "A true pneumatology is one that describes and explains life in the freedom of the Spirit and in the concrete communion of the historical Church, the essence of which lies not in the Church itself nor in its institutions." "Pneumatologie orthodoxe," in the collection *Le Saint-Esprit* (Geneva: Labor et fides / Paris: Librairie protestante, 1963), 85–106, at 91.

ple of articles "announced" the development of his thought,[11] but the publication that really began to disclose this development is the 1969 article in honor of Msgr. Gérard Philips, "Pneumatology or 'Christomonism' in the Latin Tradition?" which we have included in Part Three.[12] Congar accepted Nissiotis's critique, at least to the extent that he acknowledged that the implications of Roman Catholic pneumatology were not always well-understood or explained, and he used that critique as a tool with which to chisel out a more precise Catholic pneumatology with anthropological, Christological, and ecclesiological facets. Before the Council, Congar had sculpted one figure of the Holy Spirit, along the lines of Tertullian's "vicar of Christ." However, after the Council he began work on a different figure of the Holy Spirit, along the lines of Irenaeus's "two hands of God."[13] Famerée and Routhier write, "If the preconciliar Congarian theology is very Christocentric, the Spirit is evidently not absent in it, but the Spirit's role is clearly subordinated to Christ."[14] His post-conciliar work gave more emphasis to the work of the Holy Spirit and looked for a balance between that work and Christ's.[15]

---

11. The following articles are essentially the same: "La pneumatologie dans la théologie catholique," *Revue des sciences philosophiques et théologiques* 51 (1967): 250–58, and "Saint-Esprit en théologie catholique," in *Vocabulaire œcuménique*, ed. Yves Congar (Paris: Cerf, 1970), 197–210. The first uses footnotes, whereas the second puts all of the citations within the body of the text. Congar identifies Nissiotis as his main catalyst for writing on the Holy Spirit. Although Congar is erudite as usual, his argument is not as coherent in these articles as it is in the publication we mention next.

12. "Christomonism" designates a theological emphasis on Christ that is so strong that it undervalues the Holy Spirit and ignores or wrongly conceives the relationship between the two. Congar's article on Christomonism referred to here specifies beliefs that might typify this emphasis, as well as figures in Catholic intellectual history who evidence some Christomonist tendencies.

13. See Rémi Chéno, "Les retractationes d'Yves Congar sur le rôle de l'Esprit Saint dans les institutions ecclésiales," *Revue des sciences philosophiques et théologiques* 91 (2007): 265–84.

14. Famerée and Routhier, *Yves Congar*, 149, our translation.

15. See Groppe, *Yves Congar's Theology of the Holy Spirit*, 48, 75; Aidan Nichols, *Yves Congar*, (London: Geoffrey Chapman / Wilton, Conn.: Morehouse-Barlow, 1989), 61.

While Congar's pneumatology seemed to have benefitted from Nissiotis's criticism, not all Orthodox theologians concurred in Nissiotis's perspective. A notable, and irenic, example is that of the then Fr. John D. Zizioulas. Zizioulas accepted Congar's research and argument. Zizioulas states that it is just as true of the Western Fathers as it is of the Eastern Fathers that to speak of Christ is, at the same time, to speak of the Father and of the Holy Spirit.[16] Zizioulas continues, "[t]o speak of 'Christomonism' in any part of the Christian tradition is to misunderstand or be unfair to this part of tradition (Fr. Congar has shown this with regard to the Roman Catholic Western Tradition)."[17] Zizioulas acknowledged Congar's unique and influential position among contemporary theologians by citing the French Catholic more than any other living theologian in his book *Being as Communion*.[18]

Retrospectively, Congar believed that he had given a reply to the criticism that the whole of the Western Catholic tradition lacks a pneumatology in the theology of the Eucharist, of grace, and of the Mystical Body, and in ecclesiology generally.[19] Furthermore, he had outlined the explicit place given to the Holy Spirit by the Second Vatican Council.[20] Even more, though, he had begun after the

---

16. John D. Zizioulas, *Being as Communion: Studies in Personhood and the Church*, with a foreword by John Meyendorff (Crestwood, N.Y.: St. Vladimir's Seminary Press, 1985), 111.

17. Ibid., 127. See also John D. Zizioulas, *Communion and Otherness: Further Studies in Personhood and the Church*, ed. Paul McPartlan (New York: T&T Clark, 2006), 189, n. 30.

18. Twenty-one times. In *Communion and Otherness*, Zizioulas cites Congar's work nine times.

19. In *HS* 3:228–74, Congar refers to "Pneumatology or 'Christomonism' in the Latin Tradition?" as well as to *HS* 1:151–57, 163.

Tragically, Nissiotis's life was cut short by an automobile accident in 1986, but his published writings up to that time do not comment on Congar's reply to him, even though he multiplied his criticisms of Western Christian theology by warning that the emotion-driven charismatic movement was the result of a deep deficiency in pneumatology. See "Visions of the Future of Ecumenism," *Greek Orthodox Theological Review* 26 (Winter 1981): 290.

20. *HS* 1:167–73 and in this volume Part Four, Article 5.

Council to elaborate a full ecclesiological pneumatology.[21] "I would agree," wrote Congar in the mid-eighties, "that the criticism of 'Christomonism' in Western Catholicism is to some extent right, but I have, I think, shown that this is being corrected."[22] Again looking back upon his work, Congar stated:

> The way is now open for a real pneumatology to be developed in the Church. I must have had a premonition of what would have to be done when I wanted the first volume in my series 'Unam Sanctam' to be a new translation into French of Möhler's *Die Einheit in der Kirche*.... It is more important here to mention the developments that have led me to try to elaborate a full ecclesiological pneumatology since the Council.[23]

Almost two generations in the Church and in the world now have no living memory of Vatican Council II or of some of the great people who influenced it. Although Famerée and Routhier think that it is especially risky to mark out these giants with summary formulas, they cautiously offer the following description characterizing Congar:

> ... truth, for that was his passion and his vocation; dialogue, for it was in meeting and exchange that it was built, trying continually to expand its horizon; reform, for it was to this patient labor that he was vowed; resistance, for he never abdicated before a system that denied freedom and no longer sought the truth; servant, because it was in this spirit that he worked tirelessly for unity, his passion and his life.[24]

This small collection of Congar's work was assembled with the assumption that readers would have a certain familiarity with the Scriptures, Church history, and theological terminology. Yet, it will also introduce his ideas to a new generation lacking that background. Occasionally, Congar wrote as if he had the foresight to recognize those two audiences, and we are grateful for his legacy.

---

21. *HS* 2 and in this volume Part Two, section 3.
22. *The Word and the Spirit*, 117.
23. Ibid., 115.
24. Famerée and Routhier, *Yves Congar*, 51, our translation.

A Word about the Translation

In translating Congar's words, we have tried to remain faithful both to the substance and to the style of the French text from which we worked. Our aim has been to make Congar's ideas and his enthusiasm accessible to contemporary readers. To the extent that it has been possible to do so, we have supplemented Congar's notes by giving complete publication data and by noting, in square brackets, where passages to which he refers would be found in English translations. For those writings of St. Thomas Aquinas that are cited frequently enough to appear in our list of abbreviations, we have simply given the standard reference in the note. We have adopted the same policy when citing patristic and medieval sources for which a complete bibliographical entry, including information about English translations, appears either in Congar's General Bibliography at the end of Part Two or in our Select Bibliography (pp. 265–83). If we have noticed any errors in Congar's references, we have also noted these in square brackets unless they appear to be typographical or transcription errors (reading a handwritten IV as III, for example). Such errors we have usually corrected without drawing attention to them. All notes in our translation are numbered sequentially, starting with 1 for the first note in each section or article in a given part of the book, and when we insert our own note into our translation of Congar, we put "[trans.]" into the note immediately after the note number. When this system modifies the original numbering of Congar's own notes, we signify the original note number in square brackets at the end of each of his notes thus affected.

Congar's familiarity with the Scriptures derived from his liturgical life as much as from his scholarly tasks. His biblical references do not seem to be drawn from any one source, perhaps because he is quoting the Bible from memory or translating from the Latin. We have simply translated into English Congar's versions of the biblical passages.

Since the publication of these short pieces, theological writing has changed in at least two respects, both of which arise from a desire to acknowledge the equal dignity of all persons before God and a concern lest a more traditional use of language be experienced as hurtful. We need to say a word about how we have handled these challenges.

For one thing, out of respect for those, especially the Jewish people, who do not acknowledge the Lordship of Jesus the Messiah, many now customarily use BCE (before the Common Era) and CE (Common Era) in place of BC (before Christ) and AD (*anno Domini* [in the year of our Lord]). The new terminology, originally used only by scholars, is now becoming increasingly familiar even to the general public and so we have employed it here, even though Congar's original text employed the older terms.

Secondly, many of our contemporaries, conscious of the ways in which masculine language for God has been misused, opt for more gender-neutral language for God, whenever this can be done without a distortion of meaning. In his own writings, Congar employed masculine pronouns for the Holy Spirit. This was, of course, what was required grammatically, since in French *esprit* is a masculine noun. Three decades ago, however, the use of masculine language for God would have been more conventional and less politically charged than it is today in North America. The writings by Congar presented here were meant to focus the reader's attention on the reality of the Holy Spirit and the effects of the Holy Spirit on the individual and on the Christian community, not to make a point in a hotly contended debate over the propriety of using gendered language for God. We did not want our translations to suggest more partisanship on this issue than we think it fair to attribute to Congar. Consequently, we have aimed for translations that are as neutral as possible on this question. In most places, this has simply meant that we have substituted "the Spirit" for "il/he," using, in effect, the noun itself instead of the masculine pronoun which from time to time takes its place in the French. In the handful of places in which we could not see how to offer an unobtrusively neutral translation, we have retained Congar's masculine pronouns.[1] Also, whenever we have made use of published translations, we have retained the language used therein.

We would also like to signal the occasional appearance in our translation of a term, "theologal," that may be unfamiliar to readers. The English translation of the *Catechism of the Catholic Church* sometimes retains the distinction made in the original French text between *théologal* (that which is oriented to God) and *théologique* (that which pertains to the study of theology), employing the term "theologal" as the equivalent of the French *théologal*.[2] On the one hand, since the term "theologal" appears in the *Catechism*, we have

1. For Congar's take on God language and gender, see *ES* 3:181–218; ET: *HS* 3:133–64. Here he notes that the Bible avoids attributing sex to God but that the idea that male and female people are images of God (Genesis 1:27) implies that in God there are dimensions that correspond, respectively, to maleness and femaleness, albeit in transcendent form. He backs up this idea by noting the feminine characterizations (tenderness, wisdom) of God and of Jesus in the Bible and in the monastic tradition. He believes that Christian reflection ultimately attributes the feminine character of God to the Holy Spirit. He cites as evidence mother images of the Spirit in Jewish Christian and Syriac traditions; the Spirit-as-Eve theme in Methodius of Olympus, fourth-century Nicene theologians, and John of Damascus; and nineteenth- and twentieth-century theological developments of these two strands of Christian reflection. Finally, Congar develops his own account of the maternal functions of the Spirit in the life of Christ and of the Christian, as well as in the functioning of the Christian tradition. Throughout this treatment, he retains the use of the masculine pronoun for the Spirit and for God.

2. See, for example, nos. 2607, 2686, and 2803, but note that "vertus *théologales*" is translated, as is customary, by "*theological* virtues" in nos. 1812ff. and in no. 2656.

used it on occasion, rather than "godly," to render Congar's *théologal*. On the other hand, we have rendered Congar's *les vertus théologales* as "theological virtues."[3]

We have furnished each part of our translation with a brief introduction. These short texts were written by Mark E. Ginter, with the editorial assistance of Susan Mader Brown and Joseph G. Mueller, SJ. Mark Ginter composed the indices at the end of this volume, too.

Finally, we would like to acknowledge the assistance we have received from others. We are particularly grateful for the preliminary work done by Sr. Clare Smith, RSM, emerita of Saint Meinrad School of Theology and for the helpful suggestions on early drafts of Part One by the late Friar Thomas Potvin, OP, of the Collège dominicain in Ottawa, a former student of Congar's. And we are grateful for the contribution of Fr. Ernest Falardeau, SS, who was kind enough to look over the articles in Parts Three and Four for which Susan Brown is the sole translator, as well as for the suggestions made by those who reviewed our manuscript for the Catholic University of America Press. The deficiencies of the translation are, of course, our responsibility.

Susan Mader Brown
Mark E. Ginter
Joseph G. Mueller, SJ
Catherine E. Clifford

---

3. Congar actually uses the term "theologal" more broadly than just with reference to faith, hope, and charity. For a further explanation, see the introduction to Part Three, n. 8.

PART ONE

The Human Spirit and the Spirit of God

Overview

1. Evidence of the "Holy Spirit" in the Past and Today | 19
   1. In Israel | 19
   2. In the early Church | 20
   3. Today | 21

2. Difficulties: Critical Objections | 23
   1. The world remains unchanged | 23
   2. It encourages irrationality | 24
   3. It devalues the body | 25
   4. It is only a projection of our yearnings and our potential | 27
   5. It is only the unfolding of world history … | 30

3. The Spirit is the Source of Life in Us Personally and in the Church | 36
   1. The need for an interior life | 37
   2. The act of prayer | 39

Part One is a translation by Susan Mader Brown, Catherine E. Clifford, and Mark E. Ginter of *Esprit de l'homme, Esprit de Dieu*, Foi vivante 206 (Paris: Cerf, 1983), originally published as *Geist und Heiliger Geist* in *Christlicher Glaube in moderner Gesellschaft: Eine enzyklopädische Bibliothek in 30 Teilbänden* (Freiburg: Herder, 1982), 22:59–116.

3. Source of liberty | 41

4. Liberation that is not purely interior and spiritual | 42

5. The Spirit, joined to the Word and source of communion, gives rise to renewals and reforms that do not lead to anarchy | 46

6. The Spirit distributes "charisms" and thus gives rise to a Church that lives also from its "grassroots" | 49

4. A Theology of the Third Person | 52

1. A long and difficult history | 52

2. Three who are One | 54

3. Three "Persons"? | 56

4. The Spirit is fulfillment, the Gift that completes and perfects | 60

5. Two approaches to the mystery: East and West (*Filioque*) | 61

Conclusion | 68

This piece, a requested summary of *I Believe in the Holy Spirit*, offers a compact, contemporary defense of the claim that "God is present and active in our lives by a non-coercive Power" and of the Church's teaching about the Holy Spirit. Its value is indicated by the frequency with which it is cited by scholars,[1] as well as by the fact that it was re-issued in French in 1998 and remains in print in several languages.

Sections 1, 3, and 4 take much of their material from *HS*. How-

---

[1]. See, for example, the work of the Austrian moralist Gerhard Holotik, *Die pneumatische Note der Moraltheologie: Ein ergänzender Beitrag zu gegenwärtigen Bemühungen im Rahmen der katholischen Sittlichkeitslehre* (Vienna: VWGÖ, 1984) and that of the American systematician Elizabeth Groppe, who presents the most thorough exposition and analysis of Congar's pneumatology to date in *Yves Congar's Theology of the Holy Spirit* (New York: Oxford University Press, 2004). Out of the twenty-one references made by Holotik to Congar's writings, a third of them cite *Geist und Heiliger Geist*. Groppe makes eighteen references to *Esprit de l'homme, Esprit de Dieu*. She most frequently refers to chapters 2 and 3 of that work, as does Holotik.

ever, section 2, which summarizes the main sorts of objections made to traditional claims about the Holy Spirit, is different. The style is colloquial and recalls two of Congar's earlier writings on the Holy Spirit: his anticipated, although not realized, talk for the student pilgrimage to Chartres Cathedral for Pentecost in 1956,[2] and his "Holy Spirit and Spirit of Freedom," preached in 1958.[3] Congar had treated the Renewal in the Spirit in *HS 2* from the perspective of a defensive insider, so to speak, but in *Esprit de l'homme, Esprit de Dieu*, he takes the perspective of a sympathetic "outsider." Especially for those personally involved in, or studying, the Renewal, as Congar preferred to call it, this little work remains relevant. While there is an abundance of personal anecdote and witness about the Holy Spirit from members of the Charismatic Renewal, there is a continuing need for a contemporary theological explanation of such phenomena from a distinctively Catholic ecclesial perspective.

---

2. The exact origin of Congar's wonderful little book *La Pentecôte: Chartres 1956* (Paris: Cerf, 1956), seems unresolved. It appears that he could *not* have preached this pilgrimage to Chartres Cathedral for Pentecost in May 1956, because he was exiled in England at the time. The English translator A. V. Littledale, who put together two of Congar's books, *Esquisses du mystère de l'Église* (Paris: Cerf, 1941) [new ed., Unam Sanctam 8 (Paris: Cerf, 1953; 3d ed. Paris: Cerf, 1963; Foi vivante 18 (Paris: Cerf, 1966)] and *La Pentecôte: Chartres 1956*, in *The Mystery of the Church: Studies by Yves Congar*, added this playful note about *La Pentecôte: Chartres 1956*: "[It] purports to be a discourse delivered to a group of pilgrims as they made their dusty way towards Chartres, where they were due to arrive for the feast of Pentecost. The manner, therefore, is naturally colloquial, even breezy; we see in our mind's eye, the shorts and the loaded haversacks, which, to judge from some of the references, must have held, besides articles of more common necessity, at least some of the volumes of Migne" (p. vi). More recently, Famerée and Routhier wrote: "Regarding *La Pentecôte—Chartres 1956*, it is a booklet of 157 pages intended for the 'Chartres Pilgrimage' of Pentecost 1956 and written in January of that year just before the departure of the theologian for his English 'exile.'" Joseph Famerée and Gilles Routhier, *Yves Congar*. Initiations aux théologiens (Paris: Cerf, 2008), 209–10.

3. *Laity, Church and World: Three Addresses by Yves Congar*, trans. Donald Attwater (London: Geoffrey Chapman, 1960), 1–34.

Evidence of the "Holy Spirit" in the Past and Today

1. In Israel

In the Christian branch of religion, itself an offshoot of Judaism, a claim pervades all times and places. Its unanimity is impressive, considering the diversity of sources from which it comes. The claim is this: God is present and active in our lives by a non-coercive Power that we call the Holy Spirit. The following examples, chosen from among the hundreds available, attest to this.

There are the seventy elders who assist Moses (about 1230 BCE). "When the Spirit rested upon them, they prophesied" (Nm 11:25). There is Samuel (about 1040 BCE) who says to Saul, "You will run into a group of prophets.... The spirit of Yahweh will then come upon you, and you will enter into ecstasy with them, and be changed into another man" (1 Sm 10:5–6).

About 580 BCE, there is Ezekiel who says, "The spirit lifted me up ..." (3:12). "I shall give you," says God, "a new heart, and put a new spirit in you; I shall remove the heart of stone from your body and give you a heart of flesh instead. I shall put my spirit in you ..." (36:26–27). Prophecy, so characteristic of the history of Israel, involves this experience: "The Lord Yahweh has sent me with his spirit" (Is 48:16, about 550 BCE). This is how the prophets explain the promises of God: "I shall pour out my spirit on all flesh..." (Joel 3:1, about 330 BCE). This is the text to which Peter refers on the day of Pentecost to say: this is becoming a reality, this is what you are witnessing (Acts 2:17).

2. In the early Church

The coming of Jesus, the undisputed and indisputable one, attests to the reality of the Spirit. His birth, his mission, his actions all originate with the Spirit. And he promises the Spirit to his disciples: "When they hand you over, do not worry about what to say... for the Spirit of your Father will speak through you" (Mt 10:19–20). "Without being reborn through water and the Spirit, no one can enter the kingdom of God" (Jn 3:5). "I shall pray to the Father, and he will give you another Paraclete, the Spirit of truth" (Jn 14:16). "The Paraclete, the Holy Spirit, will teach you everything and remind you of all I have said to you" (Jn 14:26, 16:13).

This, then, is the experience of the Church. The Church is "We Christians," and so the Church's experience is the experience of disciples within it, for "we were all baptized in a single Spirit to form only one body, Jews as well as Greeks, slaves as well as free men, and we were all given to drink of only one Spirit" (1 Cor 12:13). "The very person of the Spirit is joined with our spirit to bear witness that we are children of God" (Rom 8:16).

To encapsulate twenty centuries of this history is an impossible task. Yet, one cannot fail to bring forth some testimonies from it. Irenaeus (about 180 CE) saw the Spirit unceasingly renew both the content of Christianity (the faith) and what conveys it (the Church) (*Adversus haereses* 3:24.1). Patrick (†460) recounted his experience in his famous *Confession* (§25 and 26): "Once again, I saw him [the Holy Spirit] praying within me and it was as if I were inside my body and heard him praying above me, that is, over my inner being. And he was praying there loudly with many a groan. And during all of that time, I was awestruck and astonished and kept wondering who it was that was praying within me like this. But at the end of the prayer he spoke as if he were the Spirit and thus I came to my senses and recalled the Apostle having said, 'The Spirit comes to the aid of the weaknesses of our prayer. For we do not know how to pray as we ought. But the Spirit himself asks on our behalf, with groans that are indescribable'" (Rom 8:26).

3. Today

I am obviously not going to outline here either a history of spirituality or—what would be, by the nature of things impossible—of holiness. Yet so many facts and testimonies allow one to maintain that there is such a thing as "a possession-giving [fruitive] experience of the absolute" (J. Maritain).[1] Questionable though some of these experiences may be, enough valid elements remain. Today as much as ever—and more than in many other ages—lives have been changed by the Spirit's action. Think of the Moslem proverb: "If someone tells you that a mountain has changed its location, believe it. But if someone says that a person's character has changed, don't believe it!" "Character" probably reasserts itself because one always reacts on the basis of who one is. Yet one sees men and women adopt a different life orientation and other standards of behavior, thanks to a welling up in them of a force and an inspiration that they attribute to the Holy Spirit. Among them are found once more the characteristic qualities that were already apparent to St. Paul: "love, joy, peace, patience, generosity, goodness, trust, gentleness, and self-control" (Gal 5:22).

---

1. [trans.] Maritain spoke of "une expérience fruitive de l'absolu" in "L'expérience mystique naturelle et le vide," *Études carmélitaines* 23.2 (1938): 116–39, reprinted in *Quatre essais sur l'esprit dans sa condition charnelle* (Paris: Desclée de Brouwer, 1939), 129–77; ET: "The Natural Mystical Experience and the Void" in *Ransoming the Time*, trans. Harry Lorin Binsse (New York: Charles Scribner's Sons, 1941), 255–89, or (slightly abridged) in *Understanding Mysticism*, ed. Richard Woods (Garden City, N.Y.: Doubleday [Image], 1980), 477–99.

One of the most striking features of this history is the coherence—one might say the unanimity—of the testimonies, despite a great diversity of circumstances. It could be said, of course, that this derives from common needs, or from common psychological structures. Why would we refuse to recognize this aspect? However, when lives are more balanced and fruitful, can one simply disregard what that says about the initiative of an Other?

We could press the objection further by noting that analogous accounts can be drawn from all religions, and even from this or that philosophy. We might think of Shamanism, or of the Stoicism of Chrysippus or of Seneca. Clearly this could be disputed; the coincidences or parallels are only partial, and we simply do not see the equivalent of a life completely animated and transfigured by the Spirit, or that of an ecclesial life enlivened in the same way. I have no difficulty, however, in holding that the Spirit acts outside the visible and official boundaries of the Church. In fact, this is such an important point that I will come back to it. Although another may find this idea objectionable, I do not. I locate the truth of this idea within the context of the truth we profess.

2

Difficulties: Critical Objections

The world born of the eighteenth-century Enlightenment is suspicious of our statements about the Holy Spirit. It calls them into question. Indeed, it has learned to mistrust every explanation involving a transcendent, unverifiable "cause." The spirit it favors is *ours*, not that unknown One beyond the clouds. Its suspicion takes many forms and I do not claim to deal with all of them. Nevertheless, here are five or six of its principal manifestations, from the most superficial to the most philosophically sophisticated.

1. The world remains unchanged

Christians affirm a newness of life. To be more precise, they say that, with the resurrection of Jesus and with Pentecost, the principle of a new order and the seed of a definitive future have entered into the world and are already active there. This is too beautiful, too idealized. We know the story often told by Jewish authors. Someone said to a rabbi, "The Messiah has come!" The rabbi went to the window, leaned out and looked. "No," he said, "I see no change...." Christians have waged war; they have even waged war against each other, and sometimes more cruelly than others. "Some saints approved of the Crusades and the Inquisition. I cannot avoid thinking that they were wrong. I cannot reject the light shed by conscience," wrote Simone Weil in 1942.[1] This was one of the obstacles standing in the way of her entry into the Church.

Facts are facts. I am not going to defend the indefensible. I *do* ask, however, that one evaluate matters intelligently, that is to say, historically to begin with, in the context which makes the text clear. Concerning the gift of the Spirit, St. Paul points out that we have only the first installment of it, in expectation of the future (read 2 Cor 1:22; 5:5 and Rom 6:5ff.; 8:18–25). Modern exegetes describe this situation in terms of the dialectic of the "Already" and the "Not-yet." The Spirit is already active but has not yet taken complete possession of us. It is a struggle, where the Church's "un-nature" ["malessence" in Congar's text; "un-wesen" in the original German], to take up a term used by H. Küng,[2] has more than once carried the day. It is especially this which history's public record preserves. But the sum total of the fruits of the Spirit, sometimes so dazzling and sometimes so modest as to be unnoticeable, shows that the "Already" is real.

2. It encourages irrationality

People fear that, in a certain kind of craze for the Spirit (for example, what appears in the Charismatic Renewal) the irrational takes over.[3] I would be the first to sound such a warning but not, however, without having noted the limits of the rational in the name of the truth about human beings, their balance and their well-being. It is normal for an emotional reaction to arise against the stifling of the heart's yearnings and of poetry by a milieu that is overly or-

---

1. [trans.] Letter to Fr. Jean-Marie Perrin, sometime between January 19 and April 16, 1942. For an alternate translation see *Waiting for God*, trans. Emma Craufurd (New York: G. P. Putnam's Sons, 1951), 53.

2. [trans.] See *Die Kirche*, A.II.1.c (Munich: Piper, 1977, a reprint of the 1967 Herder edition), 41–43; ET: *The Church*, trans. Ray and Rosaleen Ockendeen (New York: Sheed and Ward, 1967), 27–29.

3. See A. Woodrow, "Les résurgences équivoques de l'Esprit," *Lumière et vie* 148 (1980): 5–12. [1]

ganized, quantified, and preoccupied with how to get things done. A deep spiritual life, spontaneous prayer, and enthusiastic joy are better responses to this need to recover the dimension of the heart than violence and destructive rages. However, the Spirit ought not to diminish what it is to be human. Not too long ago, J. Dupont pointed out the importance for St. Paul of appeals to knowledge.[4] That is one of his priorities. And if I myself were to draw only one conclusion from my studies on the Holy Spirit, it would concern the Spirit's bond with the Word. There is no breath without speaking or articulating something. That would be energy without direction, rather like a whirlwind is movement that is not applied to anything. I like the approach of St. Irenaeus, who compares the Word and the Breath to God's two hands with which the clay is shaped.[5] So I am against a spirituality that proposes irrationality—an irrationality of subtraction and of disdain for the rational—as a method. But I am in favor of a spirituality that goes beyond the rational, because there is a depth of insight and breadth of possibility that reason, all by itself, cannot attain.

3. It devalues the body

If the Charismatic Renewal, because of its sentimentality and the joyous, indeed tangible, enthusiasm of its prayer meetings, represents something of a re-entry of Dionysus into our Catholic rationality,[6] is this enough to respond to the vehement reproach that Nietzsche addressed to Christianity, that it had scorned the body and covered the joy of living with ashes? Let us recognize frankly

---

4. J. Dupont, *Gnōsis: La connaissance religieuse dans les épitres pauliniennes* (Paris: Gabalda / Louvain: Nauwelarts, 1949). [2]

5. *Adversus haereses* 5:6.1 and 28.4. [3]

6. Françoise van der Mensbrugghe, *Les mouvements de renouveau charismatique: Retour à l'Esprit? Retour de Dionysos?* end-of-studies mémoire (Jan. 1978), Faculté de théologie de l'Université de Genève. [Published in book form as vol. 3 of the series *La parole et les hommes* (Geneva: Labor et fides, 1981).] [4]

that a certain asceticism based upon a dualistic vision, a certain tradition of "contempt for the world," and, finally, a remnant of Jansenism, have encouraged a spirituality that has excessively devalued the body, pleasure, sexuality, joy, and even creative freedom. But these sorts of things are deformations of a biblical spirituality of the Holy Spirit. In Scripture, the "flesh" is not the body; it is the egoistic closing in on one's self. There is, however, a certain affinity between the flesh and the body, and St. Paul sometimes switches from one term to the other (Rom 8:12–13). Spiritual experience and the spiritual tradition are very confident about this: it is impossible to have a serious spiritual life if one yields to all one's physical desires. This is because, on the one hand, the body is ambiguous. It is where change takes place, from the better or from the less good. On the other hand, what gratifies it, even perfectly legitimate satisfactions, tends to overwhelm everything else. This is especially true in the case of sexual matters. Who will challenge the testimony of Dietrich Bonhoeffer, a person who was both virtuous and clear-sighted? This is what he said:

If you set out in search of freedom, first learn to discipline your senses and your soul, so that your cravings and your body do not lead you astray.
May your mind and your flesh be pure, completely under your control, and may they, obedient to you, seek the end which has been assigned to them.
No one fathoms the mystery of freedom except through discipline.[7]

What shall one say, then, if one is concerned about the *sequela Christi*, about following in the path of Christ, about communion with the most holy God to whom the Spirit directs us and moves us? A saint, when all is said and done, stands up well against Nietzsche's Superman, who is only a poetic myth and whose dangerous ambiguities history has demonstrated. By contrast, there have never

---

7. Text printed at the beginning of Bonhoeffer's *Ethik* (Munich: Christian Kaiser Verlag, 1949). [5]

been saints who did not participate in the cross of Jesus. This, however, was followed by his return to life and by his exaltation.

4. It is only a projection of our yearnings and our potential

What Christians, and especially the Charismatic Renewal, attribute to the Holy Spirit can be explained by psychology. We project and objectify desires, feelings, budding ideas and tendencies. We attribute them to an Other and, consequently, we give them a name: Holy Spirit, Breath of God. And so we differentiate ourselves from them. Yet, in reality, they proceed from us, and in them we only find ourselves again.

One could illustrate this from the texts of St. Paul. In Rom 8:15, the Spirit makes us cry: Abba, Father! *We* are the ones who cry out. In Gal 4:6, it is the Spirit who utters this cry within us. Does the Spirit cry out, or do we? Certainly we cry out, yet we attribute it to the Spirit. In the prayer meetings of the Charismatic Renewal, one comes across instances of speaking, praying, or singing in tongues. These things are attributed to an outpouring or welling up of the Spirit. Yet certain case studies note that instances of learned behavior and imitation occur. Some behaviors induce others.[8] That is the business of psychology and is explained by it.

I acknowledge the pertinence of the objection. Yet, even if the facts, in the concrete, involve that discernment about which we will speak later, the objection does not, in principle, represent a grave difficulty, in my view. In fact, except for what is absolutely miraculous, God's action works entirely through *our* mental, psychological, and bodily capabilities. We must even avoid imagining

---

8. The most complete documentation is found in Kilian McDonnell, *Charismatic Renewal and the Churches* (New York: Seabury, 1976). Neither for the author nor for me do these instances of learned behavior and imitation exhaust what one can say about speaking (praying, singing) in tongues. [6]

that our contribution counts for, let's say, 75 percent, and that at the point where our part comes to an end, the divine contribution begins. All is from us, and all is from God. God is and acts within us; God remains transcendent in this very immanence. In the same moment that we invoke God under the affectionately familiar title of "Father," we add "who art in heaven..."

For a non-materialistic anthropology, it comes as no surprise that the Holy Spirit—if it is indeed the Holy Spirit—corresponds to what we desire. It is even less of a surprise for biblical thought, conscious as it is of the fact that humanity is in the image of God. The human person is, as spirit, open to *all* the truth that can be expressed. The human being embodies an infinite potential for knowledge and desire....[9] What psychologists call the megalomania of desire is not a defect; it is the expression of that condition of potential infinity that is our constitutive condition. "As spirit, the human being can have only a divine destination, can find definitive realization only in God. It is right to say that the nature of the human person is to be more than nature, when one thinks of the fixed and limited character of natures. 'Humanity surpasses humanity,' and infinitely" (P. R. Régamey).[10] Thus, one will not be surprised at the coincidences between the operations of God in us and our aspirations, our mental structures. One could take this even further. I will come back to the images of the Holy Trinity later. However, here is one specific example, the "theological" virtues: faith, hope, and love:

---

9. A sign of this potential for the infinite is found in languages. Each language offers limitless possibilities of combinations. Moreover, the number of languages or dialects is now [in 1983] estimated at 6,000. [7]

10. [trans.] Congar gives no citation for this quotation, but it is typical of Fr. Régamey's thought. See, for example, p. 80 of his *Pauvreté chrétienne et construction du monde*, Foi vivante 57 (Paris: Aubier, 1967), where he writes "l'esprit est ouvert à l'infini: 'l'homme passe l'homme.'" The concluding quote in both passages comes from Pascal's *Pensées*, Léon Brunschwicg, ed. (Paris: Hachette, 1971), fragment 432; ET: H. F. Stewart, ed. (London: Routledge and Kegan Paul, 1950), fragment 258.

We do not receive them from outside, as realities dissimilar to what we are, as creations of the Spirit from nothing, as the grafting into us of virtues borne independently of us. No. There is, in all more or less normally constituted people, a certain capacity to trust, without which life would be impossible. There is likewise in the human being a certain resilience turned toward the future, an expectation, a hope. And finally there is a certain gift of sympathy, the sense of solidarity with others....[11]

One could treat this question more fully using the terms and resources of K. Rahner's transcendental anthropology. Something within us renders *possible* what we affirm about the gift and action of the Spirit. That this takes place within us legitimates its attribution to ourselves as well as to the Spirit. St. Paul says that the Spirit is sent "into our hearts," that is to say, into the most intimate part of our person.

On this basis, one can, in fact, attribute to the Holy Spirit some things that come only from us. We cannot avoid this. It is easy to justify in this way doubtful initiatives, even downright deviations, and it has always been necessary to exercise discernment.[12] St. Paul is emphatic about inviting us to do this: 1 Thes 5:19–22; 1 Cor 12:10; 14:1–33. Aside from a "charism," which is of the order of an intuitive and immediate judgment, discernment uses objective rules as criteria: reference to Jesus Christ; investigation of norms in Holy Scripture (so powerful and so effective in making one grow up); conformity to God's design. If one needs some sort of practical guideline for concrete situations, one can do as St. Paul did. He took for criteria the requirements of charity or that which "edifies";[13] the acceptance of adversity, that fire which tests the quality of each one's

---

11. Pierre-Yves Émery, *Le Saint-Esprit présence de communion* (Taizé: Les Presses de Taizé, 1980), 38–39. [8]

12. See the very detailed study of discernment of V. [G.] Therrien, *Le discernement dans les écrits pauliniens*, Études bibliques (Paris: Gabalda, 1975). Compare my study *ES* 3 [2]:233–39 [ET: *HS* 2:180–83]. [9]

13. See my study "La casuistique de saint Paul," in *Sacerdoce et laïcat devant leurs tâches d'évangélisation et de civilisation* (Paris: Cerf, 1962), 65–89 [ET: "St. Paul's

work (1 Cor 3:13); the patient conversion of our subjectivity "so that it conforms and harmonizes itself more and more to the manner in which Jesus lived the Gospel";[14] finally, the quality of the life. It is charity that decides about true miracles, said Pascal.[15]

5. It is only the unfolding of world history...

I have already mentioned the Enlightenment, and we need to return to that topic. It is a story which, under relatively new forms, continues to be our own. People wanted to stop attributing what arose from nature and reason to the transcendent, unverifiable causes envisaged by religion. The consequence was a denial of the miraculous and of the supernatural, and a reduction to *this* world, to its resources and its modes of causation, of what people, in their ignorance, were attributing to so-called transcendent realities. [The Enlightenment claimed that] the Spirit is in the world; the Spirit is everywhere. And if any dynamic force exists, it is that of history.

Hegel (1770–1831) wished to dismiss the *Aufklärung* [the Enlightenment], "that vanity of understanding." He wanted to re-establish the harmony, even the unity, between religion and reason.[16] Basically, each was to be understood as saying the same thing: religion under poetic or symbolic form, philosophy through concepts. It was to be a philosophy of the spirit and of its dialectic. His view was that the spirit exists in itself, then it manifests itself—it express-

---

Casuistry," in *A Gospel Priesthood*, trans. P. J. Hepburne-Scott (London: Darton, Longman and Green, 1964), 49–73]. [10]

14. Émery, *Le Saint-Esprit*, 37. See also 53, 132. [11]

15. [trans.] *Pensées*, Brunschwicg ed., fragment 826; ET: Stewart ed., fragment 147.

16. See W. Kern, "Philosophische Pneumatologie: Zur theologischen Aktualität Hegels," in *Gegenwart des Geistes: Aspekte der Pneumatologie*, ed. W. Kasper, *Quaestiones disputatae* 85 (Freiburg: Herder, 1979), 54–90. On Joachim and the trajectory of his idea, see my *ES* 1:175–89 (footnotes) [ET: *HS* 1:126–37 (notes on 134–37)]; H. de Lubac, *La postérité spirituelle de Joachim de Flore* (Paris: Éditions Lethielleux), vol. 1, *De Joachim à Schelling* (1979) and vol. 2, *De Saint-Simon à nos jours* (1980)]. [12]

es itself and so goes out of itself—but it returns to itself in a third moment in time. The second moment is that of creation, but also of the Incarnation, of the death of God in Jesus Christ. However this death, followed by the resurrection, is a death of death, a negation of negation, the entrance into what is positive. The third moment will be when the Spirit universalizes the unique accomplishment of Christ, the Spirit is God in the community and the return to absolute Spirit is accomplished. Thus the history of the world is itself God's history. And this history is Trinitarian. Hegel develops this idea as the Reign of the Father, the Reign of the Son, and the Reign of the Spirit. Obviously, this is an allusion to the theme of Joachim of Fiore the dynamism of which reappears in every period and is still not dead today. Joachim had historicized eschatology, and the Trinity itself. Hegel writes:

The Middle Ages was the reign of the Son. In the Son, God is not yet brought to full reality; this occurs only in the Spirit. For, as Son, God is placed outside of himself and so there is a "being otherwise" which will be surpassed (*aufgehoben*) only in the Spirit, in the Return of God to himself. Just as the Son's status comprises in itself an outwardness, the Middle Ages was governed by exteriority. The reign of the Spirit commences with the Reformation; henceforth, God is truly known as Spirit.[17]

Our era has inherited from Joachim and from Hegel. It has found in them the wherewithal to formulate a theology of history: God is involved in it; the Spirit is present and active in everything and everywhere. This history is a history of the quest for freedom, a history of the liberation of humankind. After Hegel, some also saw

---

17. *Vorlesungen über die Philosophie der Weltgeschichte* (posthumous publication, 1837), ed. [Georg] Lasson, vol. 4, *Die germanische Welt* (Leipzig: Meiner, 1920), 881. For Hegel, the Reformation, in deprecating works and in scorning the world, closed itself into an abstract interiority and did not bring to reality the society reconciled by the unity of the universal and the particular, of the interior and the exterior, which was the vocation of Christianity. The State will be the heir of this failed mission...(!). [13]

in this a history of God and of God as Trinity.[18] Beginning in 1958, K. Rahner stressed the incontestable fact that, in Jesus Christ, God is the subject of a history.[19] God, immutable and impassible as God, becomes subject to suffering and change in this other in whom God's self-expression takes place. Rahner also developed what is for him a fundamental axiom, to which I will return later: the economic Trinity, that which reveals itself and communicates itself in the history of salvation, *is* the immanent, eternal Trinity, "*und umgekehrt,* and vice versa."[20] In this sense, the history of salvation is God's history.

I need not develop here the theology of the changeability of God and of suffering in God. Among Catholic authors, see H. Mühlen, H. Küng, F. Varillon, and among Protestant ones, see W. Elert, E. Jüngel, J. Moltmann. They discuss these themes in reference particularly to Christology. The history of God in the world is, above all, that of Christ and, in Christ, that of the Passion. They never mention, for example, his transfiguration.... That the economic Trinity is the immanent Trinity and reveals it follows from the patristic and scholastic theology of the "divine missions." For these "missions"— the Incarnation for the Son and the Pentecostal outpouring for the Spirit—are simply the eternal Trinitarian processions in so far as they terminate in a created effect: the assumption of a human nature in the hypostatic union and the sanctification of the disciples. But the "vice versa ('réciproquement'), *umgekehrt,*" can be held only by maintaining some distance—which it is impossible for us to bring to light—between that which God is as God and the content of God's

---

18. W. Kern, "Philosophische Pneumatologie," 78ff. [14]

19. "Réflections théologiques sur l'Incarnation," trans. Gaëtan Daoust, in *Écrits théologiques* 3:81–101 [Textes et études théologiques] (Paris: Desclée de Brouwer, 1963); also *Sciences ecclésiastiques* 12 (1960): 5–19 [ET: "On the Theology of the Incarnation," *Theological Investigations*, vol. 4, *More Recent Writings*, trans. Kevin Smyth, 105–20, esp. 112ff. (Baltimore: Helicon / London: Darton, Longman and Todd, 1966)]. [15]

20. [trans.] *The Trinity,* trans. Joseph Donceel (New York: Herder and Herder, 1970), 22.

self-communication to us in the economy of salvation, just as the specific ways in which that communication takes place also remain obscure.[21]

As for the idea that the Spirit is present everywhere, I welcome this with enthusiasm. It is true that our Catholic tradition has seen the Holy Spirit's universal presence mostly in the activity of sanctification, animation, and inspiration of persons and of the Church and, to a lesser extent, in the work of nature, as Creator. Creation was appropriated to the Father and attributed to the Substance of the living God. Obviously we need to avoid thinking of the Holy Spirit either in terms of the breath of an animal or the simple animation of nature, which we would risk doing by stringing together Old Testament passages in which the word "spirit-breath, *ruach*," is found. We ought even to avoid seeing the Holy Spirit as the vital force of the world and its evolution. For the Spirit-Paraclete of Christian revelation is not the *pneuma* of the Stoics. A distinction is to be made between the *action* of the Spirit, which obviously engages the Spirit's presence—but a simple presence of cause—and the *gift*, the indwelling of the Spirit as communication of grace that enables us to enter into a relationship of communion and familial intimacy with God.

That said, however, I am prepared to affirm a cosmic presence of the Spirit and the Spirit's role in the development of the world and its evolution. Hellenistic Judaism and the ancient Fathers up to St. Basil himself read in Gn 1:2 a cosmic function of the Spirit who hovered over the waters.[22] "For the spirit of the Lord fills the world, and the one who holds everything together knows every word said" (Ws 1:7). "You, whose imperishable spirit is in everything!" (Ws 12:1). If there is an echo of a Stoic theme in these statements, it is completely theologized. Here it is a question of the *Breath of*

---

21. See *ES* 3:37–44 [ET: *HS* 3:11–18]. [16]
22. The following lines reproduce the beginning of a paragraph from *ES* 2:279–84 [ET: *HS* 2:218–28]. [17]

Yahweh.[23] There were some antecedents for the use of this theme: the breath of God was not only extended to humankind (Gn 2:7; 6:3; Job 27:3; 33:4; Ez 37:1–14; Qo [Eccl] 12:7); it was given to all living creatures (Ps 104:28–30; Job 34:14–15). What is more, the "Breath of God" is also the Creator-breath (Jdt 16:14; Ps 33:6; 104:30). Like Wisdom and the Word, the Spirit of God is at work everywhere. "In truth," says St. Basil, "creation possesses no gift which does not come from the Holy Spirit."[24] A text of St. Paul—from which I never tire of renewing my hope—presents the world as in the labor of giving birth to its eschatological transfiguration. The faithful, *who have the first fruits of the Spirit*, share, in the midst of the world, in this yearning for life, for the freedom of the glory of the children of God (Rom 8:18–25).

I certainly extend this action of the Spirit to the works of the human spirit—discovery of truth, law, poetry and culture ... —and eventually to religions. Medieval Christianity often quoted this saying of Ambrosiaster: "Omne verum, a quocumque dicitur, a Spiritu Sancto est (All truth, by whomever it is spoken, is from the Holy Spirit)."[25] With respect to other religions, I do not hold the Holy Spirit responsible for the errors found in them, including possible temptations of idolatry or just plain syncretism. But for me it is no problem—indeed it is a necessity—to acknowledge that the Spirit is

---

23. See M[arie] E. Isaacs, *The Concept of Spirit: A Study of Pneuma in Hellenic Judaism and Its Bearing in the New Testament* (London: Heythrop Monographs, 1976). Let me quote here the following lines from P.-Y. Émery, *Le Saint-Esprit*, 104: "The witness that Christians render to God will have more meaning in the eyes of those religious beings who are not entirely wrong to represent God as the spiritual energy of the universe. Yes, one could tell them: God is that energy, but precisely in a spiritual way, that is to say, in a transcendent and personal way, as a longing for love, as a hope for communion." [18]

24. *On the Holy Spirit* (written in 375) 19:49. [The direct quote attributed to St. Basil does not appear here, although the words ascribed to him reflect the general thrust of the section.] [19]

25. PL 17:245. [The text to which Congar refers actually reads: "quidquid enim verum a quocumque dicitur, a sancto dicitur Spiritu" ("For whatever is true, by whomever it is spoken, is spoken by the Spirit").] [20]

active, not only in the prayer of the faithful of these religions, but in the message, albeit mixed and ambiguous, of the founders or leaders of these religions. It is true that some Christians have opposed this idea, not only by confessing their faith even to the point of death when they were driven to it, but also by rejecting false or ambiguous cults and by destroying idols (Polyeuctus). In the past—and this is still so clear in the sixteenth century—people maximized distinctions and oppositions, and they wanted to lead others to become like themselves. That followed from a love for the truth, but they saw truth in a rigid and uniform manner, as entirely from our side. We know today that truth is dispersed and found also among others. It is in the name of the same love of truth, but applied differently, that one believes in ecumenism, religious freedom, and respect for religions. With regard to them, the missionary Church desires to exercise hospitality and criticism simultaneously. Such is the position of the Second Vatican Council.[26] I have explained myself elsewhere on the question of knowing if and how religions can be means of salvation.[27] This is not exactly our question here, but that is the gist of a response to it.

26. See *LG*, n. 17; *AG*, n. 9. [21]

27. "Non-Christian Religions and Christianity," in *Evangelizaton, Dialogue and Development* [*Selected Papers of the International Theological Conference, Nagpur, India*, ed. Mariasusai Dhrvramony], Documenta missionalia 5 (Rome: Università Gregoriana editrice, 1972), 133–45; "Les Religions non bibliques sont-elles des médiations de salut?" in *Ecumenical Institute Year Book* (Jerusalem: Tantur, 1972–73), 77–101 [also in *Essais oecuméniques: Les hommes, le mouvement, les problèmes* (Paris: Le Centurion, 1964), 271–96]. [22]

3

The Spirit Is the Source of Life in Us Personally and in the Church

Having recalled the fact of an uncritical but constant claim that the Spirit *of God* is at work in us and in the world, I have highlighted the main difficulties to which this claim gives rise. This sequence is well known to believers: after a time of peaceful possession of the faith, they become aware of challenges to it. If not doubt, at least an ongoing questioning—what St. Thomas called the *cogitatio*—is a part of the faith. It is the passport into what Paul Ricoeur calls the second naiveté,[1] which is more or less the state of a mature and enlightened faith. I would like to reach this point with respect to the Holy Spirit, first by investigating the Spirit's action in us in the community and the Church, and then by explaining straightforwardly what theology, the science of the Word of God and of the faith, says about the Holy Spirit.

---

1. [trans.] See the final chapter ("The Symbol Gives Rise to Thought") of Ricoeur's *The Symbolism of Evil*, Part 2 of *Philosophie de la volonté* (Paris: Aubier, 1960), trans. Emerson Buchanan (Boston: Beacon Press, 1967), 347–57.

1. The need for an interior life

One needs to begin here because humankind today has a particular need and thirst for the Holy Spirit. Were one to doubt this, the literary evidence of publications in great abundance would remind one of it. At the level of reflective and articulated faith, we are emerging from what Heribert Mühlen has denounced as a pre-Trinitarian monotheism or vision of God. Books of theology, or of spirituality, liturgy, and religious poetry are Trinitarian. Even music is. Olivier Messiaen has set the *De Trinitate* of St. Thomas to music! In France, at least, this trend benefits from the presence and the influence of an Eastern Orthodoxy that has the gift of a Trinitarian spirituality and of a vibrant pneumatology.

This thirst for the Trinity and the Holy Spirit coincides with—and this is no accident—an agonizing search for identity on the part of humanity. Is this not so? A. T. Robinson has cited W. H. Auden's *Christmas Oratorio*, in which the three magi explain why they followed the star. The first says, "To discover how to be truthful today is why I follow the star." The second one says, "To discover how to be alive today is why I follow the star." The third says, "To discover how to love today is why I follow the star." Then they all say together, "To discover how to be human today is why we follow the star!"[2] The star leads to Bethlehem, to Jesus. H. Küng, who entitled the last section of his *On Being a Christian* "Christianity, Radical Humanism," resembles our magi in this view. Some found in his approach too optimistic a harmonization in which some of the more serious demands on the human side, and a certain spiritual depth and the aspect of the cross from the Christian side, had not been taken

---

2. [trans.] W. H. Auden, "For the Time Being: A Christmas Oratorio—The Summons," in *For the Time Being* (London: Faber and Faber, 1945), 85–86. In Auden's original English, the first of the magi says: "To discover how to be truthful now / Is the reason I follow this star"; the second says: "To discover how to be living now / Is the reason I follow this star"; and the third says: "To discover how to be loving now / Is the reason I follow this star." Their joint statement reads: "To discover how to be human today / Is the reason we follow this star."

sufficiently into account. Nevertheless, the fundamental thesis remains true: to be a Christian, the source of which in us is the Holy Spirit, satisfies in a radical way our quest to be fully human.

Immersed in a world of concrete, of technology, of programmed life, and of merciless competition, a person today experiences the need to have an interior life ("un dedans"), some sacred personal space and, at the same time, a connection with other human beings. People long for an interior life ("un dedans")—the word is from Teilhard—but one that does not isolate the self. Teilhard himself showed that the evolution of the world, which unfolds in the history of humanity, leads *simultaneously* toward more personalization and toward more socialization, that is to say, toward community, toward communion. However, the secret of a true relationship with others consists in really knowing that they too are *subjects*, persons, centers of emotions and aspirations. We are not alone in being such centers. To think we are, to behave as if that were the case, would lead us to treat others as objects of our desires or plans. But they, too, are persons.[3]

The Holy Spirit is that active presence in us of the Absolute who, at one and the same time, deepens our interior life by making it vibrant and welcoming and puts us in communion with others: the Spirit is what requires and is the means of communion. I recall here something a friend told me. When he was a student, not baptized and without religious education, he had developed a friendship with a young girl, a student just as he was. He asked her for a more intimate relationship. She refused. Why? "I am a Christian . . ." Then, he said to me, "I understood that she was indwelt." Yes, we are indwelt. Jesus and St. Paul were already saying this.[4] Theologians explain it. The faithful live it. We are familiar with what St. Augustine confessed in his praise of the God of grace: "You are

---

3. See the book of Dr. Fritz Künkel, [*Die Arbeit am Charakter*] trans. L. Barbey under the title *Psychothérapie du caractère* (Lyon: Vitte, 1952) [ET: *God Helps Those: Psychotherapy and the Development of Character* (New York: Ives Washburne, 1941)]. [23]

4. Jesus: Jn 14:16, 23; St. Paul: 1 Cor 3:16; 6:19, Rom 8:9, 11; 1 Jn 4:12–13, 16. [24]

within, and I am outside." How many people do not dwell within themselves! They are swept along in the movement of things, in the superficial reality of miscellaneous events and the daily routine. Yet within us there is a dimension of eternity and an affinity with the Transcendent. Those who know it from experience cannot doubt it, but they feel powerless in demonstrating it to those who are closed to that interior dimension.

2. The act of prayer

The deep dimension of our being becomes real in prayer, that admirable activity that is proper to the human being and qualifies one as human. We can experience an I-Thou relationship not only horizontally, with a human partner, but also vertically, with that partner who is at one and the same time infinitely beyond and more intimate than our deepest self. To address oneself to such a Being is so basic a need that, once again, it could be said that this seems to be a simple projection of our desire. We need some support, some help. Some people seek a crutch in alcohol, drugs, a guru... Could God be considered some kind of super drug? But if God exists—it is reasonable to *believe* this, and this can be demonstrated—it will be another thing altogether. But, once again, what presents itself as religious and even supernatural corresponds to a structure of our existence. This is entirely normal. This is the practical, concrete solution to a philosophically difficult problem: how can the *supernatural* be a response to an appeal of *nature*?

The Spirit ensures the fully Christian quality of our prayer and leads us to follow the patterns of Jesus' own prayer. This is what we have been told about him: "He was filled with joy by the Holy Spirit and said, 'I bless you, Father, Lord of heaven and of earth, for hiding these things from the learned and the clever and revealing them to little ones. Yes, Father, for that is what it pleased you to do'" (Lk 10:21). This calling upon God as Father, *Abba*, with its connotation of tenderness and familiarity, is peculiar to Jesus, as Joachim Jeremias has shown. It is truly remarkable that Paul, who had not known Jesus in his flesh and who writes in Greek, takes up the Aramaic term used by Jesus. From all the evidence, the Christian community repeated it according to Jesus' example and transmitted it to Paul. However, for Paul, it is the Holy Spirit who causes us to utter this invocation, or, indeed, who cries it out in us (Rom 8:15; Gal 4:6). The same Spirit, through whom Jesus prayed, gives rise to prayer in us. Likewise, the Spirit causes us to recognize Jesus as Lord (1 Cor 12:3). This is like a Trinitarian concert. In fact, according to our most ancient witnesses, Christians gave thanks to God the Father, through Christ the Son, in the Spirit. They applied in this sense the text of St. Paul (Eph 4:6), "one God and Father of all, who is over all, through all, and within all."[5] This has remained the fundamental sense of the liturgy.[6] All of our Eucharistic prayers end with the doxology: To you, Father, through Jesus Christ, in the unity of the Holy Spirit, all honor and all glory. The Father is the one to whom we direct our prayer, just as the Father is the absolute Source of it; Christ the Son is our Priest and Mediator; the Spirit makes us the temple of this spiritual worship. As we saw earlier, this testifies to an interiority of such a kind that we could as easily attribute the

---

5. Thus according to St. Irenaeus, between 180 and 200: *Adversus haereses* 5:18.1 (PG 7:1173; Harvey 2:374) and in the *Proof of the Apostolic Preaching* 5 (*Patrologia orientalis* 12:759): "The apostle Paul quite rightly says, 'one God, the Father, who is above all and through all and within us all.' For the one who is 'above all' is the Father, and the one who is 'through all' is the Word, because by means of Him everything was made by the Father, and the one who is 'within us all' is the Spirit, 'who cries: Abba, Father,' and who has formed and adorned man in the likeness of God." See also Hippolytus, beginning of the third century, *Contre les hérésies*, fragment published by P. Nautin, *Hippolyte contre les heresies, fragments. Étude et édition critique* [Études et textes pour l'histoire du dogme de la Trinité 2] (Paris: Cerf, 1949), 254 and 256 ([French] translation) and 255 and 257 (Greek). [25]

6. See C. Vagaggini, *Initiation théologique à la liturgie*, 2 vols. ([Bruges: Apostolat liturgique /] Paris: Société liturgique, 1959–63) [ET: *Theological Introduction to the Liturgy* (based on 4th Italian edition), trans. Leonard J. Doyle and W. A. Jurgens (Collegeville, Minn.: Liturgical Press, 1976)]. [26]

cry "Abba, Father!" to ourselves as to the Spirit. For this cry takes shape in the "heart."

3. Source of liberty

Interiority bespeaks liberty. Jesus and St. Paul link these realities: Spirit, being a son/child (of God), and liberty. "The sons are free," says Jesus (Mt 17:25–26). "If it is the Son who sets you free, you will indeed be free" (Jn 8:36). And St. Paul writes, "Where the Spirit of the Lord is, there is freedom" (2 Cor 3:17). If, as we shall see, the Spirit is the eschatological Gift, and if, as Hegel has shown, history moves toward liberty, nothing is more normal than such a connection. One must recognize the applications and dimensions of this connection.

St. Paul was speaking of liberty through faith in Christ in regard to the Law, but the commentaries, whether ancient ones (St. Augustine, Thomas Aquinas) or those of contemporary exegetes (H. Schlier, S. Lyonnet), show that it is a question of liberty with respect to all law, since obligation constrains from without.[7] It is not that one can do whatever one likes, as if one were "beyond good and evil." What is involved is not quietism, nor is it a "free spirit" movement. The Spirit does not liberate from the content of the Law, that is, from the good, but it removes the constraint of obligations because, by grace and love, the Spirit interiorizes what they command. Henceforth my conformity to the Law comes from me; it is my spontaneous movement. I act freely.

This condition of the Christian is subject to the situation of the "Already" and the "Not-yet." In Pauline terms, this is the struggle between the Spirit and the flesh. Etymologically, "asceticism"

---

7. See *ES* 2:156ff. and especially the bibliographical information on 164ff. [ET: *HS* 2:119–30, especially the bibliographical information on 131, n. 21ff.]; see also I. de la Potterie and S. Lyonnet, *La vie selon l'Esprit, condition du chrétien* (Paris: Cerf, 1965) [ET: *The Christian Lives by the Spirit*, trans. John Morriss (Staten Island, N.Y.: Alba House, 1971)]. [27]

means "training"; it is a battle. All spiritual authors, those from the East as much as those from the West, have spoken of the spiritual life as a combat, and one that lasts one's whole life. The Curé of Ars said that our concupiscence dies a quarter of an hour after we do.

Certain works of spirituality and, with all the seriousness which characterizes it, the Jansenist movement, have developed this great theme of the battle to win our liberty within a purely individualistic framework. This is necessary, because conversion is personal, but it is not sufficient. The content of the Law, which Love makes concrete (Rom 13:8–12), has to do with one's neighbor. We know that we encounter this Law on two levels. There is the level that is immediate: the neighbor is the one whom we meet, with whom we have an immediate and personal relationship. But the neighbor is also the man/woman whose life is conditioned by his/her social context, inasmuch as the neighbor is part of a group, and possibly part of a whole society. To love one's neighbor, to accomplish what the Law demands in his/her regard, might well consist, therefore, in doing something at the structural level, on the level of the social conditions of existence. Pius XI spoke of a political charity.[8] There is "flesh," in the Pauline sense of the word, also on the level of the structures and of the social conditions of life. The most recent Synods, the most recent Popes have proclaimed that liberation is part of evangelization . . .

4. Liberation that is not purely interior and spiritual

From other perspectives, as well, the liberty that the Spirit brings goes beyond the purely private spiritual realm of the personal interior life. This is so, first of all, because liberty is intended for our body, too. It is not merely a matter of a spiritual radiance, which

---

8. [trans.] Congar gives no reference, but he might have in mind a text such as n. 88 from the May 15, 1931 encyclical of Pius XI, *Quadragesimo anno*.

is sometimes so obvious and so beautiful. Still less is it a question of miraculous occurrences such as marked the lives of the saints where features similar to those of the transfiguration of Jesus or to the conditions of his resurrected body were produced.[9] These are, like (true) miracles, inbreakings of the Kingdom and of eschatology. For we aspire to that which St. Paul calls the redemption of our bodies and which he characterizes as "the freedom of the glory of the children of God" (Rom 8:21–23; see also Eph 4:30). On this earth, it is through the body that we nourish the life of our spirit. And we nourish the life of our body only by sucking the life from [vampirisant] that which surrounds us, by killing animals so as to eat them, and plants, too, which also have their own life. This is so despite the fact that life ought to radiate from the spirit to the body. That will be the eschatological situation, when the children of the first Adam, who had been made a "living soul," will become like the *eschatos Adam*, the second and last Adam, who is "life-giving spirit" (1 Cor 15:44–49: "What is sown is a natural body, and what is raised is a spiritual body"). Such is the Christian utopia. Its scope extends even beyond that, and this is natural because, through our bodies, we are a piece of the world. We may be a very small piece in terms of mass but we are a decisive one because the world's evolution has culminated in us and, thus, we draw the world into our own destiny.[10] We hope for "a new heaven and a new earth." According to St. Paul (Rom 8:19ff.), *all of creation* awaits the revelation of the children of God, that is to say, their transfiguration in glory and in glorious freedom: a liberation. Yes, I repeat, such

---

9. Motovilov's account of his visit to St. Seraphim of Sarov (+1834) is well known: Irène Gorainoff, *Seraphim de Sarov* (Bellefontaine Abbey, 1974) [ET: Constantine Cavarnos and Mary-Barbara Zeldin, *St. Serphim of Sarov*, Modern Orthodox Saints 5 (Belmont, Mass.: Institute for Byzantine and Modern Greek Studies, Inc., 1980)], and the *Théophanie* series (Paris: Desclée de Brouwer, 1979). There is also the complete fast (Marthe Robin, †1981), friendship with the wild animals, and instances of levitation (I[saias] Rodriguez, ["Lévitation"] in *DictSpir*, 9:738–41. [28]

10. *LG*, n. 48.1. How else are we to understand the announcement of a new heaven and a new earth? See Is 65:17; 66:22; 2 Pt 3:13; Mt 19:28; Acts 3:21; Rv 21:1. [29]

is the Christian utopia. It is not absurd, but to accept it one must believe in the—really quite reasonable—idea of creation. It is worth noting that the liturgy has us begin Lent—that is to say, the preparation for Easter—by the reading of Genesis, and that it takes it up again in the Paschal Vigil. If one thinks that this world is created, that it is fundamentally dependent upon the very One Who IS, as self-existent, one can admit that the world is like a rough draft and that its Creator will finish his work.

Now let us return to our present circumstances. By dwelling in a soul, the Spirit gives it the power of freedom. Hippolytus (beginning of the third century) notes that the apostles betrayed Jesus before Pentecost, whereas afterwards they preached and witnessed with that fearless assurance that the Scriptures calls *parrēsia*.[11] There exists a profound connection between the Spirit and the spread of Christian witness. The Acts of the Apostles illustrates this. There is also a similar relationship between Christian witness and Christian liberty. Recall the episode of the witness of Saints Perpetua and Felicity, whose original account we have, a journal that may have been completed by Tertullian. Before the witnesses of Jesus entered the amphitheater, their captors wanted to disguise the men as priests of Saturn and the women as priestesses of Ceres. The Christians refused. Perpetua said to the tribune, "If we are here, it is because we wished to keep our freedom. We are paying for it with our life; these are the terms of the contract between you and us."[12] The Church has always given birth to martyrs, but our era is particularly rich in them. Christians are pursued and savagely imprisoned in atheistic regimes, and they are witnesses

---

11. Hippolytus, *Contre les hérésies*, n. 25, in Nautin, pp. 256 and 257. "The Jews glorified the Father, but they did not give him thanks, for they did not recognize the Son; the disciples recognized the Son, but not in the Holy Spirit, and because of that they denied him." About *parrēsia*, see the article by H. Schlier in *TWNT* 5:877ff. [ET: *TDNT* 5:871–86]. *Parrēsia* is connected to the Holy Spirit: Phil 1:19–20, 2 Cor 3:7ff., 12ff., Acts 4:8 and see 4:31; 18:25ff. [30]

12. *Passio sanctarum Felicitatis et Perpetuae*, 18.3. [31]

to the costly demands of the Gospel concerning human rights and the rights of the poor.... Archbishop Romero is only one—but how pure and great—among thousands.

St. Paul speaks of powers, *dunameis*, to say that Christ has conquered them and that, in the end, he will be completely triumphant over them.[13] This is one more case of the "Already" but the "Not-yet." He speaks of them also to say, "It is not against flesh and blood (i.e., merely human) enemies that we have to struggle, but against the principalities, against the powers, against the rulers of this world of darkness, against the spirits of evil" (which he locates between heaven and earth) (Eph 6:12). Translated into concrete terms for us, we might think of the forces, at once or alternately personal and collective, beyond and within the general tendencies of the world and of history. These forces tend to turn creation and people away from the end desired for them by God, by pushing them to seek, by themselves alone, what they are ("quaerere quae sua sunt") and to act by their own power (*Eigenmächtigkeit*). They tend to give a purpose and meaning to things and to human life only in terms of the elements of the present world. Is it necessary to point out what these forces are? They are the idols of the "flesh": the perennial pretension to absolute autonomy (see Gn 3:5) along with its theoreticians, and also distortions of the way God is depicted. They are the false messiahs, political (or clerical!) power that wants to take the place of God and which the Apocalypse designates as the Beast. They are our modern idols: money, racial superiority, science, comfort, sex, systems of sacred knowledge, and false mysticisms. They, too, are the adversaries of spiritual persons who must have themselves guided by the Spirit (Gal 5:16); "Since the Spirit is our life, let the Spirit also make us act ..." (5:25). This is quite an undertaking!

13. Col 2:10, 15; Eph 1:21ff.; 1 Cor 15:24ff.; 1 Pt 3:22. See H. Schlier, *Mächte und Gewalten im N.T.* (Freiburg: Herder, 1958) [ET: *Principalities and Powers in the New Testament* (London: Nelson, 1961)]. There is also "The prince of this world," Jn 12:31; 16:11. [32]

5. The Spirit, joined to the Word and source of communion, gives rise to renewals and reforms that do not lead to anarchy

One cannot exclude from the liberty brought by the Spirit some, at least, of the protest movements against the excessive domination, maybe even within the Church, of fixed forms claiming to be normative. These can be abusive, and they can obstruct what the advancement of the Gospel demands. Clearly, one cannot give *a priori* the label of inspiration to every nonconformist uprising; neither can one deny *a priori* the action of the Spirit in every wave of protest or reform. Karl August Fink mentions, with approval, studies by G. Cracco, who saw the dispersed but quite homogeneous manifestations of protest against the clerical practices which marked the eleventh century as animated by charisms.[14] This raises the enormous problem of reforms, of original creations, of what new ideas contribute to the Church.[15] That, *also*, belongs to the Church. That belongs to the liberty of the Spirit. The Church must be free with regard to a certain aspect of itself, with regard to what holds it back, with regard to what it harbors that derives from the spirit of the world, from self-justification, from attachment to dead weight from its past and even from its present. The Spirit, who indwells the Church, ceaselessly raises up initiatives of reform and invention from the grassroots to the higher levels.

To the extent that something comes from the Spirit, it will be less

---

14. G. Cracco, *Riforma e eresia in momenti della cultura europea tra X e XI secolo*, in *Rivista di Storia e Letteratura religiosa* 7 (Florence/Turin: Olschki, 1971), 411–77 and *Realtà e carisma nell'Europea del Mille* (Turin: G. Giapichelli, 1971). However, Cracco takes "charism" in an excessively broad sense: active and personal participation in one's salvation and in the progress of the Christian community. [33]

15. Classic treatments of the question: *Vraie et fausse réforme dans l'Église*, 2d ed., [Unam Sanctam 72] (Paris: Cerf, 1968) [ET: *True and False Reform in the Church*, trans. Paul Philibert (Collegeville, Minn.: Liturgical Press, 2011)]; K. Rahner, *Éléments dynamiques dans l'Église* (Paris: Desclée de Brouwer, 1967 [ET: *The Dynamic Element in the Church*, Quaestiones disputatae 12, trans. W. J. O'Hara (Freiburg: Herder / Montreal: Palm, 1964)]. [34]

destructive of unity because the Spirit is, in an essential and radical way, the source of communion. It is in this way that the greeting from 2 Corinthians 13:13 creates the liturgical space of our celebrations. This property is connected to the Spirit's fundamental nature, to what the Spirit is in the mystery of God, to the fact that, one and the same Spirit is in all to animate them, and, in the first place, *in Jesus and in us*.[16] Are we not his members, his body, and is this not because of one and the same Spirit (see 1 Cor 12:12–13, Eph 4:4)? Therefore, the Spirit is at once source of an immense diversity and source of unity, because the Spirit bestows charisms in diverse forms but "for the common good" (1 Cor 12:7). Communion, precisely, is unity without uniformity, a harmony or symphony of different voices. There is nothing more sublime; there is nothing more concrete. *We live that reality*. The Church of today, rather surprisingly, brings to life chapter 12 of the first letter to the Corinthians. It would be good to quote the whole passage here! It should be read!

The Holy Spirit, at one and the same time, interiorizes or personalizes the blessings of eternal life which are offered to us in Christ, and universalizes these blessings in communicating them to a great number. Thus the Spirit makes the faithful, simultaneously, members of a whole and also personal subjects of their own activity. The Spirit is inseparable from the Word ("the two hands" of St. Irenaeus). The Word is the form, the determination of things. The Spirit is the dynamism which animates it.

---

16. On this idea, see St. Thomas Aquinas, *3 Sent.*, d. 13, q. 2, a. 1, ad 2; q. 2, a. 2; *De veritate* q. 29, a. 4; *Super evangelium s. Ioannis lectura* (*In Ioan.*), ch. 1, lectures 9 and 10 [ET: *Commentary on the Gospel of John, Chapters 1–5*, trans Fabian Larcher and James A. Weisheipl, with introduction and notes by Daniel Keating and Matthew Levering (Washington, D.C.: The Catholic University of America Press, 2010), 78–85]; *ST* 2a2ae, q. 183, a. 3, ad 3; Pius XII, encyclical *Mystici corporis*, n. 54 (*AAS* 35 [1943]: 219) [ET: *Mystici Corporis: Encyclical Letter of Pope Pius XII on the Mystical Body of Christ*, 55–56, in *Selected Documents of His Holiness Pope Pius XII 1939–1958* (Washington, D.C.: National Catholic Welfare Conference, 1958), 24–25]; *LG*, n. 7.7. This obviously involves also a "pneumatological Christology," about which there exist several good treatments. [35]

The Catholic Church holds that the fullness of the gifts of the Spirit is found wherever the fullness of what has been determined by the Word is found. In the classical categories of theology, the fullness of the spiritual reality (*res*) follows the fullness of the ecclesial *sacramentum*, the organic ensemble of the means of grace. These are, however, two different levels of reality, and their connection is not physical-mechanical. That is why there can exist *persons* who have a very profound spiritual life who belong to "churches" whose ecclesial character is weak. One thinks, for example, of the Quakers, profound moral and religious personalities—and they give a decisive place to the Spirit—who do not have much of the "Church" reality, in the sense of an organic ensemble of the means of salvation.

The Second Vatican Council put into effect, although imperfectly,[17] an ecclesiology of communion, just as it took on, imperfectly but really, a pneumatology. At least it applied both to the ecumenical problem which, along with that of the wider world, was its horizon of work. On the one hand, the Council indeed recognized not only the action of the Holy Spirit in this wider world[18] but, speaking of other Christians, it said, "To that is added . . . a genuine communion in the Holy Spirit since, by his gifts and his graces, he effects also in them his sanctifying action . . ."[19] The category used by the

---

17. See A. Acerbi, *Due ecclesiologie: Ecclesiologia giuridica e ecclesiologia di communione nella "Lumen gentium"* (Bologna: Editione Dehoniane, 1975). Concerning the pneumatology of the Council, see *ES* 1:227–35 [ET: *HS* 1:167–73]; also my contribution "Les implications christologiques et pneumatologiques de l'ecclésiologie de Vatican II," in *Les églises après Vatican II: Dynamisme et prospective; Actes du colloque international de Bologne, 1980, Théologie historique* 61 [ed. G. Alberigo] (Paris: Beauchesne, 1981), 117–30; [reprinted in *Le Concile de Vatican II: Son Église, peuple de Dieu et corps du Christ*, preface by René Rémond, Théologie historique 71, 163–76 (Paris: Beauchesne, 1984)] [ET: Part Four, Article 5, below]. [36]

18. The Spirit fills the universe: *GS*, n. 11.1; *PO*, n. 22.3; the Spirit "guides the course of time, renews the face of the earth, is present in this evolution," *GS*, n. 26.4. [The English translation published by the Vatican website says that God's Spirit, who "directs the unfolding of time and renews the face of the earth, is not absent from this development."] [37]

19. *LG*, n. 15. [The English translation published by the Vatican website reads, "Likewise we can say that in some real way they are joined with us in the Holy Spirit,

Council in connection with ecumenism—repeated unceasingly by Paul VI, for whom ecumenism was, as he said, the hidden part of his pontificate—is that of imperfect communion. One more "Already" and "Not-yet"! There is, therefore, a solid theological basis for our ecumenism. Its possibilities and consequences are far from being exhausted. I think that this will happen only through living and praxis. One often notices that at this level agreement is very substantial. From it, consequences also present themselves in the field of doctrine. Speaking very specifically of pneumatology, one can detect some promising results.[20] The very Person of the Spirit is at work, and works better than we do!

6. The Spirit distributes "charisms" and thus gives rise to a Church that lives also from its "grassroots"

Neither the hierarchy nor certain non-conformists have a monopoly on the Spirit. The Spirit gives "charisms" to all the living members of the Mystical Body of Christ. "Charism" does not necessarily mean extraordinary gifts such as miracles, healings, or speaking in tongues. These gifts have been present in the past and still exist. But "charism" means, according to St. Paul who is the author of this

---

for to them too He gives His gifts and graces whereby he is operative among them with His sanctifying power."] H. Mühlen has drawn from this text excessive consequences concerning the other churches. For the problem still remains of determining whether all the *ecclesial* fruits of the Spirit are to be found where the *ecclesial sacrament* remains imperfect. See also *UR*, nn. 19–24. [38]

20. One example is the final report of the third cycle of conversations (1977–81) of the International Catholic/Methodist Commission. It deals with pneumatology and displays some substantial convergences. The text is in *Service d'information* of the Roman Secretariat for Unity [Pontifical Council for Promoting Christian Unity] 46, no. 2 (1981): 87–100 [ET: "The Honolulu Report" in *Growth in Agreement: Reports and Agreed Statements of Ecumenical Conversations at a World Level*, Ecumenical Documents 2. Harding Meyer and Lukas Vischer, eds. (New York: Paulist / Geneva: World Council of Churches, 1982), 367–87]. [39]

term, a gift, a "talent" that is the aim of, and has as its own aim, the plan of God's grace. St. Paul lists marriage among the charisms and he proclaims, in an admirable and famous text (1 Cor 13), that the greatest charism is charity. Each person has gifts that must be put at the service of the building up of the Body of Christ.

One person will provide the catechesis for a group of children; another person will lead liturgical celebrations—in the absence of a priest, as the occasion demands; this or that man or woman will undertake to keep a Bible study going, or an ecumenical group, or a section of Catholic Action. Others will study. Still others will have a gift for personal relations and communication. Others, or perhaps the same ones, will have zeal for justice and peace, will be active in service and in the charitable works of the Church.... The Church is not built only from the top downward by the sacred functions of the hierarchical ministry, as necessary and important as they are—and these functions are no less than the celebration of the sacraments and the authentic teaching of doctrine! Sometimes these have occupied the whole of our field of vision. In the recent past we had a pyramidal vision of the Church, and I have noted numerous examples of this. A vertical re-centering on the activity of the glorified Christ and of the Holy Spirit has permitted a horizontal de-centering on the whole body. This has been the tendency of the last fifty years in ecclesiology and of the Second Vatican Council. At a time when all institutions are experiencing a crisis and when many great structures are crumbling, the Spirit is inciting revivals of the Gospel everywhere. This happens through persons. Consequently, this involves a certain precariousness, a fragmentary character, even an appearance of disorganization. But, as it is the same Spirit in all, both in Jesus and in us, a hidden but sovereign orchestra conductor will make the diversity converge in a unified work which is all his own!

This vision must be extended to the universal Church. Persons have their gifts. So do peoples, and they have their own histories.

This symphonic diversity also builds the Church which, says Vatican II, exists in and from local or particular churches.

If one cannot imagine the living God, the God of the covenant, without a people and a Church, neither can one think of the Church as a symphony of diverse gifts, of co-responsibility, of giving and receiving, and of communion without seeing God, through God's Holy Spirit, as the One who forms relationships, who communicates and makes communion happen. St. Paul characterizes the Spirit as *koinōnia*, communication, communion (2 Cor 13:13).

4

A Theology of the Third Person

1. A long and difficult history

A theology of the Holy Spirit and, in more general terms, a theology of Christ and of the tri-unity of God, took a long time to develop. There was no model to follow. The chapter was blank and yet, in a sense, its contents were already determined. Antiquity knew a broad diffusion of Stoicism, so widespread that it touched the class of ordinary people and even the world of slaves. And Stoicism envisaged a divine Breath animating the world but saw it as an element of this world itself. It tended to see the Word or Wisdom of God, and then God's Breath-Spirit (*Pneuma*), as means of creation, as simple intermediaries between God and nature, immanent in this nature. It is not surprising that some Christians, applying all their resources to express the facts of the history of salvation—the intervention and gift of the Spirit; the incarnation of the Word in Jesus—saw the Word and the Spirit either as the first links or intermediaries of creation or, at best, simply as modalities through which a creative and provident God acts. The history of Christian doctrine puts labels on these attempts, using abstract names to designate erroneous doctrines condemned as heresies, and concrete names to designate those persons who held and set forth these teachings. Beginning at the end of the first century, there was the monarchianism of Cerinthus, inspired by Jewish monotheism, and, at the end of the second century that of Theodore [or Theodotus] the Tanner/Cobbler. In the third century, there was Paul of Samosata's adoptionism: Christ was simply a man adopted as son of God at his baptism ... Then, in the middle of the third century, there was Sabellius who embraced modalism and was condemned in Rome. Father, Word, Spirit were only the modes through which one unique Subject was manifested. Then, just when the Church's peace had been proclaimed by Constantine, Arius appeared. He was a priest in Alexandria who saw the Son as intermediary between the Father and creation. Athanasius rose up against him. His unwavering defense of the Faith defined in the Council of Nicaea (325)—the Son is of the same substance as the Father—cost him five exiles.

But a false idea analogous to that of Arianism was expressed in the middle of the fourth century by Macedonius, bishop of Constantinople, and those called the *pneumatomachi* [Spirit fighters], who were opposed to the Holy Spirit. St. Basil the Great led the same sort of battle against them as St. Athanasius had led against Arius and before that against those who were calling into question the divinity of the Spirit: if the Spirit is not God, how can we be divinized? Basil wrote his treatise *On the Holy Spirit* in 375. We should, he says, praise (pray) as we believe, and believe as we have been baptized. Out of consideration for the *pneumatomachi*, and to facilitate their return to true doctrine, Basil avoids calling the Spirit "God" and expressing the Spirit's consubstantiality with the Father and the Son. The Council of Constantinople of 381 would do the same. It would be content to say (and these are the words of the Creed which we still recite), "(I believe) in the Holy Spirit, Lord and Giver of life, who proceeds from the Father. With the Father and the Son he is the object of the same adoration and the same glory. He has spoken through the prophets."[1] This was

---

1. [Trans.] Congar's French translation of the second sentence of this credal

equivalent to affirming the Spirit's divinity. But let us note here a fact emphasized by various authors:[2] the people of God think what they live; their doctrine flows from this life and, at the same time, it protects and directs it. This happens in such a way that, as a text attributed to Pope Celestine I (†432) says, the rule of worship and of prayer indicates the rule of belief (DS 246). This is not another version of the modernist position of Georges Tyrrell. For him Christianity was only a spiritual experience, theology being something built upon it. This approach neglects the fact that there exists, from the start, a Revelation made in words and in texts, which inspires and regulates practice. The two realities are interconnected. While the faithful have contact with Revelation through and in the practice of Christianity (the liturgy, among other things), the practice depends first of all on Revelation. One ought neither to confuse nor to separate the two.

2. Three who are One

The Holy Spirit is God. God is, in the unity of one same "substance" (= a concrete reality having its own existence), Father, Son and Spirit. There is no point here in raising an objection because of being scandalized that one equals three or that three are one. No mathematician would be shocked by this because he or she knows that one cannot add to the infinite. To speak of three "Persons" introduces a distinction, but it does not introduce plurality into God.

---

excerpt does not replicate exactly the words of the French Liturgy. There the formulation is: "With the Father and the Son, he receives the same adoration and the same glory"; in English we say "Who with the Father and the Son is adored and glorified." All of these wordings are renderings of the Latin "cum patro et filio coadorandum et conglorificandum" and the equivalent in Greek. See Norman Tanner, ed. *Decrees of the Ecumenical Councils* (London, UK: Sheed and Ward / Washington, D.C.: Georgetown University Press, 1990), 1: 24. Incidentally, the ET given by Tanner reads "co-worshipped and co-glorified with Father and Son."

2. For example, Edmund Schlink, "Die Struktur der dogmatischen Aussage als ökumenisches Problem," *Kerygma und Dogma* 3 (1957): 251–306 (esp. 265ff.). [40]

The Fathers of the Church explained this. Not too long ago, a Soviet (Ukrainian) mathematician reminded us of this:

> The mockeries which Tolstoy heaps on the Holy Trinity illustrate vividly his rationalism. Any peasant, he says, knows that one cannot be equal to three; consequently, the dogma of the Holy Trinity is absurd and aims only at stupefying the faithful.
>
> As a mathematician I knew one thing very well: the assertion that the part is smaller than the whole is valid only for finite quantities. For infinite quantities, this statement has no validity; the part can be equal to the whole. And upon reading a Soviet historian of Christianity, I became aware that the formulator of the theory of large numbers, Kantor, had begun his study precisely in reflecting upon the problem of the equivalence between one hypostasis of God and three...[3]

This existence of the Three adorable Ones in One unique Adorable is for Christians a fundamental element of faith, that of their baptism "in the name of the Father and of the Son and of the Holy Spirit." This triple and unique confession accompanies a triple immersion or infusion (sprinkling), and accomplishes one single baptism, since the Three are one single God. The liturgy does not celebrate the divine Persons separately. There is no feast of the Father; Christmas is not the feast of the Son, but the celebration of the *fact* of his birth into our world; Pentecost is not a feast of the Holy Spirit, but a celebration of the *fact* of the Spirit's being sent in a tangible way to the first disciples.

To make the Trinitarian mystery meaningful to our minds, various images have been proposed. One of the most common is that of the sun, its light and its warmth. These three suns are perfectly congruent. Another image is the spring, the river, and the sea—a comparison dear to the Greek Fathers. Still another is the thought, the word, and the breath. Or again, the root, the branch, and the

---

3. Leonid Plioutch [Plyushch], *Dans le carnaval de l'histoire* (Paris: Éditions du Seuil, 1977), 55 [ET: *History's Carnival: A Dissident's Biography*, ed. and trans. Marco Carynnyk (New York: Harcourt, Brace, Jovanovich, 1979), which, however, seems to lack the paragraph quoted by Congar]. [41]

fruit. These are obviously very imperfect images and ones whose adequacy must be denied even as they are being proposed.

If we are made in the image of God, it is legitimate to make cautious use of the elements most essential to our deepest being to express and construct intellectually—that is what theology does—the mystery of God, One and Three. A saintly priest, to whom ecumenism owes much, Fr. Paul Couturier, used to say, "The absolute One of infinite Being, presents itself, precisely because of that infinity, as a Trinity of Persons who exhaust the possibilities of the relation of the Infinite with Itself."[4] In the West, some great religious geniuses have taken the risk of constructing a Trinitarian theology by making use of the essential moments of life or immanent self-generativity, whether of the mind, or of love. For God is spirit (Jn 4:24)[5] and light, but also "God is Love" (St. John, 1 Jn 4:8). St. Augustine, St. Anselm (†1109), St. Thomas Aquinas and, among the Orthodox, Father Sergei Bulgakov have preferred to follow the analogy of the mind; Richard of Saint Victor (†1172), St. Bonaventure (†1274) and, among us, in an original manner, Father Louis Bouyer, have followed the theme of love.[6] Here I do not have to propose a theology of the Trinity as such. My concern is only the Holy Spirit.

3. Three "Persons"?

It is true that, in Scripture and also in Christian experience, the Spirit sometimes appears more like a force or a dynamism than like a "person." There is thus something like a self-effacement of

---

4. See M. Villain, *L'abbé Paul Couturier*, preface by A. Latreille (Tournai: Casterman, 1957), 336 (this is taken from his "Ecumenical Testament"). [42]

5. [Trans.] The passage to which Congar refers (Jn 4:24) says that God is spirit and truth. In French, "esprit" can mean either "spirit" or "mind." It is clear from the history of Trinitarian thought, as referenced by the theologians that Congar lists here, that "esprit" means "mind" in this context.

6. See *ES* 3 [ET: *HS* 3]; L. Bouyer, *Le Consolateur: Esprit-Saint et [vie de] grâce* (Paris: Cerf, 1980), see 438–39. [43]

the Holy Spirit behind the fruit produced by the Spirit. Some have spoken of the Spirit's "kenosis." However, "were the Spirit not confessed as a Person in the same sense as the Father and the Son, something would indeed be lacking in our faith. Yet our faith thus finds itself up against a barrier because the countenance of the Spirit is intentionally concealed from us and the Spirit avoids meeting us face to face. As for the images which allow us to think and to speak of the Holy Spirit and to delight in being subject to the Spirit, they have the drawback of not connoting a person."[7] There are the images of powerful action (wind, fire, flowing water), but also the image of a bird that flies and hovers. In St. Paul, however, there are a number of three-membered formulas—someone has counted forty-seven of them[8]—of which a certain number are genuinely Trinitarian. One of the most eloquent statements is that one by which we so often open our Eucharistic celebrations and which creates the sacred space within which those celebrations unfold: "The grace of Jesus Christ, the Love of God (the Father), and the communion of the Holy Spirit be with you all" (2 Cor 13:13). In several statements, the Spirit appears as the *subject* of acts concerning our spiritual life: the Spirit attests that we are children of God, the Spirit comes to the aid of our weakness, the Spirit intercedes for us (Rom 8:16, 26, 27). In St. John, the Spirit is "another Paraclete" (14:16) as Jesus had been and continues to be (1 Jn 2:1); the Spirit teaches us (Jn 14:26). We can "grieve" the Spirit (Eph 4:30). We can address the Spirit as one person addresses another by saying "thou." The Spirit, says the Creed, is adored and glorified with the Father and the Son.

Let us recognize, however, that even if the characterization of the Spirit as "person" has the advantage of going beyond the idea of an impersonal dynamism, doing so raises some questions. Already St. Augustine acknowledges that he uses the word "person" not so

---

7. Émery, *Le Saint-Esprit*, 117. [44]
8. R. Blümel, *Paulus und der dreieinige Gott* (Vienna: Mayer, 1929), 250. [45]

much to say something as to avoid saying nothing,[9] and St. Anselm used to say, "tres nescio quid," "three of I know not what."[10] The Middle Ages found itself faced with several definitions of the person. Boethius († c. 525) said a person was an "individual substance of a rational nature."[11] That united the values of a spiritual and intelligent nature, a separate existence and a distinct individuality: a being which exists by itself, distinct from others. It was very metaphysical, not very "personalist." So Richard of Saint-Victor critiqued it around 1170, and substituted for it this formula: "a being existing by itself alone, according to a certain mode of rational existence."[12] The accent is more personalist. The person, said Richard, is not a *quid*, a something, but a *quis*, someone.[13] That permits Richard to develop his whole Trinitarian theology in the key of Love. Thomas Aquinas would follow Boethius, adding elements from Richard to complete his understanding of the person.

Modern thought, however, has developed still further and enriched the personalist emphasis. Anton Günther (†1863) had already identified "person" with *Selbstbewusstsein*, self-consciousness. This had the drawback of suggesting three centers of consciousness in God, and, therefore, of bordering on tritheism. However, it is indeed by consciousness and autonomy that modern thought characterizes the person, an autonomous subject of consciousness and accountability. A number of contemporary presentations apply interpersonal psychology to the Persons of the Trinity. The idea of relation to the other, which this implies, seems particularly appropriate to

---

9. *De Trinitate* 7:6.11 (PL 42:943). [46]

10. *Monologion*, 79 [78 in some editions; (PL 158:221); ET: St. Anselm, *Proslogium; Monologium; An Appendix in Behalf of the Fool by Gaunilon and Cur Deus Homo*, trans. Sidney Norton Deane (Chicago: The Open Court Publishing Company, 1935), 142]. [47]

11. Boethius, *Liber de persona et duabus naturis*, 3 (PL 64:1343) ["Persona est naturae rationalis individua substantia"]. [48]

12. Richard, *De Trinitate* 4:24 [(PL 196:946 or SChr 63:284): "si dicimus quod persona sit existens per se solum juxta singularem quemdam rationalis existentiae modum"]. [49]

13. Ibid. 4:7 [(PL 196:934–35 or SChr 63:244)]. [50]

the divine Persons. But sometimes this approach inclines toward a simplistic anthropomorphism, if not an unconscious tritheism: the divine Persons speak to one another and love one another in the manner of individual autonomous persons.

This is why Karl Rahner proposed not to abandon the term "person," which had for him the authority of the strongest tradition, but to speak, in theology, of *Subzistensweise*, "modes of subsistence."[14] In this way, the notion of "person" is explained in a manner which avoids postulating three centers of consciousness, three loves, three centers of immanent operation. And this is not "modalism," for which there are only three roles and three names of one single person. Certainly, this approach is not satisfactory from all perspectives. Let us cite, however, as a possible antecedent, these terms from the Lateran Council of 649, presided over by Pope St. Martin I and in which St. Maximus the Confessor participated (both of them martyrs of the true faith): "Unum Deum in tribus subsistentiis consubstantialibus (One single God in three consubstantial substances)."[15] This is an excellent formula, but rather technical. It means that, in the unity of the divine Substance (only one God!), three moments of being exist, three distinct, original and specific ways of being Who God is. God, absolute spirit, exists in a threefold way: as Source and radical existence, as self-knowledge and self-expression, and as self-love.

This introduces neither quantity, nor even plurality, into God because these notions can have no place in the infinite, the infinite ocean of being. But one can speak of an order (the Greeks say *taxis*). In this sense the Spirit is third. That does not mean that the Spirit comes *after* the others in the chronological sense. The Three are ab-

---

14. K. Rahner, *Dieu Trinité, fondement transcendant de l'histoire du salut*, in *Mysterium salutis* 6:13–140 (Paris: Cerf, 1971) [ET: *The Trinity*, trans. Joseph Donceel (New York: Herder and Herder, 1970)]. [51]

15. *DS* (1965 ed.), no. 501 [ET: J. Neuner and J. Dupuis, eds. *The Christian Faith in the Doctrinal Documents of the Catholic Church*, 7th ed., rev. and enlarged (New York: Alba House, 2001), 215, no. 627/1]. [52]

solutely simultaneous, instantaneous, "consubstantial." In so far as they are distinct "Persons," they interpenetrate, exist and live one *in* the other. This is what is called in Greek *perichōrēsis*, in Latin *circumincessio*. "I am in the Father and the Father is in me" (Jn 10:38; 17:21). "Each one (of the divine Persons) is in each and all are in each, and each one is in all, and all are in all, and all make only one."[16] St. Gertrude (†1302) described one of her visions in this way: "Then the three Persons together radiated an admirable light, each seemed to cast its flame through the other and they were, however, all one with the other."[17]

4. The Spirit is fulfillment, the Gift that completes and perfects

Third in the substantial unity, the Spirit is the one who brings to completion God's self-revelation and self-communication to God's own creature made in God's image. In the New Testament, the Spirit is designated as "the Promised One" beyond the coming and the gift of Christ/Son. And the Spirit is called *par excellence* the Gift. The Spirit is the ultimate Gift that perfects the other gifts. St. Irenaeus writes, "The Holy Spirit, the Gift that through the Son, the Father grants to human persons, brings to perfection everything that the Son possesses."[18] This perfecting, this consummation, is designated by different names: becoming a child of God, a member of God's family,[19] "divinization," new creation, living eternal life or "life of the world to come." These are the last words of the

---

16. St. Augustine, *De Trinitate* 6:10.12 (PL 42:932). ["Ita et singula sunt in singulis, et omnia in singulis, et singula in omnibus, et omnia in omnibus, et unum omnia"]. [53]

17. W. Oehl, *Deutsche Mystiker* [Munich: J. Kösel'schen, 1910], 2:90. [54]

18. *Adversus haereses* 5:9.1 [= 5:8.1? Trans.—We have been unable to confirm Congar's citation. We wonder, though, if our proposed citation approximates what he intended]. [55]

19. Rom 8:14–16; Gal 4:6ff.; Eph 2:19–22. [56]

Creed. They conclude what the Protestants call the third article, that which concerns the Holy Spirit.[20] For the Creed is Trinitarian. The whole of its last part sets forth the work attributed to the Spirit. It includes eschatology, the life of the world to come, of which we have the promise while possessing only the "first installment" of it (2 Cor 1:22, 5:5; Eph 1:14).

In all of this, the Christ/Son and the Spirit work together. Objects of two "missions," they do the same work. But Christ himself executes it because, glorified, he is permeated by the Spirit: see 1 Cor 15:45; 2 Cor 3:17.

5. Two approaches to the mystery: East and West (*Filioque*)

It is common knowledge that on the question of the Holy Spirit—more precisely, on the Spirit's eternal outpouring in God (the Spirit's "procession")—a controversy exists between the Orthodox East and Catholicism, whose positions were formulated in the West. Catholics say "who proceeds from the Father and the Son." They have said this since the fourth and fifth centuries (St. Ambrose, St. Augustine, St. Leo) and on the basis of numerous councils held in the West in the sixth and seventh centuries. For a long period the Latin part of the Church and its Greek part lived in communion, albeit with some periods when relations were less harmonious.

The East retained the words of Jesus in John 15:26: "who proceeds from the Father." This is also what the Council of Constantinople (381), to which we owe our Creed, did. Its concern, its inten-

---

20. Whence this arrangement of classic dogmatics: G. Ebeling, *Dogmatik des christlichen Glaubens*, vol.1, *Der Glaube an Gott den Schöpfer der Welt*; vol. 2, *Der Glaube an Gott den Versöhner der Welt*; vol. 3, *Der Glaube an Gott den Vollender der Welt* (Tübingen: Mohr, 1979). See H. Thielicke, *Der evangelische Glaube: Grundzüge der Dogmatik* (Tübingen: Mohr, 1976–78), of which vol. 3 (1978) is entitled *Theologie des Geistes* [ET: *Theology of the Holy Spirit*, trans. and ed. Geoffrey Bromiley (Edinburgh: T&T Clark, 1982)]. [57]

tion, was to take a step, in regard to the Spirit, similar to that which Nicaea had taken in regard to the Son in 325, namely, to affirm the divine character of the Spirit and—without using this word—to affirm the Spirit's consubstantiality with the Father and the Son. Yet the Council said nothing specific about the Spirit's eternal relation to the Son. The Greek Fathers did not reflect about this article as the Latins did. They did not specify the relation that the Spirit maintains with the Son in his eternal "going forth." Several have, in this regard, formulas that suggest a positive relationship: the Spirit proceeds from the Father through the Son (St. Maximus, St. John of Damascus, Patriarch Tarasius); the Spirit comes from both (St. Cyril of Alexandria); the Spirit comes from the first, the Father, through the mediation of the one who comes immediately from the first, the Son (St. Gregory of Nyssa); the Spirit proceeds from the Father and receives from the Son (Syrian epicleses, Epiphanius, Gregory of Nyssa); the Spirit rests in the Son (Epiphanius, John of Damascus).... But the Greeks reserve strictly to the Father the quality of being first principle (*archē*) and cause (*aitia*). They insist on the "monarchy" of the Father. The Latins do this also, but without making the Father play exactly the same role, on account of the consubstantiality of the Son and the Spirit who proceed from the Father, the former by generation, the latter by ekporesis [*ekporeusis*], procession from the first principle.

What are the reasons for, what is the interest in, keeping the *Filioque*? St. Augustine invokes the fact that the New Testament speaks equally of the Spirit *of the Father* (Mt 10:28; Jn 15:26) and of the Spirit *of the Son* (Gal 4:6; see also Rom 8:9; Phil 1:19; he also refers to Jn 14:26, 20:22; Lk 6:19).[21] The Spirit is therefore the Spirit of both; the Spirit is their mutual love. Augustine's point of departure was the problem of how to harmonize the two affirmations that God is one and that God is three. Unity is expressed through abso-

---

21. [trans.] In *ES* 3:125 (*HS* 3:86 and notes on p. 93) Congar gives several references to Augustine's *De Trinitate* in connection with these biblical references.

lute terms: wise, all-powerful, good, creator. Terms such as these do not distinguish the Persons. On the other hand, Father implies a relation to Son, as Son does to Father. The Persons are distinguished, therefore, by a relation, which is a relation of origin and owes its consistency or fullness of being to the fact that it expresses the communication of the divine substance precisely within that substantial unity. For the Holy Spirit the relation is: Giver-Gift, the Father and the Son being together the Giver, and "Gift" being a name of the Spirit, often designated thus in Scripture.[22] The Spirit deserves this name even before actually *being given*—which presupposes the existence of creatures placed in time by a free act of God—for the Spirit is Generosity in God. The Spirit is the Love that proceeds from the Father and from the Son and that—if one may speak in such a human manner—goes beyond that face-to-face relation of the Father and the Son, of God and of his image, to give access to communication, to Gift, to Grace. The Gift will be effective only when there are creatures for whom this can be accomplished, but what we call the "economy" (the history of salvation) is only the expression, outside of God, of what exists in God. W. Kasper and H. Mühlen have said this better than I![23]

The theology of the "divine missions" establishes a connection, and even a continuity, between the free self-communication of God to creatures, the "economy," and the intra-Trinitarian life. The Son is sent by the Father; the Spirit is sent by the Father and the Son. These missions or gifts are the expression, in creation, of

---

22. See Acts 8:20; 2:38; 10:45; Jn 4:10; Heb 6:4; 1 Thes 4:8. See also *ES* 3:193ff. [ET: *HS* 3:144–54]. [58]

23. H. Mühlen: "The Spirit is God's being-beyond-self." *Morgen wird Einheit sein* (Paderborn: Schöningh, 1974), 128. See also W. Kasper: "[The Spirit] is that which is innermost in God, unity in himself, of sovereign freedom, and at the same time that which is the most exterior, the freedom and possibility in God of further self-communication in a new way, that is, outside God's self. Thus, the Spirit is, as much in God as between God and the world, the bond of unity, of a unity in a love which frees even as it unites" (*Kirche, Ort des Geistes* [Freiburg: Herder, 1976], 34). [59]

the intradivine processions. This theology, which is found among the Fathers and is common to the great Scholastics, has been translated, by the contemporary theologians K. Barth and K. Rahner, in what Rahner calls a *Grundaxiom*, a fundamental axiom, namely: the economic Trinity, that which is revealed to us, is the immanent or intradivine Trinity, and vice versa.[24] The concrete significance of this theology is well expressed by the Klingenthal report published by "Faith and Order": "When we invoke God, we turn ourselves toward a God who is none other than the one who is revealed in his Word.... This living God from eternity to eternity has been, is, and will be the same as the one who is revealed throughout history."[25] The "umgekehrt," the "vice versa," of Rahner must, however, safeguard the freedom of the communication and the transcendence of the eternal Trinity with regard to its self-communication. It is not certain that this requirement is honored by all Trinitarian theologies, for example, that of Jürgen Moltmann. One cannot say that the eternal Trinity *is nothing more than* the Trinity revealed in the economy of grace.

In the economy of salvation, the Spirit is sent by the Son as well as by the Father. This fact is not the only basis for the *Filioque*, but it confirms and illustrates it. If the sending and the coming of the divine Persons are the expression, in our lives and our history, of their eternal procession, the sending and the coming of the Spirit imply the Spirit's procession from the Father and the Son. More-

---

24. [trans.] See *The Trinity*, 22.

25. [Trans.] From *La théologie du Saint-Esprit dans le dialogue entre l'Orient et l'Occident*, Document foi et constitution 103, ed. Lukas Vischer (Paris: Le Centurion / Taizé: Les Presses de Taizé, 1981); ET: "The *Filioque* Clause in Ecumenical Perspective" (WCC Commission on Faith and Order 1979), in *Spirit of God: Ecumenical Reflections on the* Filioque *Controversy*, Faith and Order Paper 103 (Geneva: WCC / London: SPCK, 1981), 10. We have translated Congar's French. The official English version reads: "In calling upon God, we turn and open ourselves to the God who is none other than he has revealed himself in his Word.... The living God from eternity to eternity was, is and will be none other ('immanent Trinity') than he has shown himself to be in history ('economic Trinity')."

over, in the theological construction of the mystery, on the one hand, the Son has all that the Father has, except being Father. This is required by his perfect consubstantiality. On the other hand, the Persons are distinguished one from another by the opposition of their relations of origin: Father-Son, Giver-Gift. The Spirit, who proceeds from the Father, would not be hypostatically distinguished from the Son if there were not, between the Spirit and the Son, this relational opposition of procession.

The Orthodox reject this construction. They have another vision of the mystery that has its own internal coherence. According to them, the mode of procession from the Father suffices to distinguish the Son and the Spirit. The relations of origin certainly characterize the Persons but do not define them as such. And there exist among them relations other than the relations of origin: those of manifestation, of mutual hospitality.... The Orthodox find the Latin construction too rational. They judge also that it makes the Spirit depend upon the Word, upon Christ; that is why they say the West has drifted into what they call a "Christomonism" in which the Spirit is only a "vicar" of Christ and is not accorded a proper role in an ecclesiology of communion, an ecclesiology of a people who are, as a whole, priestly and active. A Christology not balanced by a full-fledged pneumatology results in a pyramidal and clerical vision of the Church....

Even if we deserved this criticism in the past, the current direction of our Church's life removes much of its pertinence. This criticism is also a little too simplistic and does not take into account other historical factors. But that is not the main point. The doctrinal question connected to the procession of the Holy Spirit is more fundamental. It also concerns the Protestant and Anglican churches, because they hold the procession *ab utroque* [from both], which has had no more determined a defender than Karl Barth. The issue was also on the agenda, first during the reconciliation negotiations between the Roman Church and the Orthodox Church at Nympha, near Chalcedon, in the thirteenth century and, above all, at the Council of Florence, where the question was seriously discussed and the union achieved, July 6, 1439, on the basis of the equivalence of the two phrases, "Filioque" and "per Filium" ("through the Son"), the latter being understood in the sense of the former. This was not entirely satisfactory. The question has been, for more than a century, on the agenda of various mixed conferences and, very recently, of a very interesting conference organized at Klingenthal, Alsace, by the "Faith and Order" Commission of the World Council of Churches, in 1978 and 1979.[26] Concerning the procession of the Spirit, they have insisted on this: "The Spirit proceeds from the Father, but proceeds from him only insofar as the Father is (already) the Father of the Son." "The existence of the second hypostasis is the prerequisite or the 'condition' for the existence of the third." But above all, the dialogue shows that we must not focus exclusively on this phrase to which controversy has given a disproportionate emphasis. Concerning this point, however, let us keep to the position of John Paul II in his letter to Patriarch Dimitrios of March 25, 1981, and, finally, in his homily of Pentecost 1981: the text as it has come forth from the Council of 381 is normative; it possesses the highest degree of dogmatic authority; no "Filioquist" interpretation can counter it. But the theology of the Holy Spirit encompasses many aspects besides that of a dependence, in some sense linear, of the Spirit upon the Father-Son as Source. A Cartesian or geometric mentality tends to conceive of the Person of the Father *entirely constituted before* the actual generation of the Son; likewise, that of the Son as constituted *before* the spiration of the Spirit. Yet there is simultaneity in the same existence; the Persons do not exist one without the other, but one with and in the other, influencing one another mutually in the midst of the processions coming from the

---

26. *La théologie du Saint-Esprit dans le dialogue entre l'Orient et l'Occident*. It is also interesting to refer to the anonymous report published by the historian V. Bolotov, "27 Thesen über das Filioque," *Revue internationale de théologie* 6 (1898): 681–712; French translation in *Istina* 17 (1972): 261–89. [60]

Father. Each hypostasis or divine Person lives a Trinitarian life. The contribution of Tradition and of the Orthodox theologians is, in this regard, very enriching.

There exists a whole *Trinitarian* life of the Persons with one another, within one another, in the unity of the divine substance, which *is* love. Furthermore, although not the "Son," the Spirit is the Spirit of the Son. The Spirit brought to life in Mary a being who would be called Son of God; given to Christians, the Spirit is in them the source of their existence as children of God by grace (Rom 8:15–17; Gal 4:6). The Spirit extends to a multitude the benefits of what God has done and given to us in Jesus. The Spirit universalizes this unique accomplishment, which is the center and highpoint of history.

Conclusion

I have spoken of the Holy Spirit, albeit in a very rudimentary way. However, to speak of the Spirit is less important than to live in the Spirit. The initiative belongs to the Spirit. In so far as anything depends on us under the Spirit's sovereign impulse, this will be grounded in prayer. It is worth noting that prayers to the Holy Spirit begin by this appeal: "Come!" The Spirit is already there. Indeed, the Spirit is the very one who moves us to pray. Yet we beg the Spirit to come as a visitor, as a power, and as a guest.

A visitor. Often awaited and desired, sometimes unexpected. We owe our "inspirations"—as decisive in an active spiritual life as they are in a life of intellectual service—to the Spirit. These are impulses to prayer or the suggestion of little sacrifices. It is not necessary to see them so much as means of asceticism or of moral improvement as to see them as the nourishment of our theologal life, that is, of our relationship to God. To obey these inspirations supposes a disposition of openness and of abandon without sentimentality or timidity, a confident and active faith in God who directs our life. This is not quietism; it is not contrary to a vigorous exercise of our freedom. But God becomes the active partner in our life. The door is open to God. Let the Spirit come! Let the Spirit come in!

A power. One of the terms constantly linked to references to the Spirit is that of *dunamis*, a Greek word which has produced several more in our language. In the Acts of the Apostles, the missionary impulse comes from the Holy Spirit. Everything begins with Pentecost and the movement has not stopped. The Church is still "apostolic" in that sense, too. And all of us are the Church, according to each one's gifts and vocation. Moreover all lives, no matter how diverse they may be, have a common problem, that of perseverance. The Spirit also is strength for that. This is one of the Spirit's functions as "Consoler."

A guest. If the Spirit comes, if the Spirit enters in, it is in order to stay. "*Dulcis hospes animae*," we sing, "Sweet guest of our soul." But also of our body, St. Paul loves to underscore that. The Spirit dwells in me, but do I inhabit myself otherwise than through my "carnal" occupations of this life? "Wanderers, vagabonds, deserters of your soul and fugitives from yourselves,"[1] Bossuet used to say. This indwelling of the Holy Spirit must not end in a sterile intimacy. The Spirit is Breath. The guest who dwells within us wants us to be dedicated and fruitful. There is no real contradiction between an authentic interior life and working actively at that which we are called to do. Ultimately, what we must do is given to us by God, and the Spirit, too, dwells in our doing it.

---

1. [trans.] "Sermon pour le quatrième dimanche de l'Avent, 'Sur la véritable conversion,'" from *Sermons de Messire Jacques-Bénigne Bossuet*, vol. 1 (Paris: Antoine Boudet, 1772), 330.

PART TWO

A Theology of the Holy Spirit[1]

Overview

1. Testimony about the
Holy Spirit | 75

1. The Spirit of communion | 76
2. The experience of the faithful | 78
3. Prophecy, *parrēsia*, Tradition | 79

2. The Spirit in the Personal
Prayer and in the Personal Lives
of Christians | 83

1. Salvation and messianic eschatology | 83
2. A freedom judged by its fruits | 84
3. The gifts of the Spirit | 85

3. An Ecclesiological Pneumatology | 87

1. The Church, temple of the Holy Spirit | 87
2. A Church that is, first of all, a communion | 90
3. A communion organized as a society | 97
4. No "pneumatocentrism" | 100

Part Two is a translation by Susan Mader Brown and Joseph G. Mueller, SJ, of "Pneumatologie dogmatique," in *Initiation à la pratique de la théologie*, vol. 2, *Dogmatique* 1, published under the direction of Bernard Lauret and François Réfoulé (Paris: Cerf, 1982), 483–516.

4. The Spirit Is the Breath
of the Word and the Spirit
of the Son | 102

1. The gift of the Spirit brings God's
self-communication to fulfillment | 102

2. A pneumatological Christology | 103

3. Relations between the Spirit and Christ | 106

5. The Spirit, the Eschatological
Gift, Brings the "Redemption" to
Fulfillment | 114

Bibliography | 121

"Pneumatologie dogmatique" was one of Congar's contributions to a five-volume set, *Initiation à la pratique de la théologie*, edited by Bernard Lauret and François Refoulé in 1982. The book's title might be rendered in English as "Beginning to Do Theology." Still in print, the volumes—entitled Introduction, Dogmatics 1, Dogmatics 2, Ethics, and Practice—are meant for an academic setting, especially for the Catholic seminary context in which most of Congar's teaching career was spent. Although an apologetic character is not absent from this presentation, Congar is here working more as a dogmatician than as an apologist, giving primacy to the biblical and historical testimony of revelation, following the approaches of Friars Ambroise Gardeil and Marie-Dominique Chenu, respectively. He expected this text to be a kind of summary catechesis of the mission of the Holy Spirit, and in this piece he makes clear his conviction that, although the missions of the Holy Spirit and of Christ may operate somewhat differently, they are dependent upon one another and ultimately have the same aim.

The first chapter of this piece provides Congar's central thesis. He writes at the end of the first paragraph in italics for the sake of emphasis, "the Spirit inspires people to pursue God's work," and as the chapters unfold, it becomes clear that God's work involves divine self-communication and drawing humanity into the divine life through the assimilation of believers to the incarnate Son. Testimonies about the Spirit's "inspiration" furthering this work are numerous. The Spirit enlightens people and draws them into communion with God, transforming their priorities and their wills so that they act freely in accordance with God's plan. The Spirit brings people into communion with one another as well as with God and moves them to bear witness to the joy of that communal life.

Congar presents the Holy Spirit as the principle or source of the divine life of believers who become children of God by Baptism. His presentation of the Holy Spirit shows his vast knowledge of the Catholic theological tradition and of the various ways in which the Holy Spirit has been treated by others. Still, Congar's presentation is never far removed from his pastoral concerns, which lead him to draw out the practical implications of what he says about the nature of prayer, the freedom brought by the Spirit, the gifts of the Spirit, and the way that the Spirit can prod persons—and, through them, the whole Church—toward the *eschaton* in unanticipated ways. He shows that the life of the Spirit really does lead human beings—all of whom seek some sort of interiority—to well-being or salvation. That his treatment of the relationships among the persons of the Trinity should focus on God's saving work in the world comes as no surprise.

1

Testimony about the Holy Spirit

The Third Person is not revealed to us in the way that the Son is revealed in Jesus Christ. However, the Spirit[1] has been and is made manifest by what the Spirit brings about. That is why we must examine the evidence—whether of Scripture, liturgical celebrations, or personal Christian experience. I have organized the testimonies in this section with an emphasis above all on the *practical*. One cannot say everything all at once, even about matters that are simultaneous and connected. *The Spirit inspires people to pursue God's work.*

The most constant of the testimonies we have about the Holy Spirit—for they are found already in abundance in the Old Testament—is that the Breath of God raises up and guides men and women to accomplish the plan of God: servants of the liturgy, prophets, charismatic warriors and, above all, the Davidic and messianic king. Isaiah wrote about this king, "A branch will come forth from the stump of Jesse, a shoot will grow out of his roots. On him will

---

1. Congar's original note refers readers to the abbreviation he uses for the title of his three-volume work in French on the Holy Spirit (*ES*). The same abbreviation appears above in our list of abbreviations, along with that for its English translation (*HS*).

rest the Spirit of the Lord: a spirit of wisdom and understanding, a spirit of counsel and might, a spirit of knowledge and of fear of the Lord" (11:1ff.). Some also ascribe to Wisdom the same feeling of being indwelt and guided. It comes as no surprise that the ante-Nicene Fathers thought of Wisdom and the Spirit together. Obviously this guidance by the Breath of God has to do primarily with the period *constitutive* of the People of God—with the prophets, the sacred writers, the apostles, the Fathers, and the first councils. Yet the economy of salvation continues after the constitutive period. All periods have had their founders and their prophets, ours no less than the others. "I am bound to the Spirit and it is not I, but the Lord, who bade me come" (to Ireland), St. Patrick confessed (†460).[2]

1. The Spirit of communion

"When the fullness of time came," God (the Father) sent his Son to confer on us adoption as children and to send into our hearts the Spirit of his Son (Gal 4:4–6). "Those whom the Spirit of God enlivens are sons of God" (Rom 8:14). We are sons and daughters of God in the one and only Son, by becoming his body, by being mystically identified with him. There is a fundamental connection between the unity of the body and the unity, or rather, the unicity of the Spirit: 1 Cor 12:13; Titus 3:5–6. The Spirit will do in us what the Spirit did for Christ (Rom 8:11), for it is the same Spirit, the Spirit *of Christ* (Rom 8:9). The Spirit thus assumes the role of being principle of communion (2 Cor 13:13; Phil 2:1). The Spirit, the same and only one, can be in many, creating among them a unity with neither fusion nor confusion of persons. Theologians and spiritual writers have celebrated this mystery of unity. Note the connec-

---

2. [trans.] Patrick's *Confession*, Section 43, in *Confession et Lettre à Coroticus*, SChr 259 (Paris: Cerf, 1978); ET: *The Confession of St. Patrick and Letter to Coroticus*, translated and with notes by John Skinner, prologue by John O'Donohue (New York: Doubleday, 1998).

tion drawn by St. Augustine between the Spirit of Christ and the Body of Christ: when the Spirit is in us, we are in Christ. The great spiritual writer William of Saint-Thierry (†1148), commenting on Jesus' words "so that the love with which you have loved me may be in them and I in them" (Jn 17:26), ends up composing this prayer: "Thus we love you, or more accurately, you love yourself in us, we affectively and you effectively, making us *one* in you through your own unity, through your own Holy Spirit whom you have given to us."[3] This consciousness of being united to God and of loving God with God's own love would, from a theological perspective, have to be nuanced, but as a feeling it corresponds to an experience and is found in more than one mystic.[4] The Spirit would thus be that One who is the principle of the greatest interiority and of mutual presence, not only between us and God, but among us, the faithful.

---

3. [trans.] William of St. Thierry, *On Contemplating God*, 11, *The Works of William of St. Thierry*, vol. 1, trans. Sister Penelope, CSMV, Cistercian Fathers Series 3 (Shannon, Ireland: Irish University Press, 1970), 58. (William is actually commenting on Jn 17:21.)

4. John of the Cross writes: "The soul here loves God not through itself, but through Him ... for it loves through the Holy Spirit, as the Father and the Son love each other, according to what the Son himself declares through St. John: 'that the love with which you have loved me be in them, and I in them,'" *Living Flame of Love*, [Commentary on] Stanza 3, [par. 82, *The Collected Works of St. John of the Cross*, trans. Kieran Kavanaugh and Otilio Rodrigues (Washington, D.C.: ICS Publications, 1973), 642]; "the soul loves God with the will of God, which is also her own will; and she can love God to the extent that she is loved by God, because she loves through the very will of God, in the same love through which God loves her, which is the Holy Spirit, according to the word of the Apostle: Rom. 5:5," *Spiritual Canticle* [Stanza 38, par. 4, *The Collected Works of St. John of the Cross*, 554; this passage, which Congar quotes as Stanza 37, is Stanza 38 in the ICS edition]. St. Theresa of the Child Jesus: "For me to love you as you love me, I would have to borrow your own love," *Story of a Soul:* [*The Autobiography of St. Thérèse of Lisieux*, a new translation from original manuscripts by John Clarke (Washington, D.C.: ICS Publications, 1976), 256]; St. Maximus the Confessor [*Opuscula theologica et polemica*]: "A single energy works in God and in those who are deified" (PG 91:33). [2]

2. The experience of the faithful

The faithful have an awareness and experience of this in at least two ways:

1. In their sense of the "communion of saints," where "saints, *sanctorum*," is understood to refer, not to communion in the sacraments, but to union with the saints and with the martyrs. This is perhaps the original meaning of the expression (Nicetas of Remesiana, Faustus of Riez).[5] From the beginning, Christians have had the conviction that they form, in Christ and in the Spirit, one body whose members sustain and support one another, and that this happens in a realm of life which, being that of the Lord and of the Spirit, encompasses the age to come as well as the present one. Our belief can reach beyond this world, and our love can extend into the world of God, into the heart of God: "Neither death nor life, neither the present nor the future, nor any created thing, nothing will be able to separate us from the love of God made manifest in Christ Jesus Our Lord" (Rom 8:38–39).

2. There is a presence and an influence of Christ and of the Holy Spirit that are connected to participation in the community as such. Our classic texts from the age of the martyrs attest to this: St. Ignatius of Antioch (*Letter to the Ephesians* 5.3); St. Irenaeus, "where the *ecclesia* (the assembly of the faithful) is, there also is the Spirit of God; and where the Spirit of God is, there is the *ecclesia* and all grace";[6] St. Hippolytus, "one will make haste to go to the *ecclesia* (the assembly of the faithful), the place where the Spirit flourishes."[7] The experi-

---

5. [trans.] Nicetas, *Explanatio symboli* (PL 52:871); Faustus, *De Spiritu Sancto* (PL 62:11).

6. *Adversus haereses* 3:24.1. [3]

7. *Apostolic Tradition*, 35. See P.-M. Gy ["Eucharistie et 'Ecclesia' dans le premier vocabulaire de la liturgie chrétienne,"] *La Maison-Dieu*, no. 130 (1977): 26–34, and also Heb 10:25. [4]

ence of all times, but particularly that of our own, illustrates these ancient testimonies. It is a fact that a distinctive experience of the Spirit is occurring in prayerful gatherings such as those of the "renewal" sometimes called "charismatic" today. Lives are being changed, veils fall, and men and women are being turned toward the living Lord (see 2 Cor 3:16–18).

3. Prophecy, *parrēsia*, Tradition

The Spirit speaks through the prophets (1 Pt 1:11–12; Eph 3:5). St. Justin, St. Irenaeus, St. Cyril of Jerusalem, etc., attest to this note, which characterizes the Spirit in the Creed. The Spirit as such is not speech; the Spirit is not the Word. Yet, the Spirit makes speech happen; the Spirit is the Breath that makes speech come forth and that carries it afar. This is the experience and the witness of all "missionaries" down through the ages. At the level of the New Testament, it is the promise of the "Paraclete."[8] The Spirit of truth will teach the disciples and remind them of the teaching of Jesus (Jn 14:26), will bear witness on behalf of Jesus (Jn 15:26–27), and will lead the disciples into the fullness of the truth (Jn 16:13–15). The fulfillment of these promises is indicated, throughout the whole of history and even in our own times, by the following facts:

a. As G. Haya-Prats has shown,[9] the Holy Spirit in Acts is essentially the dynamic principle of witness which assures the expansion of the Church. The Book of Revelation makes a lot of room for the spirit of prophecy, which enlivens the testimony that the faithful give about Jesus (19:10), which corresponds to Jn 15:26 and I Jn 4:3. The Spirit is the one

---

8. [trans.] Here Congar inserts a parenthetical reference to an earlier chapter of the book from which this selection is taken and to his three-volume work on the Holy Spirit: Max-Alain Chevallier, "L'Esprit de Dieu dans les Écritures," in *Initiation à la pratique de la théologie* (Paris: Cerf, 1982), 2:467–68 and *ES* 1:81–91 [*HS* 1:53–59].

9. *L'Esprit force de l'Église: Sa nature et son activité d'après les Actes des Apôtres* (Paris: Cerf, 1973). [5]

who carries forward the Gospel and the action of the Lord Jesus into the places and times open to them. The witness carried out in this way is marked by a note of assurance, *parrēsia* (Acts 4:31; 2:29; 4:13, 29; 14:3; Clement of Rome, *Letter to the Corinthians* 42:3; compare, in St. Paul, faith as a "charism," 1 Cor 12:9). The Gospel is always contested, the trial of Jesus is continued down through the ages. The Spirit is promised to the disciples to strengthen them and to make them realize that the world is wrong (Jn 16:7–11).

b. The apostolic testimony is not simply a material repetition of facts. It incorporates insight into, and articulation of, the meaning of these facts. The fourth gospel attests several times that the disciples understood the meaning of Christ's actions or words only later, and in the light of Easter.[10] It also conveys Jesus' promise that the Spirit will lead the disciples into all the truth and reveal to them everything that is to come (Jn 16:13). This is not about predicting the future, but about the promise of assistance so that fidelity to the word of Jesus will be accompanied, in the novelty of history, by new responses. That is the role of the living Tradition, whose transcendent Subject and guarantee of fidelity is the Holy Spirit.[11] Its historical subject is the whole People of God, organically structured, whose members are enlivened by

---

10. See Jn 2:22; 12:16; 13:7; 16:12ff. F. Mussner, *Le Langage de Jésus et le Jésus de l'histoire* (Paris: Desclée de Brouwer, 1969); A. M. Hunter, *S. Jean, témoin du Jésus de l'histoire* (Paris: Cerf, 1970) [English original: *According to John* (London: SCM, 1968)]; O. Cullmann, *Le milieu johannique: Sa place dans le judaïsme tardif, dans le cercle des disciples de Jésus et dans le christianisme primitif; Étude sur l'origine de l'Évangile de Jean* (Neuchâtel-Paris: Éditions Delachaux et Niestlé, 1976), 33ff. [ET: *The Johannine Circle: Its Place in Judaism, among the Disciples of Jesus and in Early Christianity; A Study in the Gospel of John*, trans. John Bowden (London: SCM, 1976), 14–19]; ES 1:81–91 (bibliographies); 2:42ff. [ET: *HS* 1:53–59; 2:28ff.]. [6]

11. See *La Tradition et les traditions: Essai théologique* (Paris: Fayard, 1960) [ET: *Tradition and Traditions: An Historical and a Theological Essay*, Part Two, trans. Thomas Rainborough (London: Burns and Oates, 1966; reprinted San Diego, Calif.: Basilica Press / Needham Heights, Mass.: Simon and Schuster, 1997)]. [7]

the Spirit according to the role each has in God's plan of salvation. Second Timothy 1:14 speaks of "guarding the deposit with the help of the Holy Spirit living in us." At this point we touch upon what the Orthodox call *sobornost,* about which I will speak under the heading of pneumatology.

c. The Church's experience is that the Spirit never stops building it up through prophecy. "Prophets" play a large role during the formative period.[12] We can understand their role during our "foundation" when we compare the statements *about* Christ contained in the epistles and in the Book of Revelation ("evangelium de Christo [the good news about Christ]") with the Synoptic writings ("evangelium Christi [Christ's good news]"). There has been a transition to an understanding of the mystery and of the definitive plan of salvation whose center has been Jesus. Only rarely was prophecy a question of prediction. It was a question of unveiling the purposes of God. The Church, being a *peregrinans* [a wayfarer], being en route, has its point of stability in the future; it walks in time toward its goal. "Prophets" blaze the trail ahead. In this sense, "prophecy" has not ceased in the Church.[13] For our time, one could think of Lebbe, Cardijn, John XXIII;[14] of certain group sharings of the Gospel; of meetings of the renewal; of the pioneers of the ecumenical

---

12. See Eph 2:20; 3:5; the lists in Rom 12:6; 1 Cor 12:28; Eph 4:11; the role in Acts 11:27; 13:1; then, in the ordinary assemblies of the faithful, 1 Cor 11:4–5; 12:10; 14:26–40; 1 Thes 5:19–20. [8]

13. For the early Church, references to the *Didache,* Clement of Rome, Justin, Hermas, Miltiades can be found in *ES* 1:95–96 [ET: *HS* 1:65–66]. And see *Vraie et fausse réforme dans l'Église* [Unam Sanctam 20] (Paris: Cerf, 1950), 196–228; 2d ed. [revised and corrected, Unam Sanctam 72] (Paris: Cerf, 1968) 179–207 [ET: *True and False Reform in the Church,* translated and with an introduction by Paul Philibert (Collegeville, Minn. / Michael Glazier, 2011), 169–95]. [9]

14. [trans.] Frédéric-Vincent Lebbe, a missionary to China, encouraged the pope to appoint indigenous bishops in mission countries. Joseph Leo Cardinal Cardijn founded the Jeunesse ouvrière chrétienne (Young Christian Worker) movement. Pope John XXIII convoked the Second Vatican Council.

movement; of all those women and men who open up and unveil the paths of God. This is the work of the Spirit, "the Unknown beyond the Word" (H. Urs von Balthasar).[15]

---

15. [trans.] "Der Unbekannte jenseits des Wortes," in *Interpretation der Welt: Festschrift für R. Guardini zum achtzigsten Geburtstag*, ed. H. Kuhn et al. (Würzburg: Echter Verlag, 1965), 638–45.

2

The Spirit in the Personal Prayer and in the Personal Lives of Christians

1. Salvation and messianic eschatology

It is a fact that prayers to the Holy Spirit begin with the cry, "Come!" Thus begin the hymn *Veni Creator* (ninth century), the antiphon and sequence *Veni, Sancte Spiritus* (twelfth century, with a sequence attributed to Stephen Langton), the great lyric prayer of Symeon the New Theologian that is placed at the beginning of his hymns, or a prayer of Jean de Fécamp, from 1060 (*ES* 2:147 and 148, n. 2 [*HS* 2:112]).[1] It is not that the Spirit is not already there, but the Spirit is implored to bring, by a new coming, what we lack. These prayers ask the Spirit precisely for what we do not have and even for the opposite of what currently exists: to straighten what is twisted, to warm what is frozen, to wash what is soiled, etc. From a biblical perspective, this is what is effected by a salvation and an *eschaton*

---

1. [trans.] For St. Symeon, see SChr 156 (Paris: Cerf, 1969), 151 and 153; for Jean de Fécamp, see Yolande Arsène-Henry, *Les plus beaux textes sur le Saint-Esprit*, nouv. éd. (Paris: La Colombe, 1968), 204 and note 33, p. 363.

that are messianic, by those foretastes of the Kingdom that the Bible expresses in terms of valleys filled in, mountains brought low, roads constructed where there were none, the blind made to see, prisoners set free, etc.[2] Let us keep this feature in mind.

2. A freedom judged by its fruits

More generally, the Spirit is the principle of our life as children of God: "all those who are enlivened by the Spirit of God are children of God" (Rom 8:14; St. Paul speaks of *huioi*, St. John uses the term *tekna*). The life of a child of God is—after Baptism which inaugurates it—a holy life under the rule of the Spirit (Rom 7:6; 8:2; Gal 5:16ff.). "God chose you ... to be saved by the Spirit who sanctifies and through faith in the truth."[3] This process of sanctification involves a combat against the "flesh" (1 Thes 4:8; Rom 8:5ff. and 13; Gal 5). The Spirit brings freedom: "wherever the Spirit of the Lord is, there is freedom" (2 Cor 3:17b). For the Spirit is interiority, and the Spirit indwells the interior of the "heart" in such a way that the prayer and the impulses the Spirit arouses in us are jointly and almost indiscernibly the Spirit's and ours. Yet this liberty is something other than an impulsiveness which remains psychological and even carnal. "No one fathoms the mystery of freedom except through discipline" (D. Bonhoeffer).[4] Such is the experience of the saints and of all those who endeavor to take the spiritual life seri-

---

2. See the references in Yves Congar, *Un peuple messianque[: L'Église, sacrement du salut—salut et libération*, Cogitatio fidei 85] (Paris: Cerf, 1975), 142–43. Is 40:3ff.; 58:6; Mt 3:3; Mk 1:3; Lk 3:4ff., etc. [10]

3. 2 Thes 2:13; 1 Thes 4:7–8 and see 5:23. The connection between the Spirit and faith is expressed frequently: see *ES* 2:135 [ET: *HS* 2:101–2]. I cannot here repeat the whole of the second part of *ES* 2 [ET: *HS* 2] which presents "the Breath of God in our personal lives," but see especially chapter 4, "Life in the Spirit and according to the Spirit," and chapter 6, "The Spirit and the Battle against the Flesh. Spirit and Freedom." [11]

4. [trans.] From "Stations on the Way to Freedom," printed at the beginning of his *Ethics*.

ously. Sometimes people have feared that the frequent insistence in the "renewal" upon an immediacy of conversion and of experience will make people forget that "ordinarily" God bestows the Spirit "after much sweat in his service and much fidelity to his grace" (Marie of the Incarnation. And see *ES* 2:216–17 [*HS* 2:167]).⁵ In the renewal, as in the personal life of anyone, the action of the Spirit is shown through its fruits: see Galatians 5:22, where the word "fruit" is in the singular, which enables L. Cerfaux to translate it as "the harvest of the Spirit" (*ES* 2:181 [*ES* 2:138]).⁶ St. Paul outlines the ideal image of a peaceful and joyful readiness to welcome the other and to love him or her in an effective way with patience and serenity, while the fruit of the "flesh" is violence, aggressive self-affirmation, and the absence of availability to others.

3. The gifts of the Spirit

St. Paul speaks of letting oneself be led by the Spirit (Gal 5:16, 18, 22, 25; Rom 8:14). This is also the experience of the men and women who are spiritual people. This experience was given systematic expression beginning in 1235 and, in particular, by St. Thomas Aquinas in a theology in which the gifts of the Spirit are distinguished from the virtues (*ES* 1:167ff.; *ES* 2:175ff. [*HS* 1:118ff.; *HS* 2:134ff.]).⁷ The idea is that only God, in person, can bring the action of a child of God to its culmination and carry it to the level which its full divine character demands. It is a question of putting into action those sources of life that are received from the grace of God according to a

---

5. [trans.] Letter to her son, in Arsène-Henry, *Les plus beaux textes sur le Saint-Esprit*, p. 242.

6. [trans.] *Le chrétien dans la théologie paulinienne*, Lectio divina 33 (Paris: Cerf, 1962), 273 and 422ff; ET: *The Christian in the Theology of St. Paul*, trans. Lilian Soiron (New York: Herder, 1967), 461ff.

7. [trans.] The references Congar gives in the volumes of *ES* mentioned here are the ones cited in the first three pages of his article in Part Three, below, "The Holy Spirit in the Thomistic Theology of Moral Action."

measure and a mode which transcend those of *our own* spirit. This happens even with the theological virtues. The "excesses" of the saints are connected to this leading by the Spirit, at least the most incontestable aspects of those excesses, for something of the human and behaviors derived from their own idiosyncrasies can be mixed in with these ... Yet inspirations and appeals to the absolute are a part of any normal life in the Spirit. So is an experience of joy in the face of trials, to which the Apostle so often bears witness (*ES* 2:161 [*HS* 2:122]).[8] And finally, so is the experience of freedom, for the most onerous demands are internalized and experienced as the demands of love. The Christian, says St. Augustine, is not lawless, but is no longer *under* the law (St. Paul, Gal 5:13 and 18; *ES* 2:165 [*HS* 2:124–25]).[9]

---

8. [trans.] Congar refers to the following NT passages: 1 Thes 1:5–6; 2 Cor 1:3–7; Rom 11:17; Gal 5:22.

9. [trans.] At the page from *ES* 2 to which he refers, Congar gives the following citation for this quote from Augustine: *In Ioannis Evangelium*, Tractate 3.2 (PL 35:1397), and he also mentions Augustine's *De spiritu et littera* 9.15 (PL 44:209).

3

An Ecclesiological Pneumatology

1. The Church, temple of the Holy Spirit

On two occasions the Second Vatican Council speaks of the Church in Trinitarian terms as the "people of God, body of Christ, temple of the Holy Spirit."[1] In St. Paul, the repeated affirmation of the Spirit's indwelling in us as in the Spirit's sanctuary (*naos Theou*) is applied simultaneously to persons and to the community as such (1 Cor 3:16–17; 6:19; 2 Cor 6:16; Rom 8:9; Eph 2:19–22). The Tradition—patristic, spiritual and medieval—has never stopped saying that every soul is the Church; the spiritual dimensions of the latter, as Temple and Spouse, are also made real in each faithful soul. If it is a question of the Church as such, the Temple idea is naturally accompanied by a dynamic nuance—the idea of being built up. If it is a question of the sanctified person (St. Paul speaks not only of the soul, but of the body), questions arise in theology about the mode of indwelling, about its appropriation—or more than a simple "appropriation"—to the Person of the Holy Spirit. On this subject there are differences, nuances at the very least, among authors, even in their interpreta-

---

1. [trans.] *LG* n. 17.3 and *AG* n. 7.

tion of the "authorities."[2] However, agreement takes shape on the following positions: (a) In the descending line of efficient causality, everything is effected by the three Persons together. (b) However, the nature which is common to them exists only as hypostasized in the Persons, starting from the "monarchy" of the Father, the Source without source. The simultaneous action of the Persons is brought about according to their order and their hypostatic particularity. (c) God's gift of self to God's spiritual creature is brought about from the Father through the Son in the Spirit; *in us* the Spirit is the first gift through which and with which, inseparably, the Father and the Son are given to us. (d) In our return to God we are made like the Son through the Spirit, who plays the role of formal exemplary cause; in this order of exemplarity, as in that of the logical priority of the gift, there is something which is proper to the Holy Spirit.

It is regrettable that our classical treatises about (created) grace do not make explicit its relationships with the Trinity and the Spirit. After the systematization of *De gratia capitis* [On the Grace of the Head] (second half of the twelfth century), the treatise was to become quite Christological. Yet in the *Summa* of St. Thomas, the Christological element is not there at all, since the treatise comes before the third part, in which Christology is developed! Some recent presentations, such as those of K. Rahner, G. Philips, and especially L. Bouyer,[3] give attention to developing the continuity between the Spirit bestowed and the life of grace or the "spiritual" life.

In the temple, the Holy Spirit makes the offering of spiritual worship possible (Phil 3:3; Jn 4:23–24). This is the consecration of life by faith (Rom 15:16); it is the prayer inspired by the Holy Spir-

---

2. See the encyclopedias: A. Michel ["Trinité (missions et habitation des personnes de la)"], *DTC*, vol. 15, bk 2, 1841–55; Roberto Moretti, ["Inhabitation, 2: Réflection théologique"], *DictSpir*, 7:1745–57; *ES* 2:112–26 [ET: *HS* 2:83–90]. L. Bouyer, *Le Consolateur, Esprit-Saint et [vie de] grâce* (Paris: Cerf, 1980), maintains an indwelling is *proper* to the Holy Spirit. [12]

3. Philips: *L'union personelle avec le Dieu vivant*[: *Essai sur l'origine et le sens de la grâce créée*. Bibliotheca ephemeridum theologicarum Lovaniensium 36] (Gembloux: Duculot, 1974). Bouyer: *Le Consolateur*. [13 and 14]

it (Eph 5:19; 6:18; Col 3:16 and especially Rom 8:26–27). This last passage is particularly pregnant with meaning, and it expresses the experience of countless souls, not only those in the "renewal," even if it is found especially there. The Spirit prays in us. The Spirit is so intimately within us, so much a gift "within hearts,"[4] that one can attribute to the Spirit as well as to us the invocation, "Abba, Father" (Gal 4:6; Rom 8:15). The Spirit comes to the aid of our weakness, because we do not know how to pray as we should (Rom 8:26). It is the Spirit who is the Desire of God, and the Spirit can make us desire in accordance with God. The Spirit animates the Church's celebration of the mystery of Christ in the liturgy; the Spirit concelebrates with the Church and, with her, sends up the cry, "Come, Lord Jesus!" (Rv 22:17 and 20). A. Vonier, asked to write a book on the Holy Spirit, could do it only by celebrating the Spirit's work in the Church: *The Spirit and the Bride*.[5] In extreme instances, the Spirit arouses in us a prayer that is foreign to our ideas and to our vocabulary, that praying or singing in tongues which is met above all in Pentecostal movements and in the "renewal," but also, occasionally, throughout history.[6]

The Spirit is at work in the liturgical life of the Church. The whole of the liturgy is animated by the praise of the Father, through the Son, in the Holy Spirit; it is a great doxology.[7] The dialogue

---

4. Gal 4:6; 2 Cor 1:22; Rom 5:5; 2:29; Eph 5:19 and 3:17; Col 3:16. [15]

5. *L'Esprit et l'épouse*, published in 1947 in Paris by Cerf, as Unam Sanctam 16, was a translation into French by K. Lainé and B. Limal of the original English edition, published in 1935 (London: Burns, Oates and Washbourne). [16]

6. Information and bibliography in *ES* 2:221–27 [ET: *HS* 2:173–77]. Contrary to K. Niederwimmer (["Das Gebet des Geistes, Rom 8:26,"] *Theologische Zeitschrift* 20 [1964]: 252–65), O. Cullmann thinks that the "groanings" of Rom 8:26 refer to praying in tongues: "La prière selon les épîtres pauliniennes," *Theologische Zeitschrift* 35 (1979): 89–101, at 95ff. [17]

7. C. Vagaggini, *Initiation théologique à la liturgie*, 2 vols. (Bruges: Apostolat liturgique / Paris: Société liturgique, 1959–63) [ET: *Theological Introduction to the Liturgy* (based on 4th Italian edition), trans. Leonard J. Doyle and W. A. Jurgens (Collegeville, Minn.: Liturgical Press, 1976)] and, for the doxology that concludes all eucharistic prayers, *ES* 2:271–91 [*HS* 2:213–30]. [18]

that opens the celebration alludes to the Spirit's presence and to the charism of the celebrant (*ES* 1:62 [*HS* 1:36 and notes on p. 43]). As much in the West as in the East, the efficacy of the sacraments, and indeed the conversion of the Eucharistic gifts into the body and blood of Christ, is attributed to the Holy Spirit (*ES* 3:320–29 [*HS* 3:250–57]). The question of the Eucharistic epiclesis will be treated later (see *ES* 3:294–315 [*HS* 3:228–41]). It is important to note here that all sacred actions call for an epiclesis (*ES* 3:343–51 [*HS* 3:267–74]).

2. A Church that is, first of all, a communion

Everything is at stake in the choice of the concept through which one enters into ecclesiology, that is to say, the discourse about the reality that is "Church." Will it be "society" or "communion"? The ecclesiology that came forth from the Counter-Reformation and from the anti-revolutionary restoration of the nineteenth century, communicated through a number of official statements and manuals, privileged "society,"[8] and even "unequal, hierarchical society" and *societas perfecta*, "complete society," that is, one having all the means of such a society, in particular, legislative and coercive power.[9] Such an option is linked to the following view of the Church:

---

8. See my investigations in "L'ecclésiologie de la Révolution française au concile du Vatican sous le signe de l'affirmation de l'autorité," in *L'ecclésiologie au XIXe siècle*, Unam Sanctam 34 (Paris: Cerf, 1960), 77–114. For the ecclesiological situation at the time of *Ecclesiam suam* and the shift toward a Church walking along the pathways of men and women, see the proceedings of the conference in Rome in October 1980 on *Ecclesiam suam* [*"Ecclesiam suam": première lettre encyclique de Paul VI. Colloque International*, Rome, 24–26 octobre, 1980 (Brescia: Instituto Paolo VI, 1982), in *Le concile de Vatican II: Son Église, peuple de Dieu et corps du Christ*, preface by René Rémond, Théologie historique 71 (Paris: Beauchesne, 1984), 7–31]; E. Germain, "À travers les catéchismes des cents cinquante dernières années," *Recherches et débats* 71 (1971): 107–31. [19]

9. K. Walf, "Die katholische Kirche—eine *societas perfecta*?" *Theologische Quartalschrift* 157 (1977): 107–18; P. Granfield, "The Church as *Societas Perfecta* in the Schemata of Vatican I," *Church History* 48 (1979): 431–46. [20]

(a) it is founded by Christ, in the days of his flesh and, in that capacity, Christ is essentially the Church's *founder*; (b) it is pyramidal, with everything coming down from the top to the base; (c) it is seen in a perspective which is completely Christological, subject to the danger of "Christomonism" (see below). The role of the Spirit, in short, pneumatological Christology, is replaced by a theology of *created grace* and of the "gratia capitis [grace of the head]." Note that the expression "gratia creata [created grace]" appears only in 1245. A pneumatological ecclesiology presupposes, on the other hand, a pneumatological Christology,[10] that is to say, the awareness of the role of the Spirit in the messianic life of Jesus, in the resurrection and the glorification that made him Lord and made his humanity, hypostatically united to the eternal Son, pass from the *forma servi* [form of a servant] to the *forma Dei* [form of God]. The result of this was a humanity entirely penetrated by the Spirit, pneumatized, capable of communicating the Spirit and of acting as Spirit (Acts 10:38; Rom 1:4; 1 Cor 15:45; 1 Cor 3:17).

A concept other than "society" is preferable for entering into the theology of the Church: that of "communion." It was used by Möhler in *Die Einheit* (1825)[11] and by F. Pilgram, in *Physiologie der Kirche* (1860;[12] curiously, he speaks very little of the Holy Spirit). The Second Vatican Council, without developing the concept of communion—except a little in connection with ecumenism—really made this its fundamental idea and key to its doctrine in showing, before everything else, that the Church is dependent upon the mystery of the Trinity and in treating the Church itself first as mystery. Its social nature and its hierarchical character come afterwards.

With pneumatological Christology, there is no longer only the

---

10. See *ES* 3:219–28 (bibliography) [ET: *HS* 3:165–73]. [21]
11. [trans.] *L'unité* (German edition published in 1825); ET: *Unity in the Church or the Principle of Catholicism: Presented in the Spirit of the Church Fathers of the First Three Centuries*, edited and translated with an introduction by Peter C. Erb (Washington, D.C.: The Catholic University of America Press, 1996).
12. [trans.] Mainz: F. Kirckheim.

historical-founder Christ; there is Christ the foundation through the faith of believers whose "we" is the Church. There is the glorious Christ acting unceasingly as Spirit to form his Body, and sending his Spirit. Or even better: the Church, even in its origins as institution and society, is brought into being by two "missions," that of the Son-Word and that of the Spirit-Breath. The Spirit is "co-instituting" in a broader sense than I indicated in *ES* 2:13–24 [*HS* 2:5–14]. With many theologians today, I recognize that Jesus laid the foundations but that the full institution of the Church was the accomplishment of the apostles after Pentecost. Had Jesus not said, using the future tense, "I will build my Church?"[13] Inspiration came into play throughout the whole foundational period, after which there was operative that "assistance" for which the Fathers, the councils and the medievals used the words *revelare, inspirare, illuminare* [to reveal, to inspire, to enlighten], which express a constant and always current action of the Spirit.[14]

The Spirit is promised and given to the *ecclesia* [assembly]. Jesus said [using the second person plural], the Father will give *you* the Spirit, will send *you* the Spirit; the Spirit will teach *you*, will lead *you*, will make *you* know ... (Jn 14 and 16); Rom 5:1–11 is all in the first person plural, "the love of God has been poured out in *our* hearts by the Holy Spirit who has been given *to us* ..." On the day of Pentecost, the Spirit is given to everyone, about 120 persons (Acts 1:15; compare Lk 24:33, "the eleven and their companions"),

---

13. There took place, during the years 1945–1960, a discussion on this point: was the Church born at the cross (S. Tromp, F. Grivec) or at Pentecost (T. Zapelena)? It is clear that it was spiritually founded at the cross and brought to birth at Pentecost. Those taking the side of the cross held that it was there that Christ had given the Spirit ... [22]

14. See *La Tradition et les traditions: Essai historique* (Paris: Fayard, 1960), 127ff., 151–66 (with notes on pp. 178–82) [ET: *Tradition and Traditions: An Historical and a Theological Essay*, Part One, trans. Michael Naseby (London: Burns and Oates, 1966; reprinted San Diego, Calif.: Basilica Press / Needham Heights, Mass.: Simon and Schuster, 1997), 93–94 and 119–37], to be supplemented by *ES* 2:44ff. [ET: HS 2:29ff.]. [23]

and yet the Spirit comes upon each one (Acts 2:3). In 1 Cor 12:4ff., there is only one body because one and the same Spirit has been given, in diverse ways, to many. The gift of unity is made to many people in one alone, the one who constitutes them members of the same "body," which is the earthly body *of Christ* in glory. As Möhler puts it:

When they received strength and light from on high, the leaders and the members of the nascent Church were not dispersed into different places, but brought together in the same place and with the same heart, forming only one assembly of brothers ... In this way each disciple was filled with gifts from on high only because he or she formed one moral unity with all the other disciples.[15]

Two noteworthy expressions translate these ideas: *epi to auto*, gathered together (in the same place),[16] *homothumadon*, in unanimity.[17] One might be surprised that it is necessary to be already in agreement to receive the Spirit of unity. Indeed, a familial and non-schismatic spirit, already aroused secretly by the Spirit, is a necessary disposition for receiving that same Spirit as divine principle of communion (*ES* 2:26 [*HS* 2:15]). Yet what the Spirit brings when given in this way transcends any simply human harmony.

The New Testament does not use the word *koinōnia*, communion, to designate the united body of believers, the (mystical) Body, the Church. Today, on the other hand, the term enjoys a wide cur-

---

15. *La symbolique*, [2d ed., trans. F. Lachat (Paris: L. Vivès, 1852–53)] §37 [German original: *Symbolik* (Mainz: F. Kupferberg, 1832); for an alternate ET, see *Symbolism: Exposition of the Doctrinal Differences between Catholics and Protestants as Evidenced by Their Symbolical Writings*, trans. James Burton Robertson, introduction by Michael Himes (New York: Crossroads, 1997)]; see also *Unity in the Church*, §63. [24]

16. Acts 1:15; 2:1; then 2:47 and 1 Cor 11:20. The function of this term in the unity ideal of the early Church: P. S. Zanetti, *Enōsis—epi to auto*, vol. 1, *Un "dossier" preliminare per lo studio dell'unità cristiana all inizio del 20 secolo*, [Università di Bologna Facoltà di lettere e filosofia, Studi e ricerche nuova, ser. 25] (Bologna: Zanichelli, 1969) (on *epi to auto*, pp. 154ff.); E. Delebecque, "Trois simples mots chargés d'une lumière neuve (Actes 2:47b)," *Revue thomiste* 80 (1980): 75–85. [25]

17. Acts 1:14; 2:1; 2:46; and then 4:24; 5:12; 15:25; Rom 15:6. [26]

rency.[18] In the New Testament, the term is used in several ways. The one that interests me the most is very close to the meaning of *metochē*, participation; believers participate in, have communion in, the good things which come from God, or in God himself.[19] And it is because they have—one and all and all together and in the same way—a share in these good things that they have communion with one another, that they are a communion (1 Jn 1:3, 6, 7; and see Gal 2:9). The Spirit is put more explicitly into relation with *koinōnia* in the New Testament. In 2 Cor 13:13, so important for us, *koinōnia tou hagiou Pneumatos* [communion in the Holy Spirit], the genitive is an objective genitive, not a subjective genitive. It does not mean the (ecclesial) communion produced by the Spirit; it means participation in the Holy Spirit.[20] Some exegetes (H. Seesemann, M. Manzarene) understand the *koinōnia* of Acts 2:42 as the putting into common ownership of material resources, but perseverance in the *koinōnia* in that text is linked with the devotion to the apostles' teaching, to the breaking of the bread, and to the prayers, all of which are of profound value for ecclesial communion (J. Dupont). In any case, the ecclesiology of the New Testament and the relationship between the Spirit and the Church go beyond, in actuality, the usage of the word *koinōnia* and what is said about the Spirit in connection with this word. C. H. Dodd rightly says: "The life of the Church is the divine life manifested ... in the incarnate Christ and communicated by his Spirit" (cited by Hamer,[21] who, for his part, says, "*koinōnia* typifies

18. W. Elert, *Abendmahl und Kirchengemeinschaft in der alten Kirche, haupsächlich des Ostens* (Berlin: Lutherisches Verlagshaus, 1954) [ET: *Eucharist and Church Fellowship in the First Four Centuries*, trans. N. E. Nagel (St. Louis, Mo.: Concordia, 1966)]; M.-J. Le Guillou, "Église et 'communion'," *Istina* 6 (1959): 33–82; J. Hamer, *L'Église est une communion*, Unam Sanctam 40 (Paris: Cerf, 1962); P. C. Bori, *Koinōnia: L'idea della communione nell'ecclesiologia recente e nel Nuovo Testamento* (Brescia: Paideia, 1972). [27]

19. *Koinōnia*, participation in the same Gospel (Phil 1:5), in the same faith (Phlm 6), in God (1 Jn 1:6), in Christ (1 Cor 1:9; Phil 3:10; 1 Cor 10:16: through the Eucharist); in the Spirit (2 Cor 13:13; Phil 2:1). [28]

20. F. Hauck, ["*Koinōn-* im Neuen Testament,"] *TWNT* 3:807 [ET: *TDNT* 3:807]. [29]

21. *L'Église est une communion*, 177. [30]

in the New Testament ... a relationship with God and with human beings that is characteristic of the Christian community"). Now this relationship—in which the horizontal dimension among believers flows from the vertical dimension with God—is wholly tied to the action of the Holy Spirit. It is the Spirit who is the principle of communion, the one and only Spirit who is there to animate these relationships in a holy way, first in Christ and then in believers and in his ecclesial body.[22] What a prodigious principle of unity and of life!

St. Basil, more than any other, has proclaimed the greatness of the unity that the Church, which celebrates the Eucharist, receives from the communion (*koinōnia*) of the Holy Spirit.[23]

The Spirit is therefore *in hearts* (Gal 4:6). The Spirit is given to persons in the most interior of ways, in a fashion so spiritual and so intimate that one scarcely distinguishes the Spirit's action from one's own: is it the Spirit or is it we who say, "Abba, Father" (see Gal 4:6; Rom 8:15)? Thus, the Spirit can be the principle of a communion without fusion or confusion, as much between us and God as among believers. We are "members of one another" (Eph 4:25). That is why the Spirit is the transcendent principle of the communion of saints,[24] which is an exchange, a sort of being for one another,

---

22. On the Spirit "unus numero in Christo et in omnibus [one in number in Christ and in all]" see St. Thomas, *3 Sent.*, d. 13, q. 2, a. 1, ad. 2; *De veritate*, q. 29, a. 4; *Super evangelium s. Ioannis lectura* (*In Ioan.*), ch. 1, lectures 9 and 10 [ET: *Commmentary on the Gospel of John, Chapters 1–5*, trans. Fabian Larcher and James A. Weisheipl, with introduction and notes by Daniel Keating and Matthew Levering (Washington, D.C.: The Catholic University of America Press, 2010), 78–85]; *ST* 2a2ae, q. 183, a. 3, ad 3; Pius XII, encyclical *Mystici corporis*, no. 54 and 77 (*AAS* 35 [1943], 219 and 230) [ET: *Mystici Corporis: Encyclical Letter of Pope Pius XII on the Mystical Body of Christ*, 55–56 and 77, in *Selected Documents of His Holiness Pope Pius XII 1939–1958* (Washington, D.C.: National Catholic Welfare Conference, 1958), 24–25 and 34.]; *LG*, n. 7.7. [31]

23. See B. Bobrinskoy, "Liturgie et ecclésiologie trinitaire de saint Basile," in *Eucharisties d'Orient et d'Occident 2*, Lex orandi 47 (Paris: Cerf, 1970), 197–240. [32]

24. St. Basil [of Caesarea], *On the Holy Spirit* 26.61 (PG 32:18[0–181]); SChr 17 bis:470–71 [ET: NPNF 2-8:38–39, or pp. 93–94 of Anderson's translation]; *Epistola 90* (PG 32:473) [ET: Letter 90, NPNF 2-8:176]; St. Thomas, *ST* 3a, q. 82, a. 6, ad 3; P. Bernard, ["Communion de saints 1: Son aspect dogmatique et historique,"] *DTC*, 3:440, 442 (Augustine). [33]

thanks to charity. It is the Spirit who brings about that rather astonishing communication in virtue of which the baby who is baptized believes in and through the faith of his or her parents, of the godparents, and of "the Church," while, in the infant, charity does not yet exist.[25]

The Spirit penetrates everything without violence or damage. The Fathers and the liturgy attribute to the Spirit what Scripture says of Wisdom: "There is in her a spirit that is intelligent, holy, unique, manifold, subtle, mobile, keen ... penetrating all minds;"[26] "the Spirit of the Lord fills the whole world and that which holds all things together knows what is said" (Ws 1:7). This nature of the Spirit permits the Spirit, who is unique and sovereign, to transcend space and time, what divides and separates. As to space, the point of the foreign tongues of the day of Pentecost is an answer to Babel.[27] The praises of the only God will be, thanks to the same Spirit, heard and sung by each people in its *own* language. The Spirit distributes the variety of talents and charisms, but "for the common good" (1 Cor 12:7); the Spirit harmonizes the particular and the whole, making real that ideal of unified plurality, another name for catholicity, which is the reality of the Body. The marvelous little work of St. Peter Damien (†1072), *Dominus vobiscum*, is worth reading.[28] Unique and sovereign, the Spirit is Lord over time. The pledge of our eternal and incorruptible inheritance (that is, the par-

---

25. St. Augustine, *De peccatorum meritis et remissione* 1:25.38 (PL 44:131) [ET: *The Punishment and Forgiveness of Sins and the Baptism of Little Ones*, introduction, translation and notes by Roland Teske, in *Answer to the Pelagians: The Works of Saint Augustine; A Translation for the 21st Century*, 1/23 (Hyde Park, N.Y.: New City Press, 1996), 55–56]; St. Thomas, *ST* 3a, q. 68, a. 9, ad 2; q. 73, a. 3. [34]

26. Ws 7:22–23, and see 9:11; 12:1. [35]

27. *AG*, n. 4; H. Legrand, "Inverser Babel, mission de l'Église," *Spiritus* 63 (1970): 323–46. This is done without erasing what is positive about the division of languages. On the Acts of the Apostles, see M.-A. Chevallier ["L'Esprit de Dieu dans les Écritures," in *Initiation à la pratique de la théologie* (Paris: Cerf, 1982), 2:448–52]. [36]

28. PL 145:231–52; partial translation in *La Maison-Dieu*, 21 (1950/1): 174–81 [ET: *The Book of "The Lord Be With You," St. Peter Damien: Selected Writings on the Spiritual Life*, trans. Patricia McNulty (New York: Harper and Brothers, 1961), 53–81]. [37]

tial presence of our future), the Spirit is the principle of what has been called "sacramental time," that time of the mysteries of salvation in virtue of which what is past is still present to us and what is in the future is already there. Because the Spirit acts in them, the sacraments belong to a distinctive form of duration within which past, present, and future are not foreign and lethal to one another as they are in human chronological succession. Time, in the history of salvation and for the Church, is a time which allows people who succeed one another to enter into communion with a unique event, dated historically and far removed from them. And that happens not only through a reference in memory and in thought, but through a presence and an action of the mystery of salvation (as in the biblical sense of "memorial").[29]

3. A communion organized as a society

Pilgram said that the Church is a communion organized as a society. We will see below how a system of law flows from the very principles of communion; it serves and protects them. What must be done here is to show how a pneumatological ecclesiology, an ecclesiology of communion, will avoid legalism, uniformity, and a purely pyramidal logic, which is thereby clerical and paternalistic. While pre-Trinitarian monotheism favors, and even gives rise to, such defects, and a purely Christological logic produces a Church emphasizing priestly authority, a Church conceived in terms of the Trinity and of pneumatology recognizes that both persons and particular communities have the nature of *subjects*:[30] subjects of what

---

29. See the reference in *La Tradition et les traditions: Essai théologique*, 272ff., n. 88 and 89 [ET: *Tradition and Traditions: An Historical and a Theological Essay*, Part Two, 259, n. 1 and 260, n. 2]. [38]

30. One could read H. Legrand, "Grâce et institution dans l'Église: Les fondements théologique du droit canonique," in [Monneron, Jean Louis et al.,] *L'Église: Institution et foi* (Bruxelles: Facultés universitaires Saint-Louis, 1979), 139–72; my

they do, having a part to play in the determination of the rules by which they live; subjects of their own history, putting into action their own gifts and charisms. This implies many things in the lived experience of the Church. For practical decisions, it implies governance by councils, by decisions taken in common, where women have their rightful place;[31] it implies a conciliar life that culminates in "ecumenical" councils which may possibly formulate "dogmas." The fathers who are assembled there are not there as "delegates" of the faithful back home, but each represents his local or particular church and is supported by its communion. Councils speak of themselves as assembled "in the Holy Spirit," they invoke the Spirit, and they are assisted by the Spirit.[32] Their decisions, once approved by the Bishop of Rome, are valid "ex sese [by their own authority]," but they must be "received" by the *ecclesia* which is, as a whole, the historical subject that carries the Tradition. "Reception" is the process through which the *ecclesia* acknowledges what is its own in a given decision.[33] "The Church's infallibility depends entirely on its double gift: the ongoing presence of Christ as head of the whole body in his emissaries, in whom, as he promised, he is present, as the Father was present in him to authorize or authenticate in him the truth, his truth; and the presence, in the whole body, of the Spirit, who keeps that truth a living one. One must again emphasize that what we call the special assistance of

---

articles "La tri-unité de Dieu et l'Église," *La vie spirituelle* 128 (1974): 687–703, and "Le monothéisme politique et le Dieu Trinité," *Nouvelle revue théologique* 103 (1981): 3–17. [39]

31. See my study "Quod omnes tangit ab omnibus tractari et approbari debet," *Revue historique de droit français et étranger* 36 (1958): 210–59; H.-M. Legrand, "Synodes et conseils de l'après-concile," *Nouvelle revue théologique* 98 (1976): 193–216. [40]

32. There are innumerable references. See, for example, *La Tradition et les traditions: Essai historique*, 151ff. and 220; *La Tradition et les traditions: Essai théologique*, 108ff. [ET: *Tradition and Traditions*, Part One, 119ff. and 172; Part Two, 346–47]. [41]

33. See my article "La 'réception' comme réalité ecclésiologique," *Revue des sciences philosophiques et théologiques* 56 (1973): 369–403 [ET: "Reception as an Ecclesiological Reality," in *Election and Consensus in the Church*, ed. Giuseppe Alberigo and Anton Weiler, *Concilium* 77 (New York: Herder and Herder, 1972): 43–68]. [42]

the Spirit, which keeps the pope who is formulating an *ex cathedra* [from the chair (of St. Peter)] definition, or all the bishops gathered together, from altering the deposit of faith would not even have a point if this deposit had not been kept alive in the catholic consciousness as a whole, whose supernatural clarity is first of all dependent upon the actual holiness of her members."[34] This reference to holiness is very important. The charism of truth is linked to the gift of holiness through the Holy Spirit.

If it is a question of ministries, the fact that we have gone from the singular to the plural is already significant. Along with the ordained ministries, a variety of services or ministries contribute to the fact that the Church exists and lives. The ordained ministries themselves are what they are, not over and above the community, but within it. The community plays a role by raising up—and possibly pointing out—vocations, by giving witness to the faith and the aptitude of those chosen, and by accompanying their consecration with prayer.[35] It is not a purely vertical descent, by "valid" succession, from the apostles, as a purely Christological logic would have it; something is done by the whole body in which the Spirit dwells and acts. "Succession" is at the same time fidelity to the teaching of the apostles and "valid" transmission of an office: both together belong to the sacramental nature of the Church.[36] In virtue of this profound quality, the whole Church is the celebrant of its liturgy and of its sacraments. The Tradition is quite firm about this.[37] If one

---

34. Bouyer, *Le Consolateur*, 419. [43]

35. H.-M. Legrand, "Le sens théologique des élections épiscopales d'après leur déroulement dans l'Église ancienne," *Concilium* 77 (1972): 41–50. [44]

36. See my study in *Ministères et communion ecclésiale* (Paris: Cerf, 1971), 51–74; J. Meyendorff, "Autorité doctrinale dans la tradition de l'Église orthodoxe," *Concilium* 117 (1976): 49–54. [45]

37. See my study "Ecclesia ou communauté des chrétiens, sujet intégral de l'action liturgique," in *La liturgie après Vatican II*, [ed. Yves Congar,] Unam Sanctam 66 (Paris: Cerf, 1967), 241–82 [ET: "The *Ecclesia* or Christian Community as a Whole Celebrates the Liturgy," in *At the Heart of Christian Worship: Liturgical Essays of Yves Congar*, translated and edited by Paul Philibert (Collegeville, Minn.: Liturgical Press/A Pueblo Book, 2010), 15–68]. [46]

adopts this corporate-sacramental perspective, which sees a communion of persons where the Spirit dwells and acts, one will have the pastoral behaviors of which Saint Augustine formulated something like a motto when he declared: "Vobis sum episcopus, vobiscum christianus—I am your bishop, but first I am a Christian along with you; I teach you, but first I am a disciple along with you; I absolve you and bless you, but first I am a sinner and a penitent along with you...."[38] To one such as Bishop Fragoso who asks, "How can we, bishops and priests, practice the fatherhood of God through the gratuity of *diakonia* [service]?" the answer is, in theological terms: by the brotherhood of Christ and the fully developed pneumatology of a Church which is a communion of persons.

4. No "pneumatocentrism"

That we lack a pneumatology is a reproach addressed to the Catholic Church by other Christians. That we practise a "Christomonism" is claimed especially by the Orthodox.[39] I take these warnings very seriously into consideration. Yet a warning against "pneumatocentrism" can also be sounded. This came to be a danger in a community like Corinth during the apostolic period. The early Church

---

38. See the references in the studies on the hierarchy as service, in *L'épiscopat et l'Église universelle*, Unam Sanctam 39 (Paris: Cerf, 1962), 67–132 at 94; A. Fragoso, ["Qu'ai-je devant les yeux lorsque je dis 'Notre Père'?"] *Concilium* 163 (1981): 167–69 at 169 [ET: "The Image Suggested by the Words 'Our Father,'" *God as Father?* ed. Johannes-Baptist Metz, Edward Schillebeeckx, and Marcus Lefébure, *Concilium* 143 (New York: Seabury, 1981), 113–14]. [47]

39. See the references in my study "Pneumatologie ou 'christomonisme' dans la tradition latine?" in *Ecclesia a Spiritu Sancto edocta* [(*Lumen gentium*, 53)]: *Mélanges [théologiques; hommages à Mgr] G.[érard] Philips*. [*Verzamelde theologische opstellen aangeboden aan Mgr. Gérard Philips*, Bibliotheca ephemeridum theologicarum Lovaniensium 27] (Gembloux: Duculot, 1970), 41–64 (previously published in *Ephemerides theologicae Lovanienses* 45 [1969]: 394–416) [ET: Part Three, Article 3, below]. Orthodox analyses have been made by N. Nissiotis, Paul Evdokimov, B. Bobrinskoy, N. Afanassieff, etc. An overview is given in W. Hryniewicz, "Der pneumatologische Aspekt der Kirche aus orthodoxer Sicht," *Catholica* 31 (1977): 122–50. [48]

reacted successfully against this, but it threatened the churches at several points in their history. The Holy Spirit does no work other than the work of Christ; the Spirit does not construct a body other than that *of Christ* (1 Cor 12:12–13; Eph 4:13). Pneumatology and Christology are principles of well-being for one another. Read again Acts 2:42 in this perspective, and also 1 Cor 12:4ff., where the diversity of gifts is not only pneumatological. The union and the complementarity of the Word-Son and the Breath-Spirit must be insisted upon.

4

The Spirit Is the Breath *of the Word* and the Spirit *of the Son*

Despite how this title might be understood, my focus remains on the economy. At issue here is not the eternal processions but the work accomplished for our salvation.

1. The gift of the Spirit brings God's self-communication to fulfillment

The gift of the Spirit is the endpoint, the *telos*, the perfection of God's self-communication to those who believe. It is linked to the mission and the gift of the Word-Son to the world (Gal 4:4–7). The two "missions," the two gifts are connected. The mission and gift of the Spirit presuppose those of the Son-Word. The mission and the gift of the Spirit aim to make us children of God; the Spirit is that of the Son and the Spirit makes people sons and daughters, members of, and coheirs with, the Son (Rom 8:14–17; Jn 1:12; 1 Jn 3:1–3). "During Christ's earthly mission, the relationship of humans to the Holy Spirit was brought about only through and in Christ. In contrast to this, after Pentecost, it is the relationship to Christ which is brought about only through and in the Holy Spirit."[1] This statement of Paul Evdokimov is correct, with the addition of some further clarifications. This is where a pneumatological Christology comes in.[2]

2. A pneumatological Christology

If the Spirit is the Spirit of the Son, the Spirit established Jesus of Nazareth as "Son of God" and did this at several points where it was a question, not of the hypostatic union—which was not an issue (see 1 Jn 1:14)—but of the economy of grace, of the role of Christ with respect to us. The New Testament is very emphatic about this. It draws our attention to three moments:

- "He will be called Son of the Most High."—"How will this be done?"—"The Holy Spirit will come upon you; therefore, the child will be holy and will be called Son of God" (Lk 1:32, 34, 35).
- Next there is the anointing at the baptism, an anointing with the Holy Spirit and with power, a messianic anointing (Acts 4:27; 10:38). "The Holy Spirit descended upon him in bodily form like a dove. And a voice came from heaven: 'You are my beloved Son; with you I am well pleased'" (Lk 3:22; Mk 1:10–11). There is here a reference to Ps 2:7: "You are my son; today I have begotten you." Jesus, at his baptism, is begotten by the Holy Spirit into his capacity as Christ, as the Son of God-*Messiah*, but in the condition of a servant and of what St. Augustine calls his "forma servi [form of a servant]."

1. [trans.] Paul Evdokimov, "Panagion and Panagia: The Holy Spirit and the Mother of God," originally published in the *Bulletin de la Société française d'études mariales* (Paris: Lethielleux, 1970), 59–71, trans. Alex Vinogradov and Michael Plekon, reprinted in the collection *In the World, of the Church: A Paul Evdokimov Reader* (Crestwood, N.Y.: St. Vladimir's Seminary Press, 2001), 155–74. The passage quoted is on p. 156.

2. See *ES* 3:219–28 [ET: *HS* 3:165–73]; J. D. G. Dunn, *Jesus and the Spirit*[: *A Study of the Religious and Charismatic Experience of Jesus and the First Christians as Reflected in the New Testament*] (London: SCM, 1975). (I do not follow him in his theological conclusions). [49]

His path will be essentially that of obedience to the Father, a filial path, even unto the cross.³

- God (the Father) raised him. And thus the Father "set him up as Son of God with power, according to the Holy Spirit" (Rom 1:4). This is a new begetting, and the New Testament applies once again to the risen Christ the passage from Ps 2:7 "You are my son; today I have begotten you" (Acts 13:32–33; Heb 1:5–6; see *ES* 3:224 [*HS* 3:168–169]). The same incarnate Son, the same Jesus Christ, is involved, but begotten into the condition of the world of God, "in forma Dei [in the form of God]," into his capacity as Lord permeated with the Spirit, the eschatological gift, the eschatological Adam, "a life-giving spirit" (1 Cor 15:45), priest according to the order of Melchizedek, having entered for us into the heavenly Holy of Holies. Of the risen Christ, it can be said that he is a man "without father, without mother, without genealogy" [Heb 7:3], for his resurrection was a new begetting of his human nature, in which neither human father nor human mother played a role, which makes him a "first-born" (Heb 1:6) without generation. "If St. Peter can say of Christians that they have been 'born again by the resurrection of Jesus Christ' (1 Pt 1:3), the same affirmation is still more valid for the Risen One himself."⁴

This three-moment chain is expressed, in Johannine theology, through the figure of the Lamb. Since it does not concern the ontology of the incarnate Word–of whom, however, we know that he was begotten of God, not of the will of the flesh or of man (Jn 1:13)–this figure begins at the baptism when, after having pointed him out as the Lamb of God who takes away the sin of the world,

3. See *ES* 2:139–42 [ET: *HS* 2:104–6 and notes on p. 110] on the filial soul of Jesus. [50]

4. A. Vanhoye, *Prêtres anciens, prêtre nouveau selon le Nouveau Testament* (Paris: Éditions du Seuil, 1980), 178 [ET: *Old Testament Priests and the New Priest according to the New Testament*, trans. J. Bernard Orchard (Petersham, Mass.: St. Bede's Publications, 1980), 157]. [51]

John saw the Spirit descend and remain upon him who was to baptize in the Spirit (Jn 1:29–34). This will be the Lamb sacrificed (Rv 5:6 and 9) "in forma servi, in forma agni paschalis [in the form of a servant, in the form of a paschal lamb]," but who will become "the first-born among the dead, the Prince of the kings of the earth" (Rv 1:5; Col 1:18) and who, always bearing the marks of his sacrificial slaughter, will reign in heaven, exercising sovereignty also over the history of the world (Rv 4:8–6:17). He is the one who gives the living water of the Spirit, which proceeds from his throne (Rv 21:6; 22:1). Moreover, St. John, with symbols that have a great fullness of meaning, expresses very forcefully the connection of the gift of the Spirit with Christ, and the sacrificed Christ, the paschal Lamb (Jn 4:10; 7:37–39; 14:16ff. and 26ff.; 16:7ff.; 19:34; 20:19–23).

This connection between the gift of the Spirit and the work of the Word incarnate springs from the Spirit's relationship to faith in the word. Already in the Old Testament, *ruah* and *dabar* are often linked or put side by side as equivalents: breath and word issue together from the mouth.[5] In the New Testament, the Word of God is the sword of the Spirit (Eph 6:17; Heb 4:12). The Spirit is active in the word (1 Thes 1:5; 4:8; 1 Pet 1:12) and the Spirit is given to faith (see Gal 3:2, 5 and 14; Eph 1:13; Jn 7:37–39 cited in *ES* 2:135 [*HS* 2:101–2]). "Through faith they establish the Spirit of God in their hearts" (St. Irenaeus, *Adversus haereses* 5:1.2 [= 5:9.2]). Active in this very faith, the Spirit makes people confess Jesus as Lord (1 Cor 12:3; 2 Cor 3:14–18; 1 Jn 4:1–3). This connection of the Spirit to faith in the word is found again in the connection between the Spirit and baptism. In *ES* 2:242–51 [*HS* 2:189–96] I analyzed the New Testament passages. That investigation showed that the Holy Spirit is given to the faith professed in water baptism. This happens in such a way that the gift of the Spirit is attributed to this baptism, even though the New Testament, in affirming a connection between the two, does not make

---

5. See Is 11:4; 34:16; Ps 33:6; 147:18; Jdt 16:14; Job 15:13. The Fathers (Irenaeus, Augustine) saw a revelation of the Spirit in Ps 33:6. [52]

the baptismal rite the instrumental cause of the gift of the Spirit. This Spirit, connected to the word and to baptism "in the name of Jesus," makes us become members of the Body of Christ (1 Cor 12:12–13). All of this obviously involves the apostolic ministry.

The two moments of the "forma servi—forma Dei [form of a servant—form of God]" in Christ correspond, for us, to the fact that we have the Spirit at present only as a pledge, as the first-fruits, under the constraints of the "flesh," of the promise of a transformation into a state of being sons and daughters of God permeated with the Spirit in the glorious freedom of the children of God. See Rom 8:1–30 and the themes "Already and Not-yet," the Spirit-flesh struggle, the cross and glory, the suffering of the Christian and of the apostle, the strength of God amidst our weakness, etc.

3. Relations between the Spirit and Christ

On the basis of these data gathered from the economy, I can present in further detail the relationship between the Spirit and Christ. I will do this in five propositions:

1. God's work is effected by two missions: that of the Word-Son and that of the Breath-Spirit.[6] By these missions whatever "proceeds" from the "monarchy" of the Father comes forth, in some fashion, out of God. The image which St. Irenaeus proposes is simple but remarkably expressive of the reality: God fashioned the human being using his two hands, who are the Son and the Spirit. In this way God fashioned the human being in his image and brought the human being to life (see especially *Adversus haereses* 4:38.3; 5:1.3 and 28.4). Less poetically St. Thomas Aquinas writes: "Salus generis humani

---

6. The Son sent (by the Father): Gal 4:4; Mt 10:40; Lk 9:48; 10:16; Jn 3:16–17 and 34; 5:37; 6:57; 7:16; 8:42; 10:36; 17:18; 20:21; 1 Jn 4:9. The Spirit sent by the Father: Jn 14:16 and 26; Gal 4:5; by Christ: Jn 15:26; 16:7; Lk 24:49. [53]

quae perficitur per Filium incarnatum et per donum Spiritus Sancti [The salvation of the human race which is brought to perfection through the incarnate Son and through the gift of the Holy Spirit]" (*ST* 1a, q. 32, a. 1, ad 3). Each of these two missions has an external or sensible form and an interior, spiritual form. However, while the sensible form for the Son is that of the Incarnation through the hypostatic union, that of the Holy Spirit is symbolic: dove, tongues of fire.

2. There are two missions, two who are sent, but for one and the same work. One can, without pretending to be exhaustive, put together a list [see Table 1] of the effects or actions that are attributed as much to Christ (left-hand column) as to the Holy Spirit.

To this ought to be added a parallel between what in the Gospel of John is attributed to the Paraclete (left-hand column) and what is attributed to Christ [see Table 2].

The parallelism extends to the point that Jesus speaks of the Spirit as another Paraclete: *allos* ["another" in the sense of "one more of the same sort"] not *heteros* ["another" in the sense of "one more of a different sort"] (Jn 14:16), and he says that the Spirit will be, as it were, his own return and his presence. Even better, St. Paul writes, "The Lord is the Spirit"–with the article *to Pneuma* [the Spirit] (2 Cor 3:17). It is not that he is confusing Christ and the Holy Spirit; the passage continues by speaking of the Spirit of the Lord, but without the article and in a fashion that can be translated "of the Lord (who is) spirit." There are more than thirty Trinitarian formulae or textual structures in St. Paul.[7] Yet there is no

---

7. See J. Lebreton, *Histoire du dogme de la Trinité*, vol. 1, 4th ed. (Paris: Beauchesne, 1919), 352–408; 565–69. I. Hermann, *Kyrios und Pneuma: Studien zur Christologie der paulinischen Hauptbriefe* [Studien zum Alten und Neuen Testament 2] (Munich: Kösel, 1961), does not deal with the Trinitarian utterances as such. Those who are concerned about the question of the Trinity note either that "Spirit" can have two meanings—the person and the action of the Holy Spirit, or the nature or character of

Table 1

Christ	Spirit
Wisdom and assurance before the courts: Lk 21:12–15	Mt 10:18-20; Mk 13:10–12
Baptism into Christ: Gal 3:27 One single body in Christ: Rom 12:5	Baptized into the Spirit: 1 Cor 12:13 to form a single body
Christ in us: Rom 8:10 and we in Christ: Rom 8:1	The Spirit in us: Rom 8:9 and we in the Spirit: Rom 8:9
Justified in Christ: Gal 2:17	Justified in the name of the Lord Jesus Christ and by the Spirit of our God: 1 Cor 6:11
The justice of God in Christ: 2 Cor 5:21	Justice, peace and joy in the Holy Spirit: Rom 14:17
Rejoice in the Lord: Phil 3:1	Joy in the Holy Spirit: Rom 14:17
The love of God in Christ Jesus: Rom 8:39	Your love in the Spirit: Col 1:8
Peace in Jesus Christ: Phil 4:7	Peace in the Holy Spirit: Rom 14:17
Sanctified in Christ Jesus: 1 Cor 1:2 and 30	[Sanctified] in the Spirit: Rom 15:16; compare 2 Thes 2:13
To speak in Christ: 2 Cor 2:17	To speak in the Spirit: 1 Cor 12:3
Filled with Christ: Col 2:10	Filled with the Spirit: Eph 5:18
To form in him (Christ) a holy temple in the Lord: Eph 2:21	To become a dwelling place for God in the Holy Spirit: Eph 2:22

---

being divine, the heavenly realm, which would be the sense here (L. Cerfaux)—or, if they are speaking within the framework of the Trinitarian doctrine, they appeal to consubstantiality and to circumincession. [54]

Table 2

Spirit	Christ
given by the Father: Jn 14:16	3:16
is with, alongside, within the disciples: 14:16ff.	3:22; 13:33; 14:20 and 26
is not received by the world: 14:17	1:11; 5:33 (12:48)
is not known by the world, only by believers: 14:17	14:19; 16:16ff.
sent by the Father: 14:26	see n. 6 above
teaches: 14:26	7:14ff.; 8:20; 18:37
comes (from the Father into the world): 15:26; 16:7, 13	5:43; 16:28; 18:37
bears witness: 15:26	5:31ff.; 8:13ff.; 7:7
confounds the world: 16:8	(3:19ff.; 9:41; 15:22)
does not speak on his own account; says only what he has heard: 16:13	7:17; 8:26, 28, 38; 12:49ff.; 14:10
glorifies (Jesus): 16:14	see 12:28; 17:1 and 4
reveals (communicates): 16:13ff.	4:25; (16:25)
leads into the fullness of truth; is the Spirit of truth: 16:13	see 1:17; 5:33; 18:37; 14:6
whoever drinks of him will never thirst: 4:10–15	whoever eats of him will never be hungry: 6:32–5

speculation on his part about the Tri-unity of God: he speaks on the level of the economy about what "God," the Lord, and the Spirit do for us and in us. On this existential level of the economy, the Lord acts in a Spirit mode, for he is "the spirit who gives life" (1 Cor 15:45), and the action of the Spirit is that of the Lord, which is, moreover, recognized and confessed as such only through the Spirit (1 Cor 12:3). The Lord and the Spirit act in the same sphere and do the same thing. The Lord acts as Spirit, and the Spirit does the work of the Lord.

3. The Spirit does the work of Christ/the Son. For here it is a matter of making sons and daughters of God in the image of the Son and by their assimilation into his "body." It is the Spirit which makes us members of the body (1 Cor 12:13; Eph 4:4) because the Spirit is the Spirit of the Son (Gal 4:6), of Christ (Rom 8:9), and because the Spirit takes or receives what is Christ's to give us a share in it (Jn 16:14). When the Spirit rested on the baptized Jesus, and anointed him as Messiah-Savior, the voice of the Father declared: "This is my beloved Son in whom I am well pleased." The whole economy of grace is related to Christ. There is no age of the Paraclete which might come after that of Jesus-Christ, as Joachim of Fiore (†1202) imagined, making a bad translation of the original and correct feeling he had that history is open to hope, to newness, and that it seeks the advent of freedom (see *ES* 1:175–90 [*HS* 1:126–37]). The movement unleashed by Joachim has had, until our own times, widespread repercussions in history. It is secularized in philosophies along the lines of Schelling or Hegel.[8]

4. Each of the divine persons sent by the Father contributes that person's hypostatic or personal stamp to a common action.

---

8. See H. de Lubac, *La postérité spirituelle de Joachim de Flore*, vol. 1, *De Joachim à Schelling* (Paris: Éditions Lethielleux, 1979). [55]

The Word is the form; the Spirit is the Breath. By way of analogy, think of the way our spoken words are produced: the content of our thought must come forth from us thanks to our breath. We have seen that Scripture links the idea of *dunamis* [motive power] with that of Spirit. In the Eucharistic celebration, the gifts are transformed by "virtus Spiritus Sancti [the power of the Holy Spirit]," but it is the institution narrative that determines *what* is being done.

In Gal 4:4–6 the Son is sent into the world to bring about the redemption, an objective work of universal value, accomplished once and for all. It is the Spirit who is sent "into hearts," into the inmost part of persons. The Spirit interiorizes and personalizes the treasury of grace acquired by Christ. The Spirit is communication, communion. St. Irenaeus speaks of "communicatio Christi [the communication of Christ]."

As we have seen, the Spirit is characterized as the one who has spoken through the prophets and who continues to do so. Jesus says that the Paraclete will lead the disciples into all the truth and tell them of the things to come (Jn 16:13). That does not mean predictions of the future, but the progressive gift of the living understanding of the work of Christ in the history of the world. The Spirit inspires a Christological reading of the Scriptures ("spiritual" exegesis) and of life. The Spirit is the Breath which pushes the Gospel out into the newness of history (see *ES* 2:50–52 [*HS* 2:33–34], for the very evocative text of Bishop Ignace Hazim[9] and H. Urs von Balthasar's phrase "the Unknown beyond the Word").[10] Scripture points to the Spirit by means of symbols which

---

9. [trans.] In *Irénikon* 42 (1968): 344–59 or in *Foi et vie* (November–December 1968): 8–23.

10. [trans.] "Der Unbekannte jenseits des Wortes," in *Interpretation der Welt: Festschrift für R. Guardini zum achtzigsten Geburtstag*, ed. H. Kuhn et al. (Würzburg: Echter Verlag, 1965), 638–45.

speak of movement: breath and wind, fire, living water, a flying dove, tongues, etc. The book of Acts shows the Spirit to be essentially prophetic and missionary.[11]

5. The Spirit does the work of Christ but is not simply a "vicar" of Christ during his corporeal absence. Tertullian called the Spirit "vicarius Christi [the vicar of Christ]" (*Adversus Valentinianos,*[12] c. 16; *De praescriptione haereticorum,*[13] c. 13 and c. 28). At a very early stage in the Church, there was a tendency to see its life as less under the rule of the charisms than under that of the hierarchical institution; this is discernible in the Pastorals, in Clement, and in Ignatius of Antioch. Balanced in the ancient Church by a sense of mystery and by a monastic influence, this tendency never stood in the way of movements of free inspiration; rather, it gave rise to them, as reactions to it. It has nevertheless become dominant, especially since the sixteenth century, as a reaction against the Reformation and the modern mind's claims of autonomy. It is a fact that all Christians who are not Roman Catholic accuse our Church of "Christomonism."[14] I have studied the question in the theology of the sacraments and of the "gratia capitis [the grace of the head]," and in ecclesiology.[15] Indeed, the Christological foundations of these realities are essential and authentic, but they must be complemented by a pneumatological contribution. The sacraments presuppose an *epiclesis,* and their celebration

---

11. The following reactions of journalists are rather significant in their convergence. When he was interviewing me in 1975, a journalist from Waldensian TV asked me whether there could be a Church of being (a Christological institution) and a Church of becoming (a work of the Spirit). H. Fesquet entitled an article about Pentecost "God in the Future Tense" (*Le monde,* May 25-26, 1980). [56]

12. [trans.] CSEL 47:177–212; SChr 280:118–20; ET: ANF 3:503–20.

13. [trans.] CSEL 70:1–58; SChr 46:106–7, 124–25; ET: ANF 3:243–65.

14. See my study "Pneumatologie ou 'christomonisme' dans la tradition latine?" [ET: Part Three, Article 3, below]. [57]

15. *ES* 1:207–26 [ET: *HS* 1:151–66]. [58]

involves the whole assembly.[16] The holiness and sanctifying power of Christ must be seen within the framework of a pneumatological Christology, and created grace must be seen in dependence upon uncreated Grace, the Holy Spirit. Ultimately pneumatology is that essential component of the ecclesiology which we have presented and to which Vatican II, followed by so many renewal initiatives, opened wide the door.[17] I am an active supporter of a rich pneumatology. However, (1) a pneumatomonism—in any case rather difficult to conceive—or, more simply, a systematic exaltation of the Spirit, would not be more authentic. Certain presentations of pneumatology—in which one senses an anti-Western animus—give the impression that a checklist of a very ideal sort, containing everything an author likes, has been put together and entitled "Pneumatology." (2) "There is no isolated doctrine on the Holy Spirit, because such doctrine always leads back to the Lord's truth" (J. Bosc).[18] There is no mystical body of the Holy Spirit: the body is Christ's. (3) The health of all renewal in the Spirit or "charismatic renewal" is to be found in the doctrine *de Christo* [about Christ], in being normed by the Word, the Scriptures, the sacraments, the apostolic pastoral institution. Christology and pneumatology assure each other's health.

---

16. For the epiclesis, see *ES* 3:294–351 [ET: *HS* 3:228–74]; for the assembly, see the preceding section, §2 "Une église qui est d'abord une communion." [59]

17. See *ES* 1:227–35 [ET: *HS* 1:167–73] and "[Les] Implications christologiques et pneumatologiques de Vatican II," in *Les églises après Vatican II: Dynamisme et prospective; Actes du colloque international de Bologne, 1980*, ed. G. Alberigo (Paris: Beauchesne, 1981), 117–30 [ET: Part Four, Article 5, below]. [60]

18. [trans.] "Le Saint-Esprit et l'Église," *Lumière et vie* 74 (1965): 39.

5

The Spirit, the Eschatological Gift, Brings the "Redemption" to Fulfillment

"Propter nostram salutem [for our salvation]": our "salvation" is the reason for the self-revelation and self-communication of God which constitutes the "economy." It is through this economy that we have some access to "theology," that is, to the knowledge of the intimate and eternal mystery of God. What "salvation" of human beings means can clarify for us what the Holy Spirit is.

Revelation and Tradition say that man (man/woman) is in the image of God. That means human beings are destined to reflect God's image, to reproduce that image as a child does that of its father. To this revealed affirmation corresponds the analysis of philosophers such as Pascal, Malebranche, M. Blondel. K. Rahner. They have demonstrated in the human person an openness toward something beyond what can be procured by the human self, an indefinite openness toward a transcendence beyond the world and beyond history. This extends as far as a desire to commune in life with God, to attain the divine order, in the sense in which one speaks of the mineral, vegetable, animal, and rational orders and the sense in which Pascal spoke of three orders (frag. 793).[1] I know that some philosophies of a contrary view are opposed to all of this: Nietzscheism (the Superman), for instance, as well as the psychoanalysts who denounce the desire to be immortal and all-powerful, like God, as the infantile illusion of megalomania.

In its current condition, humanity lives a collective history powered by a constant effort to achieve integrity and reconciliation. Integrity is the victory of life over sickness and death, of knowledge over ignorance, etc.; reconciliation is peace, communication, and communion.[2] And, through these two great goods, humanity seeks liberation from what oppresses and diminishes. This is so on the earthly or temporal level, but also in the moral order, where freedom means purity and interiority.

Redemption, "salvation," answers this deep desire for liberation, integrity, and communion, for being taken up into the order of God's life, into God's family and the enjoyment of what is God's, by a sort of inheritance. That this "salvation" is costly, that it involves the sacrifice of the Heir and the cross, does not keep it from consisting, for its beneficiaries, in the fulfillment of the hopes we have mentioned: liberation, integrity, communion, life beyond death, life attaining to the order of God's life.[3]

---

1. [trans.] This fragment speaks of the physical, the mental, and the supernatural orders: "From all bodies together we cannot extract one little thought; it is impossible and of a different order. From all bodies and minds we cannot extract a single impulse of true charity; it is impossible, and belongs to a different and supernatural order" (Brunschwicg ed. [Paris: Hachette, 1971], fragment 793; ET: H. F. Stewart ed. [London: Routledge and Kegan Paul, 1950], fragment 568).

2. *Jalons pour une théologie du laïcat*, [Unam Sanctam 23] (Paris: Cerf, 1953), 94, 133ff. [ET: *Lay People in the Church: A Study for a Theology of Laity*, trans. Donald Attwater (Westminster, Md.: The Newman Press, 1957), 66–67 and 98ff.]. [61]

3. "Christianity clarifies for us, first of all, our enslavements that are difficult and humanly insuperable because they are called death, solitude, sin; but this same Christianity (and this is precisely what the Good News is) reveals to us that the God who is free is a God who brings freedom, who derails the false destiny of our enslavements by calling us to eternity, to communion, to holiness." E. Borne, ["Liberté spirituelle et liberté temporelle,"] in *L'Église et la liberté, Semaine des intellectuels catholiques de Paris*[, May 4–10, 1952] (Paris: Flore, 1952), 103. [62]

Jesus Christ has gained all this for us, and he gained it once and for all, for all times and for all human beings. However, the Spirit brings the accomplishment of this to fulfillment, first of all, with respect to its universal relevance. The Spirit does not just act so that, in the positive institution of salvation which is the Church, the mediations of grace—the Word (Scripture), sacraments, *diakonia* [service], etc.—will be efficacious; but the Spirit acts secretly where these positive mediations and that institution do not extend, at least in a visible way. The Spirit gives rise to, and gathers toward God, this hidden desire and the groanings of creation, which St. Paul tells us is waiting to be liberated from servitude to corruption so as to enter into the freedom of the glory of the children of God.[4] If, then, one reflects upon the final goal of salvation, our being taken up into the state of sons and daughters of God, members of God's family, and heirs of what is God's (of God's glory), it is clear that this being taken up is acquired only in Christ—we are sons and daughters in the Son and his co-heirs—but it is also clear that this being taken up is made a reality by the Spirit (reread Rom 8:14–17; Gal 4:6; 1 Pt 4:13–14). It is the Spirit who completes our redemption, by assimilating us to the Son of God, to the point of resurrection, the redemption of our bodies (Rom 8:11, 23), to the point of our full assimilation to the eschatological Adam, Jesus, in his spiritualized corporeal condition (1 Cor 15:45). Thus we ourselves will no longer have to destroy plants or animals to nourish our bodies. It is the

---

4. Rom 8:21. And see *ES* 2:271–89: "Dans l'unité du Saint-Esprit, tout honneur et toute gloire" [ET: *HS* 2:213–28: "'In the Unity of the Holy Spirit, All Honor and Glory'"]. Let me quote, in addition, W. Kasper: "Henceforth God is 'all in all' through Jesus Christ (1 Cor 15:28). The ongoing action of the Holy Spirit can consist, therefore, only in making the reality of Jesus Christ universal, that is, in integrating all reality into him in such a way that the real becomes conformed to the image of God which shows through in Christ. And all of that happens according to the law of superabundant fulfillment, of creation and of full realization in Jesus Christ, through the action of the Spirit. The fullness theme is the significant theme of the history of salvation" ("Esprit-Christ-Église," in *L'Expérience de l'Esprit: Mélanges Schillebeeckx* (Paris: Beauchesne, 1976], 47–69, at 62). [63]

Spirit who, from within, will make the body live. Certain miraculous acts of the Spirit from the lives of the saints are like precarious anticipations or humble parables of this eschatological fullness.

Thus the Creed, which has a Trinitarian and "economic" structure, credits the Holy Spirit with making real a Church which is one, holy, catholic and apostolic, with making Baptism effective for the remission of sins, and with bringing about the resurrection of the dead and the life of the world to come. Some Protestant dogmatic treatises cover all of this in their presentations of the "third article" of the Creed.[5] The titles of G. Ebeling's three volumes are significant:

> *Faith in God, Creator of the World;*
> *Faith in God, Reconciler of the World;*
> *Faith in God, Perfector of the World.*

Jointly with the Word-Son, who has gained the inheritance for us, the holy Breath is the sovereign principle of the absolute future of humanity and of the creation with which humanity is connected.[6] In the Old Testament and in almost all the creeds, the Spirit is denoted as the one who has spoken through the prophets. The Spirit is the transcendent agent of the future and of hope. It is because of the Spirit that hope does not disappoint (Rom 5:5; 15:13). In the Old Testament the gift of the Spirit is predicted for a new time, for a new future (see Jer 31:31ff.; Ez 36:25ff; 39:29; Is 32:15; 44:3; 59:21; Joel 2:28ff.; 3:1ff.). The Spirit is the object of a prom-

---

5. Thus H. Thielicke, *Der Evangelische Glaube: Grundzüge der Dogmatik*, vol. 3, *Theologie des Geistes*, (Tübingen: Mohr, 1978) [ET: *Theology of the Holy Spirit*, trans. and ed. Geoffrey Bromiley (Edinburgh: T & T Clark, 1982)]; G. Ebeling, *Dogmatik des christlichen Glaubens*, vol. 1, *Der Glaube an Gott den schöpfer des Welt*; vol. 2, *Der Glaube an Gott den Versöhner der Welt*; vol. 3, *Der Glaube an Gott den Vollender der Welt* (Tübingen: Mohr, 1979). One could look, for its content, at J. Moltmann, *L'Église dans la force de l'Esprit: Une contribution à l'ecclésiologie messianique*, [trans. R. Givord, Cogitatio fidei 102] (Paris: Cerf, 1980)[; German original published in 1975)] [ET: *The Church in the Power of the Spirit: A Contribution to Messianic Ecclesiology*, trans. Margaret Kohl (Minneapolis, Minn.: Fortress, 1993)]. [64]

6. Compare *LG*, ch. 7, n. 48, on the eschatological character of the Church. [65]

ise; the Spirit is "the Promised One."[7] The economy is governed by a system of promise and fulfillment. The promise has to do with an inheritance and with the Kingdom: two terms which point to the same thing: "He saved us ... through the bath of rebirth and renewal by the Holy Spirit. This Spirit he poured out on us richly through Jesus Christ our Savior so that, having been justified by his grace, we might become heirs according to the hope of eternal life" (Titus 3:5–7). Eternal life and the Kingdom are the same thing (Jn 3:3–8), and one has to "inherit the Reign" (1 Cor 6:9–10; 15:50; Gal 5:2; Eph 5:5; Jas 2:5; comp. Mt 19:29; Mk 10:17; Lk 10:25; 18:18), a theme which is also expressed in terms of "glory" (1 Thes 2:12; Eph 1:13–14, 17–18). From Mt 12:28, it emerges that the Spirit is the principle of all of this, that it is the Spirit who is the substance of the Kingdom whose pledge we have here below. This is a theme dear to Eastern Christians.[8] Several Fathers have read the *Our Father* as saying, "may your Holy Spirit come and purify us" instead of "may your Kingdom come."[9]

---

7. Lk 24:49; Acts 1:4; 2:31; Gal 3:14; Eph 1:13. If one connects Gal 3:14–18 and 26–29 with Lk 1:55, one can see the Spirit as having been promised since the time of Abraham. [66]

8. St. Symeon the New Theologian: "The 'kingdom of heaven' consists in participation in the Holy Spirit" ["Discourse 6," In Catéchèses 6–22, ed. Basile Krivochéine, trans. Joseph Paramelle,] SChr 104:23 [(Paris: Cerf, 1964)]. [ET: Discourse 6, § 4, in *Symeon the New Theologian, The Discourses*, trans. C. J. de Catanzaro, Classics of Western Spirituality (New York: Paulist, 1980), 122]; and see *ES* 1:174 [ET: *HS* 1:94–95]. [We think this should be *ES* 2:95 (ET: *HS* 2:69) but *ES* 1 does have a whole chapter (Part 2, ch. 4) on St. Symeon]; the famous story of Motovilov's conversation with St. Seraphim of Sarov: *ES* 2:96ff. [ET: *HS* 2:70ff.]. [67]

9. Evagrius of Pontus, [*Les leçons d'un contemplatif:*] *Le traité de l'oraison* [*d'Évagre le Pontique*], ed. I. Hausherr (Paris: Beauchesne, 1960), 83 [ET: Chapter 58 of Evagrius's *Chapters on Prayer* upon which Hausherr is commenting is found in Evagrius of Pontus, *The Praktikos: Chapters on Prayer*, translated with an introduction and notes by John Eudes Bamberger (Spencer, Mass.: Cistercian Publications, 1970), 64; the page of Hausherr's commentary cited by Congar draws upon the Coptic version of Evagrius's *Commentary on the Our Father* which, like Chapter 58, equates the coming of the Kingdom with the coming of the Holy Spirit]; St. Gregory of Nyssa, *De oratione Dominica*, 3 (PG 44:1157) [ET: "On the Lord's Prayer," Sermon 3, *Gregory of Nyssa: The Lord's Prayer, The Beatitudes*, trans. Hilda Graef, Ancient Christian

One understands that, under these circumstances, the attribute of "power" is usually associated with the Holy Spirit (already in Lk 1:35; Rom 15:13, "may hope abound in you through the *dunamis* [power] of the Holy Spirit"; 1 Thes 1:5; 1 Cor 2:1–5; 12:10; Rom 15:19; 2 Tim 1:7; Eph 3:16; Acts 10:38). In the Creed, the Spirit is called "Lord." The Spirit is invoked as "creator."

The Spirit, as eschatological gift (Joel 3:1ff. = Acts 2:17), completes the final perfecting. "He brings to perfection all that he possesses," writes St. Irenaeus (*Adversus haereses* 5:9.1 [= 5:8.1]). The Spirit is *telepoios* [*teleiopoios*—"making perfect"], says Gregory of Nazianzus (PG 36:249 A), and St. Gregory of Nyssa writes, "Every action springs from the Father, progresses through the Son and reaches its completion in the Holy Spirit."[10] The Spirit is the ultimate Gift, *dōrēma teleion*, says St. Cyril of Alexandria (see *ES* 3:196 [*HS* 3:146]).[11] The liturgy, in which the Church exercises and expresses its own life most adequately, retraces, as it goes back to its source, this path of the Gift which comes to us from the Source, for the liturgy is animated by the doxological schema "To the Father, through the Son, in the Holy Spirit."[12]

Doubtless one could show a relationship between these themes and the notion, dear to the hearts of certain spiritual writers of the

---

Writers 18 (New York: Newman Press, 1954), 52–53]; St. Maximus the Confessor explains the beginning of the *Our Father* in a Trinitarian way: the Name = the Son; "the Kingdom of God the Father which subsists essentially is the Holy Spirit" (*Expositio orationis Dominicae*, PG 90:884) [ET: *Commentary on the 'Our Father,'* in *Maximus the Confessor. Selected Writings*, trans. and with notes by George C. Berthold, Classics of Western Spirituality (New York: Paulist, 1985), 106]; E.-Pataq Siman, *L'expérience de l'Esprit par l'Église d'après la tradition syrienne d'Antioch* [Théologie historique 15] (Paris: Beauchesne, 1971), 249. Compare Tertullian, *Adversus Marcionem* 4:26 [SChr 456:331–35]. [68]

10. *Quod non sint tres dii* (PG 45:129 [128c]) [ET: *On "Not Three Gods,"* NPNF 2–5:334]. See *ES* 3:200 [ET: *HS* 3:147–48]. [69]

11. [trans.] Congar cites Cyril's *Dialogues on the Trinity*, 3 (PG 75:844), SChr 250:237.

12. See C. Vagaggini, *Initiation théologique à la liturgie* [ET: *Theological Dimensions of the Liturgy*]. Compare St. Irenaeus, *Démonstration de la prédication apostolique* (SChr 62:41) [ET: *Proof of the Apostolic Preaching* 7 (Behr trans., p. 44)]. [70]

French School, that the Spirit, having no intradivine fruitfulness because of being the endpoint of the processions, becomes fruitful outside of God in the incarnation of the Word and in the sanctification of human persons.[13]

13. Pierre de Bérulle, *Grandeurs de Jésus*, 4.2 (Paris: Migne, 1856, p. 208) [ET: "Fourth Discourse on the Unity of God in this Mystery," §2, in *Discourse on the State and Grandeurs of Jesus, Bérulle and the French School, Selected Writings*, ed. with an introduction by William M. Thompson, trans. Lowell M. Glendon, Classics of Western Spirituality (New York: Paulist Press, 1989), 131ff.]; St. Louis-Marie Grignion de Montfort, *Traité de la vraie dévotion à la sainte Vierge*, 1st Part, n. 17–20 (Louvain: [publisher unknown,] 1927), pp. 23–26 [ET: "True Devotion to the Blessed Virgin," in *God Alone: The Collected Writings of St. Louis Marie de Montfort* (Bayshore, N.Y.: Montfort Publications, 1987), ch. 1, §17–20, pp. 294–95]. Compare A. Stolz, *De Sanctissima Trinitate* ([Freiburg im Briesgau]: Herder, 1941 [1939?]), 88ff. [71]

Bibliography

General Bibliography

Bouyer, L. *Le Consolateur: Esprit-Saint et vie de grâce*. Paris: Cerf, 1980.
Congar, Y. *Je crois en l'Esprit Saint*, vol. 1, *Révélation et expérience de l'Esprit*; vol. 2, *Il est Seigneur est il donne la vie*; vol. 3, *Le fleuve de vie (Ap. 22,1) coule en Orient et en Occident*. Paris: Cerf, 1979–80, 238, 296 and 338 pages.*[1] [ET: *I Believe in the Holy Spirit*. 3 vols. Trans. David Smith. London: Geoffrey Chapman / New York: Seabury, 1983. Reprinted as part of Milestones in Catholic Theology Series. New York: Crossroad Herder, 1997.]
Mühlen, H. *L'Esprit dans l'Église*. 2 vols., 470 and 374 pages (more theoretical than descriptive, sometimes open to dispute).* Translated by A. Liefooghe, M. Massart, and R. Virrion. Bibliothèque oecuménique 6–7. Paris: Cerf, 1969. [Originally published as *Una Mystica Persona, die Kirche als das Mysterium der Identität des Heiligen Geist in Christus und den Christen: Eine Person in vielen Personem* (Munich, Paderborn: F. Schöning, 1964).]
Dieu révélé dans l'Esprit. Les quatre fleuves 9 (Paris: Beauchesne, 1979), 147 pages.*
Ecclesia a Spiritu Sancto edocta: Mélanges G. Philips. Bibliotheca ephemeridum theologicarum Lovaniensium 27. Gembloux: Duculot, 1970 (600 pages, 32 articles, 17 in French).*
Actes du Congrès de pneumatologie de Rome, March 1982. [*Credo in Spiritum Sanctum = Pistemo eis to Pneuma to Agion: Atti del Congresso teologico internazionale di pneumatologia in occasione del 1600° anniversario del I Concilio di Costantinopoli e del 1550° anniversario del Concilio di Efeso, Roma, 22–26 marzo 1982*, 2 vols. Ed. José Saraiva Martins. Teologia e filosofia 6. Vatican City: Libreria ed. vaticana, 1983.]

---

1. [trans.] The comments and additional pieces of information followed by an asterisk come from Congar himself.

Textes du Séminaire de Chambésy (CH [Confédération helvétique = Switzerland]), June–July, 1981. [*La signification et l'actualité du IIe concile oecuménique pour le monde chrétien d'aujourd'hui.* Études théologiques de Chambésy 2. Chambésy-Genève: Éditions du Centre orthodoxe du Patriarcat oecuménique, 1981.]

History

In addition to Bouyer, Congar, F. Bolgiani in Les quatres fleuves, and the histories of dogma, see these classic Greek texts:

Athanasius of Alexandria. *Lettres à Serapion sur la divinité du Saint-Esprit.* Translated by J. Lebon. SChr 15. Paris: Cerf, 1947 [PG 26:525–676; ET: *The Letters of Saint Athanasius concerning the Holy Spirit.* Translated and introduction by C. R. B. Shapland. New York: Philosophical Library, 1951].

Basil of Caesarea. *Traité du Saint-Esprit.* Introduction, translation, and notes by Benoît Pruche. 2d ed. with Greek text. SChr 17. Paris: Cerf, 1947. [PG 32:67–218.] [ET: *On the Spirit*, NPNF 2-8:1–50 or *On the Holy Spirit.* Translation by David Anderson. Crestwood, N.Y.: St. Vladimir's Seminary Press, 1980.]

Gregory of Nazianzus. *Discours 27–51.* Introduction, critical text and notes by Paul Gallay. SChr 250 [Paris: Cerf, 1976, rep. 2006]. [ET: NPNF 2-7:284–328.]

and also the following:

Siman, E.-Pataq. *L'expérience de l'Esprit par l'Église d'après la tradition syrienne d'Antioch.* Théologie historique 15. Paris: Beauchesne, 1971.

Kelly, J. N. D. *Early Christian Doctrines.* London: A. C. Black, 1977. French trans.: *Initiation à la doctrine des Pères de l'Église.* [Trans. C. Tunmer.] Paris: Cerf, 1968.

Christian Life

St. Thomas Aquinas. *Summa theologiae*, 1a2ae, q. 68 on the gifts, and the corresponding article for each virtue.

———. *Somme théologique: La loi nouvelle, 1a 2ae, questions 106–108.* Trans. J. Tonneau. Paris: Cerf, 1981.

la Potterie, I. de, and S. Lyonnet. *La vie selon l'Esprit, condition du chrétien.* Paris: Cerf, 1965. [ET: *The Christian Lives by the Spirit.* Translated by John Morriss. Staten Island, N.Y.: Alba House, 1971.]

Philips, G. *L'union personelle avec le Dieu vivant: Essai sur l'origine et le sens de la grâce créée.* [Bibliotheca ephemeridum theologicarum Lovaniensium 36.] Gembloux: Duculot, 1974.

Manning, H. E. Cardinal. *The Internal Mission of the Holy Ghost.* [London:

Burns and Oates, 1875]. French trans. [of the 3d ed.]: *La mission de l'Esprit-Saint dans les âmes*, by [K.] Mac-Carthy. Paris: [Retaux-Bray], 1887.

Émery, P.-Y. *Le Saint-Esprit, présence de communion*. Taizé: Les Presses de Taizé, 1980.

Ecclesial Life

L'Esprit Saint et l'Église: Catholiques, orthodoxes et protestantes de divers pays confrontent leur science, leur foi et leur tradition; L'avenir de l'Église et de l'oecuménisme. Paris: Fayard, 1969 (a rich symposium of the Académie internationale des sciences religieuses*).

Afanassieff, N. *L'Église du Saint-Esprit*. Cogitatio fidei 83. Paris: Cerf, 1975. [ET: *The Church of the Holy Spirit*. Trans. Vitaly Permiakov. Ed. Michael Plekon. Notre Dame, Ind.: University of Notre Dame Press, 2007.]

Le Saint-Esprit dans la liturgie: Conférences Saint-Serge, 16e semaine d'études liturgiques, Paris, July 10, 1969. Bibliotheca "Ephemerides liturgicae," Subsidia 8. Paris: Institut Saint-Serge, 1977.

Moltmann, J. *L'Église dans la force de l'Esprit: Une contribution à l'ecclésiologie messianique*. Translated by R. Givord. Cogitatio fidei 102. Paris: Cerf, 1980. German original published in 1975. [ET: *The Church in the Power of the Spirit: A Contribution to Messianic Ecclesiology*. Translated by M. Kohl. Minneapolis, Minn.: Fortress, 1993.]

Orthodox, *Filioque*, Ecumenism

Evdokimov, P. *L'Esprit Saint dans la tradition orthodoxe*. Bibliothèque oecuménique 10. Série orthodoxe. Paris: Cerf, 1969.

Lossky, V. *Essai sur la théologie mystique de l'Église d'Orient*. Paris: Aubier, 1944 (a real classic).* [ET: *The Mystical Theology of the Eastern Church*. Trans. members of the Fellowship of St. Alban and St. Sergius. Cambridge: James Clarke, 1991.]

Jugie, M. *De processione Spiritus Sancti ex fontibus revelationis et secundum orientales dissidentes*. Rome: Lateran, 1936; 418 pages.*

Le Saint-Esprit en rediscussion. Concilium (fr.) 148. Paris: Beauchesne, 1979. [ET: *Conflicts about the Holy Spirit*. Edited by Hans Küng and Jürgen Moltmann. Concilium 128. New York: Seabury, 1979.]

Russie et chrétienté, no. 2 (1950).

Istina 17 (1972).

Vischer, Lukas, ed. *La théologie du Saint-Esprit dans le dialogue entre l'Orient et l'Occident*. Document foi et constitution 103. Paris: Le Centurion / Taizé: Les Presses de Taizé, 1981 (recommended).* [ET: *Spirit of God, Spirit of Christ: Ecumenical Reflections on the Filioque Controversy*. Faith and Order Paper 103. Geneva: WCC / London: SPCK, 1981.]

PART THREE

The Promise of the Father (Acts 1:4)

Overview
Article 1: Theology of the Holy Spirit
and Theology of History | 131

Article 2: The Holy Spirit in the Thomistic
Theology of Moral Action | 145

Article 3: Pneumatology or "Christomonism"
in the Latin Tradition? | 162

  1. Sacramental, especially Eucharistic,
     theology | 165
  2. The theology of Christ's capital
     grace | 182

Although the three articles that form Part Three were written and published before the works in Parts One and Two, they represent well the biblical, historical, sacramental, and pneumatological character of Congar's mature thought. All three come from the last period of Congar's scholarly life, 1969 to 1991, according to the periodization of Cornelis Van Vliet.[1] The climax of this part is arguably Congar's most important article on the Holy Spirit, "Pneumatology or 'Christomonism' in the Latin Tradition?" We have included two additional writings, "Theology of the Holy Spirit and Theology of History" and "The Holy Spirit in the Thomistic Theology of Moral Action." We titled this part "The Promise of the Father (Acts 1:4)" because Congar's several references to this Scripture point toward the transition in his own pneumatology from a dominance of Tertullian's "vicar of Christ" perspective to the Trinitarian perspective of Irenaeus's "two hands of God." It is in history, in Christian moral action, and in the sacramental economy that the Holy Spirit's personal stamp, as it were, is especially to be found.

"Theology of the Holy Spirit and Theology of History" was Congar's contribution to an academic colloquium of theologians, philosophers, and historians entitled "Theology of History: Hermeneutics and Eschatology." Co-sponsored by the International Center of Humanist Studies and the Institute of Philosophical Studies of Rome, it was held in Rome from January 5 to 11, 1971. Although Congar considered himself a "positive theologian" because of his training and intellectual propensity for history,[2] he did not consider himself

---

1. Cornelis Th. M. Van Vliet, *Communio sacramentalis: Das Kirchenverständis von Yves Congar—genetisch und systematisch betrachtet* (Mainz: Matthias-Grünewald, 1995).

2. Early in his career, Congar had proven himself a capable historian, for example, with his 1968 monograph *A History of Theology* (translated by Hunter Guthrie [Garden City, N.Y.: Doubleday]), the bulk of which he had composed and published already in 1939 in French (as "Théologie," *DTC*, 15:341–502). In the preface to *A History of Theology*, Congar identifies the "renewal of the sources" as the first principal element of the "crisis" that followed Pope Pius XII's 1950 encyclical *Humani Generis*. Although it was never made clear to Congar why he was silenced in 1954 and not rehabilitated until Pope John XXIII appointed him to the Preparatory Theological Commission of Vatican II in July 1960, the preface to *A History of Theology* about how historical research threatened the *status quo* of the theological manuals suggests an explanation for Congar's punishment. See Yves Congar, *My Journal of the Council* (a translation of *Mon journal du Concile*, 2 vols. [Paris: Cerf, 2002] by Mary John Ronayne, OP and Mary

a historian in the strict sense of the word, because as a theologian he read history with the eyes of faith and engaged in historical research from an identifiable doctrinal perspective.³ Yet, he believed that he had something important to contribute to a discussion about how history unfolds.

Congar makes three main points in this article: (1) the history of the world, the history of salvation, and the history of Revelation frequently coincide, but the Holy Spirit is behind whatever contributes to the realization of God's plan; (2) since the Spirit is creative, the Spirit often furthers the divine plan in new and unanticipated ways; (3) except for the Spirit of prophecy, human knowledge of God's plan is limited to what has already been definitively revealed through Jesus Christ as interpreted by the pastoral magisterium. It is not always easy to discern where the Spirit is acting, and one ought not to make hasty judgments in this regard. Congar here applies to the theology of history his revised perspective on the role of the Holy Spirit with respect to Christ and the Church.⁴

Congar delivered "The Holy Spirit in the Thomistic Theology of Moral Action" during a plenary session of the International Congress in Rome and Naples in April 1974 to celebrate the seventh centenary of Thomas Aquinas's death.⁵ This meeting was a veritable "who's who" of experts in Thomistic thought in the last quarter of the twentieth century. Although many specialists in the field of moral theology overlooked Congar's contributions, at this Congress

---

Cecily Boulding, OP, edited by Denis Minns, OP [Collegeville, Minn.: Liturgical Press / Michael Glazier, 2012]), 3.

3. Yves Congar, "Théologie historique," in *Initiation à la pratique de la théologie*, ed. Bernard Lauret and François Refoulé (Paris: Cerf, 1982), 1:237.

4. This article revises Congar's earlier theology of history in *Christians Active in the World*, translated by P. F. Hepburne-Scott (London: Darton, Longman & Todd, 1968).

5. *Tommaso d'Aquino nel suo VII Centenario: Congrès international Rome-Naples, 17–24.4.1974* (Rome 1976).

he was on a panel that also included the famous moral philosopher Josef Pieper and Dominican moralists Jean-Marie Aubert and Marceliano Llamera. Dominican moralist and Vatican II *peritus* Philippe Delhaye moderated the session. Congar included part of this paper in *I Believe in the Holy Spirit*.[6]

In the two main sections of this paper, Congar summarizes St. Thomas's teaching on the role of the Holy Spirit in moral action (mostly from the Second Part of the *Summa theologiae*, where Thomas treats the virtues and the gifts, fruits and charisms of the Holy Spirit, along with the beatitudes and the New Law), and he reflects on how applicable this teaching remains for today. Congar was recognized as a moral theologian by the organizers of this Congress (because of numerous writings on the matter), while, on the other hand, he was ignored by moral theologians in the U.S.[7] Congar's unique pneumatological conception of morality is summarized in this statement, "It is a *theonomy* of the living God, a *Christonomy*, which cannot be a legalism. A purely *moral* ethics is replaced by a *theologal* and *spiritual* ethics, that is to say, dependent upon the gift of the Spirit."[8]

"Pneumatology or 'Christomonism' in the Latin Tradition?" originally appeared in 1969 in the scholarly journal *Ephemerides theo-*

---

6. *HS* 1:118–19 and *HS* 2:136–7.

7. Thomas F. O'Meara, OP, "Virtues in the Theology of Thomas Aquinas," *Theological Studies* 58 (1997): 254–85, though deeply informed by Congarian thought, does not cite Congar on Thomas's views of the moral life.

8. Yves Congar, "Réflexion et propos sur l'originalité d'une ethique chrétienne," *Studia Moralia* 15 (1977): 40, my translation. In addition to his explanation of "theologal" in *Spirit of God*, see Yves Congar, OP, "Poverty in Christian Life amidst an Affluent Society," *War, Poverty, Freedom: The Christian Response*, ed. Franz Böckle, *Concilium* 15 (New York: Paulist Press, 1966), 54; Yves Congar, OP, "St. Francis of Assisi," in *Faith and Spiritual Life*, trans. A. Manson and L. C. Sheppard (New York: Herder and Herder, 1968), 33; and Yves Congar, "Poverty as an Act of Faith," in *The Poor and the Church*, ed. Norbert Greinacher and Alois Müller, *Concilium* 104 (New York: The Seabury Press, 1977), 97–104.

logicae Lovanienses, in an issue honoring the Belgian dogmatician Gérard Philips of the Theology Faculty of Louvain, the principle editor of Vatican II's *Lumen gentium*.[9] The articles were reprinted in 1970 in the book *Ecclesia a Spiritu Sancto edocta (Lumen gentium, 53): Mélanges théologiques, hommages à Mgr Gérard Philips* [*The Church Taught by the Holy Spirit (LG 53): Theological Essays in Honor of Mgr. Gérard Philips*]. The importance of this article for the development of Congar's thought is shown by the frequency with which he cited it. In the selections included in our volume, he explicitly refers to it eight times, and he often dealt with the substance of the article without citing it explicitly, as he did in the work we have included in Part One.

Congar makes two main points in this piece: (1) although the sacramental theology of the Roman Catholic Church, specifically the Eucharist, has lacked an explicit mention of the Holy Spirit since the Council of Trent, the return to the sources of Catholic theology has uncovered a rich sacramental theology revealing the unity of the Christological and pneumatological elements of the Church's sacraments; (2) the Christological element of Catholic sacramental theology, known as Christ's capital grace, is incomplete without the accompanying pneumatological element. Thus, contrary to appearances, Catholic sacramental theology does not rely upon Christ alone, and more work needs to be done by theologians and by the Church's Magisterium to implement the decrees of Vatican II so that what has been obscured for so long will be made explicit. In the end, Congar answers the criticism raised by Nissiotis: it is, in fact, imprecise to speak of "Christomonism" in the Latin tradition. While a narrow reading of Catholic theology would confirm that Christology certainly dominated Scholasticism and the subsequent centuries, Vatican II has reintroduced the pneumatology that has always been integral to Tradition. Since the whole historical

---

9. A. M. Charue, "Le Saint-Esprit dans '*Lumen gentium*,'" *Ephemerides theologicae Lovanienses* 45 (1969): 364.

background for Congar's reply to the charge of "Christomonism" in the Latin tradition still remains untranslated, many scholars remain unengaged with this material.[10] This lack of engagement keeps the originality of Congar's position from forty-five years ago as fresh today as it was then.

---

10. The two main points of Congar's article build upon research that he presents in *L'ecclésiologie du haut Moyen Âge: De saint Grégoire le Grand à la désunion entre Byzance et Rome*, Histoire des doctrines ecclésiologiques (Paris: Cerf, 1968) and *L'Église: De saint Augustin à l'époque moderne*, Histoire des dogmes 20 (Paris: Cerf, 1970; reprinted Paris: Cerf, 1996). Both books are masterful presentations of large swaths of history of, and theology about, the Church. To date, neither monograph has been translated into English. Thus, their impact upon English-speaking theology is rather mitigated.

ARTICLE 1

Theology of the Holy Spirit and Theology of History[1]

1

First of all, I must clarify the meaning of some terms. "Pneumatology" designates the ensemble of actions proper to the Holy Spirit (or appropriated to the Holy Spirit) in the life of the Church and of the world. It is obvious that what I will say on this subject makes sense only if one presupposes the traditional Christian faith. But that is true, too, for "theology of history." This expression designates, in the most general way, a consideration of history from God's point of view in so far as we know it, that is, in the light not only of reason but of faith. Thus it is a view of history *sub ratione Dei* [according to the plan of God], meaning a view according to the account of things in which the living God accompanies history as its efficient or empowering cause and as its final cause. However, it is not as simple as that. *What* history are we talking about? For God is the creator and sustainer of the natural world, which unfolds in history according to the forces belonging to the elements of creation—things and human persons who are free—but also—in view of the destiny

1. This article is a translation by Susan Mader Brown of "Pneumatologie et Théologie de l'Histoire," in *La théologie de l'Histoire: Herméneutique et eschatologie; Colloque Castelli 1971* (Rome: Aubier, 1971), 61–70.

131

of the sons of God—revealer and savior, through new and gracious interventions beyond what created beings bear within them. There is, thus, a temporal history, but there is also a history of salvation and a history of revelation.

The latter two do not coincide completely, for the history of salvation begins with creation, while that of revelation begins with Abraham, at least if one is speaking of revelation that is positive, public, and for a group. But the history of revelation and the history of salvation unfold within the natural history of the world. In fact they are intermingled with this history that, simultaneously, thwarts and serves them; its perennial ambiguity consists in that. God's plan of salvation, as it becomes a reality, enters into the history of humanity. Indeed, whether or not they know it, human persons exist within a situation of objectively assured salvation, subjectively proposed to all—even to those who have not heard of the Church, of Jesus Christ, or even, in truth, of God. We ought to speak, therefore, of a general history of salvation that the personal and secret comings of God bring to reality within the framework of a common earthly life, and of a special history of salvation, connected in an explicit and visible way to the positive, historical, and public economy of salvation—to revelation, to the Incarnation, to the institution of the Church and the sacraments.

The Church. *Which* Church? The discussions currently going on about the object and the understanding of Church history are well known. Is "Church" limited to the Catholic Church (I am speaking as a Catholic) so that whatever is out of accord with that enters in only under the titles of schism or heresy? Or does the history of the Church encompass all the baptized? Or ought it even, in a certain way, to be extended to all religions? Where should one stop? These are some of the questions currently being raised, but I will not enter into them here. Besides, for the topic we are treating, the very distinctions that must be made between general and special history of salvation are not decisive. Even if it is good to be precise, or to refer to the distinctions which the very subject under consideration forces upon one, it is possible for me to speak in quite a general way for, common or special, the history within which God's plan is realized and brings salvation about arises from the Holy Spirit.

2

The Holy Spirit is the transcendent agent of what, within history, is on God's side. We must reflect on the fact that God does not bring the divine plan to fruition by a single mission or a single work, that of the Word come in our flesh; God adds a second mission, that of the Spirit. The redemptive Incarnation is followed by Pentecost. Moreover the designation which, perhaps, best characterizes the Spirit of Pentecost is "the Promised One,"[2] the one who goes before us, whose "first installment" we receive but whose full reality is always beyond. In the same way, the most profound word, perhaps, which has been spoken by a theologian on the Holy Spirit is that of H. Urs von Balthasar: "Der Unbekannte jenseits des Wortes,"[3] the Unknown One beyond the Word.

That does not mean that an "economy" of the Holy Spirit has followed or ought to follow an "economy" of Christ. It is well known that such was the dream of Abbot Joachim of Fiore. This dream had, for several centuries, repercussions in diverse currents of ideas and in the upheavals they provoked. It was an absurd dream, for with Christ humanity entered into the regime of the new and de-

---

2. See also Lk 24:49; Acts 1:4–5; 2:33; (26:6ff.); Gal 3:14; Eph 1:13ff.; [Schniewind, Julius and Gerhard Friedrich, "*Epaggellō* im NT/*epaggelma / proepaggelomai*,"] *TWNT* 2:578ff. [ET: *TDNT* 2:581–86]. [1]

3. The title of his article in *Interpretation der Welt: Festschrift für R. Guardini zum achtzigsten Geburtstag*, ed. H. Kuhn et al. (Würtzburg: Echter Verlag, 1965), 638–45. On the succession of a mission of the Holy Spirit after the mission of the Word, there are some remarks about this in relation to the liturgical expression of this reality, in my study "Pneumatologie ou 'christomonisme' dans la tradition latine?" [ET: See Article 3, below]. [2]

finitive covenant.[4] Thus the work of the Holy Spirit is not *other* than the work of Christ, but it is the work of a divine Person, on account of which it is marked by a way of doing things about which theology must give up the desire to give a perfect account.

The Word incarnate established in history—and that is what constitutes the structure of the Church—the *forms* of New Testament revelation which dogmas make explicit in response to questions posed by the current of ideas in a particular historical and cultural context; the *forms* of those means of worship and of grace which are the sacraments;[5] and, by creating the mission that the ministry must fulfill (see Mt 28:18–20, etc.), the world-wide *forms* of apostolic and pastoral ministry. Jesus created, by his Passover—death, resurrection, ascension—the inexhaustible treasure of the new life of the children of God and a universal situation of (objective) redemption. Such a work is fitting for the Word made flesh, because the Word naturally expresses definition and form.

The Spirit is presented, first of all, in the Old Testament, as a force that acts in persons. Jesus himself speaks of the Spirit in these terms: "The wind blows where it chooses, and you hear the sound of it but you do not know where it comes from or where it goes" (Jn 3:8). The Spirit always retains something of the mysterious. The Spirit's existence is revealed by the Spirit's effects, but the Spirit *per se* is not revealed. That is why it is so difficult to speak of the Spirit. The Spirit's particular identity is revealed even less than that of the Father or that of the Son. However, the Spirit's action in the "economy" (that is, in the history) of salvation is sufficiently specific. The Spirit effects in time and space the universal salvific

---

4. See Thomas Aquinas, *ST* 1a2ae, q. 106, a. 4; *DV*, n. 4, with reference to 1 Tim 6:14 and Titus 2:13; on Joachim of Fiore, see my *L'Église: De saint Augustin à l'époque moderne*, [Histoire des dogmes 20] (Paris: Cerf, 1970; reprinted Paris: Cerf, 1996), 209ff. [3]

5. In a specific way for the two major sacraments (Baptism and Eucharist), of which Jesus himself made use; only by way of indication for the other sacraments, either by certain of his words, or by messianic actions, or by significant ways of behaving. [4]

work accomplished by Christ. The Spirit thus makes that work universal, or rather makes its universal impact effective and real. The Spirit is the effective principle of catholicity. So the Spirit animates persons and the Church itself, as such, within which the Spirit guarantees[6] the authenticity of the actions that ensure the fidelity of that Church to the forms of the New Covenant—whether in the order of faith and teaching, or in the order of sacramental life, or in the essential ministry—for the Spirit gives rise to the call to ministry (Acts 20:28). In a still more profound way, the Spirit, a unique and transcendent Person yet at the same time perfectly immanent to the whole (see Ws 1:7—the entrance prayer for the Feast of Pentecost), is the principle which brings about the particular quality of the *time of the Church*. This could be characterized as a sacramental time during which the past time of the Word and of the redemption, its eschatological future and its graced present are united, in a dynamic memorial celebrated day after day.[7] The Holy Spirit *indwells* the righteous, the friends of God, and indwells the Church of Christ, his Spouse.

All of that comes about in history, since the Church, while having its own way of measuring time, develops within the history of the world and moves forward on the very path taken by humankind, as the main theme of the World Congress of the Laity held in Rome in October 1967 said. The idea of a time specific to the Church would become the focus of a particular presentation, which con-

---

6. The "guarantee" aspect is one that has been most frequently underscored, especially since the Reformation: see my *La Tradition et les traditions: Essai historique* (Paris: Fayard, 1960), 219ff. [ET: *Tradition and Traditions: An Historical and a Theological Essay*, Part One, trans. Michael Naseby (London: Burns & Oates, 1966; repr. San Diego, Calif.: Basilica Press / Needham Heights, Mass.: Simon and Schuster, 1997), 169ff.]. F. Refoulé, "L'Église et le Saint-Esprit chez Luther et dans la théologie catholique," *Revue des sciences philosophiques et théologiques* 48 (1964): 428–70. [5]

7. See my *La Tradition et les traditions: Essai théologique*, (Paris: Fayard, 1963), 33ff. [ET: *Tradition and Traditions: An Historical and a Theological Essay*, Part Two, trans. Thomas Rainborough (London: Burns & Oates, 1966; repr. San Diego, Calif.: Basilica Press / Needham Heights, Mass.: Simon and Schuster, 1997), 259ff.] and the studies of I. Dalmais, O. Clément, J. Mouroux, cited on 272, note 89 [ET: 260, note 1]. [6]

cerned the question, just referred to above, about the nature of Church history. I cannot linger over that. Let me say simply that this era of the Church has a rhythm of visits or "missions" of the Word and of the Spirit. I want to insist here on a decisive aspect of the action of the latter, as the "Unknown One beyond the Word," namely, the aspect by which the Spirit unceasingly opens the way for and promotes the realization of the work of Christ in the time "to come," that is, in the newness or the "not-yet-come" of history. This is why, since Epiphanius, Cyril of Jerusalem, and the Creed attributed to the Council of Constantinople (381), the Spirit is denoted as the one who "has spoken through the prophets." The Spirit is characterized here as a unique [originale] Person, clearly inseparable from the Father and the Son, but one who acts with a specific and proper freedom.[8] The Spirit is actually described as the Spirit of Freedom (2 Cor 3:17), just as the Spirit is called the Spirit of Truth (Jn 16:13; 1 Jn 5:6). From the biblical point of view, as surprising as it may seem, these two titles are closely connected, as we will see in the following section (3). The role of the Spirit is, like that of the prophets, to carry forward unceasingly the realization of God's plan in history, history being, by definition, a succession of new occurrences, the coming into existence of what has not yet come. It is with joy that I will quote the speech with which Bishop Hakim [= Hazim], the Orthodox Metropolitan of Lattakia, opened the meeting of the World Council in Uppsala in August 1968:

God comes into the world as if coming to meet it. God is out in front and God calls, God upsets, God sends, God makes things grow, God liberates.... Creative newness comes into the world with the world. It does not invent itself or make a case for itself; it reveals itself. One welcomes it or rejects it but it comes as an event.... The Holy Spirit is Newness in person, at work in the world.... Without the Spirit, God is far away, Christ is in the past, the Gospel is a dead letter, the Church is simply an

---

8. See W. Kasper, *Dogme et Évangile* (Tournai-Paris: Casterman, 1967), 88ff. (also for what is said about the biblical notion of truth). See also note 16 [= 14] below. [7]

organization, authority is domination, mission is propaganda, worship is simply reminiscence.[9]

It is true that this work of the Holy Spirit is only the making current, in the newness of history, what was "once for all entrusted to the saints" (Jude 3). As we have shown elsewhere,[10] that does not imply that one remains hemmed in within the limits of a perpetual repetition of the exactly the same thing. One might say that, in one sense, that *is* what is involved, for it is a question of making current the revelation, the sacraments, the ministry, the salvation, and the grace given in Jesus Christ; it is a question of bringing about the advent of the one and only Jesus Christ who "is the same yesterday and today and forever" (Heb 13:8). He is the Alpha and the Omega (Rv 1:8; 21:6; 22:13); he fills the whole history of salvation. But—and here is where an authentic theology of catholicity enters in[11]—the Christ-Omega, the one toward whom history is moving, must undertake an application or articulation of the very same thing in the context of the events, the new things, the exercises of human freedom which are precisely what constitute the fabric of that history and which represent something other than a repetition of exactly the same thing. Catholicity is brought about simultaneously from above and from below, from the fullness *acquired* from Christ and from the fullness humanity must bring to him, obtaining it through *new acquisitions* from its whole history.

---

9. French text in *Foi et vie* (November–December 1968): 12–15, or in *Irénikon* (1968): 349–51. [8]

10. In a presentation given at the meeting of Marxists and Christians in Marienbad (to be published by Éditions Mame) or in *L'histoire de l'Église, 'lieu théologique'*, *Concilium* 57 (1970): 75–83 [ET: "Church History as a Branch of Theology," trans. Jonathan Cavanagh, ed. Roger Aubert, *Concilium* 57 (New York: Herder and Herder, 1970): 85–96], or finally in *Identité, changements et normes* (forthcoming). [We have not been able to identify this publication.] [9]

11. See my *Sante Église: Études et approches ecclésiologiques*, Unam Sanctam 41 (Paris: Cerf, 1963), 147ff., 155–80; *L'Église, une, sainte, catholique et apostolique*. Mysterium salutis 15 (Paris: Cerf, 1970). See also Testis (=M. Blondel), "La Semaine sociale de Bordeaux et le monophorisme" [a series of articles], taken from the *Annales de philosophie chrétienne* (Paris: Bloud, 1910). [10]

3

Holy Spirit, human freedom, and creativity. History is the space where the freedom of human beings made in the image of God is exercised. For God imposes neither covenant nor gifts like a *decree*. This is what André Neher did a good job of showing on the subject of the covenant and of what he called its "dialogic structure"[12]—a principle of that "anthropology oriented to God" that the Bible presents. That is what the Fathers, especially the Greeks, underscored in their vision of human freedom. Time is given to the human person so that he or she can exercise his or her freedom, the freedom of a mind condemned to a fragmentary and successive mode of knowing. From the religious point of view, time is that regime of delays left to the human person so that conversion can happen, and, from God's side, it is that regime of divine "patience" about which Scripture so often speaks.[13] The biblical notion of time corresponds to that anthropological vision. Claude Trésmontant wrote on this subject: "In biblical thought, as in Bergson, eternity coexists with creative and inventive time. Time is not the unfolding of what had already been given beyond time, so that a look liberated from temporality would be able to foresee in a single glance what had been given once and for all. Time really is the perpetual beginning of unforeseen novelty."[14] The history of revelation begins with the call of Abraham, invited to set out for an unknown country "that I will show you," God says ... (Gn 12:1).

Biblical ideas of *truth* and of *witness* also correspond to this dynamic sense of time. When Ernst Bloch writes, "true genesis is not at the beginning but at the end,"[15] he adopts a perspective that pro-

---

12. [trans.] See, for example, pp. 164 and 205 of Neher's *The Exile of the Word*, a translation of *L'exil de la Parole* (Paris: Éditions de Seuil, 1970) by David Maisel (Philadelphia: Jewish Publication Society of America, 1981).

13. See Acts 3:25–26; 14:16; 17:30; Rom 2:4; 1 Pt 3:20; 2 Pt 3:9. [11]

14. *Essai sur la pensée hébraïque* (Paris: Cerf, 1953), 41. Obviously, eternity coexists with time, and God does not *foresee* anything; God sees in God's present everything which is to come. [12]

15. *Das Prinzip Hoffnung*, vol. 3 (Berlin: Abau-Verlag, 1956 [1959]), 419 [ET: *The Prin-*

ceeds from the Bible. Indeed, for this perspective, the whole truth of something is at the end of its becoming, for then it corresponds to what the living God calls it to be.[16] This is why St. John could speak of a truth *to be done* (Jn 3:21). That is why the "Spirit of truth" is given to us. As to the *testimony* which the Spirit calls forth and accompanies (see Jn 15:26–27; 1 Jn 5:6; Lk 24:48–49; Acts 1:8), it is clearly a witness to words and deeds having to do with Christ, and in that respect it refers to the past. However, as R. Asting effectively showed, it includes, as an essential feature, a potent affirmation oriented toward the future, *vorwärtsgerichtet*.[17] It involves promoting the realization of the plan of God by affirming it in good times and in bad, even, if need be, unto death. That is what "martyrdom" is.

One can see that through one and the same movement the Holy Spirit is, within history, the principle of continuity or identity and the principle of newness, the Spirit of truth and the Spirit of freedom, the principle proper to the "new creation," which looks toward the *eschaton* [Congar writes "eschatology"] and rises toward it.

4

The Holy Spirit makes us decipher the "theology" of history. Since John XXIII and the council, people have loved to talk about reading the "signs of the times."[18] By this is understood, said Paul VI in a

---

ciple of Hope, trans. Neville Plaice, Stephen Plaice, and Paul Knight (Oxford: B. Blackwell, 1986)], 1375. [13]

16. See, among others, Kasper, *Dogme et Évangile*, 62ff; I. de la Potterie, "L'arrière fond du thème johannique de la vérité," *Studia evangelica* 73 [papers presented to the international congress on the four gospels held at Christ Church, Oxford, 1957] (Berlin: Akademie-Verlag, 1959), 277–94. [14]

17. R. Asting, *Die Verhündigung des Wortes im Urchristentum, dargestellt an den Begriffen "Wort Gottes," "Evangelium," und "Zeugnis,"* Stuttgart[: Kohlhammer], 1939), 458–712. [15]

18. The term used by Vatican II: see *GS*, nn. 4 and 11; *PO*, n. 9; *AA*, n. 14; the encyclicals of Paul VI: *Ecclesiam Suam*, 1964, Vatican edition, p. 28 [*AAS* 56 (1964): 632]; *Populorum Progressio*, n. 13 [*AAS* 59 (1967): 264]; Audience held April 16, 1969; see also *La documentation catholique* 1539 (May 4, 1969): 403b–405a [ET: "Pope

general audience of April 16, 1969, "the theological interpretation of contemporary history." And the Holy Father quoted *Gaudium et Spes*, n. 11, which speaks of discerning "the signs of the presence or of the plan of God." This belongs, therefore, well within our subject. In Catholic Action, people had already been seeking for some time to interpret the meaning of events from the perspective of the will of God and what it would require of us. To do this was to put into action that "spirit of prophecy" by which one bears witness to Jesus.[19] Indeed prophecy rarely is simply a means of predicting the future. More usually, and more usefully, it consists of reading events according to the warp of God's plan and in the light of God's will.[20] This latter is known to us through the Holy Scriptures, which is why this interpretation of the present so as to orient oneself toward the future involves looking at the past and remembering God's actions. It is always the Holy Spirit who speaks through the prophets.

The whole plan of God has to do with Jesus Christ, who, God-made-human, is the meaning and the Lord of the history of the world. Moreover "no one can say 'Jesus is Lord' except by the Holy Spirit" (1 Cor 12:3). A serious and authentic theological reading of history, and even of the Scriptures which are the memorial of fundamental salvific initiatives, is not something one can do easily. What is required is a deep-down conversion to Jesus Christ, about which St. Paul speaks in these terms: "Their minds were hardened

---

Speaks on 'Signs of the Times,'" *L'osservatore romano*, weekly ed. in English, no. 17/56 (April 24, 1969) 1, 12]. See M.-D. Chenu, "Les signes des temps," *Nouvelle revue théologique* [87] (1965): 29–39; L. [= F.] Levesque, "Les signes des temps," *Science et Esprit* [20.2] (1968): 351–62; R. Coste, *Théologie de la liberté religieuse* (Gembloux: Duculot, 1969), 354ff. [The Vatican translation of *GS* n. 11 quoted by Congar later in this paragraph reads "signs of the divine presence or purpose."] [16]

19. Rv 19:10: the passage Vatican II applies to the priesthood of the faithful (the decree *PO*, n. 2.1; compare the Dogmatic Constitution *LG*, n. 35). [17]

20. See my *Vraie et fausse réforme dans l'Église*, 2d ed. [revised and corrected], Unam Sanctam 72 (Paris[: Cerf], 1968), 183ff. (references to other studies) [ET: *True and False Reform in the Church*, translated and with an introduction by Paul Philibert (Collegeville, Minn. / Michael Glazier, 2011), 172ff.]. [18]

[it is a question of the Jews who, in rejecting Jesus Christ, remained followers of Moses]. Indeed, to this very day, when they hear the reading of the old covenant, that same veil [which covered the face of Moses] is still there. It has never been lifted, because it is Christ which makes it disappear.... It is when one turns to the Lord that the veil is removed. For the Lord is the Spirit, and where the Spirit of the Lord is, there is freedom" (2 Cor 3:14–17; see also 1 Jn 2:20 and 27). The Fathers and the Doctors from Origen to St. Bonaventure, and from the latter to the theologians of modern times, have been passionate in their treatment of this idea.[21] There, in a more profound way than in the questionable indulgence of a sometimes allegorizing symbolism, is where the meaning of a "spiritual" reading of Scripture ought to be sought. The danger is that one will turn that sort of reading into a simple literary exercise and lapse into superficiality.

5

To counter the tendency toward superficiality, I shall draw attention again to the limits of our knowledge of God, and, therefore, of our theological reading of history.

Of course, we know the broad outlines of God's plan of salvation. We know, by faith and by hope, the goal toward which the world is moving. Passages such as those from Rom 8:18–30 or Eph 1:3–23 do a magnificent job of indicating that. Our situation is, in a way, the reverse of the natural situation of a human being. This could be il-

21. Origen: see H. De Lubac, *Histoire et Esprit: L'intelligence de l'Écriture d'après Origène*, Théologie 16 (Paris[: Aubier], 1950), 303ff., 353 [ET: *History and Spirit: The Understanding of Scripture according to Origen*, trans. Anne Englund Nash (San Francisco: Ignatius Press, 2007)]; St. Jerome, *Commentariorum in Michæam prophetam* 1:10–15 [= 6:10–16?], (PL 25:1215); the Middle Ages: H. de Lubac, *Exégèse médiévale. Les quatre sens de l'Écriture*, vol. 2, bk. 1, Théologie 42 (Paris : Aubier, 1961), 291–94, 381–83 [An English translation of this work is gradually being published as *Medieval Exegesis* (Grand Rapids, Mich.: Eerdmans, 1998–)]; St. Bonaventure: E. Eilers, *Gottes Wort: Eine Theologie der Predigt nach Bonaventura* (Frieburg: Herder, 1941), 57ff., 71ff. [19]

lustrated by the case of Fabrice in *La Chartreuse de Parma*,[22] who was present at what he would later be told was the Battle of Waterloo. Holding the bridle of a horse in the middle of a field, he saw only trivial events in the little corner where he found himself; the meaning of the whole escaped him. In faith we know the meaning of the whole but the meaning of particular facts in the little corner of our everyday existence most often escapes us. This is because the history of salvation or of sanctity and the history of the secular or the cosmic are mixed without coinciding: the *kairoi* of the first are mingled with the *chronos* of the second, and it is very difficult for us to put these two together coherently except to the extent that it is indicated to us by revelation.[23] But revelation is closed and the interpretation of post-apostolic events is not guaranteed for us. Gabriel Marcel was right to say, "I don't know what God thinks of the Reformation because he did not tell me...." The unity of these two histories will be brought about in the Kingdom of God. Here below it is parceled out to a world and a Church in a partly clear and partly hidden way, and we can only grasp it in faith and hope. In this regard, we can concede what Gilbert Mury says about the "tactical inferiority" of the Christian position as compared with the Marxist interpretation, which is completely concrete and social.[24]

These observations, which proceed from a realistic recognition of the nature of things, could easily be illustrated by the example, sometimes rather pitiful, of failures in the interpretation of particular events from a point of view which was believed to be theological and providential. If St. Augustine was cautious about how he interpreted the taking of Rome by the barbarians and located this event

22. [trans.] A novel written by Stendahl (pseudonym of Marie-Henri Beyle) and first published in 1839.

23. See J. Mouroux, *Le mystère du temps*, Théologie 50 (Paris: Aubier, 1962), 245. [20]

24. See Ingo Hermann, "L'humanisme total, signal utopique entre coexistence et pluralisme," in *La foi chrétienne face aux athéismes contemporains*, *Concilium* 16 (1965):139–56 at 147–48 [ET: "Total Humanism: Utopian Pointers between Coexistence and Pluralism," in *Is God Dead? Concilium* 16 (New York: Paulist, 1966): 157–77]. [21]

within a vision so general and far-reaching that in fact it encompassed the whole of history, Bossuet was sometimes less so in his outline of universal history or politics taken from Holy Scripture.[25] The Calvinist Puritans of the Mayflower also fell under the illusion that they could identify the will of God with the place and the details of their building of a new and ideal city.... When Innocent IV died on December 16, 1254, three weeks after having withdrawn pastoral privileges from the Mendicants (the bull *Etsi animarum*, Nov. 21, 1254), Franciscans and Dominicans saw the judgment of God in this death. Believers in the Garabandal apparitions thought the same thing when the Bishop of Santander, Bishop Vincent Puchol Montis, who had rendered a negative decision on these apparitions (March 18, 1967), met his death in an automobile accident (May 6, 1967).[26]

When Bishop Fleming fell ill, and from the fact that three of those presiding over the Council of Pavia and Sienna (1423–24) experienced a premature death, John of Ragusa, a leading ecclesiologist and a conciliarist, saw therein a punishment from heaven, because those concerned had taken the side of the pope and battled against the conciliarists.[27] In the same—and, frankly, foolish—way, Cardinal Pitra thought, after the disaster in France in 1870, that the bishops belonging to the minority at the First Vatican Council had been punished, for the Prussians were occupying their episcopal city and not the city of the good bishops who were favorable to papalism![28] He did not ask himself whether or not the occupation of Rome by the Piedmontese had some sort of significance as a heav-

---

25. K. Kluxen, "Politik und Heilsgeschehen bei Bossuet: Ein Betrag zur Geschichte des Konservatismus," *Historische Zeitschrift* 179 (1955): 449–69. [22]

26. See R. Laurentin, "Bulletin sur la Vierge Marie," *Revue des sciences philosophiques et théologiques* 52 (1968): 479–551 at 528–29. [23]

27. See W. Brandmüller, *Das Konzil von Pavia-Siena, 1423–1424*, vol. 1, *Darstellung* (Münster: Aschendorff, 1968), 252. [24]

28. Letter of Nov. 15, 1870, to Mgr. Plantier, Bishop of Nîmes, in A. Battandier, *Le cardinal Jean Baptiste Pitra, évêque de Porto, bibliothécaire de la sainte Église* (Paris: Sauvaitre, 1893), 557–58. [25]

enly chastisement.... But at the council itself, as is well known, a huge thunderstorm accompanied the solemn declaration of the dogma of infallibility: "It's heaven's protest against the new idolatry, the opponents of the definition murmured in hushed tones. It's like Sinai; it's what accompanies a divine revelation, said its supporters in triumph."[29] But it was, more simply, a terrible storm. No theology or pseudo-theology could have said something reasonable about this; it involved meteorology!

Enough of that! The theologian sees things from God's point of view but the theologian is not God. The theologian is bound by what God has said. It is true that God speaks through and in events; but, except for the charism of prophecy, which neither the theologian nor the historian is assured of enjoying, we have, for interpreting the "signs of the times" in events, only the light of revelation as Scripture testifies to it and as the Church contemplates it in earthly meditation upon its Tradition, which is itself guided by its pastoral magisterium. This revelation is the work of the Holy Spirit and it is wholly centered upon Jesus Christ. It is he who is the universal and all-encompassing meaning of history. He is the door to every theology of history, and his cross is the key: it is the place of absolute Love.

---

29. Émile Olivier, *L'Église et l'État au Concile du Vatican*, 2d ed. (Paris: Garnier, 1877), 2:348–49. [26]

ARTICLE 2

The Holy Spirit in the Thomistic Theology of Moral Action[1]

I will first present the Holy Spirit's role in moral action according to St. Thomas, relying primarily on the thorough treatment in the *Summa*. I will then ask what these views can contribute to [the resolution of] certain problems of our own time in this field.

This is a very important topic. Part Two of the *Summa*, especially 2a2ae, presents us with a moral ideal so balanced, so reasonable, so nourished by categories stemming from Aristotelianism and Stoicism, that one might well wonder if this humanism fulfills what the gospel requires. Of course, Thomas has introduced into his vision of the structures of moral being the theological virtues (1a2ae, q. 62); the [evangelical] counsels, seen strictly in the service of charity ([1a2ae,] q. 108, a. 4; 2a2ae, q. 184, a. 3); the gifts of the Holy Spirit (1a2ae, q. 68); the beatitudes, seen as the supreme and per-

1. This article is a translation by Susan Mader Brown and Joseph G. Mueller, SJ, of "Le Saint-Esprit dans la théologie thomiste de l'agir moral," in *L'agire morale: Atti del Congresso internazionale; Tommaso d'Aqino nel suo settimo centenario* (Naples: Edizioni Domenicane Italiane, 1974) 9–19, reprinted in *Tommaso d'Aquino nel suo VII centenario: Congrès international Rome-Naples*, 17–24.4.1974 (Rome, 1976), 175–87 and in *Thomas d'Aquin: Sa vision de théologie et de l'Église* (London: Variorum Reprints, 1984), 9–19.

fect enactment of the virtues and the gifts ([1a2ae,] q. 69); the fruits of the Holy Spirit in us ([1a2ae,] q. 70); and the charisms ([2a2ae,] q. 171, prol.; q. 183, a. 2), considered, to tell the truth, in an excessively structured and systematic fashion. To all of the above, one must add the references to the theme of the *imitatio* [imitation] or *sequela Christi* [following of Christ], which, to tell the truth, is rather underdeveloped; later on we shall see why.[2] With respect to the role of the Holy Spirit in the Christian's moral actions—and apart from other domains such as knowledge, sacraments, ecclesiology, etc., all of which would call for their own treatments—I will speak first of the gifts of the Holy Spirit and then of the New Law. But we must begin by detailing the general framework within which Thomas situates all moral action and every role played by the Holy Spirit.

He situates them within the framework of the movement by which creatures are moved and move themselves toward their goal. St. Thomas understands movement in the broadest sense of the term as every change or passage from one state to another. Here it is a question of *motus hominis ad Deum* [the movement of the human being toward God]. The principle and goal of this movement is God, that is, God in God's properly divine life, insofar as it is communicable and is in fact communicated by grace, which communication is appropriated to the Holy Spirit.[3] Of course, God, as creator, first

---

2. References to *imitatio Christi*: Christ is "via tendendi in Deum [the way of tending toward God]" ([*ST*] 3a, prol.; q. 40, a.1). The treatises in Parts 1 and 2 are completed in Part 3, so 1a, q. 93 is completed in 3a, q. 8; 1a2ae, q. 109ff. in 3a, q. 7 and 8; 2a2ae, q. 81ff. in 3a, q. 25; etc. Christ is the exemplary and efficient-instrumental cause of grace, and grace is the grace *of Christ*: 1a2ae, q. 108, a.1; q. 112, a.1 and 2; *Ad Ephesios* cap. 4, lect. 4 (last part). Finally, there is mention of the imitation of the cross of Christ: see *3 Sent.*, d. 18 q. 1 a. 4 sol. 2 [this reference does not appear to be accurate – trans.]; *Summa contra gentiles* 3 [4]:55 toward the end; *De malo* q. 4, a. 6, ad 7; [*ST*] 1a2ae, q. 85, a. 5, ad 2; 3a, q. 69, a. 3 and parallels. [1]

3. See *Summa contra Gentiles* 4:21 and 22; *Compendium theologiae* 1.147 which reads as follows: "Hic est [igitur] secundus Dei effectus, gubernatio rerum, et specialiter creaturarum rationalium, quibus et gratiam tribuit, et peccata remittit: qui quidem effectus in Symbolo fidei tangitur, et quantum ad hoc quod omnia in finem

gave to each nature the principles of an activity that would be truly *its own*. In the case of human beings, God made them free. This means not only that they are self-determining, that they are *causa sui* [self-caused], that they construct and complete themselves through their own acts and *habitus* [habits], but also that if God moves them, God does so within their very freedom so that they act freely.[4] Thus, because of God, human beings have the principle of their movement first of all in themselves: faculties, acts, *habitus*

---

divinae bonitatis ordinantur per hoc quod Spiritum Sanctum profitemur Deum, nam Deo est proprium ad finem suos subditos ordinare; et quantum ad hoc quod omnia movet, per hoc quod dicit 'Et vivificantem.' Sicut enim motus qui est ab anima in corpus est vita corporis, ita motus quo universum movetur a Deo est quasi [quaedam] vita universi. Et quia tota ratio divinae gubernationis a bonitate divina sumitur, quae Spiritui Sancto appropriatur, qui procedit ut amor, convenienter effectus divinae providentiae circa personam Spiritus Sancti ponuntur. Quantum autem ad effectus [effectum] supernaturalis cognitionis quam per fidem in hominibus Deus facit, dicitur: 'Sanctam Ecclesiam catholicam,' nam Ecclesia congregatio fidelium est. Quantum vero ad gratiam quam hominibus communicat, [dicitur 'sanctorum communionem'; quantum vero ad remissionem culpae] dicitur 'peccatorum remissionem'" [This, then, is the second of God's effects, namely, the governance of things, and especially of rational creatures, to whom God gives grace and whose sins God forgives. This effect is touched on in the Creed through our profession that the Holy Spirit is God, insofar as all things are ordained to the end of divine goodness, for it is proper to God to order God's subjects to their end. This effect of God's governance is touched on in the Creed through the words "and giver of life," insofar as God moves all things. Indeed, as the movement flowing from the soul into the body is the life of the body, so the movement whereby the universe is moved by God is something like the life of the universe. Further, since the entire process of divine governance is derived from the divine goodness, which is appropriated to the Holy Spirit, who proceeds as love, the effects of divine providence are fittingly thought of in connection with the person of the Holy Spirit. The effect of God's governance of things, as it applies to the effect of supernatural cognition, which God produces in people through faith, is touched on in the Creed when it is said, "I believe in the ... holy catholic Church," for the Church is the congregation of the faithful. The Creed touches on the effect of God's governance of things, as it applies to the grace that God communicates to people, (when the communion of saints is mentioned. And the Creed touches on the effect of God's governance of things, as it applies to the remission of guilt,) when the remission of sins is mentioned"]. [Latin text modified according to Vivès ed. This English translation follows Vivès ed.] [2]

4. See [*ST*] 1a2ae, q. 9, a. 4 and 6; q. 68, a. 3, ad 2; 2a2ae, q. 23, a. 2 (body); q. 52, a. 1, ad 3. [3]

[habits], virtues (or vices!). However, there are also forces driving moral action that are outside human persons themselves. St. Thomas distinguishes these according to whether their influence is exercised by information or suggestion or by efficient causality.[5] The devil acts upon our freedom by suggestion; that is temptation. God acts for the sake of our return to God *per instructionem et per operationem* [through instruction and direct action],[6] whence the statement, which leads us directly into our topic, *Principium exterius movens ad bonum est Deus, qui et nos instruit per legem et iuvat per gratiam* [The external principle moving us toward the good is God, who both instructs us through the law and helps us through grace].[7]

The gifts of the Holy Spirit *per gratiam* [through grace] include not only the assistance of actual graces but also habitual gifts: *grace, the virtues and the gifts*. The distinction between the virtues and the gifts had only recently been settled in theology.[8] St. Thomas, who in the *Sentences* (*3 Sent.*, d. 34, q. 1, a. 1; see also *In Isaiam*, c. 11) was content to say that, through the gifts, the faithful person acts *ultra modum humanum* [beyond the human mode], spec-

---

5. On this distinction which Thomas often employs, compare my study "Traditio und sacra doctrina bei Thomas von Aquin," in *Kirche und Ueberlieferung*, Festschrift J. R. Geiselmann, [ed. Johannes Betz and Heinrich Fries] (Freiburg: Herder, 1960), 170–210. French text: "Tradition et sacra doctrina chez s. Thomas d'Aquin," in *Église et Tradition* (Le Puy et Lyon: X. Mappus, 1963), 157–94. [4]

6. See *1 Sent.*, d. 16, q. 1, a. 3; [*ST*] 1a2ae, q. 108, a. 1. [5]

7. [*ST*] 1a2ae, q. 90, prol.; q. 109, prol. [6]

8. See A. Gardeil's article "Dons du Saint-Esprit," in *DTC*, vol. 4, bk. 2, 1728–81 (1911); J. de Blic, "Pour l'histoire de la théologie des dons avant s. Thomas," *Revue d'ascétique et de mystique* 22 (1946): 117–79; O. Lottin, *Psychologie et morale aux XIIe et XIIIe siècles* (Louvain: Abbaye du Mont-César / Gembloux: Duculot, 1942–60), 3:329–433; 4:667–736; *DictSpir*, 3:1579–87 (in the Fathers, by G. Bardy), 1587–1603 (in the Middle Ages, by F. Vandenbroucke), 1610–35 (in St. Thomas, by M. Labourdette). The Fathers speak of gifts of the Spirit in a general sense. The first to distinguish them from the virtues was Philip the Chancellor, around 1235. Vandenbroucke does not discuss Alexander of Hales, while A. Gardeil attributes to him a first systematization in the direction that Albert the Great and Thomas would later take. [7]

ifies in the *Summa* that this follows from the fact that *movetur ab altiori principio* [one is moved by a higher principle] (1a2ae, q. 68, a. 2). St. Thomas connects his whole theology of the gifts of the Holy Spirit to the text of Isaiah 11:1–2, quoted according to the Vulgate version (which adds "piety" to the fear of Yahweh). Now Isaiah does not speak in a vague manner about "gifts" but very precisely about "spirits"—spiritus *sapientiae* [*spirit* of wisdom], etc., that is, about a motion coming from inspiration (1a2ae, q. 68, a. 1). Now St. Thomas had at his disposal, beginning in 1259 or 1260, an unexpected confirmation (he says twice et etiam *Philosophus* [*and even* the Philosopher]) in *De bona fortuna*, a little work made up of two chapters borrowed from Aristotle, the one from his *Eudemian Ethics* and the other from the second book of his *Magna moralia*. Aristotle spoke of the *hormē*, the inclination or impulse of the higher appetite. St. Thomas applies this idea to the divine impulse transcending the use of reason,[9] an application obviously foreign to Greek philosophy.... The gifts, as permanent realities distinct from the virtues, are those dispositions which make the Christian *prompte mobilis ab inspiratione divina* [readily movable by divine inspiration] or *a Spiritu Sancto* [by the Holy Spirit].[10] They are themselves only a permanent disposition, but one which, to be precise, in a permanent way, makes Christians ready to have their actions normed by something beyond the virtues, beyond reason indwelt by faith, beyond supernatural prudence—by Another, infinitely superior and supremely free, the Holy Spirit, the Third Person, to whom the operations of love and of gift are appropriated.

We are far from moral action that is purely reasonable or merely humanist. We are even far from a position that is sometimes imputed to St. Thomas, that of governance by the rigorously and timelessly fixed nature of things. Not only does St. Thomas acknowledge a

---

9. See T. Deman, "Le '*Liber de bona fortuna*,'" *Revue des sciences philosophiques et théologiques* 17 (1928): 38–58. [8]

10. [*ST*] 1a2ae, q. 68, a. 1 and 8; q. 69, a. 1; 2a2ae, q. 52, a. 1; q. 121, a. 1; etc. [9]

certain historicity in human nature, in the "natural law,"[11] but he makes room here for the *event* of the Holy Spirit. His ethical cosmos is a cosmos of the saving and sanctifying will of God, [and it moves] according to measures which surpass all rationality, even of a supernatural sort. Another is leading us, not without us and not by violence (see note 4 [3], above), but all the same beyond our ways of perceiving things and our planning. And we are being led not only beyond the perceptions and plans of our fleshly reason but beyond the ones that proceed from faith. It is not that the gifts of the Holy Spirit are above the *theological* virtues [vertus *théologales*]; the latter, uniting us *to God's own self,* are surpassed by nothing; the gifts are at the service of their perfect exercise.[12] But, to be precise, only God, in person, can give divine fullness to the exercise of the theological virtues, and only God can perfect the action of a child of God. This is true of the whole life of grace as well as of presence to God as object of knowledge and of love for which the life of grace provides the foundation.[13] And so St. Thomas endeavors to specify that the gifts remain even in the state of beatitude.

With even more reason he works at establishing the role of the gifts in the exercise of the theological or the moral virtues [vertus théologales ou morales]. And since Thomas sees the beatitudes as the perfect enactment of the virtues and especially of the gifts, he also applies himself to matching a particular gift and one of the beatitudes with each of the virtues. He even tried to attribute to each virtue, with its corresponding gift and beatitude(s), one or another

---

11. See "Historicité de l'homme selon Thomas d'Aquin," *Doctor communis* 22 (1969): 297–304. [10]

12. See [*ST*] 1a2ae, q. 68, a. 8 (body) and ad 1; 2a2ae, q. 9, a. 1, ad 3. [11]

13. This point was made clear by John of St. Thomas (*Cursus theologicus* 1, q. 43, disp. 17, a. 3) and by the Carmelite, Joseph of the Holy Spirit. See A. Gardeil, *La structure de l'âme et l'expérience mystique,* 2d ed. (Paris: Gabalda, 1927), 2:232ff.; J. Maritain, [*Distinguer pour unir; ou,*] *Les degrés du savoir,* 4th ed. (Paris: Desclée de Brouwer, 1946), Ch. 6, §15 [ET: *Distinguish to Unite or The Degrees of Knowledge,* trans. under the supervision of Gerald B. Phelan, *Collected Works of Jacques Maritain,* vol. 7 (Notre Dame, Ind.: University of Notre Dame Press, 1995)]. [12]

of the "fruits" of the Spirit about which St. Paul speaks. Thomas devoted a particular question to these fruits, insisting upon the element of spiritual combat against the "flesh."[14] Certainly a reason can always be found to justify such correspondences. So one ought neither to attribute too much value to them nor to accord them none a priori, for a great spiritual tradition also expresses itself in such a manner. Thus, the action of the Spirit, through the gift of intelligence, perfects faith to yield a *sanus intellectus* [a healthy understanding], a certain interior insight whose high point is apophatic in import, through a keen sense of the transcendence of God. The corresponding beatitude is that of the pure of heart (2a2ae, q. 8). However, the activity of faith is also brought to a greater perfection through the gift of knowledge, to which Thomas attributes the benefit of a *certum iudicium* [sure judgment] that is not discursive but simple and, as it were, instinctive, *discernendo credenda a non credendis* [in discerning what is to be believed from what is not to be believed]. Thomas makes this correspond to the beatitude of tears.[15] To hope, which awaits God's help, corresponds the gift of fear, by which one is *subditus Deo* [subject to God], and the beatitude of the poor in spirit (2a2ae, q. 19). To charity, the queen of the virtues, corresponds the gift of wisdom, which assures *rectitudo iudicii circa divina conspicienda et consulenda* [rightness of judgment about divine matters to be perceived and pondered] and the beatitude of the peacemakers (2a2ae, q. 45). Prudence is obviously completed by the gift of counsel, to which the beatitude of the merciful corresponds (2a2ae, q. 52). Justice, which gives to each what is owed to each, is transcended when it comes to what we owe to those from whom we hold being itself. It is supported and complet-

---

14. [*ST*] 1a2ae, q. 70, with reference to Gal 5:22–23. The grace of the Holy Spirit, which is the main element of the New Law, inspires in the *affectus* [the affection] the *contemptus mundi* [contempt for the world]: q. 106, a. 1, ad 1. [13]

15. [*ST*] 2a2ae, q. 9. Compare to q. 1, a. 4, ad 3; q. 2, a. 3, ad 3; *3 Sent.*, d. 24, q. 1, a. 3, qc. 2, ad 3. There are several studies, for example, G. H. Joyce and S. Harent, "La foi qui discerne," *Recherches de science religieuse* 6 (1916): 433–67. [14]

ed by the gift of piety, which *exhibet patri (et Deo ut Patri) officium et cultum* [offers to one's father–and to God as Father–dutifulness and devotion]. Thomas attributes to this the beatitude of the meek (2a2ae, q. 121). The gift of fortitude clearly comes to the aid of the virtue of fortitude, with the beatitude of those who hunger and thirst for justice (2a2ae, q. 139). That leaves temperance, to which St. Thomas seems to have trouble attributing a gift and a beatitude. This will finally be fear and either the *beati pauperes* [blessed are the poor] or the *qui esurient et sitiunt iustitiam* [those who hunger and thirst for justice]. One indeed senses that there is a certain arbitrariness in these correspondences, to say nothing of how close they come to the biblical or exegetical meaning of the beatitudes and the text of Isaiah.

Yet it is interesting to note this presence of the gifts of the Holy Spirit even within the fabric of the virtues meticulously analyzed throughout the 2a2ae. Indeed, in following these analyses where Aristotle or Cicero so often play a guiding role, one has the impression that moral action is left to follow structures of nature, set down indeed by God, but recognized by reason: a settled morality! It is good to realize that what is settled still calls for the event of the Holy Spirit. Without that, it would not be clear how the holiness made known to us by the saints is the highest form of the Christian life. This holiness consists in continually surpassing supernatural, yet human, standards by means of "inspirations" heard generously by free people giving wholly of themselves.

The New Law. Questions 106 to 108 of the 1a2ae are the most notable fruit produced, in the theology of St. Thomas, by his focus on the Gospel.[16] This is not the place to investigate to what extent Thom-

---

16. One could consult F. P. Abert, *Das Wesen des Christentums nach Thomas von Aquin: Festrede zur Feier des dreihundert und neunzehn[jährigen] Bestehens der Königl. Julius-Maximilians-Universität Würzburg gehalten an 11. Mai 1901* (Würzburg: H. Stürtz, 1901); A. M. D. Monda [A. M. Di Monda], *La legge nuova dell[a] libertà secondo s. Tommaso* (Naples: Convento S. Lorenzo Maggiore, 1954); S. Lyonnet,

as had forerunners and sources. He does not seem to have had any besides Augustine's *De spiritu et littera* and, in an even more decisive fashion, St. Paul. These questions scarcely have a parallel in the work of Thomas himself, except in his commentaries on the letters of the Apostle. St. Thomas's position is simple: the New Law or the Law of the Gospel consists primarily in the interior grace of the Holy Spirit which produces faith, which is itself active through love. This already implies that this interior dynamism of action has its effects outside of us. But the logic of the Incarnation, expressly formulated in 1a2ae, q. 108, a. 1, demands that grace come to us through exterior means that are accessible to the senses, and that interior grace, which subjects the body to the spirit, produces outside of us works which are equally perceived by the senses. This is why Gospel Law includes, on a secondary level, (1) the means of grace *inducentia ad gratiam Spiritus Sancti* [leading toward the grace of the Holy Spirit], that is, the *documenta fidei* [means of teaching the faith], among which are the Scriptures (*quaelibet scriptura extra homines existens* [whatever writing existing outside

---

"Liberté chrétienne et loi de l'Esprit selon s. Paul," *Christus* 4 (1954): 6–27 (reprinted in *La vie selon l'Esprit, condition du chrétien* [Paris: Cerf, 1965], 169–95); in English translation: *St. Paul, Liberty and Law* (Rome: Pontificio Instituto Biblico, 1962), in brochure format; M.-D. Chenu, "La théologie de la loi ancienne selon s. Thomas," *Revue thomiste* 61 (1961): 485–97; G. Soehngen, *Gesetz und Evangelium, ihre analoge Einheit, theologisch-philosophisch-staatsbürgerlich* (Freiburg-Munich: K. Alber, 1957); U. Kühn, *Via caritas: Theologie des Gesetzes bei Thomas von Aquin* (Göttingen: Vandenhoeck & Ruprecht, 1965) (about which see Froidure, "La théologie protestante de la Loi nouvelle peut-elle se réclamer de s. Thomas?" *Revue des sciences philosophiques et théologiques* 51 [1967]:53–61); P. Delhaye, "L'Esprit et la vie morale du chrétien d'après Lumen Gentium," in *Ecclesia a Spiritu Sancto edocta* [(*Lumen gentium*, 53)]: *Mélanges* [*théologiques, hommages à Mgr] Gérard Philips*[: *Verzamelde theologische opstellen aangeboden aan Mgr. Gérard Philips*, Bibliotheca ephemeridum theologicarum Lovaniensium 27] (Gembloux: Duculot, 1970), 432–43; Y. Congar, "Variations sur le thème 'Loi-Grâce,'" *Revue thomiste* 71 (1971–*Mélanges Cardinal Journet*): 429–38 (p. 426, n. 28, for a list of parallel passages); F. D'Agostino, "Lex indita e lex scripta: La dottrina della legge divina positiva (lex nova) secondo S. Tommaso d'Aquino," in *Atti del Congresso internazionale di diritto canonico: "La Chiesa dopo il Concilio,"* Rome, January 14–19, 1970 (Milan: A. Giuffrè, 1972), 2:401–15. [15]

of people]) and the sacraments; and (2) the *praecepta ordinantia affectum humanum et humanos actus* [precepts which order human affections and human actions], precepts which are also formulated in these writings. Some of these precepts have a necessary connection, positive or negative, with faith working through charity (for example, to confess the faith), while others do not have such a necessary connection, either positively or negatively, with faith working through charity. These latter precepts are left to individuals to apply to their own conduct, or they are left to the ecclesiastical or temporal authorities to apply in their regulation of the order of community life.

When, after having read these astonishing statements, one studies 2a2ae or the treatise on the sacraments, one sometimes has the impression that everything is made so precise and regulated that the *secundario* [matters which are secondary], or the *pertinentia ad* [the matters which pertain to] have smothered, and led to forgetting, the idea that *principaliter lex nova est ipsa gratia Spiritus Sancti* [the New Law is primarily the grace itself of the Holy Spirit]. It remains that if spiritual people are free with regard to rules which would be opposed to the leading of the Holy Spirit, *tamen hoc ipsum est de ductu Spiritus sancti quod legibus humanis subdantur* [nevertheless this itself, that they are subject to human laws, is from the guidance of the Holy Spirit].[17] Canon law, or rather what St. Thomas calls the *Statuta Ecclesiae* [statutes of the Church], *Statuta patrum* [statutes of the fathers], *in conciliis episcoporum statuta* [statutes of councils of bishops], are going to come back in through this door.[18] Is this not what has happened in history, apart from exceptional instances?

---

17. [*ST*] 1a2ae, q. 96, a. 5, ad 2. One could take a look at G. Salet, "La loi dans nos coeurs," *Nouvelle revue théologique* 79 (1957): 449–62 and 561–78. [16]

18. See [*ST*] 2a2ae, q. 147, a. 3, ad 3. See M. Useros Carretero, *"Statuta Ecclesiae" y "Sacramenta Ecclesiae" en la eclesiología de s. Tomás de Aquino*, Analecta Gregoriana 119 (Rome: Libreria editrice dell'Università Gregoriana, 1962), especially pp. 54ff. and 330ff. [17]

Perhaps. But that is not the teaching of St. Thomas. He sees all that is external rule, and even the letter of Scripture (1a2ae q. 106, a. 2), as wholly subsumed by grace, wholly referred to the relationship between faith and love, wholly measured by love.[19] His thesis on charity as the form of the virtues is not a hollow theory. Sacraments, Scripture, dogmas, canons and laws enter into (*pertinent ad* ... [pertain to]) the Gospel Law or New Law only in virtue of their reference to the *gratia Spiritus sancti quae manifestatur in fide per dilectionem operante* [grace of the Holy Spirit which is manifested in faith working through love]. It is under this condition that the Gospel Law or New Law can be called "the law of freedom" because it leaves a wide field open to the free determination of the human being and because it imposes nothing by constraint, but by call and by personal conviction (1a2ae, q. 108, a. 1 (body) and ad 2; a. 4; *Ad Galatas*, cap. 5, lect. 6). The one who loves is free because *qui amat ex se movetur* [the one who loves is self-moved] (*Ad Galatas*, cap. 4, lect. 8). For the "Law of faith," see 1a2ae, q. 106, a. 1 and 2; q. 107, a. 1, ad 3; for the "law of truth," see q. 107, a. 2; for the "law of the Gospel," see q. 106, a. 2, sed c. The spiritual person, doing spontaneously what God commands, is not under the law; the Holy Spirit is not under the law! (see 1a2ae, q. 93, a. 6, ad 1 with quotations from Gal 5:18 and 2 Cor 3:17). Whence comes also the reference St. Thomas frequently makes to a canon attributed to Urban II: *dignior est lex privata* (*Spiritus sancti*) *quam publica* (*lex canonum*) [a private law (of the Holy Spirit) is of higher status than a public law (canon law).[20] Here we find a touch of personalism

---

19. This is Pauline: Gal 5:14; Rom 13:8–10; 1 Cor 13:4–7: see S. Lyonnet, "Liberté chrétienne" (note 15 above). This dovetails with a Protestant position such as, for example, G. Siegwalt's *La loi, chemin du salut: Étude sur la signification de la loi de l'Ancien Testament*, Bibliothèque théologique (Neuchâtel and Paris: Delachaux & Niestlé, 1972). [18]

20. See *Mansi* 20:714[–715]; cited by Gratian c. 1 [2] C. 19, q. 2 [*Decretum magistri Gratiani* (*Concordia discordantium canonum*), pars 2, causa 19, quest. 2, canon 2], (Friedberg 1:839–840). St. Thomas, *De perfectione spiritualis vitae*, cc. 23 and 25 [Parma 15:97–100, 100–102 = LC, cc. 27 and 29, 41:B103–107, 108–110 = Vivès, cc. 25 and

and, at the same time, of pneumatology, the two obviously going together.

As I have already indicated, the Christological aspect is not absent. Is the Holy Spirit not the Spirit of Christ? Does St. Thomas not see the Holy Spirit, as such, as keeping the Church *subject to Christ*?[21] He writes, *lex nova non solum est Christi sed etiam Spiritus sancti* [the New Law is not just Christ's but also the Holy Spirit's] (1a2ae, q. 106, a. 4, ad 3). He could just as well have said *non solum Spiritus sancti sed etiam Christi* [not only the Holy Spirit's but also Christ's]. That *gratia Spiritus sancti* [grace of the Holy Spirit], which is the *principalitas* [the principal aspect] of the New Law, is the grace of Christ. Finally, the *lex nova* (evangelica) [the New (Gospel) Law] makes us follow Christ as a way, *via nova* [a new way], new and definitive like the covenant, and St. Thomas cites Heb 10:19–20.[22] There is, therefore, in St. Thomas's gospel morality a place for an *imitatio Christi* [imitation of Christ] (see above, n. 2 [1]) and, in any case, a place for a *sequela Christi* [following of Christ]. If Thomas did not Christologize more the life of grace, it was to safeguard its full divine and divinizing character, while maintaining for Christ, as the Word made human, his role as "way."[23]

What can this Thomistic theology of the role of the Holy Spir-

---

27, 29:148–52, 153–55]; *Contra retrahentes*, c. 11[, 47–50]; [*ST*] 1a2ae, q. 96, a. 5, obj. 2; 2a2ae, q. 184, a. 8, sed c.; q. 189, a. 7, sed c. and 8, sed c.; *Quaestiones de quodlibet* 3, [q. 6, a. 3] 17 [LC 25.2:267–68]. See I. Eschmann, "A Thomistic Glossary on the Principle of the Preeminence of a Common Good," *Medieval Studies* 5 (1943): 123–65; M. Duquesne, "S. Thomas et le canon attribué à Urbain II," in *Studia Gratiana* (Bologna: Institutum Gratianum, 1953), 1:417–34. [19]

21. See the treatise inappropriately called *Contra errores Graecorum*, pars. I[II], cap. 32 [LC 40:A101]. [20]

22. [*ST*] 1a2ae, q. 106, a. 4, directed against the Joachimite notion of a new *status* [age] to come; q. 108, a. 1, which is a preparation for q. 8 of Part 3; 3a, prol.: "Quia Salvator noster Dominus Jesus Christus ... viam veritatis nobis in seipso demonstravit ... [Since our Lord Jesus Christ ... demonstrated for us in himself the way of truth...]." [21]

23. See L. B. Gillon, "L'imitation du Christ et la morale de s. Thomas," *Angelicum* 36 (1959): 263–86. [22]

it in our moral action bring to the fundamental problems of our time in this area? Without prejudging any other suggestions which might be occasioned by our congress, I will draw attention to three points:

1. [Thomas's theology of the Holy Spirit's role in our moral action makes] a contribution to pneumatology for which a desire has been widely expressed. By "pneumatology" one must understand something other than a theology of the Third Person within the framework of the treatise *De Deo Trino* [On the Triune God]. "Pneumatology" is the impact of the free and sovereign action of the Third Person (action "appropriated," even though we are unable to give an account of all the reality expressed by that appropriation) in everything in the Church which is an activity of life going beyond the "Establishment."[24] Pneumatology is therefore a particular dimension of ecclesiology to the extent that the latter calls for and assumes a particular anthropology. One cannot make a Church of Christ and of Pentecost with just any kind of human being. St. Thomas, who did not write a *De Ecclesia* [On the Church] treatise, but who offers some rich components for such a work, has a spiritual anthropology, that is, a pneumatological anthropology.

   It is set forth in his theology of the New Law (see §2 below) and also in his theology of the gifts and charisms. Undoubtedly the whole of the Thomistic theology of the gifts cannot be kept as it is in every detail; even the significance given to each of them should be reviewed in the light of biblical

---

24. [trans.—The English word "Establishment" is actually the term that Congar uses here.] The Orthodox theologian Nikos Nissiotis writes: "A genuine pneumatology is one that expounds and interprets life in the freedom of the Spirit and in the concrete communion of the historical Church whose essence is neither in itself nor in its institutions," ["Pneumatologie orthodoxe,"] in *Le Saint-Esprit* (Geneva: Labor et fides / Paris: Librairie protestante, 1963), 85–106, at 91. I have touched on this question in seven or eight of my publications. [23]

exegesis. However, the notion of a level of moral action given over to the metarational initiatives of God, which, as we have seen, Thomas inscribes even into law, is a precious datum. So is the way in which St. Thomas connects the gifts to the virtues as their perfection beyond themselves (if it is a question of moral virtues), or as serving their perfection (if charity is in question).

As for the charisms, one must confess that excessive rationalization and systematization results in their being treated in a narrow and rigid way (see [ST] 2a2ae, q. 171, prol.; q. 176ff.; q. 183). Yet, in principle, space is amply and legitimately made for them, especially in the theme, which frequently recurs in St. Thomas, of the *subministratio ad invicem* [service to one another], those mutual services that Christians render to one another when they set themselves up as servants of one another.[25] To put it simply, what St. Thomas interprets and distributes according to the ideal of a society that is stable and fixed, hierarchical and

---

25. This theme is expressed in this way with regard to situations in which charisms are present: "diversitas statuum et officiorum non impedit Ecclesiae unitatem, quae perficitur per unitatem fidei, et charitatis et mutuae subministrationis, secundum illud Apostoli, *Ad Ephesios* 4:16: 'Ex quo totum corpus ... per omnem iuncturam subministrationis,' dum scilicet unus alii servit [a diversity of states and offices does not impede the unity of the Church, which is perfected by the unity of faith, of charity, and of mutual service, according to what the Apostle says, Eph 4:16: 'from whom the whole body ... by means of every ligature of service,' while, that is, one serves another]" ([ST] 2a2ae, q. 183, a. 2, ad 1); "in corpore Ecclesiae conservatur pax diversorum membrorum virtute Spiritus sancti qui corpus Ecclesiae vivificat ... [in the body of the Church peace among diverse members is preserved by the power of the Holy Spirit, who vivifies the body of the Church]" (ad 3). On the "subministratio ad invicem," see *4 Sent.*, d. 19, q. 2, a. 2, sol. 1; *De veritate*, q. 29, a. 4; *Contra impugnantes*, c. 8; [ST] 1a2ae, q. 112, a. 4 (body); 2a2ae, q. 183, a. 2, ad 1; *In symbolum apostolorum* 9; *Ad Romanos*, c. 12, lect.1 [=2]; *1 ad Corinthios* c. 12, lect. 1 and 3; *Ad Ephesios* c. 4, lect. 5; *Ad Colossenses* cap. 2, lect. 4. St. Thomas applies this notion to the idea of "populus [people]" (*Ad Hebraeos* c. 8, lect. 3; [ST] 1a2ae, q. 100, a. 5) and to the unity of the Church (*Contra impugnantes* c. 8; [ST] 1a2ae, q. 112, a. 4; 2a2ae, q. 183, a. 2, ad 1 and 3). [24]

"graded," articulated in "estates" and clearly distinguished dignities, must be envisaged by us in a way that is freer, more dynamic, more mixed together, within the framework of particular churches in communion within the *Catholica*.

2. St. Thomas offers us, not a morality of law but an ethics of the personal use of our freedom under grace. That corresponds much better, not just to the truth of Christianity, but to the situation in which modern philosophical reflection finds itself and to current demands. It is not that every part of this reflection or of those demands ought to be accepted uncritically. The theological [théologal] and theonomic character of St. Thomas's moral theory resists being reduced to a pure anthropology or to a "morality without sin." It leads us toward a "theological humanism," with which J. Maritain dealt well, and to a conception of sin *coram Deo* [before God] with regard to the law of the covenant, that is, to the requirements of grace (the "cost of grace" about which D. Bonhoeffer speaks) and of the calls of the Holy Spirit.

Obviously such a morality will always have something that is not finished, not settled in advance, open. It corresponds better to the morality and religion of aspiration than to the morality and religion of constraint, in the sense of H. Bergson in *Les deux sources de la morale et de la religion* (1932). This greatness is also a source of weakness. I have myself come to realize this better after associating with religious Jews. I have been struck by the strength, the certitude, the absence of self-doubt which the fact of being bound, submitted, assimilated to a law and to fixed traditions gives them. In the face of that, the situation of Catholics, at least as we know it today, appears to me full of incertitude. One must take account of the taste for calling everything into question and for uncertainty which is one of the characteristics of the current generations under 45 years of age. Yet it must also be acknowledged that a moral theory such as that of St. Thomas, one in which "Christ is the Way" and the Holy Spirit inspires our actions and moves our wills without constraining them, is an *open* morality, where the normative determination of action is not entirely given in precepts. There still are laws for the Christian, but it is a law *of grace*, a law of the covenant of grace: as wholly valid, necessary and beneficial as it might be, grace always goes beyond it.

3. The law is also measured by grace. My third and very important point concerns the critique, not of law, but of legalism, and the true situation of law in the Church. There is legalism, said Cardinal Cushing, when, instead of affirming "charity is the purpose of the law," one holds that the purpose of the law is the law itself [26]—in short, when the people are made for the Sabbath. Legality and law have their place. St. Thomas is precise about this: they belong to the *secundaria* [secondary elements] which are part of the New Law on account of their orientation to the grace of the Holy Spirit. They either dispose to that grace or direct the use that ought to be made of it ([*ST*] 1a2ae, q. 106, a. 1; q. 108, a. 1). This fact, that the connection to the grace of the Holy Spirit grounds and also norms the existence of juridical laws, seems to me to be of interest for treating a problem which I have encountered more than once these last years and which is a very delicate one. Shouldn't the way in which the *purpose* of governing power and of the law and the way in which the *good* of the faithful and of human beings is secured both influence the recognition of that power or the "reception" of laws? There is indeed something of this in the medieval canon law tradition.[27] This must justify neither anarchy nor permanent protest, but it

---

26. Speech to the canon law convention held in Boston, Oct. 12–13, 1954; see *Herder-Korrespondenz*, December 1954, pp. 110–11. [25]

27. See L. Buisson, *Potestas und Caritas: Die päpstliche Gewalt im Spätmittelalter* (Cologne and Graz: Böhlau Verlag, 1958). [26]

could call into question an unconditionality of the juridical form in itself. After all, the unanimously professed teaching is that a bad law is no law and carries no obligation....

St. Thomas is very respectful of the *Statuta Ecclesiae* (*vel Patrum*) [statutes of the Church (or of the Fathers)], of the *consuetudo* [custom] or *usus Ecclesiae* [practice of the Church]. This is apparent particularly in his treatise on the sacraments. In the absence of better historical information, he did not himself apply what he says on the level of principles about the relativity and historicity of these decisions, obligations, and prohibitions.[28] This is a plant which has, since his time, invaded everything, until the Council and current reformist tendencies opened up an era of revisions and simplifications that is obviously not without its abuses but is in itself evangelical and salutary. We still have to work out a satisfactory conception of legality (of the law) and of its status in the Church of the Incarnation and of Pentecost.[29] St. Thomas did not say everything, but, by what he has already said, he is still our teacher in such an enterprise.

> Commissione Teologica Internazionale
> Parigi
> [International Theological Commission
> Paris]

---

28. See [*ST*] 1a2ae, q. 107, a. 4 with the citation from the famous letter of St. Augustine to Januarius (*Epist.* 55.19.35; PL 33:221); q. 108, a. 1 and 2; *Quaestiones de quodlibet 4*, [q. 8. a. 2], 13 [LC 25.2:333–34]. [27]

29. In addition to the interesting work of M. Useros Carretero, cited above (n. 18 [17]), I should like to refer to the studies of Hoffmann, of E. Corecco, and of A. M. Rouco-Varela cited in my article "Rudolph Sohm nous interroge encore," *Revue des sciences philosophiques et théologiques* 57 (1973): 201–34. [28]

ARTICLE 3

Pneumatology or "Christomonism" in the Latin Tradition?[1]

The observers at the Second Vatican Council often made the reproach that the schemas, in particular those of the dogmatic constitutions *Lumen Gentium* and *Dei Verbum*, lacked a pneumatology.[2] One of them, Nikos A. Nissiotis, currently [in 1970] director of

1. This article is a translation by Susan Mader Brown and Joseph G. Mueller, SJ, of "Pneumatologie ou 'christomonisme' dans la tradition latine?" in *Ecclesia a Spiritu Sancto edocta (Lumen gentium, 53): Mélanges théologiques, hommages à Mgr Gérard Philips; Verzamelde theologische opstellen aangeboden aan Mgr. Gérard Philips*, Bibliotheca ephemeridum theologicarum Lovaniensium 27 (Gembloux: Duculot, 1970), 41–64.

2. I heard this reproach in numerous conversations and in the course of the Tuesday meetings at the Secretariat for Unity. See, for example, W. Vischer, "L'Église, communauté de l'Esprit: Réflexions sur la seconde session du concile du Vatican," *Lumière et vie* [13,] no. 67 (1964): 25–46 at 45; J. K. S. Reid ["Le Saint Esprit et le mouvement oecuménique"], *Lumière et vie* 13, no. 67 (1964): [65–86, at] 80; Vilmos Vajta, "Renewal of Worship: De sacra liturgia," in *Dialogue on the Way*[: *Protestants Report from Rome on the Second Vatican Council*], ed. G. Lindbeck (Minneapolis: Augsburg, 1965), 107; H. Roux, "Le décret sur l'activité missionaire de l'Église," in *Vatican II: Points de vue de théologiens protestants*, Unam Sanctam 64 (Paris: Cerf, 1967), 112ff. See also G. Westphal, *Vie et foi du protestant* (Paris: Éditions du Centurion, 1966), 134 (*Lumen Gentium* is said to be only "sprinkled" with pneumatology). O. Clément, "Quelques remarques d'un Orthodoxe sur la constitution *De Ecclesia*," in *Oecumenica* [1] (1966): 97–116 at 108ff. [1]

the Ecumenical Institute in Bossey, voices the same reproach.[3] He has returned insistently to what he calls the "Christomonism" of the Latins and an "ecclesiological pneumatology" which the Latins lack and which is said to be the soul of Orthodox ecclesiology. The Latins tend to make the Holy Spirit merely one of Christ's functions—the function of bringing salvation to personal appropriation (what is sometimes imprecisely called "subjective redemption") or of assuring the harmony of ecclesial life, its development, its fidelity to its origins by institutional and personal charisms—in short, of effecting, in the Church, the work *of Christ*. Does Tertullian not call the Holy Spirit *"vicarius Christi* [the vicar of Christ]" (*De praescriptione haereticorum*,[4] c. 28; see also c. 13)? This is to misunderstand the fully personal character of the Holy Spirit's Pentecost mission, that mission's importance for constituting the Church after and along with the work of Christ, and finally the personal action of the Third Hypostasis in the historical life of the Church. Along with V. Lossky, N. Nissiotis locates the source of these misunderstandings in the theology of the *Filioque*. The Latins establish a basis for this doctrine by transposing the economic and functional relationship of the *sending* of the Paraclete by Christ, the Word Incarnate, into an ontological relationship of procession *a Filio* [from the Son].[5] In so doing, they set themselves up to see the action of the Holy Spirit

---

3. "Pneumatologie orthodoxe," in the collection *Le Saint-Esprit* (Geneva[: Labor et fides / Paris: Librairie protestante], 1963), 85–106; "Is the Vatican Council Really Ecumenical?" *The Ecumenical Review* 16 (1964): 365; "Report on the Second Vatican Council," *The Ecumenical Review* 18 (1966): 193ff.; "The Main Ecclesiological Problem of the Second Vatican Council and the Position of the Non-Roman Churches Facing It," *Journal of Ecumenical Studies* 2 (1965): 31–62 at 48; "Rapport au Comité central du Conseil oecuménique des Églises," Geneva, February 1966, text in *Istina* 11 (1965–66): 249ff.; "L'Église, monde transfiguré," in *L'Église dans le monde*, Églises en dialogue [2] ([Tours:] Mame, 1966), 31ff.; "La pneumatologie ecclésiologique au service de l'unité de l'Église," *Istina* 12 (1967): 323–40. [2]

4. [trans.] CSEL 70 (1942): 1–56; SChr 46; ET: ANF 3:243–65.

5. V. Lossky has often returned to these ideas in our meetings. See his *Essai sur la théologie mystique de l'Église d'Orient* (Paris[: Aubier], 1944), 156, 181 and "Du troisième attribut de l'Église," *Dieu vivant* 10 (1948): 79–89. [3]

as dependent in everything upon the Son, and, finally, as a simple matter of bringing the Son's work to fruition.

I believe these criticisms to be exaggerated and insufficiently substantiated. Neither from the biblical point of view nor from the dogmatic can one propose an economy of the Paraclete which would be autonomous with respect to the economy of the incarnate Word. There is a mission of the Spirit; there is no hypostatic incarnation of the Holy Spirit. So, the Spirit is not manifested in a personal way. This is so evidently the case that Orthodox or Protestant theologians—and sometimes the very ones who accuse us of a lack of pneumatology—end up speaking as we do of the connections between the Holy Spirit and the work of Christ.[6] The ecclesiological pneumatology developed by N. Nissiotis presents, along with some very interesting suggestions, many statements that are insufficiently tested and precise, even with regard to the Eastern theological tradition. It is, in short, an enthusiastic translation of the *sobornost* ideal, and I gladly acknowledge the profundity and great importance of everything positive that it articulates: "A genuine pneumatology is one that describes and comments on life in the freedom of the Spirit and in the concrete communion of the historical Church whose essence is found neither in itself nor in its institutions."[7]

It remains the case that so many concordant criticisms, so many remarks inspired by deep reflection, invite us to self-criticism based upon knowledge of the past and present in our theology. Even if the accusation of "Christomonism" seems to us so massive that we must reject it, we cannot but profit from a critical second look at our Latin tradition. That is what I would like to attempt or to outline in con-

---

6. Thus N. Nissiotis in *Le Saint-Esprit*, 92–93; J. Bosc, "Le Saint-Esprit et l'Église," *Lumière et vie* 74 (1965): 29–39; the report of the European section on Christ and the Church, prepared for the Faith and Order Conference in Montreal (July 1963), reads almost like *Lumen Gentium* no. 7: see the French text in *Verbum caro* 67 (1963), especially 293–94, and H. Mühlen, "Die Ekklesiologie der Kommission f. Glauben u. Kirchenverfassung d. oek. Rates der Kirchen und das Vaticanum II," in *Volk Gottes* (*Festgabe J. Höfer*) (Freiburg: Herder, 1967), 603–38. [4]

7. Nissiotis, *Le Saint-Esprit*, 91. [5]

nection with two rather crucial points: sacramental, especially Eucharistic, theology and the theology of Christ's capital grace, which also has implications for ecclesiology. The first of these points will take us back to the high Middle Ages, the second to the Scholastic period (twelfth to thirteenth centuries).

1. Sacramental, especially Eucharistic, theology

The name of St. Isidore (†636) sometimes provokes a smile on account of the naïve views encountered in his philological work. He deserves more esteem. Not only did he transmit to the Latin Middle Ages a part (impoverished, alas!) of the cultural heritage of antiquity—linked to the councils of Toledo and to the Hispano-Visigothic liturgy from which he cannot be separated—but he also handed on some very profound insights having to do with the Christian mystery. This is the case with his theology of the Eucharist.[8]

As Geiselmann notes, Isidore's Eucharistic pneumatology already corresponds to, and has its basis in, a soteriological pneumatology.[9] For Isidore, the consecration of the offerings is effected by what he calls the *oratio sexta* [sixth prayer], which includes the ensemble of prayers contained between the *Sanctus* [Holy, Holy] and the *Pater* [Our Father]. He does not specify the exact moment of the conversion

8. See J. R. Geiselmann, *Die Abendmahlslehre an der Wende der christlichen Spätantike zum Frühmittelalter: Isidor von Sevilla und das Sakrament der Eucharistie* (Munich: Max Hueber, 1933); J. Havet, "Les sacrements et le rôle du Saint-Esprit d'après Isidore de Séville," *Ephemerides theologicae Lovanienses* 16 (1939): 32–93. For the literary history of the *Post pridie* of the Hispano-Visigothic liturgy before and after Isidore, see W. S. Porter, "The Mozarabic *Post pridie*," *Journal of Theological Studies* 44 (1943): 182–94. [6]

9. After having quoted Jn 1:33, Isidore writes, "... carnem Christi *Spiritui Sancto sociatam* per mysterium passionis sacrificium Deo in odorem suavitatis accipimus [... we understand the flesh of Christ, *which is associated with the Holy Spirit* to be, through the mystery of the passion, a sacrifice to God unto an odor of sweetness]." See Isidore, [*Mysticorum expositiones sacramentorum seu quaestiones in Vetus Testamentum:*] *In Leviticum*, c. 6, 4 (PL 83:523 [323]). [7]

of the bread and wine into the body and blood of the Lord. As we shall see, that is not the most interesting issue for us. That issue arises from the distinction drawn between the following two moments or aspects: that of *sacrifice* or the consecration of the gifts by the *prex mystica* [mystical prayer] in remembrance of the Passion; and that of the sanctification, which makes the sacrifice a *sacrament* by the invisible action of the Holy Spirit. A sacrament, according to this understanding, consists of a celebration which signifies something and also a sanctifying impact linked to the hidden operation of the *virtus divina* [divine power]. That sanctifying impact is attached to the sacrament celebrated in the Church *because the Holy Spirit, who indwells the Church, secretly brings about its effect.*[10] Thus, according

---

10. *De ecclesiasticis officiis*, 1:18.4: "Haec autem dum sunt visibilia, sanctificata tamen per Spiritum sanctum in sacramentum divini corporis transeunt [However, while these are visible, sanctified nevertheless through the Holy Spirit, they turn into a sacrament of the divine body]" (PL 83:755). *Etymologiarum*, 6:19.38–41: "Sacrificium dictum, quasi sacrum factum, quia prece mystica consecratur in memoriam pro nobis Dominicae passionis: unde, hoc eo jubente corpus Christi et sanguinem dicimus. Quod, dum sit ex fructibus terrae, sanctificatur, et fit sacramentum, operante invisibiliter (Migne: visibiliter!) Spiritu Dei ... Sacramentum est in aliqua celebratione, cum res gesta ita fit ut aliquid significare intellegatur, quod sancte accipiendum est ... Quae ob id sacramenta dicuntur, quia sub tegumento corporalium rerum virtus divina secretius salutem eorundem sacramentorum operatur ... Quae ideo fructuose penes Ecclesiam fiunt, quia sanctus in ea manens Spiritus eundem sacramentorum latentur operatur effectum [A sacrifice is so called because it has been made sacred, for by the mystical prayer it is consecrated into a memorial for us of the Lord's passion. For this reason, at Christ's command, we call it his body and blood. While it does come from the fruits of the earth, it is sanctified and becomes a sacrament by the invisible operation of the Spirit of God.... There is a sacrament in a given celebration because an action is accomplished in such a way that that action is understood to signify something that is to be received in a holy way.... These things are called sacraments because, under the veil of bodily things, the divine power of these same sacraments works salvation in a hidden manner.... These things are accomplished fruitfully in the Church because the Holy Spirit remaining in it works the same effect of the sacraments in a concealed way]" [text from *Isidori Hispalensis episcopi Etymologiarum sive Originum libri 20, recognovit brevique adnotatione critica instruxit W. M. Lindsay*, Scriptorum classicorum bibliotheca Oxoniensis (Oxford: Clarendon Press, 1911), vol. 1]; PL 82:255). One could cite here several *Postpridie* prayers from the Hispano-Visigothic liturgy, and even some texts from ancient Gallican liturgies, which can be found in Geiselmann and Havet, in the publications already mentioned. [8]

to Isidore, if it is to produce its fruit of sanctification and salvation, the Christological structure of the sacrifice must be completed by a pneumatological action. It is not simply a question of attributing to the Holy Spirit, at least by appropriation, the conversion of the bread and wine into the body and blood; it is a question of the effect of sanctity and salvation at which the Eucharist aims, through and beyond the blessed elements. That effect involves the action of the Holy Spirit who indwells the Church.

In this essay I cannot go into the very complex history of the Eucharistic epiclesis in the East and in the West. For my purposes, this is not necessary. My conviction, gained after my reading of many primary sources and a large number of studies, is that the epiclesis emerges neither chiefly nor first from sacramental theology but from *theo*-logy pure and simple, that is, from the doctrine of the Trinity and then from the doctrine of the *economy* of salvation, which reflects that theology. Still less can the problem of the epiclesis be reduced to the question of the moment of the consecration. Besides, the polemic on this subject between Latins and Greeks is extremely late. By the time it arose, the churches had been engaged in the practice of the epiclesis for a millennium and had commonly attributed the conversion of the gifts into the body and blood of the Lord to the Holy Spirit.[11] Indeed sometimes, as with St. Ambrose and St. Augustine, the manner in which writers speak of it would allow one to suppose that there existed a formal epiclesis, even

---

11. The main sources can be found collected in the "Épiclèse" articles in the *DTC*, vol. 5, [bk. 1,] 194–300 (["Épiclèse eucharistique" by] S. Salaville) and the *Dictionnaire d'archéologie chrétienne et de liturgie*, vol. 5 [bk.1, *Encaustique—Feu*, edited by Fernand Cabrol and Henri Leclercq], 142–84 (F. Cabrol). See also, for its references, K. Goldammer, *Die eucharistische Epiklese in der mittelalterlichen abendländischen Frömmigkeit* (Bottrop, Westphalia: Buch und Kunstdruckerei, 1941). Also M. Jugie, *De forma Eucharistiae, de epiclesibus ecclesiasticis* (Rome: Officium Libri Catholici, 1943) and G. C. Smit, "Épiclèse et théologie des sacrements," *Mélanges de science religieuse* 15 (1958): 95–136. For Thomas Aquinas, see [*ST*] 3a, q. 66, a. 11 [Article 11 deals with the three types of baptism, not the Eucharistic epiclesis]; q. 82, a. 5 and 6; *In Epistolam 1 ad Corinthios*, [cap.] 12, lect. 3. [9]

though the actual texts for this may not be known to us. Finally, let me add that the theological problem of the epiclesis is not simply a question of the liturgical form of the Eucharist. It concerns the other sacraments, baptism in particular, and, indeed, the whole life of the Church, the ministry of the word and that of pastoral leadership or of authority.

It has long been noticed that anaphoras have a Trinitarian structure, just as the Creed does.[12] The Fathers, Greeks as well as Latins, knew that all of the works *ad extra* [outside of the Trinity] are common to the three Persons. Cyril of Jerusalem attributes the transformation of the bread and wine to the invocation *of the Trinity*.[13] However, even in this matter, the Greeks uphold statements expressing the intra-Trinitarian structure and even the economic involvement of the Persons, according to the attributions to which Revelation and the history of salvation bear witness. The Father is praised for creation; the Son effects salvation by his Incarnation and his Passover; the Holy Spirit is given interiorly in order to sanctify. "As for the *economy* having to do with humankind, which has become a reality according to the goodness of God through our great God and Savior Jesus Christ, who, then, will deny that it is to be brought to completion by the Spirit's grace?"[14]

---

12. Nicolas Cabasilas had already noted this in his *Explication de la divine liturgie*, ch. 27, (SChr 4, trans. S. Salaville [Paris: Cerf; Lyon: L'Abeille, 1943], 143–44) with comments by S. Salaville on p. 146); [ET: *A Commentary on the Divine Liturgy*, trans. J. M. Hussey and P. A. McNulty (London: SPCK, 1960)]; F. Cabrol, in the article cited in n. 11 [9] above, col. 174ff. [10]

13. *Catechesis 19, Mystagogica 1*, 7 (PG 33:1072) [ET: Catechetical Lecture 19, First Lecture on the Mysteries, NPNF 2-7:146]; later (*Mystagogica 5*, 7; PG 33:1113–16) [ET: Catechetical Lecture 23, On the Mysteries 5, NPNF 2-7:154] he speaks of the Holy Spirit as consecrating the gifts, for "everything which the Holy Spirit touches is sanctified and changed." [11]

14. St. Basil, *On the Holy Spirit* 16:39 (SChr 17:180; PG 32:140 B) [ET: NPNF 2-8:25, or Anderson trans., p. 65]. On the sanctification which comes from the Holy Spirit: Gregory of Nyssa, *In Baptismum Christi* (PG 46:582) [ET: *On the Baptism of Christ*, NPNF 2-5:519]; Cyril of Jerusalem, *Catechesis 23, Mystagogica 5*, 7 (PG 33:1113) [ET: NPNF 2-7:154]; Cyril of Alexandria, *Thesaurus* and *De* [*sancta et consubstantiali*] *Trinitate* (see *Revue d'histoire ecclésiastique* [9] (1909): 31 and 479); according to him,

It is already the Spirit, as the Third Person, who anointed, consecrated, and sanctified Christ in view of his salvific mission: a first time, by constituting Christ by the Incarnation (Lk 1:35); a second time, by anointing him for his ministry at the moment of his baptism: "Therefore the Spirit of God descended upon him," writes St. Irenaeus,[15] "the Spirit of the One Who had promised through the prophets to give him his anointing so that we ourselves, receiving from the abundance of that anointing, could be saved." It is through the Spirit that the words and the flesh of Christ are life-giving.[16] In

---

everything comes from the Father, through the Son, in the Holy Spirit (PG 74:555 D–556 A [ET: Cyril of Alexandria, *Commentary on the Gospel according to S. John*, vol. 2, *S. John 19–21*, A Library of Fathers of the Holy Catholic Church, Anterior to the Division of the East and West, trans. Thomas Randell (London: Walter Smith [Late Mozley], 1885), 468; 481]). [12]

15. *Adversus haereses* 3:9.3 (PG 7:871–2; Harvey, 2:33; trans. Sagnard, SChr 34:161) [ET: ANF 1:423]. On the baptism of Christ, from the biblical point of view, see H. Braun, in *Gesammelte Studien zum N[euen] T[estamentum] und seiner Umvelt]* (Tübingen: J. C. B. Mohr, 1962), 168–72; L. Turrado, "El bautismo in Spiritu sancto et igni," in *Miscellanea Biblica A. Fernandes*, *Estudios eclesiásticos* 34 (1960): 807–17; I. de la Potterie, "L'onction du Christ," *Nouvelle revue théologique* 80 (1958): 225–52. From the patristic and liturgical point of view: L. Koch, "Die Geistessalbung Christi bei der Taufe im Jordan in der Theologie der alten Kirche," *Benediktinische Monatschrift* 20 (1938): 15–20; the information in J. Lecuyer, *Le sacerdoce dans le mystère du Christ*, Lex orandi 24 (Paris: Cerf, 1956), 99ff. A. Orbe, *La unción del Verbo*, Estudios Valentinianos 3 (*Analecta Gregoriana* 113) (Rome: Libreria editrice dell'Università Gregoriana, 1961). From the theological point of view: H. Volk, "Das Wirken des Hl. Geistes in den Gläubigen," *Catholica* 9 (1952): 13–35. [13]

16. See St. Athanasius, *Epistula 4 ad Serapionem*, 19 (PG 26:665–69). [In *Lettres à Sérapion sur la divinité du Saint-Esprit*, trans. J. Lebon, SChr 15: 202–4 (Paris: Cerf, 1947); ET: *The Letters of Saint Athanasius concerning the Holy Spirit*, trans. and introduction by C. R. B. Shapland (New York: Philosophical Library, 1951)] for a demonstration that Christ is God and therefore divinizing [Shapland does not include this paragraph because he believes that the authentic *Fourth Letter to Serapion* is only seven paragraphs long; a compatible reference might be in the *First Letter to Serapion*, 24–26, in Shapland, pp. 125–33]; Augustine, *In Ioannis Evangelium*, Tract. 27, 5 (PL 35:1617). Cyril of Alexandria, *In Ioannis Evangelium*, Book 4 (PG 77 [73]: 601–5) [ET: Cyril of Alexandria, *Commentary on the Gospel according to S. John*, vol. 1, *S. John 1–8*, A Library of Fathers of the Holy Catholic Church, Anterior to the Division of the East and West, trans. P. E. Pusey (London: James Parker & Co., 1874), 435–38], although, against Nestorius, Cyril willingly attributes the power to vivify which the flesh of Christ has to the fact that it is the *very own* flesh of the Word, united substantially to

the theology of the Greek Fathers, "life-giving" means "divinizing." It is no longer even the epiclesis alone which, in the Eastern rite, expresses the role of the Holy Spirit; there is also the symbolism of the *Zeon*. Nicolas Cabasilas explains this as a sort of Eucharistic Pentecost, in reference to the place occupied by Pentecost in the economy of salvation.[17] The *Zeon* brings together the twofold symbolism of water and fire, the latter often serving, in the Fathers and among spiritual writers of every age, to express the divinizing transformation of the soul.[18] In both cases, it is the Holy Spirit who brings about in communicants the effect of divinization that is the purpose of the Eucharistic sacrifice. Theodore of Mopsuestia, around 400, expressed this Eucharistic theology in the following way, drawing a connection between the Eucharist and the glorified body of Christ: "Even if the bread does not have such a nature, when it has received the Holy Spirit and the grace which comes with that, it is able to

---

the Word: letter to Nestorius and the 12th anathema in *Conciliorum oecumenicorum generaliumque decreta*, ed. G. Alberigo et al., [Basilae: Herder, 1962], 43, line 25ff. and 49–50 [ET: Norman P. Tanner, ed. *Decrees of the Ecumenical Councils* (Sheed & Ward and Georgetown University Press, 1990), 1:41 and 49–50. For the text of the 12th anathema of the Council of Ephesus, see Alberigo, p. 61 and the ET in Tanner, p. 61]. [14]

17. *Explication de la liturgie divine*, ch. 37 (SChr 4:206–8) [ET: Hussey and McNulty, 90–91]. According to L. H. Grondijs, the rite of *Zeon* symbolizes the fact that the divinity did not abandon the dead Christ on the Cross: *L'iconographie byzantine du Crucifié mort sur la croix* (Bruxelles: Éditions de Byzantion, Institut de sociologie, 1941); *Autour de l'iconographie du Crucifié mort sur la croix* (Leiden: Brill, 1960). On the divinizing purpose of the Eucharist, see Samonas of Gaza, middle of the eleventh c. [*De sacramento altaris*] (PG 120:824 B) and my *Ecclésiologie du haut moyen âge* (Paris: Cerf, 1968), 331. [15]

18. See Cabasilas, *Explication de la liturgie divine*, ch. 38 (SChr 4, p. 211 and p. 56, where there is a passage from *De vita in Christo*) and, in note 1, the texts cited on the fire comparison in the theology of divinization. On the other hand, the Eucharistic action of the Holy Spirit called forth by the epiclesis is unceasingly compared to the fire coming to give divine sanction to Elijah's sacrifice on Mt. Carmel (1 Kgs 18:38): see the numerous source texts in the works of Goldammer, Salaville and Jugie, cited above. Undoubtedly it is to this biblical foundation of the theology of the epiclesis that it is fitting to refer the expression "legitima," applied to the Eucharist beginning with St. Isidore, to signify the sacrament "in so far as it is sanctifying." See Geiselmann, *Die Abendmahlslehre*, 94, 189; Havet, *Les sacrements*, 69ff. [16]

bring those who eat it to the enjoyment of immortality.... And it is not because of its nature that it does this, but on account of the Holy Spirit who dwells in it, just as the body of Our Lord, whose symbol the bread is, received immortality by the power of the Spirit and gave it to others, even though it itself, by its own nature, absolutely did not possess it."[19]

It is through the Spirit that the words of Christ are life, just as his body is. Basically, the theory and the practice of the early Church on the topic of how to read Scripture proceeds from the same principle as that to which the epiclesis harks back. There is the letter or the body, which the Fathers often saw as an incarnation of the Word. It needs to become life-giving, sanctifying, and salvific through the Spirit who makes it attain the spirit. Fr. de Lubac's studies abundantly illustrate this application of the economy of the divine missions, which economy expresses the sequence of the intra-Trinitarian processions.

Fr. de Lubac also showed how the error of Berengarius of Tours had led people, in reaction, to shift the theology of the Eucharist

---

19. *Homélie catéchétique 15, 1re sur la Messe*, 11–12, [in *Les homélies catéchétiques: Réproduction phototypique du ms. Mingana Syr. 561 (Selly Oak Colleges' Library, Birmingham)*,] ed. and trans. Raymond Tonneau and Robert Devreesse [Studi e testi 145 (Città del Vaticano: Biblioteca Apostolica Vaticana, 1949)] 477ff. See also *Homélie catéchétique 16, 2e sur la Messe*, 12, [in the same collection,] p. 553: "The body of Christ our Lord, too, which is of our nature, was at first mortal by nature, but by means of the resurrection it passed over to an immortal and unchangeable nature. Thus when the high priest [the bishop] says that this bread and this wine are the body and blood of Christ, he clearly reveals that they have become that through the coming of the Holy Spirit, and that through the Spirit they have become immortal because the body of our Lord also was clearly revealed in this way when he was anointed and received the Spirit. In the same way, still now, when the Holy Spirit comes it is like a sort of anointing by the grace which has broken in and which, we think, is received by the bread and wine that are presented. And from then on we believe them to be the body and blood of Christ, immortal, incorruptible, impassible and unchangeable by nature as happened to the body of Our Lord by means of the Resurrection." [For an alternate ET, see *Commentary on the Lord's Prayer and on the Sacraments of Baptism and the Eucharist*, trans. A. Mingana, Woodbrooke Studies 6 (Cambridge: Heffer, 1932; Piscataway, N.J.: Gorgias Press, 2009).] [17]

in the direction of an obsession about the real presence in the consecrated species.[20] It was Cardinal Humbert de Silva Candida who composed the profession of faith imposed upon Berengarius at the Roman synod of 1059; it is a text characterized by a quasi-physical realism, that comes close to Capernaism.[21] When it passed into the collections of Yves of Chartres and Gratian, it exercised a notable influence upon the sacramental thought of early Scholasticism.[22] On the other hand, in the presence of Chancellor Frederic of Lor-

---

20. *Corpus mysticum: L'Eucharistie et l'Église au moyen âge*, Théologie 3 (Paris: Aubier, 1944; 2d ed., 1949) [ET: *Corpus mysticum: The Eucharist and the Church in the Middle Ages* (London: SCM, 2006)]. The Eucharistic theology of Berengarius has recently been the object of several studies: P. Engels, ["De Eucharistieleer van Berengarius van Tours,"] *Tijdschrift voor Theologie* 6 (1965): 363–92; R. B. C. Huygens, ["A propos de Bérenger et son traité de l'eucharistie,"] *Revue bénédictine* 76 (1966): 133–39 (textual criticism). [18]

21. [trans.] This term comes from the name of the town, Capernaum, where Jesus pronounced his Eucharistic discourse in Jn 6. At the time of the Reformation, the term came to be used in doctrinal disputes to designate those who endorsed erroneous positions on the presence of Jesus in the Eucharistic bread and wine. Most often the term has been used, as here, to designate an excessively physical interpretation of that presence.

22. Text in *DS*, 690: the body of Christ is able "sensualiter, [...] in veritate[,] manibus sacerdotum tractari vel frangi, vel fidelium dentibus atteri ["to be sensibly, ... and really, touched or broken by the hands of the priests or ground by the teeth of the faithful." Congar mistakenly quotes from the part of the text in which the position of those who deny that the body and blood of the Lord are tangibly broken and chewed—the view Berengarius had to deny—was described. The corresponding positive assertion in Berengarius's own profession of faith has the following wording: "in veritate manibus sacerdotum tractari et frangi et fidelium dentibus atteri." [ET: Lanfranc of Canterbury, *On the Body and Blood of the Lord*, trans. Mark G. Vaillancourt, The Fathers of the Church, Medieval Continuation 10 (Washington, D.C.: The Catholic University of America Press, 2009), 33]. On what happened to this formulation in twelfth-century Scholasticism: L. Hödl, "Die confession Berengarii von 1059: Eine Arbeit zum früscholast. Eucharistietraktat," *Scholastik* 37 (1962): 370–94. The second profession of faith imposed on Berengarius by Gregory VII in 1079 is more satisfactory: *DS* 700 [ET: J. Neuner and J. Dupuis, eds., *The Christian Faith in the Doctrinal Documents of the Catholic Church*, 7th ed., rev. and enlarged (New York: Alba House, 2001), 1501]. St. Thomas interprets the first text in the right way, but it was not Humbert's way: [*ST*] 3a, q. 77, a. 7, ad 3. On this topic, see also G. Geenen, "Bérenger de Tours dans les écrits de saint Thomas d'Aquin," in *Miscellanea André Combes* (Rome: Libreria ed. della Pont. Università Lateranense, 1967) 2:43–61. [19]

raine, Humbert had had, in 1053–54, a discussion with the Greeks about unleavened bread.[23] Leo of Ohrid said that the unleavened loaves were not a participation in the Father, the Son, and the Holy Spirit.[24] Nicetas of Stethatos said that in unleavened bread would be found only a lifeless body, of the same quality as our own, not the living and life-giving body of Christ in a living bread "immutatus per Spiritum [changed through the Spirit]."[25] As for Humbert, he certainly admitted that the bread was consecrated "fideli invocatione totius Trinitatis [by the faithful invocation of the whole Trinity]." However, once the consecration was completed, he understood the Eucharist only within a Christological framework. This Eucharist contains only the sacrificed Christ, "verum et singulare corpus Christi ... quod septemplici gratiae subnixum ... per passionem crucis in mortem resolvendum ... [the real and individual body of Christ ... which, supported by the sevenfold grace, ... (was) to be delivered unto death through the passion of the cross]."[26] The almost physical realism with which Humbert interpreted the presence of Christ sacrificed on the altar is well known.

The ancient notion that the Spirit played a role in completing in the communicant the work of sanctification for which the Body and Blood of Christ are given as food disappears in the West at the dawn of Scholasticism. In general, it will still be said, as Humbert admitted, that the consecration is accomplished by the power of the Holy Spirit, but the spiritual reality of grace which is the aim of

---

23. Humbert, *Dialogus*, in C. Will, *Acta et scripta quae de contoversiis ecclesiae graecae et latinae saec. XI composita exstant* (Lipsiae et Marpurgi: N. G. Elwerti, 1861), 93–126 and [*Adversus Græcorum calumnias*] PL 143:931–74; *Responsio ad Nicetam*, in Will, 136–50 and [*Contra Nicetam*] PL 143:983–1000. A. Michel, "Die 'Accusatio' des Kanzlers Friedrich von Lothringen (Papst Stephen IX.) gegen die Griechen," *Römische Quartalschrift* 38 (1930): 153–208. [20]

24. See Humbert, *Dialogus*, c. 31; Will, *Acta et scripta*, 108; PL 143:950 B. [21]

25. *Libellus contra Latinos*, 2 and 3; PL 143:974 and 975. [22]

26. *Dialogus*, c. 31; PL 143:950; Will, *Acta et scripta*, 108; Geiselmann, *Die Abendmahlslehre*, 76ff. [23]

the Eucharist is connected only to the active presence of *Christ*.[27] It is not the Holy Spirit but the Eucharist itself, in its full Christological reality, which brings about the effect of grace. As we shall see, the theology of *gratia capitis* [the grace of the head], developed in the twelfth century, corroborated this point of view. Stephen Langton (†1228), a link between early and high Scholasticism, writes these significant lines: "Tria esse circa hoc sacramentum attendenda, scilicet formam et veritatem sacramenti, hoc est corpus domini et gracia spiritus sancti, quae dicitur eucharistia, quasi bona gratia; tamen hoc nomen appropriatur Christo emphatice, eo quod ipse dator est illius gratiae, quae scilicet est res sacramenti [Three things are to be considered with respect to this sacrament, namely, the form and the truth of the sacrament, and this is the body of the Lord and the grace of the Holy Spirit, which is called Eucharist, since it is a sort of good grace. Nevertheless, this name is appropriated emphatically to Christ, because he is the giver of this grace, which is precisely the thing symbolized by the sacrament]."[28] In an even more explicit way, Albert the Great will exclude the position of Isidore when he will speak of the union which the Eucharist effects *ex vi rei contentae* [from the power of the thing contained], that is, by the real presence of Christ.[29]

We know that early Scholasticism, which unfolds between St. Anselm or Abelard and the 1220s, developed, or even created, a treatise on the sacraments and a question about Christ's capital grace. Thanks to a current that can be followed in theology in general and especially in ecclesiology, the reflection became more and more focused, in its quest for precision, upon the consideration of things in themselves. From a mere affirmation of the transcendent

---

27. J. R. Geiselmann has retraced this history: *Die Abendmahlslehre*, 79ff.; *Die Eucharistielehre der Vorscholastik* (Paderborn: Schöningh, 1926). [24]

28. *Summa* (cod. Bamberg. Patr. 136, fol. 68ᵛ), quoted by Geiselmann, *Die Abendmahlslehre*, 78, n. 6. [25]

29. *Sententiae* 4, d. 9, a. 6 (Borgnet edition, 29:222). See d. 8, a. 11, p. 206: "Unitas est effectus corporis Christi veri [Unity is the effect of the true body of Christ]." [26]

cause, reflection moves more and more, in its quest for precision, towards a study of that cause's mediations; from an overall and, in any case, synthetic approach, reflection moves toward an analysis of elements, at the risk of separating them from each other.

Theologians analyzed the sacrament, the agents and moments of the Eucharistic celebration. The controversy with the Greeks about unleavened bread and about the meaning and importance of the symbolic aspects of the rite, brought about the introduction of a distinction between the essential and the non-essential (St. Anselm, William of Champeaux) as a result of which, profound symbolic meanings ran the risk of being neglected. Attention was concentrated on the words of institution, to which even a genius as well informed and imbued with the Tradition as Thomas Aquinas attributed a sort of autonomy and sufficiency.[30] Yves of Chartres, Anselm of Laon, and the *Summa sententiarum* declare that the words of institution are the *forma* [form] and the *modus* [manner of occurrence] of the consecration; the rest is *decor sacramenti* [adornment of the sacrament].[31] Peter of Poitiers applied to them the idea of efficient causality.[32] Not only have thinkers forgotten that the consecration is a matter for the whole of the anaphora, but they wonder whether the consecration of the bread and that of the wine were each brought about by the indicative formula proper to each, *hoc est, hic est* [this is (over the bread), this is (over the cup of wine)], independently of the other (Praepositinus). It is the position of Peter the Cantor on this point which brought about the institution of the rite of the elevation of the host before the words were pronounced over the chalice.[33] Édouard Dumoutet, a historian of this devotion, has

---

30. [*ST*] 3a, q. 78, a. 1, ad 4; see also q. 82, a. 5. For the history which I am summarizing here, see Geiselmann, *Die Abendmahlslehre*, 115f. [27]

31. Roland Bandinelli, Omnebene, Peter Lombard, Master Simon, Gandolph, Huguccio, Peter the Cantor, Sicard of Cremona, Praepositinus. [28]

32. *Sententiae* 5:11 (PL 211:1243 C), around the year 1175. [29]

33. See É. Dumoutet, *Le désir de voir l'hostie et les origines de la dévotion au Saint Sacrement* (Paris: Beauchesne, 1926), 37ff. and *Corpus Domini: Aux sources de la piété eucharistique médiévale* (Paris: Beauchesne, 1942). [30]

expressed in the following terms the consequences of the introduction of this rite into the canon: "For us to realize this, we must recall what the external structure of the Eucharistic Action had been prior to this. It had a 'straight-line' character[34] because the consecration itself was underscored only by very discreet gestures. For the best-informed and the most attentive, the consecration was less a point of arrival than the beginning of an action whose solemn development was followed by their fervent piety until its consummation by communion. And see how, beginning around the twelfth century—to the extent that a precise date can be given—this harmony seems broken. The axis of the canon seems to be relocated from the communion to the consecration, which henceforth becomes, thanks to the elevation, a sort of culminating point toward which everything converges. More accurately, it is the elevation itself which runs the risk of passing, in the opinion of the faithful, for the true high point of the sacrifice and its rite risks being taken for the most essential."[35]

That the institution narrative effects the consecration, concurrently with the action of the Holy Spirit, is indeed the content of the most common tradition. Moreover, this is what the great Scholastics continue to affirm. It seems indisputable, however, that the absence of a formal epiclesis in the Roman Canon diminished the chances of a Eucharistic pneumatology in the Western tradition.[36]

To insist upon the causality of the words of institution was to become involved in a consideration of how the person of the priest functions. Already among the Greek Fathers, St. John Chrysostom is the one who most underscores the role of the words of institution in the consecration and, by the same profound logic, the one

---

34. [trans.] That is, it ran straight through to communion without interruption.

35. [Édouard Dumoutet,] *Le Christ selon la chair et la vie liturgique au moyen-âge* (Paris: Beauchesne, 1932), 149–50. [31]

36. St. Thomas himself speaks more readily of the Holy Spirit's operation in Baptism than in the Eucharist. The article, "Esprit-Saint 3: Dans la liturgie," *DictSpir*, vol. 4, bk. 2, 1283–96 (by F. Vanderbroucke), has not one word about the Eucharist. [32]

who best articulates the sacramental value of the priest's functioning person.[37] As A. Chavasse has shown clearly,[38] the problem is always how to apply to the bread and the wine set down as an offering at a particular moment, on a particular altar, the power of the consecration accomplished once by Christ in the Upper Room, the power that everyone acknowledges as the sole decisive and sovereign one here. Western theology recognized in the priest, as sacramentally representing Christ, the principle that applies to the offerings the consecration that Christ accomplished once and must accomplish each time in the Church's celebrations. This is very clear in Master Simon (around 1150), whose importance for early Scholasticism has been shown.[39] This is the position which Thomas Aquinas holds in his *Sacerdos gerit personam Christi* [the priest functions in the role of Christ], language that is not peculiar to him.[40] This doctrine was taken on in a rigid manner in the *Decree for the Armenians* from the Council of Florence.[41] It is clear that all this is linked to the idea of "character," which the East has not developed as has the West. The priest is himself a sacramental sign of Christ. The West likes to underscore the meaning that a priest's gestures take on in order to signify a sacramental representation of Christ's sacrifice.

A very Christological conception of the Eucharist comes from everything I have just presented. The pneumatological moment could have found its place there—and, indeed, it did find there a certain

---

37. See *De proditione Iudae*, Hom. 1. 6 (PG 49:380). See *De sancta Pentecoste*, Hom. 1. 4 (PG 50:458–59), where the aspect of prayer, of the suppliant role, is underlined more. [33]

38. "L'épiclèse eucharistique dans les anciennes liturgies orientales: Une hypothèse d'interprétation," *Mélanges de science religieuse* 3 (1946): 197–206. [34]

39. See the text of his *Tractatus de sacramentis*, in Geiselmann, *Die Abendmahlslehre*, 127 or in H. Weisweiler, *Maître Simon et son groupe "De sacramentis,"* Spicilegium sacrum Lovaniense 17 ([Université catholique de] Louvain, 1937), 25ff. [35]

40. See [ST] 3a, q. 82, a. 1, 3 and 5. There are other references to Thomas and to the great Scholastics in B. D. Marliangeas, "'In persona Christi,' 'in persona Ecclesiae,'" in *La Liturgie après Vatican II*, Unam Sanctam 66 (Paris: Cerf, 1967), 283–88. [36]

41. D 698; DS 1321 [ET: Neuner and Dupuis, 1510]. [37]

place—but one needs to assess to what extent and under what conditions this happened.

The distinction, classic in Scholasticism, between *res contenta* [the thing contained] and *res non contenta* [the thing not contained] could have occasioned a pneumatological development. In line with Peter Lombard, theologians generally took *res contenta et significata* [the thing contained and signified] to mean the *caro Christi* [the flesh of Christ], the real presence. *Res significata et non contenta* [the thing signifed and not contained] meant the unity of the Church or of the mystical Body.[42] The *res non contenta* is that which is not given immediately through the valid celebration of the sacrament but which, becoming real in a living and free subject outside the sacrament, requires on the part of that subject a spiritual act. An intervention that is new in relation to the celebration itself is required here. One could locate here the activity of the Holy Spirit, which the Hispano-Visigothic and Gallican liturgies required so that a Eucharist would be *legitima* [sanctifying], so that it might have its fruit of sanctification. M. Lienhard says that is Luther's position.[43]

But this is also the reality behind what Thomas Aquinas and the

42. Peter Lombard, *Sententiae* 4, d. 8, c. 6 [= c. 4 in PL 192:857, and c. 7 in *Magistri Petri Lombardi sententiae in IV libris distinctae*, 3d ed., vol. 2, bks: 3–4, Spicilegium Bonaventurianum 5 (Rome: Grottaferrata, 1981), 284–85; ET: Peter Lombard. *The Sentences, Book 4: On the Doctrine of Signs*, trans. Giulio Silano, St. Michael's College Mediaeval Sources in Translation 48 (Toronto: Pontifical Institute of Mediaeval Studies, 2010), 44 (d. 8, c.7)]; see also *In 1 Cor. 11* (PL 191:1642 A). I say "generally" because St. Thomas, for example, *In Epistolam 1 ad Corinthios*, cap. 12, lect. 1 and cap. 15, lect. 1, sees grace in the *res significata et contenta* and the resurrection in the *res significata et non contenta*. Ordinarily St. Thomas says that the *res* of the Eucharist is *caritas* [charity] or *unitas corporis mystici* [the unity of the mystical Body]. [38]

43. "La doctrine du Saint-Esprit chez Luther," *Verbum caro* 76 (1965): 11–38 at 26. R. Prenter's exposition on the Holy Spirit and the sacraments (*Spiritus Creator: Studien zu Luthers Theologie* (Munich: Kaiser Verlag, 1954), 133–72 [ET: from the Danish original with drastic reduction in the number of footnote references, *Spiritus Creator*, trans. John M. Jensen (Philadelphia: Muhlenberg Press, 1953), 130–72] does not contribute very much to a genuine pneumatology. Luther remains very Christological. [39]

great Scholastics, following St. Augustine, call "eating the sacrament *spiritually*," which they distinguish from a simple *sacramental eating*.[44] It is the *spiritual* eating which obtains the *res tantum* [ultimate effect] of the sacrament.[45] It corresponds to the "*digne sumere* [consume *worthily*]" of which St. Paul speaks (1 Cor 11:27 and 29).[46] It consists, according to St. Thomas, in the exercise of living faith and of *credere in Christum* [believing in Christ], with the dynamic meaning which was given to this expression by St. Augustine and which corresponds to what St. Paul tells us about the movement by which the members of the Body of Christ "grow *toward* the One who is the head, the Christ."[47] There is, therefore, a movement, a *spiritual* movement, over and above the pure celebration and reception of the sacrament. Through this movement, St. Thomas says, one comes to participate in the Holy Spirit.[48] It is not apparent, however, that our author goes beyond the general idea, unceasingly affirmed, that every effect of grace is appropriated to the Holy Spirit at the level of its primary causality, which involves the Triune God; the secondary, instrumental cause is the holy humanity of Christ.

---

44. Augustine, *In Ioannis Evangelium*, Tractate 25.12 and Tract. 26.11–12 (PL 35:1602 and 1611–12); Thomas Aquinas, [*ST*] 3a, q. 80, a. 1 and parallels; *In Ioan.*, cap. 6, lect. 7. 2 [ET: Larcher and Weisheipl, *Chapters 6–12*, pp. 45–46]; Cajetan, *In IV Evangel … comm.* (Lyon[: apud haeredes J. Junctae], 1558), fol. 381ff.; *De erroribus contingentibus in Eucharistiae sacramento*, 1525; republished by [Franciscus] A. Von Gunten [*Scripta theologica*] (Rome: Angelicum, 1962). [40]

45. St. Thomas, [*ST*] 3a, q. 80, a. 1; *In Epistolam I ad Corinthios*, cap. 11, lect. 7. [41]

46. St. Thomas, *De articulis fidei et ecclesiae sacramentis, Op. omnia*, Parma ed., 16:121^a. [42]

47. Eph 4:15–16; see 2:15ff., 21–22 and 4:12; Col 2:19. We are baptized *eis Christon* [into Christ], Rom 6:3; *eis hen sōma* [into one body], 1 Co 12:13; Thomas Aquinas, [*ST*] 3a, q. 80, a. 2; *In Ioan.*, cap. 6, lect. 7[.3] [ET: Larcher and Weisheipl, *Chapters 6–12*, n. 972, pp. 46–47]. This creates, in the sacramental perception of Christ as well as in the perception of faith, a tension and a reference that are eschatological: [*ST*] 3a, q. 79, a. 2; q. 80, a. 2; and the general theology of the triple reference of the sacraments so remarkably well formulated, with respect to the Eucharist, in the collect for the Feast of Corpus Christi and in the antiphon *O sacrum*. [43]

48. *In Ioan.* cap. 6, lect. 7. 4 [ET: Larcher and Weisheipl, *Chapters 6–12*, n. 973, pp. 47–49]. [44]

The Eucharistic theology of St. Thomas remains very Christological and it is even perhaps less pneumatological than his theology of baptism, which could be explained by the fact that the Eucharist, as he likes to repeat, contains Christ himself substantially in the mystery of his Passover, while baptism is the locus only of his *virtus* [power].

However, in his theology—so profound—of the relationships between humanity and divinity in Christ, Thomas Aquinas sat largely at the feet of the Greek Fathers, in particular of St. John Damascene and St. Cyril of Alexandria.[49] In studying the theological history of the first four centuries, one notices that things were first approached in a strongly Christological perspective: divinization was connected to the humanity of Christ to the extent that Christ's humanity was united to the Logos and filled with the Holy Spirit.[50]

---

49. See I. Backes, *Die Christologie des hl. Thomas v. A. und die griechischen Kirchenväter* (Paderborn: Schöningh, 1931). J.-M. R. Tillard, *L'Eucharistie: Pâque de l'Église*, Unam Sanctam 44 (Paris: Cerf, 1964), 77–83 [ET: *The Eucharist: Pasch of God's People*, trans. Dennis L. Wienk (New York: Alba House, 1967), 94–102]. [45]

50. For the second century, compare G. Kretschmar, "La doctrine du S.E. du N.T. à Nicée," *Verbum caro* 88 (1968): 5–55 (see pp. 26ff.) and St. Irenaeus, *Proof of the Apostolic Preaching* 7 [SChr 62:41–2 or SChr 406:92–3]: "(Baptism) granting us the grace of rebirth in God the Father, through His Son, in the Holy Spirit (the same wording is found in Justin, *First Apology* 61.3 and 66.1 [SChr 507:290 and 306; ET: St. Justin Martyr, *The First and Second Apologies*, trans. Leslie William Bernard, Ancient Christian Writers 56 (New York: Paulist, 1967), 66 and 70].) ... But the Son, according to the Father's good pleasure, administers the Spirit as a minister as the Father wills, to those to whom he wills" [ET: ACW 16:51 or Behr trans., p. 44]. For St. Athanasius grace comes from the Father through the Son in the Spirit: "The Son, through the Spirit who is in him, unites us to the Father" (*Letters to Serapion* 1:24 [PG 26:585], trans. J. Lebon, SChr 18 [15]: 126. [ET: *The Letters of Saint Athanasius Concerning the Holy Spirit*, trans. and intro. Shapland, 126]). Speaking of the Eucharist, St. Ephraem writes, "He called the bread his living body and filled it with himself and with the Holy Spirit.... This is my body, whoever eats it with faith eats with it the fire of the Holy Spirit." [Congar gives the reference for this quotation as *Opera*, Lamy ed. 4:173, which we have been unable to find. The text cited is, however, found in "Sermo IV in hebdomadam sanctam," alternatively named, "Sermone quarto de passione," in Sancti Ephraem Syri, *Hymni et sermones*, ed. Thomas Joseph Lamy (Mechliniæ: H. Dessain, Summi Pontificis, S. Congregationis de Propaganda Fide et Archiepiscopatus Mechliniensis Typographus, 1882) 1:415–18.] The institution narrative of the Liturgy of St. James says,

It is the difficult discussions about the personal divinity of the Holy Spirit, as well as the work of the Cappadocians and the Council of Constantinople in 381, that led to a new doctrinal *and liturgical* development in the pneumatological direction.[51] That is said without at all calling into question either the validity or the profundity of the development secured in this way for theology.

It is well known that the Second Vatican Council once again highlighted in a remarkable way a Trinitarian vision of the Church. The ancient formula "to the Father, through the Son, in the Holy Spirit" comes back twice in the conciliar documents.[52] We already have studies about the Council's pneumatology, but one will be able to assess its vigor and real impact only when the work of theologians will have more comprehensively responded to the stimulus that this pneumatology has provided. As of now we have one of its fruits in the new texts of the Eucharistic prayer, namely Canons Two, Three, and Four (Canon One being the Roman Canon).[53] These are beautiful texts, especially Three and Four. Anaphora Two has a very brief prayer to the Holy Spirit after the consecration, to ask that the communicants be "gathered together by the Holy Spirit into a single body" (p. 29 [16]). This is an echo of St. Paul (1 Cor 12:13) and also of the anaphora of Hippolytus. What is said is genuinely

---

"He took the cup ... blest it and filled it with the Holy Spirit, gave it...." There is no question there of a *personal* action on the part of the Holy Spirit, who is rather considered as the gift *which Christ gives*. [46]

51. This emerges from studies on the epiclesis within the blessings of baptismal fonts: J. Quasten, "The Blessing of the Baptismal Font in the Syrian Rite of the Fourth Century," *Theological Studies* 7 (1946): 309–13. A. Baumstark does well to note (*Liturgie comparée*, 3d ed. [Chevetogne: Éditions de Chevetogne, 1953], 27–28 and 52) [ET: *Comparative Liturgy*, revised by Bernard Botte, English edition by F. L. Cross (Westminster, Md.: Newman Press, 1958), 25–26] that an epiclesis, properly so called, presupposed the development of the theology of the Holy Spirit approved by the Council of 381. [47]

52. M. Philipon, "La T. S. Trinité et l'Église," in *L'Église de Vatican II*, ed. G. Barauna, Unam Sanctam 51b (Paris: Cerf, 1966), 275–98. [48]

53. *Preces eucharisticae et praefationes*, (Vatican City: Typis Polygl. Vaticanis, 1968); *La Maison-Dieu* 94 (1968/2). In what follows, the first number refers to the page in the Vatican edition, the second, in brackets, to *La Maison-Dieu*. [49]

pneumatological. Anaphora Three has a brief consecratory epiclesis before the consecration: "sanctify them [the offerings] through your Spirit" (p. 31 [21]), and, after the consecration, a prayer so that, filled with the Holy Spirit, the faithful may form a single body and a single spirit in Christ and so that "the Spirit may make of them an eternal offering to your glory" (p. 33 [32]). This is an allusion to texts such as Rom 15:16. Finally, Anaphora Four has a consecratory epiclesis before the institution narrative (p. 38 [32]) and, after the institution narrative, a prayer asking that the Holy Spirit gather the communicants into a single body (pp. 39–40 [34]). This indication could be very pneumatological if it were more explicit. The gathering together into one body (of Christ) and the exercise of the royal priesthood are attributed to the action, not of the sacrament itself, but *of the Spirit*. One finds here, therefore, the possible beginning of a truly ecclesiological pneumatology.

2. The theology of Christ's capital grace[54]

The twelfth century did not create the theology *de Christo capite* [on Christ the head] but elaborated upon it. That century did create the treatise *De gratia capitis* [On the Grace of the Head]. The Scholasticism of the thirteenth century, including its treatise on the mystical Body, had, as a result of the great attention paid to these two themes, a decidedly Christological character. Before these elaborations, the notion of the "Body of Christ" resulted simply from the putting together of two ideas: a multitude of members

---

54. Refer to E. Mersch, *Le Corps mystique du Christ: Études de théologie historique*, 2d ed. (Brussels and Paris: Desclée de Brouwer, 1936), 2:162ff.; A. Landgraf, "Die Lehre vom geheimnisvollen Leib Christi in den frühen Paulinenkommentaren und der Frühscholastik," *Divus Thomas* (Fr.) 24 (1946): 217–48, 393–428; 25 (1947): 365–94; 26 (1948): 160–80, 291–323, 395–434; Z. Alszeghy, *Nova creatura: La nozione della grazia nei commentari medievali di s. Paolo* [Analecta Gregoriana 81] (Rome: apud aedes Universitas Gregoriana, 1956), 158 ff. [50]

having diverse gifts, made into one body by the Holy Spirit who is the principle of life and, at the same time, the principle of unity.[55] The developments to which I have referred clearly took place under the influence of Christology.

In his *De sacramentis christianae fidei* [On the Sacraments of the Christian Faith] (perhaps before 1137), Hugh of Saint Victor remains within an Augustinian perspective. When one is united to and, in that sense, incorporated into Christ by faith and baptism, one can receive the Holy Spirit from Christ, and thus participate in the *life* of his body.[56] The Holy Spirit is given *through Christ*, as the spirit which makes a person's body live descends to the members from the head: *sicut spiritus hominis mediante capite ad membra vivificanda descendit, sic Spiritus Sanctus per Christum venit ad christianos* [Just as the spirit of a human person descends by means of the head to the members to be enlivened, so the Holy Spirit comes through Christ to Christians].[57]

Everyone obviously held that Christ is *caput ecclesiae* [head of the Church] on the basis of his divinity, that is to say, on the same basis as the Father and the Spirit. Nascent Scholasticism asks if he is also head in his own right on account of his humanity, and the response was affirmative.[58] By the idea of *caput* [head], they mean only what St. Augustine meant. At most they add that *unius naturae sunt caput et corpus* [the head and the body are of one nature]. They

---

55. I give references in *L'histoire des doctrines ecclésiologiques*, forthcoming from Herder and les Éditions du Cerf in the History of Dogmas series. [With a slightly different title for the book, see *L'Église: De saint Augustin à l'époque moderne*, Histoire des dogmes 20 (Paris: Cerf, 1970; reissued Paris: Cerf, 1996), 160ff.] [51]

56. "Quando [ergo] christianus efficeris, membrum Christi efficeris, membrum corporis Christi, participans Spiritum Christi [When you are made a Christian, you are made a member of Christ, a member of the body of Christ, participating in the Spirit of Christ]." [*De unitate Ecclesiae*], Bk 2, Pt 2, ch. 2; PL 176:417A. [52]

57. Ibid., Bk. 2, Pt. 2, ch. 1; PL 176:415D. [53]

58. So, for example, Hervé de Bourg-Dieu (†1150), Gilbert de la Porré and his school, Peter Lombard, Peter of Poitiers, etc. [54]

do not attribute to Christ's *humanity* an efficacy in causing grace.[59] They did sometimes use formulations such as *omnia* (Peter the Cantor even said *omnia dona gratiae* [all the gifts of grace]) *in se habet et ab eo defluunt in membra ecclesiae* [he has all things in himself and from him they flow down into the members of the Church].[60] The full flowering of a treatise *De gratia capitis* [On the Grace of the Head] presupposed a theology of *created* grace. The expression *gratia creata* [created grace] appeared only with Alexander of Hales in 1245.[61] The idea behind the expression had arisen earlier from questions raised by the baptism of infants. The treatise *De gratia capitis* [On the Grace of the Head], which was taking shape in the *Sentences* of Peter of Poitiers (4:20; PL 211:1215–1219), appeared complete in William of Auxerre, toward 1220–25.[62] This would be the basis of the treatises of the great Scholastics on the mystical Body. Henceforth, they deal with this by beginning with the capital grace of Christ, whereas before the twelfth century thinkers spoke of it in connection with and starting from the Eucharist.

I am not writing a history of dogmas here. We know that the theology *de Christo capite, de gratia capitis* clarifies the vision which Alexander of Hales and especially Bonaventure had of the Church as Body of Christ.[63] The well-known verse of St. John summarizes

---

59. G. Philips did a good job of shedding light on this point of Augustinian theology: "L'influence du Christ-Chef sur son Corps mystique suivant saint Augustin," in *Augustinus magister* [*Congrès international augustinien, Paris, 21–24, September 1954*], (Paris: Études augustiniennes / Besançon: Imprimerie de l'Est, 1954), 2:805–15. [55]

60. Thus Ralph of Laon in the study by A. Landgraf cited above, n. 50 [54] [*Divus Thomas* (Fr.)] (1946): 232, n. 3; Peter the Cantor, [*Divus Thomas* (Fr.)] (1946): 246, n. 1 and [*Divus Thomas* (Fr.)] (1947): 393. [56]

61. See C. Moeller and G. Philips, *Grâce et oecuménisme* (Chevetogne: Éditions de Chevetogne, 1957), 30. [57]

62. *Summa aurea*, Bk 3, tr. 1, cap. 4 (Paris: Pigouchet edition, folio CXVI^v) [reprint edition: Magistri Guillelmi Altissiodorensis, *Summa aurea*, ed. Jean Ribaillier, *Spicilegium Bonaventurianum* 18 A (Paris: Editions du Centre national de la recherche scientifique / Roma: Editiones Collegii S. Bonaventurae ad Claras Aquas, 1980)]. [58]

63. S. Lisiecki, "Die gratia capitis nach Alexander von Hales," *Jahrbuch für Philosophie und spekulative Theologie* 27 (1913): 343–404. D. Culhane, *De Corpore mystico doctrina Seraphici*, ([S.T.D. Thesis, St. Mary of the Lake Seminary], Mundelein, Ill.,

it (1:16): "of his fullness we have all received." Thomas Aquinas has basically the same vision, with one new and original element which was, however, of the greatest importance. Beginning with the last part of *De veritate* (in 1258), Thomas Aquinas applied the concept of instrumental causality to the humanity of Christ, and then to the sacraments. Even more than Aristotle, it was the Greek Fathers Cyril of Alexandria and John Damascene who gave him the idea of the holy humanity of Christ as an organ of divinity.[64] Yet, on the other hand, Thomas Aquinas had the most *theo*-logical and the most theologal conception of the Christian life. Grace really does make us participate in the life of the divine Persons; it comes from these Persons, by appropriation from the Holy Spirit, who is Gift and communication. St. Thomas often uses the expression *gratia Spiritus Sancti* [grace of the Holy Spirit].[65] He says that the Holy Spirit produces *active* grace or charity.[66] Thus, the Thomistic vision of the Church is arranged on two levels united by the concrete economy of grace: a level of absolutely *divine* causality, simultaneously final, exemplary, and efficient, and a level dependent upon the Incarnation of the Word-Son, that is both exemplary and efficient. Therefore, there is a pneumatological divine level and an Incarnation level.[67] How do these two levels fit together? Before see-

---

1934). R. Šilić, *Christus und die Kirche: Ihr Verhältnis nach der Lehre des Heiligen Bonaventura* (Breslau: Müller und Seiffert, 1938); H. Berresheim, *Christus als Haupt der Kirche nach dem Heiligen Bonaventura: Ein Betrag zur Theologie der Kirche* (Bonn: Ludwig, 1939). [59]

64. See I. Backes, *Die Christologie* (see n. 49 [45]), 214ff., 247ff., 270–86. See also Th. Tschipke, *Die Menschheit Christi als Heilsorgan der Gottheit: Unter besonderer Berücksichtigung der Lehre des Heiligen Thomas von Aquin* (Freiburg: Herder, 1940). [60]

65. Thus [*ST*] 1a2ae, q. 106, a. 1 (body), ad 1 and 3; a. 2; a. 3; q. 108, a. 1; q. 113, a. 7, sed c.; 3a, q. 72, a. 2; *In Ioan*, cap. 4, lect. 2.1 [ET: Larcher and Weisheipl, *Chapters 1–5*, n. 577, pp. 214–215]; *1 ad Cor*, cap. 6., lect. 3. [61]

66. [*ST*] 1a2ae, q. 110, a. 1, ad 2; 2a2ae, q. 23, aa. 2 and 3; *Quaestiones disputatae de caritate*, [*De virtutibus*, Q. 2], a. 1, ad 1. "Ipsum donum gratiae est a Spiritu Sancto [the very gift of grace is from the Holy Spirit]": [*ST*] 1a, q. 43, a. 3, ad 2; see also q. 38, a. 2. [62]

67. See, among other passages, [*ST*] 1a2ae, q. 108, a. 1; see also 3a, q. 8, a. 1, ad 1; q. 16, a. 11, ad 2; q. 19, a. 1, ad 2. The Holy Spirit as *principal cause*: [*ST*] 3a, q. 66, a. 11;

ing how this happens in the Church, and in order to see well how this happens in the Church, it makes sense to see how it happens in Christ, the incarnate Word.

The "grace of union" is, as a gracious willing, the uncreated act of the three Persons. As a reality in the creature, it is the assumption of a human nature, body and soul, by the Person of the Word. It is also the ontological consecration of that human nature. Because it is ordered to a work of salvation and sanctification, the grace of union calls for a created grace which is given, as an operative principle, to Christ in the greatest fullness not only for himself in his individuality, but for all those whom he must save and sanctify.[68]

The humanity of the Word, thus consecrated, sanctified and sanctifying, is—in all its human truth of corporeality and sensibility, intelligence and will—the instrument of divinity, or rather its organ. The Word's humanity is a conjoined instrument, as my hand is conjoined to my will in the unity of my bodily personality.[69] It is an instrument that is animated, intelligent, and free, not simply mechanically *used*, but one that *serves* knowingly and freely the

---

In Epistolam 1 ad Corinthios, cap. 12, lect. 3. Among the studies on the ecclesiology of St. Thomas, let me mention particularly M. Grabmann, *Die Lehre des hl. Thomas von Aquin von der Kirche als Gotteswerk* (Regensberg: Manz, 1903); M. Useros Carretero, *"Statuta Ecclesiae" y "Sacramenta Ecclesiae" en la eclesiología de S. Tomás de Aquino*, [Analecta Gregoriana 119] (Rome: Librería editrice dell'Università Gregoriana, 1962).

We know that St. Thomas applied the images of heart and head to the role of the Holy Spirit and of Christ in the mystical body, respectively: *De veritate*, q. 29, a. 4, ad 7; [*ST*] 3a, q. 8, a. 1, ad 3. This is because the Holy Spirit is (by appropriation) the cause, at once *universal* and *hidden* of all the movements of grace, just as the heart is of all the vital movements in the human being, according to Aristotle and Avicenna. The head is the *visible* cause of voluntary orientation. Compare Grabmann, *Die Lehre des hl. Thomas von Aquin*, 184–93; Šilić, *Christus und die Kirche* (see n. 63 above [59]), 53ff. [63]

68. *De veritate*, q. 29, a. 5, ad 7; [*ST*] 3a, q. 7 and 8, with article 5 on the essential identity of the grace of Christ as an individual and as head of the Church: q. 26, a. 2, ad 1; q. 59, a. 3 obj. 2; *Compendium theologiae* 1:214. [64]

69. See *Summa contra Gentiles* 4:41 [n. 10]; [*ST*] 3a, q. 64, a. 3 and 4. Tschipke, *Die Menschheit Christi* (see n. 64 [60]), 146ff. Ch.-V. Héris, *Le mystère du Christ* (Paris: Éditions de la Revue des jeunes, 1927), 129ff. [ET: *The Mystery of Christ: Our Head, Priest and King*, trans. Denis Fahey (Westminster, Md.: Newman Press, 1950), 79–89]. [65]

plan of God's grace.[70] And so there is no spiritual gift, no movement of grace, which does not depend, in subordination to the Divinity, on the *human* intelligence and knowledge, will and love of Jesus Christ, who is Head of the redeemed people. One could say, according to an authorized symbolism, that all spiritual gifts or movements of grace depend on the Sacred Heart of Jesus. Indeed, the development of devotion to the Sacred Heart could well be a sign of our Christocentricism. Thomists are right to note that this intervention of the will of Christ (perfectly in harmony with that of his Father) in the gift of every grace gives to the causality of Christ the concreteness of a principal cause, that is, of origin and authority.[71] This is important for appreciating the Christological character of this *effectus gratiae* [effect of grace] which is, for St. Thomas, the mystical Body.[72] One can consider it at the level of divine causality and at the level of what the assumption of a human nature as an organ permits one to attribute to the Person of the Word.

St. Thomas identifies the gift of grace given to us with the invisible mission of the Holy Spirit (*ST* 1a, q. 43). In classical terms, the expression "giving the Holy Spirit" is equivalent to "giving grace." See, for example, *ST* 3a, q. 8, a. 1, ad 1; *Ad Galatas*, c. 3, lect. 2. We know that every work of producing something outside of God is common to the three Persons. On this point, the Greek Fathers are as definite as the Latins. It is just that they love to affirm, within the common action of the Persons, the structure of their relations. But this is true of Thomas Aquinas, as well. It is for that very reason that he calls the Son *sanctificationis actor* [agent of sanctification].[73] This is because the Spirit proceeds from the Son united to

---

70. [*ST*] 3a, q. 7, a. 1, ad. 3; q. 8, a. 5, ad 1; q. 18, a. 1, ad 2; q. 69, a. 5; *Quaestio disputata de unione Verbi incarnati*, a. 5, ad 4; *Ad Ephesios*, cap. 4, lect. 5. Tschipke cites, in the same sense, St. Gregory of Nyssa (*Die Menschheit Christi*, p. 39) and St. John Damascene (*Die Menschheit Christi*, p. 65). [66]

71. Each sending forth of grace involves a personal act of Christ: [*ST*] 3a, q. 8, a. 5, ad 1. [67]

72. *3 Sent.*, d. 25, q. 1, a. 2, ad. 10; *De veritate*, q. 29, a. 5 (body). [68]

73. [*ST*] 1a, q. 43, end of a. 7, where the uncertainty of the text found in some

the Father in the spiration of the Spirit. Christ is obviously not the co-principle of the Spirit in his humanity, but the Word made flesh is, so that the Holy Spirit is the Spirit of Christ,[74] and the latter is *Verbum spirans amorem* [the Word breathing forth love].[75] This is where the question arises of knowing what impact the doctrine of the *Filioque* [and the Son] could have on ecclesiology.

More than one contemporary Orthodox theologian states that such an impact exists and that it is indeed decisive.[76] From the perspective according to which the procession of the Holy Spirit is *a Patre solo* [from the Father alone], one might well think that the Paraclete seems to be freer, the personal principle of an action less linked to the work and to the institution of the Word incarnate. Thus, the Church could have a more charismatic style and be less closely linked to determinate institutional forms. The question would require an attentive and critical study. On any hypothesis, the Orthodox, like us, admit the community of divine operations *ad extra* [outside the Trinity] and the fact that the Holy Spirit is sent by the Son or at the request of the Son.[77] We know also that St. Paul speaks of the Spirit of the Lord or of Jesus.[78] Does that not di-

---

manuscripts does not change anything; ad 4 of the same question. See also [*ST*] 3a, q. 7, a. 9 (body) and ad 1: Christ "universale principium in genere habentium gratiam [universal principal in the genus of those having grace]," "auctor gratiae [author of grace]." [69]

74. [*ST*] 2a2ae, q. 124, a. 5, ad 1. St. Thomas applies this consideration even to the formation of the body of Jesus in the womb of Mary: [*ST*] 3a, q. 32, a. 1, ad 1 gives a very Christological interpretation of Lk 1:35. [70]

75. [*ST*] 1a, q. 43, a. 5, ad 2. [71]

76. In addition to the works of N. Nissiotis mentioned above (n. 3 [2]), see V. Lossky, "Du troisième attribut de l'Église," (n. 5 [3]), p. 86. Hiéromoine Sophrony, "L'Église, image de la sainte Trinité," *Vestnik* [*Russkogo Zapadno-evropejskogo patriarsevo ekzarkata*]: *Messager de l'exarchat du patriarche russe en Europe occidentale*, n. 5 (1950): 33–69 at 66; Anonymous, "Note sur le 'filioquisme,'" *Lumière et vie* 67 (1964): 102–14. G. Every affirms this notion, but without any specific documentation: *The Byzantine Patriarchate 451–1204* (London: SPCK, 1947), 195–96. [72]

77. The Son sends or asks the Father to send the Spirit: see Lk 24:49; Acts 1:4ff. and 8; 2:33; 5:30–32; 11:16; Jn 7:39 and 16:7, and then 3:34; 15:26; 16:7; Phil 1:19. [73]

78. Rom 8:9 (cited by St. Thomas in [*ST*] 2a2ae, q. 124, a. 5, ad. 1); Gal 4:6; Phil 1:19; see 2 Cor 3:17. [74]

minish notably the independence one might like to see in the Holy Spirit's activity? Yet I recall the joy of V. Lossky, of the Confraternity of St. Photius, when I made him aware of the following text from St. Thomas ("I always thought," he told me, "that St. Thomas was a true and great theologian."): *Similis autem error est dicentium Christi vicarium, Romanae ecclesiae pontificem, non habere universalis Ecclesiae primatum, errori dicentium Spiritum Sanctum a Filio non procedere. Ipse enim Christus Dei Filius suam Ecclesiam consecrat et sibi consignat Spiritu Sancto quasi suo caractere et sigillo, ut ex supra positis auctoritatibus manifeste habetur; et similiter Christi vicarius suo primatu et providentia universam Ecclesiam tamquam fidelis minister Christo subiectam conservat* [The error of those who say that the vicar of Christ, the pontiff of the Roman Church, does not have primacy over the universal Church is similar to the error of those who say that the Holy Spirit does not proceed from the Son. For Christ himself, the Son of God, consecrates his Church and seals it for himself with the Holy Spirit as if by his own character and seal, as is manifestly seen from the authorities mentioned above; and similarly, as a faithful minister, the vicar of Christ keeps, by his primacy and provident care, the universal Church subject to Christ].[79]

In this passage, what needs to be underscored is *ecclesiam suam sibi* [his Church for himself], which clearly corresponds to the gospel expressions *"ecclesiam meam* [my church]" (Mt 16:18), *"pasce oves meas* [feed my sheep]" (Jn 21:15–16). The Church is truly that *of Christ*, his body, not the body of the Holy Spirit. For St. Thomas, the error of the "Greeks" on the procession of the Holy Spirit belongs to the series of those errors which *ad hoc principaliter videntur tendere ut Christi derogent dignitati* [seem to tend mainly toward detracting from the dignity of Christ].[80]

---

79. *Contra errores Græcorum*, part 2, ch. 32, critical [LC] edition, Rome, 1969, 40: A101. One could compare St. Bonaventure, [*Quaestiones disputatae*] *de perfectione evangelica*, q. 4, a. 3, n. 12 (*Opera* [*omnia, opuscula varia theologica* (Ad Claras Aquas [Quaracchi]: Ex Typographia Collegii S. Bonaventurae, 1891)], 5:197). [75]

80. *Contra errores Græcorum*, part 2, prol., LC 40:A87. A little later he writes:

What needs to be considered is not only the eternal Procession, but also the assumption, in our time, of a human nature by the Person of the Word, that is, the visible "mission" of the Son. By means of that, the Person of the Word, *as the incarnate Word*, becomes the principle of a proper causality of salvation or the principle of a structure of sanctification, to which neither the Jordan theophany nor that of Pentecost are an equivalent for the Holy Spirit. For there is no union in being of the dove or of the tongues of fire with the hypostasis of the Holy Spirit; what we have there are simply *signs* of an invisible, and altogether decisive, mission.[81] The union of the Holy Spirit with the apostolic institution and with the Church is a covenantal union. The Spirit is *given* as *the Promised One* proper to the new and eternal covenant; the Spirit is not united to a creature in such a manner as to make of the latter the Spirit's conjoined, animated and free *organ*.[82] In this way the causality of the Holy Spirit in the gift of grace remains within the mysterious order of appropriation, while the instrumental causality of the *incarnate* Word is a causality proper to him. In addition, this causality is the origin of the institution of salvation which is the Church, in which creatures are taken up, by a sharing at once sacramental and juridical,

---

"Dum enim dicunt Spiritum Sanctum a Filio non procedere, eius dignitatem minuunt qua simul cum Patre est Spiritus Sancti spirator. Dum vero unum caput Ecclesiae esse negant, sanctam scilicet Romanam ecclesiam, manifeste unitatem Corporis mystici dissolvunt.... [For when they say the Holy Spirit does not proceed from the Son, they diminish the dignity by which he is, together with the Father, spirator of the Holy Spirit. But when they deny that there is one head of the Church, namely, the holy Roman Church, they manifestly dissolve the unity of the mystical Body....]" [76]

81. *1 Sent.*, d. 16, a. 1, ad 1; [*ST*] 1a, q. 43, a. 7. [77]

82. See my study "Le Saint-Esprit et le Corps apostolique, réalisateurs de l'oeuvre du Christ," [*Revue des sciences philosophiques et théologiques* 36 (1952): 613–25, and 37 (1953): 24–48, reprinted in Yves M.-J. Congar,] *Esquisses du mystère de l'Église*, Unam Sanctam 8, 2d ed. (Paris: Cerf, 1953); 129–79 [ET: "The Holy Spirit and the Apostolic Body, Continuators of the Work of Christ," in *The Mystery of the Church: Studies by Yves Congar*, trans. A. V. Littledale (London: Geoffrey Chapman, 1960), 147–86]; Dom A. Vonier, *L'Esprit et l'épouse*, trans. L. Lainé and B. Limal, Unam Sanctam 16 (Paris: Cerf, 1947) [English original: *The Spirit and the Bride* (London: Burns, Oates and Washburn, 1935]. [78]

to be—following and depending on Christ—"a universal sacrament of salvation." *Oportet quod virtus salutifera derivetur a divinitate Christi per eius humanitatem in ipsa sacramenta* [It is necessary that saving power flow out from the divinity of Christ through his humanity into the sacraments themselves].[83] The mystical Body is seen as dependent upon the capital grace of Christ, as well as upon his redemptive acts: this is the grace which divinizes.[84] There is no incarnation and no "mystical Body" of the Holy Spirit.

However, Thomas Aquinas attributes to the Holy Spirit the role of being the seal or final completion of the mystical Body, including its Head, Christ as the *incarnate* Word. The members of the mystical Body, he says, *habent pro ultimo complemento Spiritum Sanctum qui est unus numero in omnibus* [have the Holy Spirit, who is the same one in all, as ultimate completion].[85] It is the same Spirit who is in Christ and in Christians. St. Paul supports this supremely important affirmation (Rom 8:15; Gal 4:6). St. Bonaventure and St. Albert have similar formulations.[86] Along with St. Thomas and other less

---

83. [*ST*] 3a, q. 62 a. 5. [79]

84. In terms of divinization, see *De virtutibus*, q. 1, a. 2, ad 21. [80]

85. *3 Sent.*, d. 13, q. 2, a. 2, sol. 2, ad 1; see *De veritate*, q. 29, a. 4 (quoted by the encyclical *Mystici Corporis*, *AAS* 35 (1943), 222); *In Ioan.* cap. 1, lect. 10, n. 1 [ET: Larcher and Weisheipl, *Chapters 1–5*, n. 202, pp. 82–83] and cap. 6, lect. 7 [ET: Larcher and Weisheipl, *Chapters 6–12*, n. 972, pp. 46–47]; *Compendium theologiae* 1:147; [*ST*] 2a2ae, q. 183, a. 2, ad 3. See E. Vauthier, "Le Saint-Esprit, principe d'unité de l'Église d'après saint Thomas d'Aquin: Corps mystique et habitation du Saint-Esprit," *Mélanges de science religieuse* 5 (1948): 175–96; 6 (1949): 57–80. And see H. Mühlen, n. 89 [85] below. It was only after having written the present study that I became aware of the work of P. Galvis, OP, on the Holy Spirit in the *Summa theologiae* (in Spanish, 2 vols., 1967). The first volume gathers together basically all the passages where the Holy Spirit is named, and it gives a list of the biblical passages to which reference is made; the second volume attempts a synthesis of Thomistic pneumatology. It was unfortunately impossible for me to benefit from this work. [We have been unable to identify this two-volume work. Was Congar entirely accurate in his recollection of the author's surname?] [81]

86. Bonaventure, *Sent.* 1: d. 14, [a.] 2, [q.]1 fund. 4 (*Opera* 1:249a.). It is not clear that he includes Christ in this, as St. Thomas does. Albert, *Sent.* 3: d. 24, B a. 6; [Albert], *Quaest. de Incarnatione* (before 1250), ed. I. Backes, *Florilegium patristicum* 40 (Bonn: Hanstein, 1935) 20: "Proprie loquendo, propter unam fidem ecclesia non

ingenious scholastics, they also affirm the unity of the article concerning the Holy Spirit and the article concerning the Church in the Creed, especially when the latter article is read as in *unam ... ecclesiam [in one ... church]*. They join these two articles into a single one which reads: *Credo in Spiritum Sanctum vivificantem (unientem, sanctificantem*; it would be necessary to say *catholicizantem, apostolicizantem) Ecclesiam* [I believe in the Holy Spirit enlivening (uniting, sanctifying, catholicizing, and apostolicizing) the Church].[87] The promise of an ecclesiological pneumatology seems close enough to touch. But there is no doubt that among the Scholastics this is to be understood within the framework of the *appropriation* to the Holy Spirit of everything which is gift and grace, at the level of *divine* causality. There exists no proper and autonomous personal operation of the Holy Spirit. From the point of view of efficient causality, even the "gifts" and charisms which are attributed to the Spirit are a matter for the three Persons conjointly and for Christ-the human being instrumentally. One is therefore brought back to Trinitarian theology and to the realism with which one must understand this difficult doctrine of appropriation. We know that St. Thomas inter-

---

dicitur una, sed propter unum Spiritum [properly speaking, the church is not said to be one because of one faith but because of one Spirit]." [82]

87. Alexander of Hales, *Summa*, part 3, [inq. 2], tr. 2, q. 2, t. 1, no. 16 (Quaracchi edition, 4:1131); Albert, *Sent.* 3: d. 24, B a. 6 sol. (Borgnet edition, 18:457–58); 4: d. 39, a. 3 (30:429); *De sacrificio Missae*, 2: q. 9, a. 9 (38:64); *Quaest. de Incarnatione*, edition cited (see n. 86 [82] above), p. 20, 1.8–13; Thomas, *3 Sent.* d. 25, q. 1, a. 2 sol. and ad 5, which (as does Alexander of Hales) cites St. Anselm as source or reference (passage not identified); [*ST*] 2a2ae, q. 1, a. 9, ad 5. M. Grabmann, *Die Lehre des hl. Thomas von Aquin* (see n. 67 [63]), 122 cites similar passages from Peter of Tarantaise and Richard Middleton. Sebastian Tromp writes the history of "credo (in) ecclesiam [I believe (in) the Church]": *Corpus Christi quod est Ecclesia* (Romae: Universitas Gregoriana, 1937), 1:89–91 (2d ed., 1946, 97–98); see especially J. E. L. Oulton, "The Apostles' Creed and Belief concerning the Church," *Journal of Theological Studies* 39 (1938): 239–43. On the connection between the article on the Holy Spirit and the article on the Church in ancient Christianity and in the Fathers, see P. Nautin, *Je crois à l'Esprit dans la sainte Église pour la résurrection de la chair*, Unam Sanctam 17 (Paris: Cerf, 1947); J. Jungmann, "*Die Gnadenlehre im Apostolishen Glaubensbekenntnis*," *Zeitschrift für katholische Theologie* 50 (1926): 196–217. [83]

prets it along the lines of the assimilation to an essential attribute which manifests what is proper to a Person.[88] And so, every effect of love, of gift, of communion, makes one like what, in God, is love, and thus it makes one like the Holy Spirit, in so far as the Spirit proceeds through the mode of love and is the bond of love between the Father and the Son.

This doctrine leaves an indisputable feeling of dissatisfaction with whoever tries to get back to the letter of scriptural pronouncements. From time to time, some theologians have attempted to go beyond this doctrine and to attribute to the Holy Spirit a *proper* fruit of indwelling and of sanctification: Petau, Scheeben, Schauf, H. Mühlen. The last-mentioned thinker carries out one of the most interesting efforts to go beyond every appearance of leaving to the Holy Spirit only the role of being a function of Christ. In doing so, Mühlen attempts to attribute to the Spirit a proper personal function: with regard first to Christ (baptismal anointing), then to Christians and to the Church. Mühlen bases his account of this proper function on what the Spirit is within the Godhead, namely, the Person-link, the *Wir in Person* [We in Person].[89] He does this by

---

88. [*ST*] 1a, q. 39, a. 7; his remarkable application to the Holy Spirit: *Summa contra Gentiles* 4:21. See also *1 Sent.*, d. 14, q. 2, a. 1, sol. 1 ("per dona eius ipsi Spiritui Sancto coniungimur [through his gifts we are conjoined to the Holy Spirit himself]"; see also [*ST*] 1a, q. 43, a. 3); [*ST*] 2a2ae, q. 23, a. 3, ad 3 (charity = "quaedam participatio Spiritus Sancti [a certain participation in the Holy Spirit]"; [*ST*] 3a, q. 7, a. 13 (the Spirit is said to be sent because the Spirit inhabits the soul by charity). [84]

89. *Der Heilige Geist als Person: Beitrag zur Frage nach der Heiligen Geiste eigentümlichen Funktion in der Trinität, bei der Inkarnation und im Gnadenbund*, [Münsterische Beiträge zur Theologie 26] (Münster: Aschendorff, 1963); *Una Mystica Persona: Die Kirche als das Mysterium der Identität des Heiligen Geistes in Christus und den Christen; Eine Person in vielen Personen* (Munich-Paderborn: Schöningh, 1964) [French translation: *L'Esprit dans l'Église*, trans. A. Liefooghe, M. Massart and R. Virrion (Paris: Cerf, 1969)]; "Person und Appropriation[: Zum Verständnis des Axioms: In Deo omnia sunt unum, ubi non obviat relationis oppositio]," *Münchener theologische Zeitschrift* 16 (1965): 37–57; "Das Verhältnis zwischen Inkarnation und Kirche in den Aussagen des Vaticanum II," *Theologie und Glaube* 55 (1965): 171–90; "Die Kirche als geschichtliche Erscheinung des übergeschichtlichen Geistes Christi: Zur Ekklesiologie des Vaticanum II," *Theologie und Glaube* 55 (1965): 270–89; "Der eine Geist Christi und die vielen Kirchen[: Zur Frage nach den dogmatischen Prinzipien einer ökume-

making use of the phenomenology of interpersonal relationships as a conceptual tool. Thus, without abandoning either the dogma (*Filioque*) or the Latin tradition,[90] Mühlen succeeds in coming much closer to someone like V. Lossky and to the Greek Fathers. But should one not recognize two irreducible ways of constructing theologically one identical faith, no human interpretation of which is adequate to the reality of the mystery revealed and lived?

The information collected on two points, as fragmentary as it is, permits me to draw a conclusion which touches upon the question that was addressed to me. To speak of "Christomonism" seems not only imprecise; one might wonder what it means exactly. The Latin tradition has a theology of the Holy Spirit, of the Spirit's operations, and of the Spirit's sanctifying indwelling in souls. It remains the case that during the Scholastic period, where something like the classic moment of this tradition can be seen, it showed its predilection for developing the Christological aspect of the Christian mystery. It was led in this direction by its pursuit of notional clarity—the mystery of the Spirit offers little that a conceptualized discourse can grab hold of[91]—and also by its tendency to pass from a consideration of the Economy to a consideration of ontology.

I could have extended my research by an investigation of ecclesiology. Nothing is more instructive in this regard than the teaching of the popes linking the institution of the Church to the Holy Spirit, not through the event of Pentecost but through that event in virtue of which *Christ* instituted the Church as the dispenser of

---

nischen Ganzheits-Ekklesiologie]," *Theologie und Glaube* 55 (1965): 329–66; and see above n. 6 [4]. [85]

90. He never stops quoting Thomas Aquinas, but uses some pneumatological statements out of (against?) the general context of the *principles* of Thomistic Trinitarian theology. [86]

91. See St. Augustine, *De fide et symbolo*, 9.19 (PL 40:191) [ET: *Faith and the Creed*, trans. Michael G. Campbell, OSA, in *On Christian Belief*, The Works of St. Augustine: A Translation for the 21st Century, vol. 1, no. 8, ed. Boniface Ramsey (Hyde Park, N.Y.: New City Press, 2005), 168–70]; Thomas Aquinas, [*ST*] 1a, q. 36, a. 1, ad 2; q. 37, a. 1. [87]

grace.[92] Nothing is more instructive than the path Möhler followed in going from *Die Einheit* (1825) to *Symbolik* (1832). Now if, in the nineteenth century, Möhler had such an influence on the Roman School and, through it, even on the First Vatican Council, it was the Möhler of *Symbolik*, with the link he made between the *Incarnation* and the Church as Mystical Body. Publications of that time commonly insist upon the fact that the Holy Spirit is the Spirit *of Christ*.[93] Could one say anything else? A large number of Protestant authors express themselves, when all is said and done, as we do.[94] Is this be-

    92. S. Tromp (his article entitled "L'Esprit Saint, 4: Esprit Saint âme de l'Église," *DictSpir*, vol. 4, bk. 2, 1297) quotes in this sense Boniface IX (*Ab origine mundi*, Oct. 7, 1391), Callistus III (*Summus Pontifex*, January 1, 1456), Pius II (*Triumphans pastor*, April 22, 1459), Innocent XI (*Triumphans pastor*, Oct. 3, 1678), Pius XII [*Mediator Dei*, *AAS* 39 (1947): 527; ET: *Encyclical Letter of His Holiness Pius XII on the Sacred Liturgy*, in *Selected Documents of His Holiness Pope Pius XII 1939–1958* (Washington, D.C.: National Catholic Welfare Conference, 1958), n. 18]. [88]

    93. Even one such as F. X. Dieringer, who nevertheless makes an explicit connection between the Church and the article on the Holy Spirit: *Lehrbuch der katholischen Dogmatik* (Mainz: Kirchheim, Schott und Thielmann, 1847). Let me cite H. Schell, *Das Wirken des dreieinigen Gottes* (Mainz: Kirchheim, 1885), 548, 550ff.; K. Adam, *Das Wesen des Katholizismus* (Dusseldorf: L. Schwann, 1924); H. Dieckmann, *De Ecclesia* (Freiburg: Herder, 1925), 2:241–46; E. Mura, *Le Corps mystique du Christ*, 2 vols (Paris: Blot, 1934);. R. Grosche, *Pilgernde Kirche* (Freiburg im Breisgau: Herder, 1938), 33; E. Przywara, "Das Dogma von der Kirche: Eine Aufbau," *Scholastik* 19 (1944): 1ff.; S. Tyszkiewicz, *La sainteté de l'Église christoconforme: Ébauche d'une ecclésiologie unioniste* (Rome: Pontificium institutum orientalium studiorum, 1945). Charles Journet's great body of work remains strictly within the framework of Thomism. [89]

    94. For example, H. E. Weber, "Theologisches Verständnis der Kirche," *Theologische Literaturzeitung* 73 (1948): 449–60, who writes in col. 459: "Die Kirche ist theologisch nur von der Christologie her zu verstehen. Bedeutsam, wie diese Einsicht—gegenüber der pneumatologishen Sicht—einem Denker aus der Ostkirche aufdrängt (Florovsky [Florowsky]). Reformatorische Theologie sollte darin eigenstes Erbe erkennen. Das Geheimnis, das Wesen, die Wirklichkeit der Kirche Christi ist das *Gegenwärtigwerden der Wirksamsein Christi* als immer neues Ereignis [The Church is theologically to be understood starting only from Christology. It is significant how this insight—over against the pneumatological view—imposes itself on a thinker from the Eastern Church (Florowsky). Reformed theology should recognize in this its most proper heritage. The mystery, the essence, the reality of the Church of Christ is the *becoming contemporary of Christ's being active* as an ever new event]...." We have already mentioned J. Bosc (see n. 6 [4]), who writes very accurately on p. 39: "It has often been heard, in the recent past, that certain Christian Churches lacked an

cause they are Westerners? Would it not be rather because the New Testament revelation leads us to this? I think so, but I repeat that that same revelation also offers a great number of passages that naively attribute an action to the Person of the Holy Spirit. Having remained closer to proclamations about the economy [of salvation], the Eastern tradition is here much more spontaneously at ease.

The Second Vatican Council made an important effort to move in a pneumatological direction. To measure the significance of this, studies will need to be done on the successive stages of the drafting of its texts, and also on the consequences that theological elaboration will draw from its constitutions.[95] Theology has not said its final word. The one to whom the Council's doctrinal commission owes, in great part, the fact that it did such remarkable work knows this better than anyone.[96]

---

elaborated doctrine of the Holy Spirit. I am not sure that this remark is absolutely accurate. It could be, indeed, that in calling for an isolated doctrine of the Holy Spirit, one would be going against what one was seeking. There is not, indeed, an isolated doctrine of the Holy Spirit, for that doctrine always refers back to the truth of the Lord." [90]

95. H. Mühlen has already tried to make several advances. C. Moeller has shown a growing influence of pneumatology in *Lumen Gentium* (in [*Vatican II: An Interfaith Appraisal;*] *Theological Issues of Vatican II*, ed. John H. Miller (Notre Dame, Ind.: University of Notre Dame Press, 1967), 125–26. He promises a study on the subject in *Temi conciliari*, and he refers back to *L'Église de Vatican II*, ed. G. Barauna, Unam Sanctam 51b (Paris: Cerf, 1966), 39–45, 102–4, 110 and n. 51C, pp. 1281ff. See also H. Cazelles, "Le Saint Esprit dans les textes de Vatican II," in H. Cazelles, P. Evdokimov, A. Greiner, *Le mystère de l'Esprit-Saint* (Tours: Mame, 1968), 161–86. [91]

96. [trans.] Congar is likely here referring to the Belgian theologian Mgr. Gérard Philips, who was elected vice-secretary of the Vatican II Doctrinal Commission in 1963. According to Congar's Vatican II journal, "[w]ithout any doubt, Mgr. Philips is the architect No.1 of the theological work of the council" (*My Journal of the Council*, trans. Mary John Ronayne, OP, and Mary Cecily Boulding, OP, ed. Denis Minns, OP [Collegeville, Minn.: Liturgical Press / Michael Glazier, 2012], 510). In the same work, Congar wrote, "Philips has been crucial. Without him the work of the Theological Commission would never have been what it has been" (p. 751).

PART FOUR

Pneumatological Ecclesiology

Overview

Article 4: Pneumatology Today | 203

Article 5: Christological and Pneumatological Implications of Vatican II's Ecclesiology | 225

1. What Christ did, as far as the Church is concerned, while he was on the earth | 226
2. What the glorified Christ does | 229
3. What comes from the Holy Spirit | 232
4. *Ecclesia de Trinitate* [The Church of the Trinity] | 240

Article 6: The Third Article of the Creed: The Impact of Pneumatology on the Life of the Church | 243

Introduction | 243
1. The Third Person | 246
2. The Spirit as Co-Institutor of the Church | 250
3. The Rediscovery of Pneumatology | 255
4. Conclusions | 261

Here we present three significant articles on ecclesiology primarily from the point of view of Congar's post–Vatican II pneumatology. They can all be read in light of his contributions to the Council.[1]

"Pneumatology Today" was delivered at a special 1982 Vatican celebration of the 1550th anniversary of the Third Ecumenical Council (in Ephesus in 431) and the 1600th anniversary of the Second Ecumenical Council (in Constantinople in 381). Congar was invited to speak to the contemporary status of pneumatology because the Second Ecumenical Council had expanded the third article about the Holy Spirit in the Nicene Creed. On this occasion, he was given an honorary plaque by Pope John Paul II for all of his contributions to theology and to the Church, especially those he made to the Second Vatican Council and to John Paul personally.

The American ecclesiologist Fr. Joseph A. Komonchak relates the following insightful memory about Congar's original delivery of this paper:

My favorite personal memory of Fr. Congar, however, goes back to the international symposium on pneumatology that was held at the Urbaniana in March 1982. Congar lectured there on "L'actualité de la pneumatologie." His back problems kept him confined to a wheelchair, and his ill-health perhaps made him more emotional than when he was younger. His voice broke as he spoke of how painful it had been for him, in the aftermath of Vatican II, to watch the decline and even disappearance of so many of the movements for theological and pastoral renewal in which he had participated or which he had encouraged in the 1930s,

---

1. For Congar's summary account of his role at the Council, see *My Journal of the Council*, a translation of *Mon journal du Concile*, 2 vols (Paris: Cerf, 2002) by Mary John Ronayne, OP, and Mary Cecily Boulding, OP, edited by Denis Minns, OP (Collegeville, MN: Liturgical Press / Michael Glazier, 2012), 870–71. See also, on his role in the liturgy constitution, *Fifty Years of Catholic Theology: Conversations with Yves Congar*, [a translation of *Entretiens d'automne, présentés par Bernard Lauret* (Paris: Cerf, 1987)], trans. John Bowden (London: SCM, 1988), 57.

1940s, and 1950s. These were for him the embodiment (or "incarnation," a word he loved) of the "true reform" in the Church which he had defended in his great book and which had made Vatican II possible, a realization of dreams beyond his hopes.

But, whereas other theologians at the time were content with this lament, Congar went on: "But," he said, his voice again cracking: "But I see so many signs of the Spirit in movements and developments since the Council." And he used a metaphor that has never left me since. He compared the Holy Spirit to an aquifer, a source of fresh water lying hidden beneath the ground until here or there, so often unexpectedly, from it bubbles up a spring to water the earth again and make it fruitful in new places. Everyone who heard it understood it as a great testimony of faith.[2]

A witness to both the pre-conciliar and post-conciliar approaches, Congar was particularly well-qualified to address the situation of pneumatology in 1982. He did what he was expected to do: he explained contemporary trends in pneumatology in the light of the trends of the past and in anticipation of the trends he foresaw. Congar expressed the belief that the Council had gone only halfway in planting seeds for more developed treatment of the Holy Spirit and for an increasingly pneumatological and Trinitarian model for the Church that would balance the paternal and Christological models, without doing away with anything valuable in them. He was hopeful that progress would be made.

The 1600th anniversary of the Council of Constantinople also provided an occasion for making progress toward reunion between Catholic and Orthodox churches, notwithstanding the historical divisions occasioned by theological differences over the *Filioque*. Congar, who earnestly desired the reunion of these two churches, expressed here his conviction that it is possible for the different

---

2. "Yves M.-J. Congar, OP, Reflections by Joseph A. Komonchak," in Mark E. Ginter, "Special Program, Centenarian Commemoration: A Time to Reminisce, A Time to Celebrate Four Theological Giants of the 20th Century," CTSA Banquet, June 12, 2004, *Catholic Theological Society of America Proceedings* 59 (2004): 165–66.

conceptions of the Trinity held by Eastern and Western parts of the Church to co-exist.

"Christological and Pneumatological Implications of Vatican II's Ecclesiology" was presented at an invitation-only colloquium entitled "The Ecclesiology of Vatican II: Dynamism and Prospective," April 8–12, 1980. It was held in Bologna, Italy, and was co-sponsored by the Faculties of Theology of Leuven and Louvain-la-Neuve, the Institut catholique of Paris, and the Institute of Religious Studies of Bologna. Thirty-six experts from all parts of the world participated, representing Catholic, Orthodox, and Protestant perspectives, as well as the disciplines of theology, history, canon law, and sociology. Even though the whole colloquium was an evaluation of Vatican II, participants were preoccupied with the issue of how Vatican II was going to be implemented,[3] given the threat to continuity represented by 1978, which had been the year of three popes: Paul VI, John Paul I, and John Paul II.

Congar's main points are four: (1) *Lumen Gentium* did not deny the foundational work of the incarnate Christ with respect to the Church, but it did complement that work by teaching that the community founded by the pre-paschal Christ was to be animated by the Holy Spirit; (2) the Council presents the risen Christ as continually present to and active in the community of believers he founded, through the Holy Spirit (and this is why, even as he desires to connect the ministry of the ordained priesthood to the Spirit-enlivened ecclesial community, Congar wants to retain the idea that the ordained act *in persona Christi*); (3) the Council sees the Holy Spirit as animator of the Church who accomplishes this task in a variety of ways—through enlivening not only the institutional aspects of the universal Church but also individuals and diverse local churches,

---

3. Introduction, *Les églises après Vatican II: Dynamisme et prospective; Actes du Colloque international de Bologne–1980*, ed. Giuseppe Alberigo, Théologie historique 61 (Paris: Beauchesne, 1981).

each of which contributes gifts to the wider community—so that no one in the Church is simply on the receiving end of things but each is a subject and, because the Holy Spirit works in each and every believer as a subject, even the institution founded by Christ has a qualified open-endedness about it; (4) the Trinitarian perspective of the conciliar documents envisages the Church as a communion of subjects, whether persons or local churches, rather than as a primarily juridical institution.[4]

"The Third Article of the Creed: The Impact of Pneumatology on the Life of the Church" was actually the result of an earlier plea made by Congar for Catholics to think of the Creed as containing three articles to reflect the Trinity, rather than following the medieval innovation that divided the Creed into twelve articles reflective of the twelve apostles. This shift of emphasis reattaches the Holy Spirit to the life of the Church in place of emphasizing the hierarchy as the origin of the Church. So this article appropriately concludes Part Four on pneumatological ecclesiology.

While repeating many familiar themes in this article, Congar makes the point that the Creed is a liturgical, doxological, dogmatic expression of faith. To say, "I believe ... " or "We believe ..." expresses personal involvement. To "believe in ..." orients the Church in the direction of a mystery toward which faith builds a bridge. As the "third" person simply because of the order of procession within the co-equal and co-eternal Trinity, and as "Lord" and "Giver of Life" who has "spoken through the prophets" of old and who speaks in the Church now, the Holy Spirit is the eschatological gift that carries this historical world into the life of the world to come, bringing Christ's work to completion.

---

4. For background, see James B. Anderson, *A Vatican II Pneumatology of the Paschal Mystery: The Historical-Doctrinal Genesis of Ad gentes I, 2–5* (Rome: Analecta Gregoriana, 1988).

ARTICLE 4

Pneumatology Today

(*Relazione*, March 22, 1982)[1]

Each Tuesday during the Second Vatican Council, the Secretariat for Christian Unity held a meeting with the observers in the Unitas Residence on the via dell'Anima. There they explained and discussed the questions with which the conciliar assembly was currently dealing or that it expected to take up. Now the observers—Protestant, Orthodox, Anglican—frequently found fault with the conciliar texts for their lack of pneumatology. Account was taken of these critical comments, and Paul VI noted that there are 258 references to the Holy Spirit in the documents of Vatican II.[2] But is that all that is required to construct a pneumatology? One Protestant author used to say, for example, that *Lumen Gentium* had been "sprinkled" with the Holy Spirit, the way one puts powdered sugar on a cake.[3] I believe—indeed, I am certain—that that comment is

---

1. This article is a translation by Susan Mader Brown of "Actualité de la Pneumatologie," in *Credo in Spiritum Sanctum*, International Theological Congress on Pneumatology 1 (Vatican: Libreria Editrice, 1983), 15–28.

2. Paul VI, general audience of May 23, 1973, *La documentation catholique*, 70/1634, June 17, 1973, 552 [ET: *L'osservatore romano*, weekly ed. in English 22/270, May 31, 1973, 1]. [1]

3. Gaston Westphal, *Vie et foi du protestant* (Paris: Centurion, 1966), 134. And see my study "Pneumatologie ou 'christomonisme' dans la tradition latine?" in *Ecclesia*

unjust, as we shall soon see in a formal presentation of this conference. Yet, at the very least, it tells us that one must do more than make mention of the Holy Spirit to have a pneumatology.

What was the situation during the modern period until twenty years ago [the article dates from 1982]? From the Fathers and from High Scholasticism we inherited a theology of the Third Person in which debate with the Orthodox gave priority to the question of the procession of the Holy Spirit "a Patre Filioque [from the Father and the Son]." As for the work attributed to the Holy Spirit, two aspects of this were being developed. With respect to the Church as such, the Spirit was seen above all as the guarantor of the infallibility of the Church and the continuity of its tradition. With respect to the faithful, attention was focused upon the indwelling of the Holy Spirit in souls and, in particular, upon the seven gifts. The treatise on grace still had little connection to the Holy Spirit; one spoke rather of the grace of Christ. Nothing was more characteristic of this allocation of the Spirit between the institutional Church and the interior life of individual souls than the work of Cardinal Manning, who had taken upon himself the task of speaking of the Holy Spirit.[4]

Apportioning the Creed into twelve or fourteen articles, inherited from the Middle Ages, risks being harmful to a theology of the Holy Spirit by breaking up the text of the Creed. Much to be preferred, and in harmony with the structure of this Creed, is the division into three articles, with the third beginning "I believe in the Holy Spirit" and including all that follows up to "the life of the world to come." The Spirit then appears as the one who makes the Church one, holy, catholic, and apostolic and who is, until the *es-*

---

a Spiritu Sancto edocta [*Lumen gentium*, 53]: *Mélanges* [*théologiques, hommages à Mgr G[érard] Philips. Verzamelde theologische opstellen aangeboden aan Mgr. Gérard Philips*, Bibliotheca ephemeridum theologicarum Lovaniensium 27 (Gembloux: Duculot, 1970), 41–64 [ET: See Part Three, Article 3, above]. [2]

4. [Henry Edward Cardinal] Manning, *The Temporal Mission of the Holy Ghost, or Reason and Revelation* (London: Longmans, Green, 1865); *The Internal Mission of the Holy Ghost* (London: Burns and Oates, 1875). See also Ch. 9 of my *ES* 1 [ET: *HS* 1]. [3]

chaton [Congar writes "l'eschatologie"], the driving force behind the fulfillment of the world. The third article thus has a cosmic scope. Yet our theology used to be enlivened but little by an eschatological orientation, for eschatology itself was broken up into the four chapters entitled *De ultimis rebus* [the last things].

The Second Vatican Council began to give back to us the pneumatological aspect of the Church, something inseparable from the Church in itself and from its connection to the cosmos.[5] I say "began." Here, as in many things, Vatican II remained, as it were, at the halfway point, but it sowed in the Church living seeds that have since borne fruit. I am thinking of the place accorded to charisms, to a theology of the local churches, to the start of a discussion about ministries, to what is said about the *sensus fidei* [sense of the faith], to the action of the Spirit in world history ... I do not know—such a study would be worth doing—what Vatican I's operative view of God was. Was it, perhaps, what Heribert Mühlen calls "a pre-Trinitarian monotheism"?[6] Vatican II has a vision that is explicitly Trinitarian. It went back to the vision of the Fathers of the fourth and fifth centuries, as John Paul II has emphasized. This point of departure is one of those things that gives it such great ecumenical importance.

Since the Council, the cause of the Holy Spirit has experienced advances that are indeed remarkable. This is so, first of all, on the level of sources: the Bible, the liturgy, the Fathers, the magisteri-

---

5. "Implicationi cristologiche e pneumatologiche dell'ecclesiologia del Vaticano II," *Cristianesimo nella Storia* 2 (1981): 97–110 (= "Les implications christologiques et pneumatologiques de l'ecclésiologie de Vatican II," in *Les églises après Vatican II: Dynamisme et prospective; Actes du colloque international de Bologne, 1980*, ed. G. Alberigo, Théologie historique 61 [Paris: Beauchesne, 1981], 117–30). [ET: Part Four, Article 5, below]. Already we have *ES* 1:227–35 [ET: *HS* 1:167–73]. And compare A. Laminski, "Die Entdeckung der pneumatologischen Dimension der Kirche durch das Konzil und ihre Bedeutung," in *Sapienter ordinare: Festgabe für Erich Kleineidem*, ed. Fritz Hoffman et al., Erfurter Theologische Studien 24 (Leipzig: St. Benno, 1969), 392–403. [4]

6. [trans.] See *Morgen wird Einheit sein: Das kommende Konzil aller Christen, Ziel der getrennten Kirchen* (Paderborn: Schöningh, 1974), 117–50, and also Part Four, Article 6, note 19, below.

um.⁷ Some theological studies, benefitting from the encouragement and the contributions of ecumenical dialogue, have brought to light the pneumatological momentum of Christology,⁸ have taken up again the question of the procession of the Spirit,⁹ have looked at the mystery of the Spirit and the Spirit's activity,¹⁰ and have, at last, developed the Spirit's relationship to history, to eschatology, and to the Kingdom of God.¹¹ On several occasions I have personal-

7. It is impossible to cite everything, even what is most important. Solely by way of example, I mention M. Chevallier, *Souffle de Dieu: Le Saint-Esprti dans le Nouveau Testament*, vol. 1 (Paris: Beauchesne, 1978); E.-P. Siman, *L'expérience de l'Esprit par l'Église d'après la tradition syrienne d'Antioche* [Théologie historique 15] (Paris: Beauchesne, 1971); "Le Saint-Esprit dans la liturgie," Conférences de Saint-Serge, [15e Semaine d'études liturgique, Paris, 1-4 juillet 1969, *Bibliotheca ephemerides liturgicae*, Subsidia 8] (Rome: Ed. Liturgiche, 1977); St. Basil, *On the Holy Spirit* (SChr 17); N.-J. Jaschke, *Der Heilige Geist im bekenntnis der Kirche: Eine Studie zur Pneumatologie des Irenäus von Lyon* [im Ausgang vom altchrislichen Glaubensbekenntnis, Münsterische Beiträge zur Theologie 40] (Münster: Aschendorff, 1977). Edward O'Connor, *Pope Paul and the Spirit* ([Notre Dame, Ind.:] Ave Maria Press, 1978); Daniel-Ange, *Paul VI: Un regard prophétique*, vol. 2, *L'éternelle Pentecôte* (Paris-Fribourg: Saint- Paul, 1981). [5]

8. Information about this is found in my article "Pour une christologie pneumatologique," *Revue des sciences philosophiques et théologiques* 63 (1979):435-43 (reprinted in *ES* 3:219-28 [ET: *HS* 3:165-73]). [6]

9. See my *ES* 3 and "Pour le centenaire du concile de 381: Diversité de dogmatique dans l'unité de foi entre L'Orient et l'Occident," *Irénikon* 54 (1981): 25-35; *La théologie du Saint-Esprit dans le dialogue entre l'Orient et l'Occident* [Document foi et constitution 103], ed. Lukas Vischer (Paris/Taizé: Le Centurion / Les Presses de Taizé, 1980 [ET: *Spirit of God, Spirit of Christ: Ecumenical Reflections on the Filioque Controversy* (Geneva: WCC / London: SPCK, 1981)]. [7]

10. The *Mélanges G. Philips* (see note 3 above); my *ES* 1, 2, 3 [ET: *HS* 1, 2, 3]; L. Bouyer, *Le Consolateur: Esprit-Saint et vie de grâce* (Paris: Cerf, 1980); *Erfahrung und Theologie des Heiligen Geistes*, C. Heitmann and H. Mühlen, eds. (Hamburg-Munich: Rauhen Hauses, 1974). On the abundant pneumatological work of H. Mühlen, see J. B. Banawiratma, *Der Heilige Geist in der Theologie von Heribert Mühlen* [Europäische Hochschulschriften, Reihe 23, Theologie 159 (Frankfurt am Main: Lang, 1981)]. [8]

11. In particular Jürgen Moltmann, *L'Église dans la force de l'Esprit: Une contribution à l'ecclésiologie messianique*, trans. R. Givord, Cogitatio fidei 102 (Paris: Cerf, 1980), German original published in 1975. [ET: *The Church in the Power of the Spirit: A Contribution to Messianic Ecclesiology* (New York: Harper and Row, 1977)]. Other important protestant contributions: H. Thielicke, *Die evangelische Glaube*[: *Grundzüge der Dogmatik*], vol. 3, *Theologie des Geistes* ([Tübingen: Mohr], 1978); G. Ebeling, [*Dogmatik des christlichen Glaubens*,] vol. 3, *Der Glaube an Gott den Vollender der Welt* (Tübingen: Mohr, 1979). [9]

ly put together a "report on Pneumatology," where I have presented a number of German publications.[12] From an overall perspective, the Trinitarian inspiration of spirituality is very noticeable. Among us this is due, at least in part, to the presence of the Orthodox, but also to having the liturgy in one's mother tongue. However, this spirituality reaches only a modest part of the faithful. I have been struck, and concerned by the fact that, in a number of Professions of Faith proposed by faithful individuals and sometimes by groups, the Holy Spirit is often forgotten. In several, "God" is scarcely even mentioned. They are almost solely Christological, if not indeed "Jesuanical," which is to say, centered upon "Jesus of Nazareth," the man-for-others . . .[13]

Yet how can one not locate the current called charismatic, better labeled "Renewal in the Spirit," within this context? It spread like a brush fire. It is something other than a fad. It is related, as a form of Christian activity, to what existed in the Protestantism of the nineteenth century and at the beginning of this [i.e., the twentieth] century, namely, on the one hand, to what Rouse and Neill call "voluntary movements," upsurgings of service of the Gospel and of the kingdom of God in the lives of men and women, and on the other, to movements of "Awakening." By one feature, in particular, it shows

---

12. *Revue des sciences philosophiques et théologiques* 62 (1978): 421–42; 64 (1980): 445–51; 65 (1981). [The final reference should perhaps be 66 (1982): 128–36. There does not appear to have been a review of books on pneumatology by Congar in the volume he cites. The material in the subsequent volume is, however, dated September 24, 1981, so perhaps he anticipated its publication in the final issue for 1981]. [10]

13. This is the case for most of the formulae gathered together in *Glaube elementar: Versuche einer Kurzformal des Christlichen*, [Thesen und Argumente 1,] ed. J. Schulte (Essen: Fredebeul und Koenen, 1971). Nor is there more of the Holy Spirit in the *Misa campesina nicaraguense*. On the other hand, the formulae proposed by the reader of *Informations catholiques internationales* 471, January 1, 1975, 12, are Trinitarian.—"Jesusism" was denounced by J. Millet [= Milet], in *Dieu ou le Christ* . . . (Paris: Trévise, 1980 (see my review in the *Revue des sciences philosophiques et théologiques* 64 (1980): 268–71). The (very lovely) lyrical compositions of H. Oosterhuis (see *Tijdschrift voor Theologie* 19 (1979): 124–46) are Trinitarian examples. The *Roman Catechetical Directory* (Easter 1971) requires that Christocentrism and Trinitarian theocentrism be united. [11]

its kinship to these Awakenings, namely, the public and observable character of a spiritual action that changes lives. But the difference in terminology already suggests that this is not the same thing as a Protestant Awakening. One speaks of "renewal," as if to refer to youthfulness, freshness, and new possibilities for the Church of old, our mother. Indeed, save for exceptions that are undoubtedly very rare, the Renewal locates itself *within* the Church and, far from calling into question its standard institutions, brings them to life again. I will return shortly to its conditions of well-being.

The occasion of our present conference, the centenary of the Council of 381, obtained for us very remarkable expressions of unanimity in faith and in the glorification of the Spirit. The council convoked in Constantinople by the emperor brought together only the eastern bishops, except, indeed, for Egypt. Damasus, the Bishop of Rome, had not been invited.... This council only became "ecumenical," in the theological sense of the term, by "reception." Yet its faith was already that of Damasus and of the entire Western Church. And see how ecumenical, in the sense of our modern ecumenism, the celebration of its sixteenth centenary has been. To my eyes, there is more here than a blessed and joyous fact; it is also an indication that there is one fundamental Faith, almost in the sense of "fundamental articles." In my view this is relevant to the problem that is, theologically, the most pressing in ecumenism: under what conditions would communion be able to be re-established, within the framework of the admirable formula of St. Cyprian and St. Augustine: "Licet, salvo iure communionis, diversum sentire [It is permissible to think differently, provided the law of communion is preserved]"?[14] It is noteworthy that this community of faith understands itself in terms of the classical epoch of the Fathers and the ecumenical councils of the undivided Church (if that is an acceptable expression). Even our Holy Father, John Paul II, has declared

---

14. [trans.] *De Baptismo* 3.3.5 (PL 43:141–42). Augustine cites Cyprian as an authority for this view.

several times that the text of the Council of 381 is normative.[15] It is the norm of his own teaching office. This fact cannot but stand out as having great ecumenical and ecclesiological importance. It is a victory that belongs to the Holy Spirit and we give the Spirit the glory for it.

What I have just been recalling in an oversimplified way will clarify the import of what Paul VI declared on June 6, 1973, when he said: "The Christology, and especially the ecclesiology, of the Council must be followed by a new study and a new devotion to the Holy Spirit, precisely as an indispensable complement of the conciliar teaching."[16] What encouragement! This is indeed what is already being done, under two headings that I will entitle "triadology" and "pneumatology." I am about to consider these.

Triadology. We have inherited some very rich theologies of the Holy Trinity. One must speak of a plurality because there are those of the Eastern tradition and those of the Western tradition. The latter comes from the Scriptures; it is quite unjust to see in it some sort of rational deduction starting from the nature of things. Yet it is true that the Latin tradition, in building something intellectually coherent from what is given in the revealed mystery, makes use of the analogy of the structure of the human mind, made in the image of God. Within this framework, two paths of development, both connected with St. Augustine, St. Anselm, and St. Thomas Aquinas, continue the analysis of the mind, which is awareness of its identi-

---

15. [trans.] There are numerous examples of this in recent years but one of the early instances was at a celebration in Rome marking the 1600th anniversary of the Council of Constantinople and the 1550th anniversary of the Council of Ephesus, at which the pope used the Greek text of the creed without the *Filioque*. See Part One, p. 66, above and also Michael Fahey, "Current Theology: Orthodox Ecumenism and Theology: 1978–83," *Theological Studies* 44 (1983): 625.

16. *La documentation catholique,* 70/1635, July 1, 1973, 601 [ET: *L'osservatore romano,* weekly ed. in English, 24/272, June 14, 1973, 1]. The apostolic exhortation *Marialis cultus* of March 22 [= Feb. 2], 1974, also contains, after developing the pneumatological aspect of the Marian mystery (no. 26), an invitation to "deepen reflection on the action of the Spirit in the history of salvation" (no. 27) [*AAS* 66 (1974):136–9; ET: "Devotion to the Virgin Mary," 26–7, *The Pope Speaks* 19/1 (1974): 49–87, esp. 66–8]. [12]

ty, intelligence and will. Richard of St. Victor and St. Bonaventure follow the analysis of love, indeed of its perfect personal form, the love of friendship. They give more importance to the augustinian theme, little known in the Eastern Church, of the Holy Spirit as the bond of love between the Father and the Son.[17]

This theme is very frequently developed in contemporary books of spirituality or popular theology. It is indeed very easy to grasp and it readily benefits from the contributions of interpersonal psychology. That also is very easy to understand but must be handled with discretion and a deep sense of the transcendence of a mystery that we cannot master. I have more than once drawn attention to the danger of anthropomorphism and even of latent tritheism that could be present. It is as if the Father and the Son are conversing with one another and one sees three centers of consciousness in God.... Are there not three Persons? But this "person" category, certainly traditional and valuable, must be used with prudence. St. Augustine used to say that he made use of it not so much to say something as not to say nothing,[18] and St. Anselm wrote "*tres nescio quid* [three of I know not what]."[19] A certain kind of iconography, forbidden, by the way, by Benedict XIV, that represents the three Persons as three similar individuals, could promote this incipient tritheism ... There is, however, the icon of Andrei Rublev, perhaps the most beautiful Christian image in the whole world.

One must be wary of yet another graphic image, the linear type. One might imagine the Father existing before the Son and the Son before the Spirit to make them proceed one from the other. It is in-

---

17. [trans.] See *ES* 3, Part 1, Chapter 2.B for Congar's presentation of the development of this aspect of Trinitarian theology in the Latin tradition.

18. *De Trinitate* 7:6.11 (*PL* 42: 943). [The New City Press translation by Edmund Hill divides Book 7 into four rather than seven chapters but retains the same section headings as Migne. So the passage appears in his translation as 7:4.11.] [13]

19. *Monologion*, 79 [(*PL* 158:221); ET: St. Anselm, *Proslogium; Monologium; An Appendix in Behalf of the Fool by Gaunilon and Cur Deus homo*, trans. Sidney Norton Deane (Chicago: The Open Court Publishing Company, 1935), 142; the passage appears in some editions as section 79, in others as section 78, as in this translation]. [14]

deed true that there is an order of emanation. One of the interesting conclusions of the ecumenical colloquium organized by "Faith and Order" is that, if the Spirit proceeds or emerges from the Father, as Jn 15:26 and the Creed of 381 say, it is from the Father-of-the-Son.[20] But this is the point at which to examine the rich triadology of the Orthodox. It obviously knows of the relations of procession but it does not *define* the persons by them; it makes a point of mentioning other relations: of manifestation, of mutual welcome. Their divine hypostases are, in the absolute simultaneity of their existence, one within the other (*perichōrēsis, circuminsession*). Their relations are always Trinitarian, not linear-binary. This is what the icon of Andrei Rublev suggests in a visual way.

> Look. Already from afar, one perceives the heads that incline
> toward one another
> as if to embrace one another in a grasp
> that nothing will ever be able to undo.
> One might say that they want to curl up One within the Other.
> Do you not believe that I am in the Father
> And that the Father is in me?
> Yes, they live One within the Other.[21]

---

20. "Just as the Son is connected to the Father and receives his being from him without coming after him with respect to his existence, so the Holy Spirit, in turn, receives from the Son who is regarded as before the hypostasis of the Spirit only from the point of view of causality, but without there being room for intervals of time in that life eternal. Thus, therefore, except from the point of view of causality, the holy Trinity includes within itself no distinction whatsoever." St. Gregory of Nyssa, *Contra Eunomium* 1, conclusion (*PG* 45: 464 A [= C]) [ET: *Against Eunomius*, Book 1, NPNF 2–5: 100, reads, "For as the Son is bound to the Father, and, while deriving existence from Him, is not substantially after Him, so again the Holy Spirit is in touch with the Only-begotten, Who is conceived of as before the Spirit's subsistence {hypostasis} only in the theoretical light of a cause. Extensions in time find no admittance in the Eternal Life; so that, when we have removed the thought of cause, the Holy Trinity in no single way exhibits discord with itself; and to It is glory due."]. [15]

21. Daniel-Ange, *L'étreinte de feu: L'icône de la Trinité de Roublov* (Paris: Descleé de Brouwer, 1980), 125ff. [16]

With regard to the procession of the Holy Spirit, we know that there is a dispute between the Eastern Orthodox and us. It is, in fact, a twofold one: there is the doctrinal affirmation of the *Filioque*, and there is the unilateral insertion of this term into the Creed of 381. I hope that our Congress will deal with these two problems in a way that makes use of the remarkable approaches that have been made to them and that it will produce some constructive resolutions. Personally, I have come to the following firm conclusions:

1. There are two different approaches and each one is coherent within its own principles of conceptualization. At this level, they do not correspond to one another, but each expresses the same faith that is the source of the same life. And, at the level of life in and through the Spirit, one cannot find any opposition.
2. Neither of the two formulations is absolutely perfect. That of the Creed does not express the connection—neither the connection in the economy nor the eternal connection—between the Spirit and the Son-Word. For doing that, there are many clues in the Greek Fathers, but they do not seem to have been pursued (developed) or put together in a manner that is entirely satisfactory. Is it even possible? As to the *Filioque* formula, it does not express the monarchy of the Father, even though that is understood by its *que*, which implies that the Son depends on the Father so as to be, with the Father, the source of the Spirit, but not a source without a source. The "principaliter [in the first place]" that St. Augustine applied to the Father is not expressed.... It is muffled by the "tanquam ab uno principio [as if from a single source]," and I understand very clearly that our explanation of this formula appears to the Orthodox not only unsatisfactory but marked by an injudicious rationalism.
3. These two different approaches can coexist. They can do so because they have done so. For five centuries at least, and

maybe for longer, the East and the West lived in communion, albeit a communion sometimes difficult and precarious, while the *Filioque* was held by St. Ambrose, St. Augustine, St. Leo and so many others and by a number of Spanish or other councils. It was the recollection of that and the reference to St. Maximus the Confessor that permitted union to be negotiated at Florence in 1439. I do not believe that one could take up again, just as it was, Florence's formula of union, which has not escaped some well-founded criticisms. Would it be necessary, in preparing for a future new reunion council, to seek a common formula that would synthesize the two approaches? Is that possible? I have come to doubt that it is. Each group would read it according to its own perspective. Would it not be better for them to have a discussion in peace and in mutual love, to acknowledge convergences with hands held out to one another, and to accept that they are different within the context of a deep, perhaps complementary, unity? We know that the idea of complementarity was launched by the physicist Niels Bohr and that it was even extended by him to theological domains.[22] Niels Bohr also had the following idea that I would like to welcome: "The opposite of a true statement is a false statement, but the opposite of a profound truth can be another profound truth."

4. The Orthodox have always put forth, as a condition of establishing communion, the suppression of the *Filioque* in the Creed. At Ferrara-Florence that was, at the start, their sole condition. In the thought of Marc Eugenikos, that implied the disavowal of this doctrine. On the other hand, St. Leo, in 810, had refused to insert the *Filioque*, despite holding to

---

22. See the chapter "Une structure de dualité dans l'unité: Orient et Occident, 'complémentarité,'" in my *Diversités et communion: Dossier historique et conclusion théologique*, Cogitatio fidei 112 (Paris: Cerf, 1982) [ET: "A Structure of Duality in Unity: East and West, 'Complementarity,'" in *Diversity and Communion*, trans. John Bowden (London: SCM, 1984), 70–76]. [17]

the teaching about it. Would it not be necessary to do again what he did? I am aware that the question is very sensitive. In bringing about a remedy for a great rift, one would run the risk of provoking another, smaller one, among ourselves. However, even Latin Catholics have made this gesture in Greece on the occasion of the translation of their liturgy into Greek, and their hierarchy, in January 1978, gave a most interesting explanation and justification for it.[23] I hope that our congress will propose a way of settling this matter.

Pneumatology. Today we understand this term to mean not a theology focused only upon the Third Person, but upon the impact that ongoing attention to the Spirit has upon the way people see the Church, its life and its members. One's view of the Church can, in fact, be dominated by a paternal model or by a Christological model. The latter ultimately brings a pneumatological principle to bear upon the subject, which leads one toward a Trinitarian model. I am going to give this point of departure a try.

A purely paternal model would give rise to a Church and a society of a patriarchal sort, with what is masculine being dominant and with an inclination toward "paternalism."[24] I know of no better expression of paternalism than this 1848 statement of Donoso Cortés, the Spanish convert: "Everything for the people; nothing by the people."[25] Human beings among this people would be consid-

---

23. See F. Rouleau, "A propos du 'Filioque,' un document: Instruction pastorale de l'épiscopat catholioque de Grèce," *Dieu révelé dans l'Esprit*, Les quatre fleuves 9 (1979): 73–78. [18]

24. I quoted several important passages and gave some references in "Le monothéisme politique et le Dieu Trinité," *Nouvelle revue théologique* 103 (1981): 3–17. [19]

25. [trans.] Juan Donoso Cortés (1809–53) had at first had been sympathetic to Enlightenment ideals, but by the end of his life, especially after 1848, was firmly opposed to them. He became convinced that the Catholic Church, where divine grace moves those who govern to act for the salvation of their subjects, harmoniously combines monarchy, aristocracy, and democracy and thus presents "the most beautiful spectacle the world can offer." *An Essay on Catholicism, Authority and Order Considered in Their Fundamental Principles*, trans. Madeleine Vincent Goddard (London:

ered *objects* of Power's solicitude, but they would not be treated as *subjects* of their own life. In the case of societies, this would result in a colonial system. In the case of particular churches, they would be "subjected" but would not, any more than the colonized, be *subjects* of their own life.

In a purely Christological model, Christ would be considered the founder of a Church-understood-as-a society. And I am not denying that he is this. To demonstrate this was the big concern of our apologetic treatises on the Church. They wanted to establish that Christ founded the Church in the form of a *society* that was *complete* ("societas perfecta"), a society that was *unequal* or *hierarchical* including, before all else and by divine right, a distinction between clergy and lay people.[26] This is how one got a vision of the Church as a pyramid. I could offer in support of that a good fifteen quotes, among which one or another would even use the word "pyramid." Some images found in books of religious instruction would illustrate the same idea. The pope, of course, was at the top of the pyramid. One went down, through the bishops, the priests—pastors, then curates—until one reached the laity, who had no other obligation but to obey. We all have memories of pronouncements of this sort. I will quote only two pearls that are, however, rare pearls, thanks be to God:

The passive infallibility of the faithful consists in listening as they should to the magisterium.[27]

Herder/New York: Joseph F. Wagner, Inc., 1925), 39. He became an ardent supporter of hierarchical authority and papal infallibility.

26. I will refer this time, with apologies for citing myself so often, to my essay from the Roman Colloquium on *Ecclesiam suam*: "Situation ecclésiologique au moment de *Ecclesiam suam* et passage à une Église dans l'itinéraire des hommes" [in *Ecclesiam suam: Première lettre encyclique de Paul VI; Colloque international, Rome, 24–26 octobre 1980* (Brescia: Instituto Paolo VI, 1982), 103–25] (Italian translation in *Il Regno* 436 [March 1, 1981]: 170–77). [20]

27. A.-A. Goupil, *La règle de foi*, 2d ed. Paris: Paillard, 1941, n. 17, 48. [21]

Are not the parish priest with regard to his bishop and the bishop with regard to the pope, the "Church taught," like the faithful?[28]

This Christological model dominated, with even more justification and seriousness, the idea of the priest that we had and lived. That topic would demand a broader and appropriately documented treatment. To be brief, limited as I am to the current topic, the treatise on the sacrament of Orders was linked directly to the one about Christ-as-Head, without any mention of the Church or the ecclesial community. This is how it is in the *Summa* of St. Thomas. So the priest is seen only as one who is distinguished personally and forever by a character and a power that fit him to consecrate the bread and the wine and to act *in persona Christi* [in the person of Christ]. That is certainly not false, but any connection to the community of faithful is neglected in this approach. The last fifteen years of reflection about the priest and about ministries has focused upon the significance of this connection.

I speak of ministries, putting the word in the plural. The Council began to do this, but formerly it was unusual. The basis for this reality is the existence of what St. Paul proclaims in a passage that is remarkably Trinitarian: "There are varieties of gifts (*charistmatōn*), but the same Spirit; varieties of service (*diakoniōn*), but the same Lord; and there are varieties of activities (*energēmatōn*), but it is the same God who activates all of them in everyone. To each is given the manifestation of the Spirit for the common good" (1 Cor 12:4–7). This common good is the building of the Body of Christ which is the Church. The latter will therefore be constructed through the contributions of everyone. St. Paul lists a certain number of gifts-services-activities of women and men who make these contributions and build up the ecclesial organism by being members of one another and by all being members of Christ.[29] These lists are not

---

28. [Centre catholique des intellectuels canadiens (Université de Montréal),] *Le rôle des laïcs dans l'Église: Carrefour 1951* (Montreal: Fides, 1952), 9. [22]

29. Rom 12:4–8; 1 Cor 12:8–11 and 27–30; Eph 4:7 and 11–12. Compare 1 Pet 4:10. [23]

exhaustive. All of them begin with the office of apostle and speak of services of instruction and leadership. But all attribute the building up of the Body of Christ, the point of *diakonia* [service], to all of the "saints," that is, to the baptized (Eph 4:12).

We have in this way a model of the Church that is a communion without ceasing to be a society, one that is built up horizontally, from the bottom up, without ceasing to be built from above. This is what happens in reality, whether it be in Brazil with the base communities or in Zaïre with the communities where the "Mokambi" preside, or in the Congo with the "Mabundu," or in France, where the lack of priests is compensated for by the involvement of laypeople—women and men—who, in so far as they can, devote themselves to bringing to life the people of God, the Church of Jesus Christ. And so there are a hundred to a hundred and fifty thousand catechists. It pains me, certainly, to see the disappearance or weakening of so many of the institutions and so much of the organization that I knew as flourishing concerns, but I am amazed to see more and more of the upsurgings of the Gospel that the Spirit brings forth in the lives of men and women. It is as if a subterranean layer of living water were unceasingly rising up again as a well-spring through the faith and the generosity of all the faithful. In this way Christians are once again becoming the *subjects* of their life as Church.[30] They carry this life forward, along with the gifts of nature and grace they have received, in cooperation with the ordained ministries.

What we say of persons in the framework of the local community is true, "positis ponendis [making the same presumptions]," of particular churches within the universal framework. Vatican II

---

30. For a theological elaboration of this obviously essential idea: H. Legrand, "Le développement d'Églises-sujets, à la suite de Vatican II: Fondements théologiques et réflexions institutionelles," in *Les églises après Vatican II: Dynamisme et prospective; Actes du Colloque international de Bologne*, ed. G. Alberigo (Paris: Beauchesne, 1981), 149–84. Italian and German editions for the same colloquium are available (Bologne, 1980). [24]

rediscovered local churches as an actualization of the one, holy, catholic and apostolic Church. The Holy Spirit is always mentioned in the definition that it gives of them.[31] Each local church is the Church, but it is not that by itself, for it is in communion with the others, each of which has its own history, its own gifts and, possibly, its own language and culture.... This is what the Pentecost miracle, where each heard the others celebrating the marvels of God in his or her own language, foreshadowed. "There is a variety of gifts, but the same Spirit." My colleague Hervé Legrand was able to write an article entitled "To be Catholic, the Church must be particular."[32] Open to others and to the requirements of communion, each local or particular church is thus the *subject* of its own life, the resources for which are placed in it by the God-who-is-Trinity.

Certain images, certain ways of expressing ourselves, that come to us from an era in which the paternal or Christological models dominated too exclusively, will have to be revised. These revisions are already underway. This is what is happening to the distinction, which borders on a disjunction, between the "Church teaching" and the "Church taught." In a vision of the Church that is Trinitarian and pneumatological, the entire body appears as animated, each member for the role he or she plays. The ideal formula is that of St. Augustine that *Lumen Gentium* quotes: "Vobis sum episcopus, vobiscum christianus." "For you I am a bishop; but first I am a Christian along with you."[33] Augustine also said, "Vobis pastores sumus, sed

---

31. See *LG*, n. 26.1; *CD*, n. 11.1. [25]

32. *Cahiers saint Dominique* 127 (April 1972): 346–54. [26]

33. *Sermo* 340.1 (PL 38:1483) [ET: *Sermons 306–340A on the Saints.* Trans. and notes by Edmund Hill, OP, ed. John E. Rotelle, OSA, The Works of St. Augustine: A Translation for the 21st Century, vol. 3, no. 9 (Brooklyn, N.Y.: New City Press, 1994), 292]. See also *Enarrationes in Psalmos* 126.3 (PL 37:1669) [ET: *Exposition of Psalms 121–150*, trans. and notes by Mary Boulding OSB, ed. Boniface Ramsay, The Works of St. Augustine: A Translation for the 21st Century vol. 3, no. 20 (Brooklyn, N.Y.: New City Press, 2004) 86]; *De gestis cum Emerito*, 7 ([PL] 43:702); *Sermones ineditae. Sermo XVII in solemnitate ss. Machabœorum*] 17. 8 ([PL] 46:880); *Sermo Denis* 17. 8 ["Sancti Augustini sermones post Maurino reperti," *Miscellanea Agostiniana* (Rome: Typis polyglottis vaticanis, 1930)],1:88] [ET: *Sermons 273–305A on the Saints.* Trans. and notes by Ed-

sub illo Pastore vobiscum oves sumus. Tanquam vobis ex hoc loco doctores sumus, sed sub illo unico Magistro in hac schola vobiscum condiscipuli sumus." "We are pastors for you but we are, with you, sheep under the crook of this same Pastor. From this pulpit we are your teachers, but in this Church we are, with you, disciples of this one Master alone."[34] In short, the teaching Church is also taught!

Similarly, according to a pneumatological and Trinitarian model of communion, the whole assembly forms, with its president, a single subject of liturgical actions.[35] With respect to ordinations, what Tradition presents is not a purely linear, vertical model in which the action is that of a single person. The faithful used to be involved in the "election" of their minister, in bearing witness to his faith, and in calling upon the Holy Spirit in the act of ordination. For the latter, several bishops concelebrated, contributing the witness and grace of the body or the college of bishops and, through them, of the churches.[36]

This pneumatological model, it is urged, also avoids a patriarchal approach. It is open to the recognition of a better place for women in the Church. This is a very pressing problem whose importance ought not to be minimized.

In the course of speaking, as I must, of the pneumatological model, I certainly do not want to neglect the truth of the Christological model. If, from my lengthy study of the Holy Spirit, I had to keep but a single conclusion, it would be this: Christology ensures

---

mund Hill, OP, ed. John E. Rotelle, OSA, The Works of St. Augustine: A Translation for the 21st Century, vol. 3, no. 8 (Brooklyn, N.Y.: New City Press, 1994), 296–97]. [27]

34. *Enarrationes in Psalmos* 126, 3 (PL 37:1669), etc. [28]

35. See Y. Congar, "Ecclesia ou communauté des chrétiens, sujet intégral de l'action liturgique," in *La liturgie après Vatican II*, ed. Yves Congar, Unam Sanctam 66 (Paris: Cerf, 1967), 241–82 [ET: "The *Ecclesia* or Christian Community as a Whole Celebrates the Liturgy," in *At the Heart of Christian Worship: Liturgical Essays of Yves Congar*, translated and edited by Paul Philibert (Collegeville, Minn.: Liturgical Press / A Pueblo Book, 2010), 15–68]. [29]

36. See H. Legrand, "Le développement d'Églises-sujets, à la suite de Vatican II: Fondements théologiques et réflexions institutionelles," 163ff. [30]

the well-being of pneumatology. There is no Word without Breath; it would remain in the throat and would address no one. There is no Breath without a Word: it would have no content and would transmit nothing to anyone. According to St. Irenaeus, the Word and the Holy Spirit are like the two hands with which God fashions humankind and does all that God does.[37] I would say that most especially to the members of the Renewal in the Spirit or to the groups called "charismatic." I would affirm it as a general rule, without claiming that each and every personal impulse would need to be anticipated in doctrine or authorized by it.[38] For the Spirit calls us forward and makes the Gospel a reality in the newness of history. Certainly, however, for groups and for each faithful person in general, it is the Word and doctrine that guarantee the authenticity of the Spirit. St. Theresa used to prefer a spiritual director who was a good theologian to a more pious but less well instructed confessor.

The union and mutual dependence of the two hands of God are, for the Church and for the whole economy of salvation, the constitutive law. There are actually two missions and two gifts—those of the Son-Word and of the Spirit-Breath—but only one work. This work, the goal of the divine design or plan of which St. Paul speaks (see Rom 8:28–30; Eph 1:3–14; etc.), is to bestow adoption upon us as children, to make us into sons in the Son, to form us into the family of God, with the glory and the freedom of God's children. That is accomplished through the one-time historical sending of the Son into the world, that is, through the redemptive Incarnation, and through the sending of the Spirit into hearts, through which the one and only Son becomes many sons and heirs—many and one-and-only, the one-and-only being extended to many through

---

37. *Adversus haereses* 5:6.1 and 5:28.4. [31]

38. It is in this sense that I welcome the following statement of Fr. Etienne Garin: "The great temptation for those who have been reborn in the Spirit is, little by little, to dispense themselves from obedience to the Spirit by taking refuge behind the Word or by submitting themselves unconditionally to a 'guide.'" ("D'abord obéir à l'Esprit," *Tychique* 34 [1981]: 18). [32]

the Spirit, who is communication, *koinōnia*, communion.[39] It is the Word-Son incarnate who is the Head, the source of the body. But, first of all, he is established as the source of holiness by the Holy Spirit. In Jesus' conception, his baptism, his healing ministry, his sacrifice, his resurrection, his glorification, which turns him into a "life-giving spirit," in all of that the Spirit is at work. Hence the necessity of a pneumatological Christology (see note 8 above). Second, the Word-Son becomes the communal or "mystical" body only through the Spirit, who is *koinōnia* or communion. However, what the Spirit builds is the body *of Christ*; there is no body of the Holy Spirit.

The Holy Spirit is at work in the activities that build up the body of Christ. Shall I enumerate the most important of these? Is it a question of the confession of faith that is a response to the word? "No one can say 'Jesus is Lord' except by the Holy Spirit" (1 Cor 12:3). Is it a question of Baptism? "We were all baptized with one Spirit so as to become one body ... and we were all made to drink of one Spirit" (1 Cor 12:13). Is it a question of the Eucharist? The Latin West, quite as much as the East, has attributed its consecration to the Spirit just as it has also attributed to the Spirit the spiritual efficacy of all the sacraments.[40] But I have tried to show that the Spirit is active in our reception of Communion;[41] for me this is extremely important. Is it a question of the mission [of the Church]? This is led entirely by the Spirit, who is the Breath that pushes the Gospel forward into new ages and places. The book of Acts offers a striking illustration of that. Is it a question of prayer? It is so very obvious that the Spirit gives rise to prayer and, indeed, that the Spirit *is* prayer in us more profoundly than our words or our conscious thoughts are.[42] This is the meaning of the text of Rom 8:26ff.,

---

39. Not only Gal 4:4–6 but a number of texts must be cited in this connection: Rom 8:14ff.; Jn 3: 13–16; 2 Cor 13:14 (*koinōnia*). [33]
40. See my *ES* 3:320–29 [ET: *HS* 3:250–57]. [34]
41. *ES* 3:330 [331]–341 [ET: *HS* 3:258–66]. [35]
42. See my *ES* 2:147–55 [ET: *HS* 2:112–18]. [36]

which one cannot tire of hearing: "The Spirit comes to the aid of our weakness, for we do not know how to pray as we ought, but the very Spirit intercedes for us with sighs too deep for words, and God, who searches the heart, knows the mind of the Spirit, for indeed it is according to the will of God that the Spirit intercedes for the saints." This personalized interiority of the Holy Spirit is what ensures that there exists within the framework of the Church, and even beyond its visible framework, a community of prayer that is beyond the control of the clerical institution. There exists in this way a sort of Church of the Spirit that is also an ecumenical communion. It is communion in the "res," in the spiritual reality, as it were, beyond the "sacramentum [the sacramental sign]" of it. It is indeed the Spirit who brings forth, through unanticipated initiatives, spiritual renewals that do not fit within the framework. I cannot resist quoting this passage from Alexander Ogorodnikov,[43] the founder of the religious and philosophical seminar in Moscow, written when he was nearly dead after fifteen years of the most severe concentration camp and prison.

The current religious renaissance arises not from the circles of official theology or from the hierarchy or even from ecclesiastical circles; it has no connection to them. It is the lay people, the newly converted, the persons who are the most free in the Church who are the carriers of this spirit of renewal...[44]

This happens because the Spirit is the eschatological power that acts in history but through an energy that gives history a direction and ushers it into the *eschaton*.[45] The passage from St. Paul on the prayer of the Spirit that I quoted belongs to that marvelous

---

43. [trans.] See Koenraad De Wolf, *Dissident for Life: Alexander Ogoridnikov and the Struggle for Religious Freedom in Russia* (Grand Rapids, Mich.: Eerdmans, 2013).

44. Alexandre Ogorodnikov, "Sources et espérance," *Obshchina* 2, reprinted in *Istina* 26 (1981): 304. [37]

45. See the article of John Zizioulas, "Christologie, pneumatologie et institutions ecclésiales: Un point de vue orthodoxe," in *Les églises après Vatican II* (see n. 30 [24] above), 131–48. [38]

Chapter 8 of the Letter to the Romans, where Paul shows the Spirit animating the cosmic maturation of creation toward the *eschaton* [Congar writes "l'eschatologie"]. Together with us, creation waits for deliverance, that of the liberty and the glory of the children of God. As for ourselves, we recognize this. We are what Peter Berger calls the cognitive minority. Priests of the world, we must offer and praise. As for creation, it does not know it but, on its own level, it also is bringing the *eschaton* [Congar writes "l'eschatologie"] to birth. The Spirit works on creation and leads it secretly to that end. But the Word, which the patristic apologists saw at work in all people, works with the Spirit. There are always two hands of God fashioning the human being.... I appreciate (although I have some criticisms for him on other points) the pages where Jürgen Moltmann shows the cosmic scope of what is preparing the Kingdom: "Christian eschatology is not simply an eschatology for Christians; it ought also to be developed as an eschatology of Israel, an eschatology of [world] religions, an eschatology of social structures and as an eschatology of nature, if it is to be an eschatology of the global Kingdom."[46] Since I have quoted one Protestant theologian, I will also call to mind another, Gerhard Ebeling, who entitled the third volume of his dogmatic theology, dedicated to the third article of the Creed, "I believe in God, who leads the world to its perfection/fulfillment" (see n. 11 above).

The Spirit is the eschatological Gift. The Spirit is the one who perfects the work of God and "accomplishes all sanctification." The Fathers understood the Spirit in this way. And I, their humble disciple, will conclude this introductory session as I conclude every day, with the whole Church, the eucharistic prayer, namely by turning into a doxology that theology that unites the Spirit and the Son in returning everything to the Father: "In him, through him, with him, all honor and all glory to you, God the Father almighty, in the

---

46. J. Moltmann, *L'Église dans la force de l'Esprit*, 179 [ET: *The Church in the Power of the Spirit*, 135].

unity of the Holy Spirit"[47] He is the One who, entering quietly into everything everywhere, nourishes the sprout of all that, visibly or in secret, is on the side of God in the world.[48]

> 47. [trans.] Congar's formulation here differs slightly from that used in the French Liturgy: "Par lui, avec lui et en lui, à toi, Dieu le Père tout puissant, dans l'unité du saint-Esprit, tout honneur et toute gloire," as well as from that used in English: "Through him, with him, and in him, in the unity of the Holy Spirit, all glory and honor is yours, Almighty Father, for ever and ever."
> 48. See the conclusion of *ES* 2:271–89 [ET: *HS* 2:213–28]. [40]

ARTICLE 5

Christological and Pneumatological Implications of Vatican II's Ecclesiology[1]

I agreed to treat this subject without giving it very much thought. When I began to write, I wondered exactly what it might include, what was expected of me in the overall context of this colloquium. So I sketched out for myself an outline that unfolded, it seemed to me, from the very statement of the theme, and then I re-read all the conciliar documents, pencil in hand.[2] Here is what, as a result, I propose to consider: (1) what Christ did, as far as the Church is concerned, while he was on the earth; (2) what the glorified Christ does; (3) what comes from the Holy Spirit; (4) as a conclusion, the Trinitarian character of the ecclesiology of Vatican II. In each of these sections, after reporting on the conciliar statements, I will try to show what was at stake in the debates, what that contributed in

1. This article is a translation by Susan Mader Brown of "Les implications christologiques et pneumatologiques de l'ecclésiologie de Vatican II," in *Les églises après Vatican II: Dynamisme et prospective. Actes du Colloque international de Bologne—1980*, ed. Giuseppe Alberigo, Théologie historique 61 (Paris: Beauchesne, 1981), 117–30.

2. [trans.] Congar's original note indicates the abbreviations he uses for the various Vatican II documents. These are the same as those given in the list of abbreviations found at the beginning of this volume. [1]

the post-conciliar period, and what that means for the current state of research, spiritual movements, and people's aspirations.

1. What Christ did, as far as the Church is concerned, while he was on the earth

Antonio Acerbi has shown that, until Vatican II, the dominant ecclesiology was that of a Church founded by Christ and present on the earth as a hierarchical, juridical, institution.[3] Christ had founded the Church as a society. This society was complete in itself (*societas perfecta*), an unequal society where, by divine right and as a fundamental feature, a distinction existed between clergy and laity, between those doing the governing and those being governed. Even Pius XII's encyclical *Mystici Corporis* (June 29, 1943—a date significant in itself),[4] despite restoring value to the spiritual aspect and even to charisms, fitted the spiritual aspect into the narrow confines of the institution, solicitous as it was to exclude any opposition between the Church of love and the Church of law. The schema of the preparatory commission of the Council followed the same line. There were other currents which, beginning from diverse starting points and with diverse ways of elaborating matters, saw the Church *in the first place* as a communion in the divine life, that is, as a supernatural community composed *first of all* of Christians, although ordained ministers most certainly had their place in it. Acerbi showed that these two visions competed with one another at the Council, with the latter winning out over the former, but without eliminating it—would this not undoubtedly have been

---

3. A. Acerbi, *Due ecclesiologie: Ecclesiologia iuridica e ecclesiologia di communione nella "Lumen gentium,"* (Bologna: Edizioni Dehoniane, 1975). [2]

4. [trans.] June 29, the Feast of St. Peter and St. Paul, has a special significance for those concerned about church unity. It was also on June 29 (in 1931) that Pius XI issued his encyclical *Non abbiamo bisogno* in reaction against Mussolini's attempt to suppress the youth wing of Catholic Action.

both impossible and undesirable?—with the result that *Lumen Gentium* reads like a compromise or a text in transition.

Having re-read it carefully, I maintain that one cannot accuse *Lumen Gentium* of "Christomonism." Christocentric it may be, but only if that label has a specific meaning: Vatican II is Christocentric in the way that St. Paul is and not otherwise, meaning that our communion with God is brought about only through union with Christ, who has accomplished the work which the Father entrusted to him (*SC*, n. 5). Christ is also presented very often as the perfect model.[5] Certainly, he is *founder*. He founded the Church as a social entity (*LG*, n. 8). He installed the Twelve as a stable group, the origin of the body or college of bishops (see Mk 3:13),[6] and in this way he established them as leaders, pontiffs, and pastors (*CD*, n. 2). He arranged for the ministries.[7] By sending forth the apostles with Peter at their head, Christ established the form pastoral power would take in the Church, a form continued in the college of bishops with the roman pontiff at its head (*LG*, nn. 18; 22; 27; and *Nota praevia* §2). This is a foundation the Church received from Christ in the flesh. However, people often refer to the commission given by the resurrected Jesus, with a reference to Mt 28:18–20.[8] This corresponds well to the dynamic and missionary character to which Vatican II gave priority in the whole economy of grace: Christ, Church—people of God.

Nobody can overlook or deny the anticipation or institution of a Church, at least in the person of the Twelve, by the pre-paschal Christ.[9] Certain recent ecclesiological presentations seem to me to

---

5. See *LG*, nn. 40–42; 46; *DV*, nn. 2; 7; 15 and 17; *GS*, nn. 10.2 [7?]; 22.1; 32; 38; 41; 45. [3]

6. See *LG*, n. 19; *AG*, n. 5; *UR*, n. 2.3; *DH*, n. 1.2 [n. 1.4? n.11?]. [4]

7. *LG*, nn. 7; 18; *CD*, n. 20; *AG*, nn. 4 and 5. [5]

8. Whether for the founding of the *college* (*LG*, nn. 19 and 20) or to affirm the continuity of mission: *DV*, n. 7; *AG*, n. 5; *LG*, n. 17; *SC*, n. 9; *PO*, n. 4.2; *DH*, nn. 1.2 [1.4?]; 13.2; 14.1. Look again at *LG*, n. 1; *AG*, n. 2; *PO*, nn. 2; 5; 12. [6]

9. The most one can say, exegetically or historically, in that sense has been said by Bishop A.-L. Descamps, "L'origine de l'institution ecclésiale selon le Nouveau

minimize this fact. One example of this is H. Küng, for whom "by his preaching and what he did, the *pre-paschal Jesus created foundations favorable* for the appearance of the post-pascal Church (emphasis in the original),"[10] but it is especially true of Leonardo Boff, who writes: "Jesus did not preach about the Church but about the Kingdom of God. That did not come, as he hoped up to the end that it would, because of the refusal of the Jews.... The Church-as-institution is not based, as is commonly said, upon the incarnation of the Word, but upon faith in the power of the apostles inspired by the Holy Spirit, who moved them to transpose eschatology to the time of the Church and to translate the doctrine of the Kingdom of God into the doctrine about the Church...."[11] It is the Holy Spirit and the apostles who formed the Church-as-community; making Church-as-community a reality is always an open possibility before the Church and before us ...

That was certainly not the view of the Council, even though it had espoused neither the "continued Incarnation" idea of the Roman school nor the schema of Billot and Journet, to which I had to pay homage, which saw the hierarchy as efficient cause: Christ→the apostles and their successors→the Church. The Council gives an active role to ordained ministers, but it does not construct its vision of the Church according to this schema. It sees the Church as a people, a community of grace dependent upon the Trinity through the missions of the Son and the Spirit. To be sure, the people and the community are visible and rooted in history and they make use of means accessible to the senses, but all of that is seen within the

---

Testament," in [Jean-Louis Monneron et al.,] *L'Église: Institution et foi* (Bruxelles: Facultés Universitaires St.-Louis, 1979), 91–138. [7]

10. H. Küng, *L'Église*, trans. H. Rochais and J. Évrard ([Paris:] Desclée de Brouwer, 1968), 1:71–151. The quotation is from p. 112 [ET: *The Church*, trans. Ray and Rosaleen Ockenden (New York: Sheed and Ward, 1968, [1967]), 74]. [8]

11. L. Boff, *Église en genèse: Les communautés de base réinvente l'Église*, trans. F. Malley (Paris: Relais Desclée, 1978), 79–80 and 84 [ET: *Ecclesiogenesis: The Base Communities Reinvent the Church*, trans. Robert Barr (Maryknoll: Orbis, 1986), 56, 58]. [9]

context of the sacramentality of grace and of the present action of Christ.

2. What the glorified Christ does

For Vatican II, Christ is not only a *founder*; he is a permanent *foundation*, actively present to the never-ending building up and life of the Church. This ongoing character of the Christological connection was evident in Paul VI's discourse opening the second phase of the Council on September 29, 1963. I can still hear its tone of intense and enthusiastic faith. "To three questions of prime importance in their extreme simplicity, there is but one answer to give: Christ. Christ is our origin; Christ is our path and our guide; Christ is our hope and our final destination.... We are his elect, his disciples, his apostles, his witnesses, his ministers, his representatives and, with all other faithful people, his living members, united in that immense and unique mystical Body, which He, by means of the faith and the sacraments, is in the process of building up over the course of the generations of humankind."[12] The first words of the constitution on the Church correspond well to that vision. John XXIII, on October 11, 1962, had spoken of the Church as "lumen gentium [light of the nations]," while making reference next to the *"lumen Christi* [light of Christ]" of the Paschal Vigil. The Council constructed the title of its dogmatic constitution on the Church from these words but connected them to Christ through an unconventional Latin construction: "Lumen gentium cum sit Christus [The light of the nations, since it is Christ] ..." Then there is, in n. 3 this echo: "Omnes homines ad

---

12. Paul VI, "Discours prononcée par S. S. Paul VI lors de l'ouverture de la deuxième session du concile," *La documentation catholique*, 1963, col. 1349 and 1350 [ET: "At the Opening of the Second Session of the Ecumenical Council," *The Pope Speaks* 9/2 (1964): 129, 130]. The text of John XXIII, which receives too little notice: John XXIII, "'Ecclesia Christi lumen gentium': Message de S. S. Jean XXIII au monde entier un mois avant l'ouverture du concile (11 sept. 1962)," *La documentation catholique* 59, no. 1385 (October 7, 1962): 1217–22. [10]

hanc vocantur unionem cum Christo, qui est lux mundi, a quo procedimus, per quem vivimus, ad quem tendimus [All humankind is called to this union with Christ who is the light of the world, from whom we go forth, through whom we live, and toward whom we are straining]," and, in n. 8, "Unicus Mediator Christus [Christ, the only mediator]," an idea made more explicit in n. 60 in connection with the well-known Marian title.

This ongoing character of the activity of the glorified Christ is highlighted in the Council's sacramental theology and, in the first place, in its theology of the Church as primordial and universal sacrament: "Christ, having been lifted up from the earth, has drawn all people to himself (see Jn 12:32 in the Greek text). Risen from the dead (see Rom 6:9), he sent his life-giving Spirit upon his apostles [lat. "discipulos"]. Through the Spirit he established his Body, the Church, as the universal sacrament of salvation. Sitting at the right-hand of the Father, he is continually active in the world ..." (*LG*, n. 48). This is developed using the idea of "presence" and by a brief analysis of the various forms of that presence in the *Constitution on the Liturgy* (*SC*, n. 7) which concludes: "rightly, then, the liturgy is considered as an exercise of the priestly office of Jesus Christ ..." a text to which *PO*, n. 5 returns when it speaks of priests who "in performing sacred functions, act as ministers of the one who, through his Spirit, unceasingly exercises for us, in the liturgy, his priestly office."

We can, in passing, take note of the ecumenical implications of these statements, whether with regard to the Orthodox East, which expresses in its celebrations the transcendent action *of God*,[13] or with regard to the Reform tradition with its famous "ubi et quando visum est Deo [where and when it pleases God]," which does not signify an unpredictable freedom of God with respect to the sacraments themselves, but a freedom with regard to divine grace as it affects the faithful who make use of the sacraments.[14]

13. Refer to *ES* 3 [ET: *HS* 3]. [11]
14. The expression comes from the *Confessio Augustana*, 5 [ET: The Augsburg Con-

From two sides, however, people criticize and even repudiate the expression, often employed by Vatican II, about the bishop or the priest acting *in persona Christi* [in the person of Christ]. I show elsewhere (*ES* 3 [ET: *HS* 3]) that this expression has a sacramental, iconic, meaning. Moreover it takes for granted that it is Christ who is the sovereign and principle agent. See *LG*, n. 21: "In the person of the bishops assisted by the priests, it is the Lord Jesus Christ, Supreme High Priest, who is present in the midst of believers. Seated at the right-hand of the Father, he never ceases to be present to the gathering of his high priests...."[15]

That being said, one could connect to this i*n persona Christi* [in the person of Christ] a whole development in research about the identity of the priest that followed the Council and is not yet finished. What Scholasticism, the Counter-Reform and the anti-revolutionary restoration had neglected (on the theological level of things), namely, the priest's connection to the community, is being taken into decisive consideration. The priest presides at the Eucharist because he has been ordained to preside over the community. Scholasticism used to define the priest by his "potestas conficiendi [power to confect (the Eucharist)]," identified with the "character" imprinted through ordination and personally possessed in a never-to-be-lost fashion and which configures the priest to Christ-the-Priest in a manner which is absolutely unique. I understand very well that one might want to go beyond Scholasticism, and even that one might criticize Vatican II, which oriented the definition of the priests toward the whole of the apostolate and toward mission. But I would be afraid to abandon, or even to diminish, the vertical Christological con-

---

fession (1530), 5, in "The Office of the Ministry," in Mark A. Noll, ed. *Confessions and Catechisms of the Reformation*, 89 (Grand Rapids, Mich.: Baker Book House, 1991)]. The explanation comes from M. Kwiran, "Der Heilige Geist als Stiefkind? Bemerkungen zur Confession Augustana," *Theologische Zeitschrift* 31 (1975): 223–36 at 234. [12]

15. [trans.] The Vatican translation reads: "In the bishops, therefore, for whom priests are assistants, Our Lord Jesus Christ, the Supreme High Priest, is present in the midst of those who believe. For sitting at the right hand of God the Father, he is not absent from the gathering of His high priests."

nection. The women's ordination movement would profit from this approach, because of its congruence with the movement's starting points and attitudes, but that is not what concerns me. I would like to see a strenuous attempt to integrate and to synthesize the rather individualistic Christological sacramental theology of Scholasticism and the community aspect of things (with the pneumatology it involves) and, finally, the emphasis of the Council, so clearly indicated by biblical references that had not been hitherto taken into account: John 10:36 (cited four times by the Council) and Romans 15:16 (also cited four times).

3. What comes from the Holy Spirit

To be sure, the primary thing that comes from the Holy Spirit is the enlivening of the institution of the Church. Four words are important in n. 14 of *LG*. It is concerned with the connection between the Catholic faithful and the Church-as-society. Behind this classic question, what is really at stake is a *definition* of the Church. The Council said, and I underscore the four words in question: "Illi *plene* Ecclesiae societati incorporantur, qui *Spiritum Christi habentes*, integram eius ordinationem ... accipiunt [They are *fully* incorporated into the society of the Church who, *possessing the Spirit of Christ*, accept her entire system ...]." Thus, Church-as-society or the society-that-is-Church can define itself only by embracing the Spirit of Christ. This is the beginning of going beyond "Christomonism." But it is only the beginning; it is going to continue. Those elements which Christ instituted, the realities of the Church-as-society, are *at the service of the Spirit* of Christ: "Just as, indeed, the nature assumed by the divine Word is at the Word's service as a living organ of salvation inseparably united to the Word, so the whole visible social structure that constitutes the Church is at the service of the Spirit of Christ who vivifies it for the building up of the body (see

Eph 4:16)" (*LG*, n. 8.1). It is therefore energized "ad augmentum corporis [for the growth of the body]."

If the Holy Spirit is not the one who *institutes*—which the Spirit risks being if one follows Leonardo Boff all the way—the Spirit is the one who *co-institutes*.[16] The Church was founded by Christ and on this account it exists in a determined form. But the Church is also an open-ended institution. Vatican II speaks of promptings the Holy Spirit gave to the apostles (among them, that of *writing* what we call the New Testament);[17] it speaks of the mystery unveiled, in the Holy Spirit, to the holy apostles and prophets (Eph 4:4–6 in the Greek text).[18] The Spirit gives rise, in the historical life of the Church, to *events*, that is, happenings that cannot be *reduced* to what was anticipated, to recurrent patterns, or to a natural order. Thus the modern liturgical movement was presented as "a movement of the Holy Spirit in the Church of God" (*SC*, n. 43). If it is a question of apostolic or missionary initiatives, *Ad Gentes* recognized, with reference to the Acts of the Apostles (the Cornelius episode), that sometimes the Holy Spirit precedes the action planned out by human beings (*AG*, n. 4, concluding section; n. 29.3).

One of the great novelties of Vatican II *in the realm of documents of "the magisterium"* was the introduction of the eschatological point of view, and therefore, also, of historicity. This had been lacking, and the deficiency was a grave one. It was partly connected to the predominance of the juridical aspect. Vatican II sees the Spirit of God as leading the course of temporal events, as renewing the face of the earth, since the Spirit is involved in the evolution of the human community (*GS*, n. 26.4; see also n. 39.3). There is room "with the assistance of the Holy Spirit, to examine closely, to distinguish and to interpret the multiple languages of our time ..." (*GS*, nn. 44.2; 11.1).[19] The disciples of Christ, led by the Holy Spirit, are in-

---

16. See *ES* 2:13–24 [ET: *HS* 2:5–14]. [13]
17. See *DV*, nn. 7; 9; 11; *PO*, n. 11. [14]
18. *DV*, n. 17; and see nn. 18; 19; 20. [15]
19. [trans.] The Vatican translation renders the Latin "auscultare" as "to hear";

volved in a history that is a march toward the Kingdom of the Father (*GS*, n. 1). Making use, if necessary, of resources that the world offers (*GS*, n. 44), the Church pursues, with the assistance of the Holy Spirit, an understanding of what was transmitted to it "constantly moving towards the fullness of divine truth, until the words of God be fulfilled in it" (*DV*, nn. 8.2; 23; see also n. 12.3). This guidance of the Holy Spirit is guaranteed to the whole of the people of God who, taken in a global sense, have received the Spirit's anointing (*LG*, n. 12 which refers to 1 Jn 2:20 and 27). *Presbyterium Ordinis* speaks of this especially for priests (nn. 12.2 and 3; 17.5; 18.2). The Spirit impels people toward missionary work (*LG*, n. 17); the Spirit preserves the "*viva vox Evangelii* [living voice of the Gospel]" (*DV*, n. 8 and see also n. 21) and makes it relevant through the apostolic preaching.

K. Rahner could say that the newest idea conveyed by Vatican II was that of the local church as the realization of the one, holy, catholic and apostolic Church.[20] E. Lanne speaks on this subject of a "Copernican revolution:" no longer is it the local churches that gravitate around the universal Church, but the Church of God is found to be present in the celebration of each local church.[21] Indeed that is a rediscovery of something whose full consequences have yet to be developed. Moreover, this rediscovery is connected to pneumatology, just as an ecclesiology of the universal Church had been linked to a certain "Christomonism." That was not very explicitly clarified in the Council. In the beautiful n. 13 of *Lumen Gentium* on catholicity, the Spirit intervenes instead as a principle of communion and unity. However, reference is made to the vari-

---

Congar translates this term into French as "scruter" ("to examine"). The Vatican translation renders "varias loquelas nostri temporis" as "the many voices of our age"; Congar translates as "les multiples langages [the many "languages" or "modes of expression"] de notre temps."

20. K. Rahner, "Das neue Bild der Kirche," in *Schriften zur Theologie*, Vol. 8 (Einsiedeln: Benziger, 1967), 329–54 at 333ff. [ET: "The New Image of the Church," *Theological Investigations*, vol. 10 (London: Darton, Longman and Todd, 1973), 3–29]. [16]

21. E. Lanne, "L'Église locale et l'Église universelle,"*Irénikon* 43 (1970): 481–511 at 490. [17]

ous gifts proper to each people and to the traditions proper to each particular church, which enrich the others by mutual exchanges in a common effort toward fullness. And one does not tire of quoting these beautiful definitions of the local church:

> They are, each in its locality, the new people called by God in the Holy Spirit.... In them, the faithful are gathered together by the preaching of the Gospel of Christ and the mystery of the Lord's Supper is celebrated.... In these communities ... Christ is present, and, in virtue of his presence, the Church is made one, holy, catholic and apostolic (*LG*, n. 26.1 and see also n. 28.2).

> A diocese is a portion of the people of God entrusted to a bishop to be shepherded by him, with the help of his presbytery. Thus the diocese, being bound to its pastor and gathered together by him in the Holy Spirit through the Gospel and the Eucharist, constitutes a [particular church in which the] church of Christ, one, holy, catholic and apostolic [is truly present and operative].[22] (*CD*, n. 11.1)

These are wonderful passages. In them the Holy Spirit is said to be rather like the principle whereby people are gathered together. But, and we see this better today, the Holy Spirit is the source of interior life for persons, in the diversity of their gifts, charisms, and vocations, so that each one will be freely himself or herself in communion with the others. And that holds true not only for individual persons but also for peoples and for churches. *That* aspect was not developed very much at the Council except in *Unitatis Redintegratio* for the duality—providentially structural, in my opinion—between the East and the West: two traditions of the same faith, which the Council connected not only to catholicity but also to apostolicity, all of which is very powerful.

Since the Council, we have had a development of consciousness about particular churches—I would adopt this terminology, calling dioceses "*local* churches."[23] We have had national synods;

---

22. [trans.] Congar (inadvertently?) omits the words in square brackets.
23. We know that the vocabulary used by the Council was tentative and not fixed. I

we have had the 1974 synod of bishops; we have had, finally, the crisis of Eurocentrism—a process in which the final word has yet to be spoken—and even a crisis of the West and the rise of Africa and of Asia. To all this one must add a new development in pneumatology, linked in part to ecumenism and to listening to the East. As soon as *Ad Gentes Divinitus* was published, the conciliar document received some criticism: it was too much a reflection of the vision of missionary institutes and it was still under the influence of the "church planting" idea, which involves, in the concrete, the transplanting to another land of a cutting from our western churches.[24] Today one says that it is not a question of sending missions but of acting so there will be a church, of bringing a church to birth, in a place and in a people.[25] This is obviously connected to the request that the gifts proper to each people be better accepted, together with their culture and their customs. The Council made this request its own (*LG*, n. 17; *AG*, n. 8), although without envisaging all the implications of it and without developing the pneumatology that is at the base of it.

Another fruit of pneumatology has been evoked, at least in part—namely, the bilateral and reciprocal character of the relations

---

take a stand opposed to the view championed by H. de Lubac (*Les églises particulières dans l'Église universelle*, Paris: Aubier, 1971) and Cardinal Baggio (October 5, 1974) toward the propositions of J.-M. Lachaga, *Église particulière et minorités ethniques* [*: Jalons pour l'évangélisation des peoples minoritaires*] (Paris Centurion, 1978). [18]

24. Thus, A.-M. Henry, "Missions d'hier, mission de demain," in *L'activité missionaire de l'Église*, Unam Sanctam 67[, ed. Johannes Schütte et al.] (Paris: Cerf, 1967), 411–40. [19]

25. J. Amstutz, "Pour la légitimité des missions," *Concilium* 134 (1978): 45–53 [ET: "Towards a Legitimation of the Missions," trans. Miranda Chaytor, in *Evangelization in the World Today*, ed. Norbert Greinacher and Alois Müller, *Concilium* 114 (New York: Seabury, 1979): 30–37]. "Allen claims that the reason for St. Paul's success as a missionary was that he established *Churches* and not a single *Mission*. That is to say, he established indigenous communities which were provided from the start with all the spiritual authority required and who were responsible for their own maintenance, their decisions and their expansion." D. R. Cochran, "Churches or Missions?" *Anglican Theological Review* (September 1974): 23, cited by M. Hebga[, "Églises dignes et églises indigne,"] in *Concilium* 150 (December 1979): 127–34, at 127. [20]

between the leaders and the body. A hint of something in this sense is found where the relations between priests and their bishop,[26] between the laity and priests (and even bishops) is mentioned.[27] The pneumatological foundation, namely the fact that the Spirit indwells and enlivens also the body, that the Spirit distributes charisms to the body, and that the work of God thus intends that the base also *contribute* and cooperate actively, is suggested clearly enough with regard to priests (*PO*, n. 7), more indirectly with regard to laypeople (*AA*, nn. 3.2 and 4). This is one aspect that more recent studies often develop by making reference to some fine ancient testimonies (St. Cyprian, St. John Chrysostom, etc.). Indeed, here or there, an application to the connections between the body of the Church (or the body of bishops) and the Church's Roman head, the pope, is proposed. It will certainly be necessary, one day, to emerge from the constraints of the "plenitudo potestatis [fullness of power]" which has so often been an objection against this. If it is true that, in the purely juridical order, the supreme power cannot be limited (except by divine law, natural law, respect for the "Status ecclesiae [state of the Church]" and for Tradition[28]—and that offers still more support for the thesis that the supreme power *is collegial* . . .), it remains the case that, if the Church is considered from the perspective of communion, the supreme power is conditioned. A heretical pope would cease to be the pope; he is thus conditioned by the faith of the *Church*. People have also begun to value the fact of "reception"[29] and to take it into account. For all these issues, it is

26. See *LG*, n. 28.2 (on their being friends); *PO*, n. 7 (on their being brothers and friends; on listening to them; on consulting them); *CD*, nn. 16.3 (the same idea); 28.2 (dialogue). [21]

27. See *LG*, n. 37.3; *PO*, n. 9.2; see also *AA*, n. 25.1. [22]

28. See the collection of texts in Excursus C of *La Tradition et les traditions: Essai historique* (Paris: Fayard, 1960), 271–78 [ET: *Tradition and Traditions: An Historical and a Theological Essay*, Part One, translated by Michael Naseby (London: Burns & Oates, 1966), 221–29; reprinted San Diego, Calif.: Basilica Press / Needham Heights, Mass.: Simon & Schuster, 1997]. On the "status Ecclesiae," see my article "Status Ecclesiae," *Studia Gratiana* 15 (Bologna: Institutum Gratianum, 1972), 1–31. [23]

29. A. Grillmeier, "Konzil und Rezeption: Methodische Bemerkungen zu einem

essential that history be heard, either to contribute facts or to help us to bring to life again, not, of course, the material nature of ancient situations, but the inspiration, point of view, and underlying motivations of the ancient Tradition.

There were few historians at the Council, and yet I have spoken of the emergence at Vatican II of an eschatological sense and an awareness of historicity. This influence had been rather generally lacking in theology—a focus on "De ultimis rebus [of the last things]" is something other than that![30]—and in the documents of the "magisterium," in encyclicals such as *Quas Primas* on Christ the King or *Mystici Corporis*, for example. One chapter in particular (the seventh) was added in *Lumen Gentium*: "De indole eschatologica Ecclesiae peregrinatis eiusque unione cum Ecclesia coelesti [On the Eschatological Nature of the Pilgrim Church and Its Union with the Heavenly Church]." To tell the truth, the draft text dealt only with the cult of the saints and of the union between the earthly Church and the heavenly Church, but an initial section (48) was introduced, which spoke of the eschatological character of the Church in its condition of being on the way.[31] The Spirit appears there as the first installment of our inheritance, as the first-fruits which will not stop us from groaning in expectation of the glorious manifestation of the Lord. And so, therefore, we have a situation of "Already" and "Not-yet."

The Council is also able to put some distance between the

Thema der ökumenischen Diskussion der Gegenwart." *Theologie und Philosophie* 45 (1970): 321–51. I have added considerably to my documentation since "La 'réception' comme réalité ecclésiologique," *Revue des sciences philosophiques et théologiques* 56 (1972): 369–403. [24]

30. Acerbi, *Due ecclesiologie*, 53, quotes these lines from one of my reviews of Garrigou-Lagrange on this topic: "Eschatology is becoming once again, in contemporary theological thought, what it is in Scripture and what is was for the Fathers: the very meaning of history's movement, what clarifies the whole mystery of the Church. Eschatology is therefore something that is at work in the present order, itself, of things and something that cannot really be understood except as the end-point of history's movement..." (*Revue des sciences philosophiques et théologiques* 33 [1949]: 463). [25]

31. Acerbi, *Due ecclesiologie*, 421ff. [26]

Church and Christ: the Church is just the sacrament of salvation. It can point out the distance between the Church and the Kingdom; there also we have a condition of "Already" and "Not-yet" (see *LG*, n. 5, especially the end; *UR*, n. 2.5). Because the Church is not fully the Kingdom, it can renew and reform itself unceasingly: *LG*, the end of n. 8.3; the end of n. 9; *GS*, n. 21.5 ("under the guidance of the Holy Spirit" ["ductu Spiritus sancti"]); n. 43.6 ("guided by the Spirit" ["a Spiritu sancto ducta"]). But the Spirit also impels the Church to find new forms, to mark out new paths (*PO*, nn. 18.1; 22; *AG*, n. 40.4). The Church professes not to want to prejudge the Spirit's initiatives with regard to ecumenism.[32]

Ecumenism is precisely one of those "Already" and "Not-yet" activities marked by our sinful condition and oriented toward eschatological fullness or perfection. The Council saw therein the fruit of a grace and an activity of the Holy Spirit (*LG*, n. 15; *UR*, nn. 1.2; 4.1; *GS*, n. 92.3). *Lumen Gentium*, after listing some major realities in and through which Christians from other churches or ecclesial communities are united with us, adds these words which are laden with meaning: "To that is added communion in prayer and in other spiritual blessings; moreover, *a genuine union in the Holy Spirit*, since, through the Spirit's gifts and graces, the Spirit's sanctifying action is brought about also in them" (15; emphasis mine).[33] This is a union in the *res* (possessed, however, only as a first installment). All the difficulties come from the *sacramentum*, which consists of the confession of faith, the Eucharist, the sacrament of Orders, the episcopacy, the primacy of Peter.... H. Mühlen took from this passage an extremely positive appreciation of the ecclesial value of non-Catholic communions.[34] The theological problem is therefore

---

32. *UR*, n. 24.2. See the message to artists on December 8, 1965: "Do not close your mind to the breath of the Holy Spirit!" [27]

33. [trans.] The Vatican translation reads: "They also share with us in prayer and other spiritual benefits. Likewise we can say that in some real way they are joined with us in the Spirit, for to them, too, He gives His gifts and graces whereby he is operative among them with his sanctifying power."

34. H. Mühlen, *L'Esprit dans l'Église*, vol. 1 [originally published as *Una Mystica*

to know whether the Spirit imparts all the Spirit's *ecclesial* effects, where the ecclesial sacrament is imperfect. It remains the case that a pneumatological ecclesiology of the local churches allows for a more positive evaluation of the other churches.[35]

4. *Ecclesia de Trinitate* [The Church of the Trinity]

In the Theological Commission of the Council, it was proposed by some (or someone) that Chapter 1 of *Lumen Gentium* not be entitled "On the Mystery of the Church," but "On the Nature of the Church" (which was the title in the Preparatory Commission's schema ...). It was also proposed that "De populo Dei [On the People of God]" be replaced by "De aequalitate et inaequalitate membrorum in Ecclesiae [On the Equality and Inequality of the Members of the Church]"...! "De [ecclesiae] mysterio [On the Mystery of the Church]" stayed and conveys something of profound significance. *Ad Gentes Divinitus* as much as *Lumen Gentium* showed the Church as the result, in humankind and in the "coming-to-be of the world," for the sake of humankind and for the world, of the intradivine life, of the Trinitarian processions. The end of *Lumen Gentium* 4, with references to St. Cyrpian, St. Augustine, and St. John Damascene, summarizes all that: "Sic apparet universa Ecclesia sicuti 'de unitate Patris et Filii et Spiritus Sancti plebs adunata' [Thus, the universal Church has been seen as a 'people made one with the unity of the Father, the Son and the Holy Spirit']." The concrete number of formulae is not necessarily significant, but it is in this case, and all the more so since these formulae are found in different docu-

---

Persona, die Kirche als das Mysterium der Identität des Heiligen Geist in Christus und den Christen: Eine Person in vielen Personem (Munich, Paderborn: F. Schöning, 1964), trans. A. Liefooghe, M. Massart, and R. Virrion], Bibliothèque oecuménique 7 (Paris: Cerf, 1969), 9–114. [28]

35. Philip J. Rosato, "Called by God in the Holy Spirit: Pneumatological Insights into Ecumenism," *The Ecumenical Review* 30 (1978): 110–26. [29]

ments coming from commissions that communicated little with one another. The idea, which is the soul of patristic thought and the soul of the liturgy: to the Father, through the Son, in the Holy Spirit, appears nine times.[36] Twice the Church is represented in Trinitarian fashion as People of God, Body of Christ, Temple of the Holy Spirit: *LG*, n. 17; *PO*, n. 1. Once, at least, it is said explicitly that "the highest exemplar and source of this mystery (of the Church) is in the Trinity of Persons, the unity of one God, the Father, and the Son in the Holy Spirit" (*UR*, n. 2, par. 6).

The meaning of all that is clear: a vision of the Church as a communion of persons and a communion of local churches in a Trinitarian perspective has been substituted for a vision primarily juridical and, by that fact, dominated purely by Christology. To speak of "Christomonism" for Vatican II, particularly for *Lumen Gentium*, or to say that Holy Spirit passages have simply been "sprinkled" over it, would suggest that one had not read the documents or that one had read them with a preconceived attitude.[37] It is true that the pneumatological aspect was, at Vatican II, connected to the Christological reality, but that translates the truth as the inspired Scriptures reveal it to us.[38] The Spirit is a unique hypostasis, the

---

36. *LG*, nn. 4; 28; 51; *DV*, n. 2; *SC*, n. 6; *PO*, n. 6; *OT*, n. 8; *AG*, n. 7.3; *UR*, n. 15.1. The "soul of the liturgy": C. Vagaggini, *Initiation théologique à la liturgie*, adapted by P. Rouillard, 2 vols. (Bruges: Apostolat liturgique / Paris: Société liturgique, 1959–63) [ET: (based on 4th Italian edition) *Theological Dimensions of the Liturgy*, trans. Leonard J. Doyle and W. A. Jurgens (Collegeville, Minn.: Liturgical Press, 1976)]. [30]

37. If I may be permitted to refer once again to my own works: "Pneumatologie ou 'christomonisme' dans la tradition latine?" [ET: Part Three, Article 3, above]; *ES* 1:227–35 (footnotes) [ET: *HS* 1:173 (notes)] and *ES* 3 [ET: *HS* 3] which appeared in 1980. [All three volumes of the English translation appeared together in 1983.] In addition: B. De Margerie, *La Trinité chrétienne dans l'histoire*, Théologie historique 31 (Paris: Beauchesne, 1975), 304–19; A. Laminski, "Die Entdeckung der pneumatologischen Dimension der Kirche durch das Konzil und ihre Bedeutung," in *Sapienter ordinare: Festgabe E. Kleineidam*, Erfurter theologische Studien 24 (Leipzig: St. Benno-Verlag, 1969), 392–403. [31]

38. An acknowledged fact (my "Pneumatologie ou 'christomonisme'..." p. 63, note 90 [ET: Part Three, Article 3, note 93, above]) which struck me in the course of the study that led to *ES* [ET: *HS*]. Christology is what is required for the well-being of pneumatology. [32]

object of a proper "mission," but the Spirit does not do a work other than that of Christ. I acknowledge that Vatican II is, in many areas, imperfect. Many of its views are, if not compromises, at least draft-sketches, and they keep, in a way, to half measures. Paul VI said, in the June 6, 1973, general audience: "The christology, and especially the ecclesiology, of the Council must be followed by a new study and a new devotion to the Holy Spirit, precisely as an indispensable complement of the conciliar teaching."[39] I am hereby working to do my modest part in this! The Council, which John XXIII often presented as a new Pentecost, is the *historical* origin of that paradoxical Pentecost at which it has been given to us to be present and to participate ...

---

39. *La documentation catholique*, 1635 (July 1, 1973): 601 [ET: *L'osservatore romano*, weekly ed. in English, n. 24/272 (June 14, 1973) 1]. In the fine apostolic exhortation of March 22 [= Feb. 2], 1976, *Marialis cultus*, Paul VI also invites us "to a deeper reflection upon the action of the Spirit in the history of salvation" (27) [*AAS* 66 (1974): 136–39; ET: "Devotion to the Virgin Mary," 26–27, *The Pope Speaks* 19/1 (1974/1975): 49–87 at 66–68]. [33]

ARTICLE 6

The Third Article of the Creed: The Impact of Pneumatology on the Life of the Church[1]

Introduction

The history of the Council of 381, its historical context and the part played by each of its "personae dramatis [role players]," is easily read, and I am not going to recall it. I am going to take the Creed as we have received it. I am even going to accept, along with the majority of today's historians, that it really does come from the Council.

The Creed

A creed is, in the domain of expression of the faith, a specific genre different from the "confessions of faith" of Protestant communions. The latter are specific responses made in a context determined by the posing of a question. We might think of the *Barmen Declara-*

---

1. This article is a translation by Susan Mader Brown of "Le troisième article du symbole: L'impact de la pneumatologie dans la vie de l'Église," in *Dieu, Église, Société*, ed. J. Doré (Paris: Le Centurion, 1985), 287–303.

tion of 1934. Those from the sixteenth and seventeenth centuries, however, are not liturgical formulations; they are documents of theologians. We sing the Creed during the celebration of the Eucharist; nobody would think of singing the *Thirty-Nine Articles* or the *Augsburg Confession*. This liturgical, doxological character gives the dogmatic statement its particular quality as an expression of faith.

The impact of the Creed as an expression of faith is noticeable from its first words: *Credo*, I believe, *in* ... , In the Latin and its translations, the verb is in the first person singular. That expresses personal commitment. However, in the liturgical celebration, the commitment is communal. In Greek, creeds are usually in the first person plural ("we believe") as one can see from Hahn's collection. We profess belief *in* ... , *eis* in Greek, in the direction of a mystery toward which faith erects a bridge and with which it thus connects, "yet this is in the dark." This "credo *in*" expresses a commitment of more than intelligence alone. St. Augustine, who distinguished among "credere Deo [to believe by means of God]," "credere Deum [to believe God]," and "credere in Deum [to believe in God]" used to speak, in connection with this last form of faith, of "credendo in Deum ire [proceeding by believing in God]."[2] This is the starting point of a movement that, from the perspective of my own existence, must extend as far as God, gathering up my whole life in its train, but for which the conclusions of knowledge, even if positive and true, remain within faith's absence of evidence. Everything that follows the "credo in," and that makes up the body of the Creed, states what defines the content of my faith, in propositions that encircle this content authentically, without enabling me to grasp the full reality of it. There is an admirable definition of

---

2. [trans.] Congar may be relying here on Henri de Lubac who had made the same point, and in almost the same words, in *The Splendor of the Church* (San Francisco, Calif.: Ignatius Press, 1999 [1987], reprint of the 1956 Sheed and Ward translation of *Méditations sur l'Église*, 2d ed. [Paris: Éditions Montaigne, 1953]), 36. De Lubac gives several references to the works of Augustine.

an article of faith attributed by the great Scholastics to St. Isidore: "perceptio veritatis tendens in ipsam," a perception of the truth oriented toward that truth itself.³

The Third Article

We know that the Creed is Trinitarian. We need to stop apportioning it into the twelve articles that the High Middle Ages attributed to the twelve apostles, giving each his own. This is clearly an idea without historical merit. Besides, even St. Thomas Aquinas took his own liberty with regard to it, since he argued for a division into fourteen articles, which is even less satisfactory to us. Protestant theology's practice of speaking of three articles and dividing dogmatics accordingly seems to me to be much more worthy of consideration. I am thinking, among contemporary theologians, of Helmut Thielicke. The third volume of *Der evangelische Glaube* [*The Evangelical Faith*] is entitled *Theologie des Geistes* [*A Theology of the Spirit*] (1978).⁴ It says relatively little about the Person of the Holy Spirit, but much about the Spirit's work, that is, about the realities wherein the Spirit intervenes: faith, hope and charity, charisms, the Word, the Church, sacraments, ultimately, the whole of eschatology ... I am thinking of Gerhard Ebeling, whose three volumes of dogmatic theology [*Dogmatik des christlichen Glaubens*] are entitled *Der Glaube an Gott den Schöpfer der Welt, ... an Gott den Versöhner der Welt, ... an Gott den Vollender der Welt* [*Faith in God, Creator of the World, ... in God, Reconciler of the World, ... in God, Perfector of the World*] (1979).⁵ Here again, the whole economy of the working out of redemption up to the life of the world to come is treated. Already, however, in Anglicanism, Charles Gore

---

3. [trans.] St. Thomas Aquinas (*ST* 2a2ae, q. 1. a. 6, s.c.) attributes this statement to St. Isidore but gives no reference.
4. [trans.] Tübingen: Mohr.
5. [trans.] Tübingen: Mohr.

had published *Faith in God, Faith in Christ* and *The Holy Spirit and the Church*, which he brought together in 1926 under the title *The Reconstruction of Belief*.[6] All of that is very thought-provoking. And, since we come to suspect something about the mystery of the divine Persons by the design they stamp on the economy of grace, these ways of developing the third article enable us to understand something about the very mysterious Holy Spirit. However, before describing the most important points of the economy of grace, the Creed tells us something precisely about the Third Person.

1. The Third Person[7]

The Council of 381 wanted to affirm and confess the Holy Spirit's consubstantiality with the Father and the Son *just as* Nicaea had affirmed and confessed the consubstantiality of the Son with the Father. It did not, however, make use of the same term, "consubstantial," any more than it declared the Spirit to be "God." God was the Father,[8] and, in reciting the Creed, we ought to state in one single proposition "I believe in only one God the Father ..." But the Council proclaimed that the Spirit is worshipped and glorified together with the Father and the Son. That proclamation also put the Spirit third, not as if there were number in God but simply an order of procession within the unicity of substance. People have

---

6. [trans.] London: Murray.

7. Studies abound: biblical (M.-A. Chevallier [*Souffle de Dieu: Le Saint-Esprit dans le Nouveau Testament*, vol. 1 (Paris: Beauchesne, 1978)]), historical, theological. Let us highlight only the following: A. De Halleux, "La profession de l'Esprit dans la confession de Constantinople," *Revue théologique de Louvain* 10 (1979) 5–39; L. Bouyer, *Le Consolateur: Esprit Saint et vie de grâce* (Paris: Cerf, 1980); *ES* 1, 2, 3 [ET: *HS* 1, 2, 3]; P. Vallin, *L'Église dans la profession de foi* (photocopied) (Paris: Centre Sèvres, 1981); Yves Congar, *La Parole et le Souffle*, Jésus et Jésus-Christ 20. Paris: Desclée, 1984 [ET: *The Word and the Spirit*, trans. David Smith (London: Geoffrey Chapman, 1986)]. [1]

8. One needs to have read K. Rahner, "Dieu dans le Nouveau Testament: La signification du mot 'Theos,'" *Écrits théologiques*, vol. 1 (Paris: Desclée de Brouwer, 1959), 11–111 [ET: *Theological Investigations*, vol. 1, trans. Cornelius Ernst (Baltimore: Helicon Press, 1961), 79–149]. [2]

often spoken of a sort of *kenōsis* of the Holy Spirit, since the Spirit is not revealed as a Person and is designated for us by terms used in common; for the Father is also spirit and holy, and so is the Son. In the Creed, nothing is specified about the mode of the Spirit's "going forth"; the Creed simply repeats the term used in Jn 15:26, which the Greek tradition read in the sense of "proceeding as from its primary source." For that reason, people have recently taken up the practice of simply transferring that meaning to "ekporesis" [*ekporeusis*] because "procession" has a broader and vaguer meaning. A. de Halleux notes that the past participle *ekporeuomenon* is not in the aorist tense as is *gennēthenta*, which expresses the Son's mode of procession.[9] Thus, despite the certainty of it, the eternity of the ekporesis is not emphasized.[10] As in Jn 15:26, where the context is clear, the affirmation has to do with the "economy," but implies something about the eternal and immanent being of the divinity. Nothing is specified about the eternal relationship of the Spirit with the Son, no more, by the way, than what is said about their relation in the economy. Maybe they wanted to avoid giving an opening to those who understood this relationship in a subordinationist sense. At the end of our exchanges between Orthodox and Latins, we agreed to acknowledge this lack of precision. Only an ecumenical council bringing all of us together would be able to be precise on this point, but is that possible? Is it desirable?

The Spirit is described by two terms and a statement that also refer to the economy, namely to the self-communication of God to humankind "propter nos homines et propter nostram salutem [for us human beings and for our salvation]." The Spirit is described as

---

9. [trans.] See his article mentioned in note 7, above.

10. [trans.] The full theological impact of the statement about the Son, whose generation is not confined by time as we know it, is felt when the adverbial phrase *"pro pantōn tōn aiōnōn"* [before all ages] modifying the aorist form is kept in mind. The participle *ekporeuomenon* does not inevitably point to the Holy Spirit's procession originating beyond time but can be so read, especially when interpreted in conjunction with the other statements in the Creed.

"Lord," *to Kurion,* in the neuter, whereas *Kurios* is masculine. This term, in Scripture, is connected to power, military strength, and freedom; it is a term indicating sovereignty. The Creed links to this the descriptor *zōopoion,* "giver of life." These two descriptors must be held together; they modify one another. Together they express immanence and transcendence in the same way that in the "Our Father" we do not invoke God as Father with the tone of tenderness and intimacy that the term "Abba" connotes without also adding immediately "who art in heaven." I cannot subscribe to a Hegelian conception of the Spirit, as, for example, M. Merleau-Ponty, quite close to us, describes it. He sees the Spirit simply as God's immanence in history and in the community.[11] There is immanence because there is gift, but it is the immanence of the Paraclete who remains Lord and is not identical to the life and movement that the Spirit makes real in us.

These two linked attributes of the Spirit justify the characterization of the Spirit as being Uncreated Gift and Grace. The Son is also *given* to us. Moreover, in the economy, the Son-Jesus Christ and the Spirit are inseparable. They are the two means and modalities through which God's self-revelation and self-communication are brought about. St. Irenaeus sees them as the two hands through which the Father does his work of creation and salvation; this is an especially appropriate and expressive analogy.[12] After Irenaeus, St. Hippolytus, in a very beautiful passage from his *Contra Noetum*

11. M. Merleau-Ponty, "Foi et bonne foi," in *Sens et non-sens* (Paris: Nagel, 1948; 2d ed. 1965), 305–21 [ET: "Faith and Good Faith" in *Sense and Non-Sense,* trans. and with a preface by Hubert L. Dreyfus and Patricia Allen Dreyfus (Evanston, Ill.: Northwestern University Press, 1964), 172–81]; [Georg Wilhelm Friedrich] Hegel, *Leçons sur la philosophie de la religion,* trans. J. Giberlin (Paris: J. Vrin, 1954), 3d part "La religion absolu," ch. 5, 173 [ET: *Lectures on the Philosophy of Religion Together with a Work on the Proofs of the Existence of God,* trans. E. B. Speirs and J. Burdon Sanderson from the 2d German edition (New York : Humanities Press, 1962), 106–7]; *La phénoménologie de l'esprit* (1806), trans. J. Hyppolite (Paris: Aubier Editions Montaigne, 1941), 7 C., 284–90 [ET: *The Phenomenology of Mind,* trans. and with an introduction and notes by J. B. Baillie, 2d edition revised and corrected (London/New York: George Allen and Unwin/Macmillan, 1955 (1949), 778–85]. [3]

12. *Adversus haereses* 5:6.1 and 5:28.4 (SChr 153:73 and 361) [ANF 1:531, 557];

14.2–8,[13] highlights the mysterious character of the Spirit who is, as it were, without a personal face, but he concludes by saying, "That is what Grace is."

If the Son is "given" to us (Jn 3:16; Rom 8:32), it is to the Spirit that the New Testament applies the title "Gift" in a preeminent way, whether under the noun form or by applying to the Spirit the verbs "to give" and "to receive."[14] The Spirit, who is the ultimate expression of the intradivine communication beginning from the monarchy of the Father, is also, in the realm of the economy of grace, the eschatological Gift, the fulfillment/perfection ["consommation"], "der Vollender der Welt." Such is the Spirit's role, such is the Spirit's place in the Creed. The Spirit is the Gift that suffices until the *eschaton* [Congar writes "eschatologie"] to make this historical and precarious world, the one in which Jesus "suffered under Pontius Pilate," pass into the definitive Kingdom that is already there and is still to come,[15] the life of the world to come (*zōēn tou mellontos aiōnos*), which is itself also already in the process of coming here below.

Still in the realm of the economy, the Creed adds "who has spoken through the prophets." This is one of the characteristics of the Spirit that is attested earliest and unanimously. It is undoubtedly connected with what St. Peter says in 1 Pt 1:10–12. There [in the Creed] and in this very passage [of Scripture], there is not simply a reference to the past. If there is one statement made frequently among the Fathers and in Tradition, it is that the Spirit of prophecy is always at work in the Church. The Spirit's activity is also always directed toward the proclamation and understanding of the mys-

---

J. Mambrino, "Les deux mains du Père dans l'oeuvre de saint Irénée," *Nouvelle revue théologique* 79 (1957): 355–70. [4]

13. [trans.] Hippolytus of Rome, *Contra Noetum*, intro., ed., trans. Robert Butterworth (London: Heythrop Manuscripts, 1977), 74–76.

14. See the references and texts in *ES* 3:193ff. [ET: *HS* 3:144ff.]. [5]

15. St. Gregory of Nyssa liked to read in the *Our Father*, in place of "Thy Kingdom come," "send your Spirit that he may purify us." [6]

tery *of Christ*.[16] The Spirit reveals Christ, who reveals the Father. In a way parallel to this process of coming to understand, the Church lives a doxological life, that life that animates the whole of the liturgy: to the Father, through the Son, in the Spirit.[17] All of that is essential, even for our activity as theologians.

2. The Spirit as Co-Institutor of the Church

There again, God works through two hands. Certainly Christ put into place the foundations of the Church, not only in a mystical and ongoing sense (1 Cor 3:10ff.) but in the historical sense as its "founder." He did this by instituting the Twelve, baptism, and the Eucharist, and by revealing the Gospel. But it is the Spirit who gave life, who gave breath, and who unceasingly makes Christ's work real in the present. Again, it is the work *of Christ*, of his body. There is no Mystical Body of the Holy Spirit; it is the Spirit who enlivens Christ's Body that is made up of us (see 1 Cor 12:13).

Since one could say "credo *in* . . ." only with reference to God, the Scholastics used to gloss the words of the third article "et unam, sanctam, catholicam et apostolicam Ecclesiam [and one, holy, catholic and apostolic Church]" in the following way: "I believe in the Holy Spirit unifying, sanctifying, catholicizing, apostolicizing the Church." I shall not get involved in explaining that theology;[18] rather, I will consider just the impact of a genuine pneumatology on the question of ministries and on the guiding model of ecclesiology.

---

16. This is a very important point. Besides 1 Pt 1:10–12, see 1 Cor 12:3; 1 Jn 4:1–13; Jn 14:26; 16:8–11; Rv 1:2–3; 19:10. That was how Jesus interpreted it: Lk 24:25–27. [7]

17. See C. Vagaggini, . *Initiation théologique à la liturgie*. 2 vols. Bruges: Apostolat liturgique / Paris: Société liturgique, 1959–63. [ET: (based on 4th Italian edition) *Theological Dimensions of the Liturgy*, trans. Leonard J. Doyle and W. A. Jurgens. Collegeville, Minn.: Liturgical Press, 1976.] On the doxology that concludes our Eucharistic Prayers, see the Conclusion of *ES* 2 [ET: *HS* 2:213ff.]. [8]

18. See *ES* 2 [ET: *HS* 2], and even *Mysterium salutis* 15 (Paris: Cerf, 1970). [9]

By "pneumatology" I understand specifically, over and above a theology of the Third Person, the impact upon the life of the Church and, consequently, upon the way of seeing the Church, of taking the Holy Spirit and the Spirit's activity into consideration. The way of seeing the Church will be Trinitarian.

I can first of all indicate why a purely paternal model [of the Church], or a "pre-Trinitarian monotheism"[19] which amounts, for all practical purposes to the same thing, is insufficient. Everything derives from on high, from a single source. This easily leads to paternalism, to that sort of solicitude of which Donoso Cortés seems to me to have given an ideal description: "everything for the people, nothing by the people."[20] Others are not really treated as subjects. Thus one would have a patriarchal or purely masculine model.

Even a purely Christological model [of the Church] would present some deficiencies and even disadvantages. Certainly the model needs to be Christological; it is not a question of forgetting the Christological model but of completing it. In a *purely* Christological approach, Christ would be seen (he has been seen) as the founder of a society and, first of all, of a hierarchy at the origin of that society. The Church would be defined and presented as a hierarchical or unequal society, a complete society (*societas perfecta*).[21] By "society" is meant the relationships between those in charge and those who are subordinate to them "secundum sub et supra [according to what is below and what is above]," and so we have the possibility of

---

19. See my article "Le monothéisme politique et le Dieu Trinité," *Nouvelle revue théologique* 103 (1981): 3–17, and at H.-M. Legrand, "Le développement des Églises-sujets à la suite de Vatican II: Fondements théologiques et réflexions institutionelles," in *Les églises après Vatican II: Dynamisme et prospective, Actes du colloque international de Bologne, 1980*, ed. G. Alberigo, Théologie historique 51 (Paris: Beauchesne, 1981), 149–84. [10]

20. [trans.] See the mention of Donoso Cortés above, Part Four, Article 4, note 25.

21. See this time my presentation from the *Ecclesiam suam* Colloquium, Rome, October 1980: "Situation ecclésologique au moment de *Ecclesiam suam* et passage à une Église dans l'itinéraire des hommes" [*Ecclesiam suam: Première lettre encyclique de Paul VI: Colloque international, Rome, 24–26 octobre, 1980* (Brescia: Instituto Paolo VI, 1982)]. [11]

a pyramidal vision. In fact, that did exist, whether in pictures or in writing, sometimes even using the word "pyramid." I have collected some seventeen texts or references where one finds an analogous conception of society. And I am not counting the use made, up to the time of Leo XIII in 1878, of the hierarchical model of the angelic choirs.... But let us get back to the Christological model.

Its influence has been felt in the theology of what has often been called the ministerial or hierarchical priesthood. It has been the dominant view since the second half of the twelfth century, since Peter Lombard's *Sentences*, let us say. The ordained priest was distinguished by the share he had been given in a power, "potestas conficiendi [the power to confect (the Eucharist)]," and by the "character" that gave him, personally and in an indelible way, a participation in the priesthood of Christ and thereby conferred this power upon him.[22] Thus the ordained priesthood was defined by, and the priest was characterized by, a personal and purely vertical reference to Christ without reference to the community. In the writings of St. Thomas, the treatise on the sacraments follows immediately upon the treatise on Christ without a treatise on the Church. As celebrant of the Eucharist and of the sacrament of penance, the priest acts *in persona Christi* [in the person of Christ]—which is true— without any room being made for the *in persona Ecclesiae* [in the person of the Church], which will be recognized only in the realm of prayer.[23] The tendency today would be rather to situate the *in*

---

22. One could look at *L'Église: De saint Augustin à l'époque moderne*, [Histoire des dogmes 20] (Paris: Cerf, 1970), 169ff. where I quote J.-F. Von Schulte, "Die geschichtliche Entwicklung des rechtlichen 'Character indelebilis' als Folge der Ordination," *Revue internationale de théologie* 9 (1901): 17–49; C. Vogel, *Ordinations inconsistantes et caractère inamissible* (Turin: Bottega, 1978) and articles in a variety of journals; Edward Schillebeeckx, *Le ministère dans l'Église: Service de présidence de la communauté de Jésus Christ*, trans. N. Kesteman (Paris: Cerf, 1981) [ET: *Ministry: Leadership in the Community of Jesus*, trans. John Bowden (New York: Crossroad, 1981)]; see my critical review: *Revue des sciences philosophiques et théologiques* 66 (1982) : 101–3. [12]

23. See B.-D. Marliangeas, *Clés pour une théologie du ministère: "In persona Christi," "in persona Ecclesiae,"* Théologie historique 51 (Paris: Beauchesne, 1978). [13]

persona Christi within the *in persona Ecclesiae* and to say that the priest presides at the Eucharist because he is ordained to preside over the community.[24] However, Pius XII, in his important encyclical on the liturgy, *Mediator Dei* (November 20, 1947), justified a solitary celebration of the Eucharist, with neither server nor community, by this consideration: the priest represents the Christian people only because, acting *in persona Christi*, he represents the Head of all the members. It is worth the trouble of quoting the original text:

> But we deem it necessary to recall that the priest acts for the people only because he represents Jesus Christ, Who is Head of all His members and offers Himself in their stead. Hence, he goes to the altar as the minister of Christ, inferior to Christ but superior to the people (footnote reference to St. Robert Bellarmine [*De Missa*, 2, c. 4]).[25]

The reason put forward reminds me of the response given by Bishop Gasser, in the discussions at Vatican I, to the minority who did not want to separate the bishops from the pope and therefore wanted to state that the latter needed to be united with the former. There could be no separation, responded Bishop Gasser, because the members must always follow the head....[26] There we have an application of the *caput-corpus/membra* [head-body/member] schema. The history of doctrines of the Church in the West, especially from the Roman point of view, could be written under the heading of this schema and under the influence of what I will call "capital-

---

24. See H. Legrand, "La présidence de l'Eucharistie selon la tradition ancienne," *Spiritus* 69 (1977): 409–31. [14]

25. "... [I]n memoriam revocandum esse ducimus sacerdotem nempe idcirco tantum populi vices agere, quia personam gerit Domini nostri Jesu Christi, quatenus membrorum omnium Caput est, pro iisdem[que] semet ipsum offert, ideoque ad altare accedere ut ministrum Christi, Christo inferiorem, superiorem autem populo," *AAS* 39 (1947): 553 [ET: *Encyclical of Pope Pius XII on the Sacred Liturgy*, in *Selected Documents of His Holiness Pius XII on the Sacred Liturgy* (Washington, D.C.: National Catholic Welfare Conference, 1958), n. 84, p. 33]; *DS* 3850 [ET: J. Neuner and J. Dupuis, eds., *The Christian Faith in the Doctrinal Documents of the Catholic Church*, 7th ed., rev. and enlarged (New York: Alba House, 2001) no. 1734, p. 733]. [15]

26. *Mansi* 52:1213–14, intervention of July 11, 1870. [16]

ity." This was to persist right up to certain texts from Vatican II, to the extent that the council went only halfway and retained many ways of thinking that are sometimes foreign to its fundamental thrust. H. Legrand noted, for example, that "the predominance, in certain texts, of the body/head schema to explain the notion of *communio hierarchica* [hierarchical communion], also points to an excessive attachment to a Christological approach..."[27]

This brings us back to the accusation of "Christomonism" that has so often been made to us by Orthodox and Protestants.[28] I do not deny that the accusation has some basis in fact. It was by a rather sound instinct that, wanting to replace juridical ecclesiology by a vision more in harmony with the deepest roots of our tradition, I had wanted to inaugurate the "Unam Sanctam" series with Möhler's *L'unité dans l'Église*, which was a pneumatological synthesis. The situation today is improving greatly.[29] The Council already attempted to unite Christology and pneumatology.[30] We are in the process of shaping the contemporary life of the Church, and the theology that articulates it, according to a pneumatological and Trinitarian model.

---

27. See p. 160 of H. Legrand, "Le développement des Églises-sujets à la suite de Vatican II: Fondements théologiques et réflexions institutionelles" (see note 19 [10], above) which has, in its note 3, a review of *LG* 21 and 22; *PO* 7 and 15; *CD* 4; and the "Nota praevia." Then there is some faultfinding addressed to O. Saier for a vision too narrowly Christomonist in his *"Communio" in der Lehre des Zweiten Vatikanischen Konzils* (Munich: Max Hueber, 1973). [17]

28. See my article "Pneumatologie ou 'christomonisme' dans la tradition latine?" in *Ecclesia a Spiritu Sancto edocta (Lumen gentium, 53): Mélanges théologiques, hommages à Mgr Gérard Philips; Verzamelde theologische opstellen aangeboden aan Mgr. Gérard Philips*, Bibliotheca ephemeridum theologicarum Lovaniensium 27 (Gembloux: Duculot, 1970), 41–64 [ET: Part Three, Article 3, above]; *ES* 1:207ff., 218–19 [ET: *HS* 1:151ff., 159–60]; *La Parole et le Souffle* [ET: *The Word and the Spirit*], ch. 6 and 7; H. Legrand article cited above (notes 19 and 27), 159–60. [18]

29. See P. Vallin, *L'Église dans la profession de foi*, 48ff. [19]

30. On this topic, see my contribution ["Les implications Christologiques et pneumatologique de Vatican II"] in *Les églises après Vatican II: Dynamisme et prospective*, Actes du Colloque international de Bologne, ed. G. Alberigo (Paris: Beauchesne, 1981), 117–30 [ET: Part Four, Article 5, above]. [20]

3. The Rediscovery of Pneumatology

That occurs first of all—the Council opened the way—by a rediscovery of charisms and ministries. The guiding text, noticeably Trinitarian, is well known:

> There is, to be sure, a variety of spiritual gifts, but the same Spirit; and a variety of services, but the same Lord; and a variety of activities, but it is the same God who activates all of them in everyone. To each is given the manifestation of the Spirit for the common good (1 Cor 12:4–7).

And St. Paul offers some examples. One could contribute others taken from the current life of the Church. There are the thousands of men and women who take on the catechetical task of the Christian community. There are those men and women who are working, sometimes with great sacrifice and to the point of martyrdom, *for humanity*, in and through the Spirit of Jesus Christ. There are the initiatives involving biblical or ecumenical circles. There is the liturgical animation of celebrations. There is the immense realm of *caritas* [charity]. And how can one not make room for the Renewal in the Spirit, often called "charismatic" in a specific way, even though it clearly does not have, and does not pretend to have, a monopoly on charisms? Can one speak of "ministries"? Under what circumstances? Undoubtedly not in every instance. For a ministry to exist, at least three conditions must all be fulfilled: it must involve an activity essential to the Church; it must be something that is guaranteed, stable, something that can, above all, be relied upon; and it must be recognized, made public, officially authorized, possibly by a liturgical rite or by the intervention of the bishop, but also by an official appointment or an announcement.[31]

---

31. The motu proprio *Ministeria Quaedam* of August 15, 1972 in *La documentation catholique* 1617 (October 1, 1972): 852–54 [*AAS* 64 (1972): 529–34; ET: The Ministries of Lector and Acolyte, *The Pope Speaks* 17/2 (1972): 257–61]) takes this position. Its interesting theological foundation was to distinguish between ministries that are based upon sacramental ordination and those that are based upon baptismal

If each one can have his or her charisms, that is also true, positis ponendis [the same presumptions being made], of local or particular churches, of peoples and of their cultural possessions. Each people must celebrate the marvels of the Lord in *its own* language. That is the meaning of the Pentecost miracle. In this sense, "to be catholic, the Church must be particular" (H. Legrand). One of the most interesting steps taken by the Council—according to Karl Rahner it was the most notable one in ecclesiology—was the rediscovery of the local or particular church (the vocabulary is a bit in flux with regard to how these adjectives are used). The Council's definition is remarkable; I emphasize its mention of the Spirit:

> This Church of Christ is truly present in all legitimate local congregations of the faithful that, united with their pastors, are themselves called churches in the New Testament [the note refers to Acts 8:1; 14:22–23; 20:17 and passim]. For in their locality, these are the new People called by God *in the Holy Spirit* and in much fullness (see 1 Thes 1:5). In them the faithful are gathered together by the preaching of the Gospel of Christ, and the mystery of the Lord's Supper is celebrated "so that, by the flesh and blood of the Lord, the whole brotherhood may be drawn together into a single Body" [the Mozarabic Eucharistic Prayer]. In any community of the altar, under the sacred ministry of the bishop [Ignatius of Antioch], there is exhibited a symbol of that charity and "unity of the mystical Body without which there can be no salvation" [St. Thomas]. In these communities, though frequently small and poor, or living in the Diaspora, Christ is present, and in virtue of His presence, there is brought together one, holy, catholic and apostolic Church [St. Augustine].[32]

A diocese is a portion of the people of God entrusted to a bishop to be shepherded by him with the help of his presbytery. Thus the diocese,

---

consecration. It also recalls the distinction made by St. Hyppolytus' *Apostolic Tradition* between ministries involving a consecration by the imposition of hands and those simply instituted (sub-deacon, acolyte, widow) ... One can refer to "L'avenir des ministères: Diversifier et unir," in the journal *Vocation* 278 (April 1977). [21]

32. *LG*, n. 26.1 [in the passage he quotes, Congar indicates in square brackets the content of the document's footnote references]. See also n. 13 on catholicity. [22]

being bound[33] to its pastor and *gathered together* by him *in the Holy Spirit* through the Gospel and the Eucharist, constitutes a particular church in which the one, holy, catholic and apostolic Church of Christ is truly present and operative.[34]

We have there some fine *Trinitarian* texts. Each particular church has its own gifts and its own role to play; each one *is* the Church, but not by itself. It is Church in communion with the others. The Holy Spirit, who is the source of variety by the diversity of the Spirit's gifts, is also the principle of communion and unity. For the Spirit is one and the same in all, without suppressing originality or infringing upon the freedom of any, since it is the particular role of the Spirit to be subtle and to be of universal value. What the Book of Wisdom states about this subject is precisely to the point. With the liturgy, I apply it to the hypostasis of the Holy Spirit and to the Spirit's activity:

The Spirit of the Lord indeed fills the world, and the one that holds all things together knows what is said (1:7).

There is in her (Wisdom), indeed, a spirit that is intelligent, holy, unique, manifold, subtle, mobile, penetrating, unpolluted, clear, invulnerable, loving the good, keen, irresistible, beneficent, humane, steadfast, sure, free from anxiety, all powerful, overseeing all, and penetrating through all spirits, all those who are intelligent, pure and altogether subtle. For Wisdom is more mobile than any motion; because of her purity she pervades and penetrates all things (7:22–24).

This penetrating Spirit is love, the Spirit is communion, making what is diverse come together in unity, a unity that is not uniformity. The Spirit does this by acting on what is innermost and from within. In this coming together, where each church brings its own particular talents, these churches are, in the communion of

---

33. [trans.] The Vatican translation reads "adhering."
34. See *CD* on the ministry of bishops, n. 11.1. See also chapter 3 of *AG* (more descriptive and without a mention of the Holy Spirit) but see also n. 4 of its first chapter. [23]

all, responsible *subjects* of their life (see H. Legrand's study, cited above, note 19). Churches, communities, and the faithful are animated and alive within the spiritual organism. They are also active agents. Pneumatology grounds, in a balanced way, ecclesial practices and the theological views that correspond to them. Here are some of these.

Consider the "Teaching Church/Church Taught" pair. These terms come from the first third of the eighteenth century. Even though they express an authentic reality that must always be recognized, they have also given rise to some abusive notions such as that at which George Tyrrell poked fun when he said the Church was considered infallible "because it has an infallible pope, a little like a flock of sheep could be said to be intelligent because it was in union with its shepherd."[35] A caricature? All the same, one could read things such as this: "the passive infallibility of the faithful consists, therefore, in listening as they should to the magisterium."[36] Vatican II said something completely different![37] And here is another: "The pastor with respect to his bishop, the bishop with respect to the pope, are they not part of the Church taught, just like the faithful?"[38] The question must therefore be taken up again and reformulated.[39] The Church, animated by the Spirit of Christ, is, as a whole, listening, celebrating, loving, praying and confessing, but in an organic manner; each one in it is enlivened so as to exercise his or her own function. The

---

35. *Medievalism*[: *A Reply to Cardinal Mercier*], translated into French as *Suis-je catholique?* (Paris: E. Nourry, 1909), 91 [the passage quoted is on p. 85 of the 1994 Burns and Oates edition]. [24]

36. A.-A. Goupil, *La règle de foi*, n. 17, 2d ed. (Paris: Paillard, 1941), 48. [25]

37. See *LG*, n. 12, which speaks specifically about charisms. [26]

38. [Centre catholique des intellectuels canadiens (Université de Montréal),] *Le rôle de laïques dans l'Église: Carrefours, 1951* (Montreal: Fides, 1952), 9. [27]

39. Among the most recent contributions that deal with this, one could consult those of B. Bobrinskoy, Leonardo Boff, L. Sartori, and even mine, in *Concilium* 148. (1981): *Qui a la parole dans l'Église?* [ET: *Who Has the Say in the Church?* ed. Jürgen Moltmann, Hans Küng and Marcus Lefébure, *Concilium* 148 ([Edinburgh: T & T Clark / New York: Seabury, 1981), with Congar's contribution, "Towards a Catholic Synthesis," trans. John Maxwell, on 68–80]. [28]

whole Church learns, the whole Church teaches, but in a differentiated manner. The secret of a balanced position is given in the formula of St. Augustine often taken up again by him under different forms: "For you I am a bishop; with you I am a Christian," or better still, "From this spot [the bishop's cathedra?] I am your teacher, but I am a disciple along with with you (*condiscipulus*) of the one who teaches all of us."[40] The bishop is, at one and the same time, within the Church and standing before it. So is the pope. A purely juridical approach to his function affirms only his "plenitudo potestatis [fullness of power]" and admits no reciprocity. According to this way of thinking, the head governs the body and does not depend upon it; this is a biological error but also an ecclesiological error. For the Church must be seen, not only as a society with relationships "secundum sub et supra [according to what is below and what is above]," but as a communion of spiritual life. It is obvious that from the communion perspective the head is in the body and also depends upon it; the life of the body does not come from the pope as the impact of juridical rules can come from him. The "vobis sum episcopus [For you I am a bishop]" requires, as its presupposition a "vobiscum christianus [I am a Christian along with you]." That is the truth conveyed by a model that is pneumatological and Trinitarian, not purely paternal and Christological. This is the truth of a Church seen as a communion of all that God gives to all its members, and not simply as an "unequal and hierarchical" society.

There is a connection between the communication, and thus the presence or indwelling, of the Holy Spirit, and community. This is seen in Acts by the way the related terms *epi to auto* [in one place] and *homothumadon* [with one heart] are used. Möhler expressed this connection well when he wrote, alluding to Acts 2:1, "When they received strength and enlightenment from on high, the leaders

---

40. Thus *Sermo 340*, 1 (PL 38:1483) [ET: *Sermons 306–340A on the Saints*, trans. and notes by Edmund Hill, OP, ed. John E. Rotelle, OSA, The Works of St. Augustine: A Translation for the 21st Century, vol. 3, no. 9 (Brooklyn, N.Y.: New City Press, 1994), 292] and in many other places. [29]

and the members of the emerging Church were not dispersed in different locations, but united in one place and with one heart, forming one single assembly of brothers...."[41] The Fathers from the period of the martyrs kept alive an awareness that the Spirit indwelt the assembly. St. Irenaeus writes: "Where the *ecclesia* [the assembly of believers] is, there the Spirit of God is; and where the Spirit of God is, there is the *ecclesia* and every grace."[42] And St. Hippolytus writes: "One will hasten to go to the *ecclesia*, the place where the Spirit flourishes."[43] Let us not be astonished that this *ecclesia*, made up of members of the High Priest and indwelt by the Spirit, is the subject, as a whole, of liturgical actions, even of the celebration of the Eucharist and of penance.[44]

The Christian community also plays a role in the ordination process. I speak of a "process" because this begins before the liturgical ceremony. Formerly this was by election, but today this occurs by the maturation of a vocation in which the life-community of the future minister cooperates. The ordination of a bishop or a priest is not ordinarily the solitary act of transmitting "power" according to a vertical logic, from the top down. It requires the cooperation of several bishops and of the presbyterium [priests of the diocese]. It takes place before the people, who bear witness to the aptness

---

41. The beginning of §37 of *La symbolique* [2d ed., trans. F. Lachat (Paris: L. Vivès, 1852–53)]; [ET: *Symbolism: Exposition of the Doctrinal Differences between Catholics and Protestants as Evidenced by Their Symbolical Writings*, trans. James Burton Robertson, introduction by Michael J. Himes (New York: Crossroad, 1997)]. [30]

42. *Adversus haereses* 3:24.1 (SChr 211, 475). On the practical meaning of *ecclesia* = assembly, see P. M. Gy, "Eucharistie et 'Ecclesia' dans le premier vocabulaire de la liturgie chrétienne," *La Maison-Dieu* 130 (1977): 19–34 at 31. [31]

43. *Apostolic Tradition*, 35. [32]

44. See my study "Ecclesia ou communauté des chrétiens, sujet intégral de l'action liturgique," in *La liturgie après Vatican II*, ed. Yves Congar, Unam Sanctam 66 (Paris: Cerf, 1967), 241–82 [ET: "The *Ecclesia* or Christian Community as a Whole Celebrates the Liturgy," in *At the Heart of Christian Worship: Liturgical Essays of Yves Congar*, translated and edited by Paul Philibert (Collegeville, Minn.: Liturgical Press / A Pueblo Book, 2010), 15–68]. With regard to Penance, see my Preface to K. Delahaye, *Ecclesia Mater chez les Pères des trois premiers siècles*, Unam Sanctam 46 (Paris: Cerf, 1964). [33]

of the chosen one and who associate themselves, in silence, with the epiclesis.[45] And thus a pneumatological and Trinitarian model is made real.

Let me highlight, in passing, the significance of everything we have just explained, too briefly, for the urgent problem of the recognition of the place that belongs to women in the Church. *Ministeria Quaedam* excluded them (n. 8) from the liturgical ministries that were being renewed. Yet they were doing and do much more than these rather formal ministries, and a variety of declarations came forth immediately saying that they could continue [to fulfill these tasks], even within the liturgy (reading, distributing Communion).[46]

4. Conclusions

If, by way of conclusion, I were to try to articulate an overall view of the image that an active pneumatology gives to the Church, I could say the following:

First of all, this is the fulfillment of the movement that asserted itself among us between 1925 and the 1950s under the label "Mystical Body," a movement toward an organic and supernatural conception of the Church where the faithful (the "laity") would have their active place. It is true that at the First Vatican Council the *De Ecclesia* schema, distributed to the Fathers in January 1870, began with this statement: "The Church is the Mystical Body of Christ." But that had been criticized by a number of Fathers who wanted a definition of the Church "*ab extremis* [from the outside]" (the ter-

---

45. H. Legrand, "Le développement des Églises-sujets à la suite de Vatican II: Fondements théologiques et réflexions institutionnelles" (note 19, above), 163ff., reveals all of that, with references to his work and his own articles. [34]

46. ["Mise au point du Saint-Siège sur le role des femmes dans la liturgie,"] *L'osservatore romano*, October 8, 1972 (*La documentation catholique*, Nov. 5, 1972); the instruction *Immensae Caritatis* from the Congregation for the Discipline of the Sacraments, January 29, 1973 [ET: *The Pope Speaks* 18.1 (1973): 45–51]. [35]

minology is that of Bishop Dupanloup), as a society. The Mystical Body idea reemerged in a rather triumphal form. But Vatican II, in the first chapter of *Lumen Gentium* and similarly in the first chapter of *Ad Gentes Divinitus*, gave a Trinitarian structure to the Church. With respect to the liturgy, there was also the transition from a primarily Christological vision, admittedly very deeply rooted and true, to a greater consideration of the Holy Spirit. So, while Pius XII's encyclical *Mediator Dei* (1947), and the conciliar constitution on the liturgy that came from the preparatory Commission prior to the council, define the liturgy, with great insight, as the act of Christ the Leader and of his body, someone like Jean Corbon, in *Liturgie de source* (Paris: Cerf, 1980),[47] speaks unceasingly, with regard to the liturgy, of "the synergy of the Spirit and the Church." The two visions are not contradictory and both are necessary and true, but the second points toward what one could call an epicletic vision and practice of the liturgy. This pneumatological complement of a necessarily christic liturgy is shown most particularly in the new Eucharistic Prayers, whereas the Roman Canon used to have no epiclesis, at least none that was explicit. The epiclesis is not limited to the Eucharist. The whole of the Church's life is epicletic!

It is therefore by a renewal of pneumatology, without undermining the essential and very deeply rooted Christological aspect, that we are today, in accordance with the most ancient tradition, renewing an organic vision of the Church. This can take on much of what the Orthodox put under the difficult-to-translate term *sobornost*: communion, conciliarity, collegiality, being and living together in an organism of grace and love....

The fact that the whole Body is animated is shown also, today, by the innumerable instances of the resurgence of the Gospel in the lives of men and women. It is as if a hidden layer of water were

---

47. [trans.] ET: *The Wellspring of Worship*, trans. Matthew O'Connell (New York: Paulist, 1988).

coming to the surface in a multitude of places and becoming there, in each locale, a wellspring of life. The net result of this is that there is inserted into the midst of the frameworks, always present and active, of the ancient institution, a kind of Church from below, that comes to birth from the ground up. The Renewal in the Spirit is but one element of this bubbling up of living water. I have compared it to the extraordinary flourishing of initiatives that marked the life of Protestant communions during the nineteenth century, which Rouse and Neil describe as "voluntary movements."[48] Examples of these instances of resurgence of the Gospel correspond a little to what I have said about the charisms or talents given "for the common good," to contribute to the building up of the Body of Christ, the common task of ministry (Eph 4:12). Here, a couple welcomes delinquents or drug addicts; there a man or a woman starts a meeting focused on prayer or Bible study or ecumenism. Or better, they fan the flame of faith and of the praise of God where there was a desert. Or there are people who, animated by God's "love of mankind" (Titus 3:4), are involved in promoting justice, or opportunities for people, for development and liberation....

There has been speculation about whether the Western teaching about the *Filioque* has not inspired or supported an evolution of the Church in the direction of a predominance of hierarchical organization to the detriment of the role of the whole people, and in the direction of a rationalization of thought and of life to the detriment of Christian liberty, of inspiration, and of a more global and organic feeling. The Orthodox readily hold this polemical position. What they say rings true enough for a certain influence, or at least a certain coherence, to be conceded, but it is also sufficiently open to dispute for one to regard that causal connection as doubtful.[49] The difference between East and West in ecclesial vision and practice

---

48. R. Rouse and S. Neill, *History of the Ecumenical Movement* I (London: SPCK, 1958). [36]

49. See ES 3:271–76 [ET: *HS* 3:208–12] and *La Parole et le Souffle* [ET: *The Word and the Spirit*], ch. 7. [37]

arises from a great number of historical, cultural, and theological factors. The difference between their theological constructions of the mystery of the Trinity is but one of these factors. Yet things have their coherence and I admit that, within this coherence, the *Filioque* plays a part. However, it is more Christomonism than the *Filioque* that must be called into question.

I am not dealing here with the *Filioque* itself. I have done that elsewhere and so have others. But I am adamant about underscoring that, with or without the *Filioque*—and better with than without—Christology guarantees the well-being of pneumatology. Pneumatology without an operative Christology would be the sort of adventure about which the embodiments of Joachimism and the history of certain sects—the Brothers of the Free Spirit or others—give us an inkling. I have outlined the limits and disadvantages of a purely Christological model. The limits and disadvantages of a purely pneumatological model would perhaps be worse. The Word without the Breath would produce legalism; what would Breath without the Word yield? "No one knows whence the Spirit comes nor where the Spirit is going." Concretely, the Word is the form: the spoken Word, the doctrine, the structures. The truth is in the hinging of the two together. For, without Breath, the Word cannot emerge from the throat and the Gospel cannot fill the history that lasts until the *eschaton* [Congar writes "eschatologie"].[50]

---

50. Reread at this point the intervention of Bishop Ignace Hazim, Orthodox Patriarch of Lattakia, at the ecumenical conference in Uppsala, August 1968. The text is in *Irenikon* 42 (1968): 344–59; extracts are to be found in *ES* 2:51–52 [ET: *HS* 2:33–34]. [38]

Selected Bibliography

(in addition to sources listed in Bibliography at the end of Part Two)

1. Congar's Publications on the Holy Spirit (in chronological order)

"L'appel œcuménique et l'œuvre du Saint-Esprit." *La vie spirituelle* 82 (1950): 5–12. Reprinted in Yves M.-J. Congar. *Chrétiens en dialogue: Contributions catholiques à l'œcuménisme.* Unam Sanctam 50, 71–78. Paris: Cerf, 1964. ET: "The Call to Ecumenism and the Work of the Holy Spirit." In Yves M.-J. Congar. *Dialogue between Christians: Catholic Contributions to Ecumenism.* Translated by Philip Loretz, 100–106. London: Geoffrey Chapman, 1966.

"Le Saint-Esprit et le corps apostolique, réalisateurs de l'œuvre du Christ." *Revue des sciences philosophiques et théologiques* 36 (1952): 613–25 and 37 (1953): 24–48. Reprinted in Yves M.-J. Congar. *Esquisses du mystère de l'Église.* New ed. Unam Sanctam 8, 129–179. Paris: Cerf, 1953. ET: "The Holy Spirit and the Apostolic Body, Continuators of the Work of Christ." In Yves M.-J. Congar. *The Mystery of the Church: Studies by Yves Congar.* Translated by A. V. Littledale, 147–86. London: Geoffrey Chapman, 1960; "The Holy Spirit and the Apostolic College: Promoters of the Work of Christ." 2d rev. ed., 105–45. London: Geoffrey Chapman, 1965.

"L'Esprit-Saint dans l'Église." *Lumière et vie* 10 (June 1953): 51–74. Reprinted in Yves M.-J. Congar. *Les voies du Dieu vivant: Théologie et vie spirituelle,* 165–84. Paris: Cerf, 1962. ET: "The Holy Spirit in the Church." In Yves M.-J. Congar. *The Revelation of God.* Translated by A. Manson and L.C. Sheppard, 148–67. London: Darton, Longman and Todd, 1968.

La Pentecôte: Chartres 1956. Paris: Cerf, 1956. ET: "The Church and Pentecost." In Yves M.-J. Congar. *The Mystery of the Church: Studies by Yves*

Congar. Translated by A. V. Littledale, 1–57. London: Geoffrey Chapman, 1960. 2d rev. ed. 146–85. London: Geoffrey Chapman, 1965.

"Saint-Esprit et esprit de liberté." *Revue nouvelle* 29 (1959): 3–24. Reprinted in Yves, M.-J. Congar. *Si vous êtes mes témoins ... : Trois conférences sur laïcat, Église et monde,* 9–55. Paris: Cerf, 1959. ET: "Holy Spirit and Spirit of Freedom." In Yves M.-J. Congar. *Laity, Church and World: Three Addresses by Yves Congar.* Translated by Donald Attwater, 1–34. London: Geoffrey Chapman, 1960. Reprinted in *Yves M.-J. Congar, OP.* Edited by Martin Redfern. 11–46. Theologians Today. London / New York: Sheed & Ward, 1972.

"Le Saint-Esprit, sujet transcendant de la Tradition: Son actualité dans l'Église-Corps du Christ." In Yves M.-J. Congar. *La Tradition et les traditions: Essai théologique,* 101–9. Paris: Fayard, 1963. ET: "The Holy Spirit, the Transcendent Subject of Tradition, His Active Presence in the Church the Body of Christ." In *Tradition and Traditions: An Historical and a Theological Essay,* Part Two. Translated by Thomas Rainborough, 338–47. London: Burns & Oates, 1966. Reprinted San Diego, Calif.: Basilica Press / Needham Heights, Mass.: Simon & Schuster, 1997.

"Le Saint-Esprit, sujet transcendant de la Tradition." In Yves M.-J. Congar. *La Tradition et la vie de l'Église.* 2d ed. Traditions chrétiennes 18, 43–48. Paris: Cerf, 1984. First published 1963 by Fayard, Paris. ET: "The Holy Ghost: Transcendent Subject of Tradition." In Yves M.-J. Congar. *The Meaning of Tradition.* Translated by A. N. Woodrow, 51–58. Twentieth Century Encyclopedia of Catholicism 126. New York: Hawthorn Books, 1964. Reprinted with a foreword by Avery Cardinal Dulles, San Francisco: Ignatius Press, 2004, 51–58.

"Avant-propos." In I. de la Potterie et S. Lyonnet. *La vie selon l'Esprit, condition du chrétien,* 7–11. Paris: Cerf, 1965. ET: "Preface." In I. de la Potterie and S. Lyonnet. *The Christian Lives by the Spirit.* Translated by J. Morriss, v–ix. Staten Island, N.Y.: Alba House, 1971.

"Ecclesia ou communauté des chrétiens, sujet intégral de l'action liturgique." In *La liturgie après Vatican II.* Edited by Yves Congar. Unam Sanctam 66, 241–82. Paris: Cerf, 1967. ET: "The *Ecclesia* or Christian Community as a Whole Celebrates the Liturgy." In *At the Heart of Christian Worship: Liturgical Essays of Yves Congar.* Translated and edited by Paul Philibert, 15–68. Collegeville, Minn.: Liturgical Press, 2010.

"La pneumatologie dans la théologie catholique." *Revue des sciences philosophiques et théologiques* 51 (1967): 250–58.

"Saint-Esprit en théologie catholique." In *Vocabulaire œcuménique.* Edited by Yves Congar, 197–210. Paris: Cerf, 1970.

"Pneumatologie ou 'christomonisme' dans la tradition latine?" *Ephemerides theologicae Lovanienses* 45 (1969): 394–416. Reprinted in *Ecclesia a Spiritu Sancto edocta (Lumen gentium, 53): Mélanges théologiques, hommages à*

Mgr Gérard Philips. *Verzamelde theologische opstellen aangeboden aan Mgr. Gérard Philips*, 41–64. Bibliotheca ephemeridum theologicarum Lovaniensium 27. Gembloux: Duculot, 1970.

"Dans la communion et la communication du Saint-Esprit." *Unité des chrétiens* 1 (1971): 8. ET: "On the Communion and Communication of the Holy Spirit." Translated by Mark E. Ginter. *Forefront* 3 (Spring 1996): 27–28.

"Pneumatologie et théologie de l'Histoire." In *La théologie de l'Histoire: Herméneutique et eschatologie; Colloque Castelli 1971*, 61–70. Rome: Aubier, 1971.

"Renouvellement de l'esprit et réforme de l'institution." *Concilium* 73 (March 1972): 37–45. ET: "Renewal of the Spirit and Reform of the Institution." Translated by John Griffiths. In *Ongoing Reform of the Church*. Edited by Alois Muller and Norbert Greinacher, 39–49. *Concilium* 73 (New York: Herder and Herder, 1972).

"Actualité renouvelée du Saint-Esprit." *Lumen vitae* 27 (1972): 543–60. ET: "Renewed Actuality of the Holy Spirit." Translated by Olga Prendergast. *Lumen vitae* 28 (1973): 13–30.

"Actualité d'une pneumatologie." *Proche-Orient chrétien* 23 (1973): 121–32. Reprinted without notes in Yves M.-J. Congar. *Appelés à la vie*. Épiphanie, 69–82. Paris: Cerf, 1985. ET: "Pneumatology Today." Translated by William Burridge. *The American Ecclesiastical Review* 167 (1973): 435–49. Reprinted without notes as "The Spirit in Action." In Yves M.-J. Congar. *Called to Life*, 60–74. Slough: St. Paul Publications / New York: Crossroad Publishing, 1987.

"Charismatiques ou quoi?" *La Croix*. January 19, 1974. Reprinted in *ES* 2:207–20. ET: *HS* 2:161–72.

"Le Saint-Esprit dans la théologie thomiste de l'agir moral." In *L'agire morale: Atti del Congresso internazionale; Tommaso d'Aqino nel suo settimo centenario*, 9–19. Naples: Edizioni Domenicane Italiane, 1974. Reprinted in *Tommaso d'Aquino nel suo VII centenario: Congrès international Rome-Naples*, 17–24.4.1974, 175–87. Rome, 1976.

"Rénovation dans l'Esprit et vie religieuse." *La Croix*. July 12, 1974.

"La tri-unité de Dieu et l'Église." *La vie spirituelle* 12, no. 604 (August–September 1974): 687–703.

"De lastering tagen de Heilige Geest (Mt 9, 32–34: 12, 22–32; Mc 3, 20–30; Lc 11, 14–23; 12, 8–10)." In *Leven uit de Geest: Theologische Peilingen aangeboden aan Edward Schillebeeckx*, 17–31. Hilversum: Gooi en Sticht, 1974. ET: "Blasphemy against the Holy Spirit." Translated by Paul Burns. In *Experience of the Spirit; Healing and the Spirit*. Edited by Peter Huizing, William Bassett, Georges Combet, and Laureat Fabre, 47–57. *Concilium* 99 (New York: Seabury, 1974).

"Participation à questions sur le Renouveau charismatique." *La France catholique* 1480 (April 25, 1975): 18–19.

"Renouveau dans l'Esprit et institution ecclésiale: Mutuelle interrogation." *Recherches d'histoire et philosophie religieuses* 55 (1975): 143–56. Reprinted in *ES* 2:193–205. ET: *HS* 2:149–60.

"Bulletin de théologie: Aperçus de pneumatologie." *Revue des sciences philosophiques et théologiques* 62 (1978): 421–42.

"Méditation théologique sur la troisième Personne." *Proche-Orient chrétien* 29, nos. 3–4 (1979): 9–12. Reprinted in *ES* 3:193–205. ET: *HS* 3:144–54.

"S. Syméon le Nouveau Théologien: Une expérience de l'Esprit." *La vie spirituelle* 629 (Nov.–Dec. 1978): 864–79. Reprinted in *ES* 1:131–45. ET: *HS* 1:93–103.

"L'Eglise de Corinthe et les charismes d'après S. Paul. " *Tychique* 18 (1979): 27–31. Reprinted in *ES* 1:50–68. ET: *HS* 1:29–43.

"Pour une christologie pneumatologique." *Revue des sciences philosophiques et théologiques* 63 (1979): 435–42. Reprinted in *ES* 3:217–28. ET: *HS* 3:165–73.

Je Crois en l'Esprit Saint. 3 vols. Paris: Cerf, 1979–80. ET: *I Believe in the Holy Spirit*. Translated by David Smith. 3 vols. London: Geoffrey Chapman / New York: Seabury, 1983. Reprinted as part of Milestones in Catholic Theology Series. New York: Crossroad Herder, 1997.

"Chronique de pneumatologie." *Revue des sciences philosophiques et théologiques* 64 (1980): 445–51.

"Le monothéisme politique et le Dieu Trinité." *Nouvelle revue théologique* 103 (1981): 3–17.

"Sur la maternité en Dieu et la féminité du Saint-Esprit." *Escritos del Vedat* 11 (1981): 115–21. Reprinted in *ES* 3:206–18. ET: *HS* 3:155–64.

"Les implications christologiques et pneumatologiques de l'ecclésiologie de Vatican II." In *Les églises après Vatican II: Dynamisme et prospective; Actes du colloque international de Bologne, 1980*. Edited by G. Alberigo, 117–30. Théologie historique 51. Paris: Beauchesne, 1981. Reprinted in *Le concile de Vatican II: Son Église, peuple de Dieu et corps du Christ*, 163–76. Théologie historique 71. Paris: Beauchesne, 1984.

"Le Saint-Esprit dans la consécration et la communion selon la tradition occidentale." *Nicolaus* 9 (1981–82): 383–86. Reprinted in *ES* 3:320–30. ET: *HS* 3:250–57.

"Le Saint-Esprit dans les prières de sainte Catherine de Sienne." In *Atti del Congresso internazionale di studi Cateriniani, Siena-Roma 24–29 aprile 1980*, 333–37. Rome: Curia generalizia O.P., 1981.

"Renouveau charismatique et théologie du Saint-Esprit." *La vie spirituelle* 646 (Sep.–Oct. 1981): 735–49. Reprinted as "Théologie du Saint-Esprit et renouveau charismatique." In Yves M.-J. Congar. *Appelés à la vie*. Épiphanie, 83–94. Paris: Cerf, 1985. ET: "Theology of the Holy Spirit and Charismatic Renewal." In *Called to Life*. Translated by William Burridge, 75–87. Slough: St. Paul Publications / New York: Crossroad Publishing, 1987.

"Grace et pneumatologie." *Revue des sciences philosophiques et théologiques* 66 (1982): 128–36.

"Synthèse générale de la problématique pneumatologique: Réflexions et perspectives." In *La signification et l'actualité du IIe Concile œcuménique pour le monde chrétien d'aujourd'hui*, 365–76. Études théologiques de Chambésy 2. Chambésy and Genève: Éditions du Centre orthodoxe du Patriarcat œcuménique, 1982.

"Actualité de la Pneumatologie." In *Credo in Spiritum Sanctum: Atti del Congresso internazionale di pneumatologia*, 1:15–28. Vatican: Libreria Editrice, 1983.

Esprit de l'homme, Esprit de Dieu. Foi vivante 206. Paris: Cerf, 1983. Reprinted 1998.

"Pneumatologie dogmatique." In *Initiation à la pratique de la théologie*. Edited by B. Lauret and F. Refoulé, 2:483–516. Paris: Cerf, 1982.

La Parole et le Souffle. Jésus et Jésus-Christ 20. Paris: Desclée, 1984. ET: *The Word and the Spirit*. Translated by David Smith. London: Geoffrey Chapman, 1986.

"Le troisième article du symbole: L'impact de la pneumatologie dans la vie de l'Église." In *Dieu, Église, Société*. Edited by J. Doré, 287–309. Paris: Cerf, 1985.

"Introduction." In *L'Esprit Saint: Lettre encyclique de Jean Paul II, 'L'Esprit qui donne la vie,'* vii–xv. Paris: Cerf, 1986.

"Esprit de conseil et de sagesse." *Tychique* 82 (July 1986): 13–16.

2. Secondary Material on Congar and His Pneumatology

Beauchesne, Richard J. "Yves Congar Leaves Rich Legacy." *National Catholic Reporter* 31 (July 14, 1995): 2.

Chéno, Rémi. "Les retractationes d'Yves Congar sur le rôle de l'Esprit Saint dans les institutions ecclésiales." *Revue des sciences philosophiques et théologiques* 91 (2007): 265–84.

Congar, Yves M.-J., O.P. "My Path-Findings in the Theology of Laity and Ministries." *The Jurist* 32 (1972): 169–88.

———. "Poverty as an Act of Faith." Translated by V. Green. In *The Poor and the Church*. Edited by Norbert Greinacher and Alois Müller, 97–105. Concilium 104 (New York: Seabury, 1977).

———. "Reflections on Being a Theologian." Translated by Marcus Lefébure, OP. *New Blackfriars* 62 (1981): 405–9.

Dulles, Avery. "*In Memoriam*: Yves Congar: In Appreciation." *America* 173, no. 2 (July 15, 1995): 6–7.

Famerée, Joseph. *L'Ecclésiologie d'Yves Congar avant Vatican II: Histoire et*

Église. Analyse et reprise critique. Bibliotheca Ephemeridum Theologicarum Lovaniensium 107. Louvain: Peeters Press, 1992

———. "Formation et ecclésiologie du 'premier' Congar." In *Cardinal Yves Congar 1904-1995: Actes du colloque réuni à Rome les 3-4 juin 1996.* Edited by André Vauchez, 51-60. Paris: Cerf, 1999.

——— and Gilles Routhier. *Yves Congar.* Initiations aux théologiens. Paris: Cerf, 2008.

Flynn, Gabriel, ed. *Yves Congar: Theologian of the Church.* Louvain Theological & Pastoral Monographs 32. Louvain: Peeters Press / W. B. Eerdmans, 2005.

———. *Yves Congar's Vision of the Church in a World of Unbelief.* Aldershot: Ashgate, 2004.

Ford, David F., ed. *The Modern Theologians: An Introduction to Christian Theology in the Twentieth Century.* 2d ed. Cambridge / Oxford: Blackwell, 1997.

Fouilloux, Étienne. "Congar, témoin de l'Église de son temps (1930-1960)." In *Cardinal Yves Congar 1904-1995: Actes du colloque réuni à Rome les 3-4 juin 1996.* Edited by André Vauchez, 71-91. Paris: Cerf, 1999.

———. "Friar Yves, Cardinal Congar, Dominican: Itinerary of a Theologian." Translated by Christian Yves Dupont. *U.S. Catholic Historian* 17 (Spring 1999): 63-90.

Ginter, Mark E. "The Holy Spirit and Morality: A Dynamic Alliance," *Catholic Theological Society of America Proceedings* 51 (1996): 165-79.

———. "Special Program, Centenarian Commemoration: A Time to Reminisce, a Time to Celebrate Four Theological Giants of the 20th Century." CTSA Banquet, June 12, 2004. *Catholic Theological Society of America Proceedings* 59 (2004): 161-66.

Granfield, Patrick. "Interview with Yves Congar." *America* (May 6, 1967): 676-80.

Groppe, Elizabeth Teresa. "The Contribution of Yves Congar's Theology of the Holy Spirit." *Theological Studies* 62 (2001): 451-78.

———. *Yves Congar's Theology of the Holy Spirit.* New York: Oxford University Press, 2004.

Henn, William. *The Hierarchy of Truths according to Yves Congar, OP.* Rome: Gregorian University Press, 1987.

———. "Yves Congar, OP (1904-95)." *America* 173 (Aug. 12, 1995): 23-25.

Holotik, Gerhard. *Die pneumatische Note der Moraltheologie: Ein ergänzender Beitrag zu gegenwärtigen Bemühungen im Rahmen der katholischen Sittlichkeitslehre.* Vienna: VWGÖ, 1984.

———. "Spiritualität und Moraltheologie-Pneumatologie und Ethik." In *Pneumatologie und Spiritualität.* Edited by Walter Kirchschläger, 157-81. Theologische Berichte 16. Zürich: Benziger, 1987.

Jossua, Jean-Pierre. "La mort du 'pere' de Vatican II," *Le Monde* (24 juin 1995): 1, 13.

———. *Yves Congar: Theology in the Service of God's People.* Translated by Sr. Mary Jocelyn, OP. Chicago: The Priory Press, 1968.

Kerr, Fergus. *Twentieth-Century Catholic Theologians: From Neoscholasticism to Nuptial Mysticism.* Malden, Mass. / Oxford / Carlton, Victoria: Blackwell, 2007.

Koskela, Douglas M. *Ecclesiality and Ecumenism: Yves Congar and the Road to Unity.* Milwaukee, Wisc.: Marquette University Press, 2008.

LeGrand, Hervé, OP. "Yves Congar (1904–1995): Une passion pour l'unité," *Nouvelle revue théologique* 126 (2004): 529–54.

MacDonald, Timothy I. *The Ecclesiology of Yves Congar: Foundational Themes.* Lanham, Md.: University Press of America, 1984.

McBrien, Richard P. "*I Believe in the Holy Spirit.* The Role of Pneumatology in Yves Congar's Theology." In *Yves Congar: Theologian of the Church.* Edited by Gabriel Flynn, 303–27. Louvain Theological & Pastoral Monographs 32. Louvain: Peeters Press / W. B. Eerdmans, 2005.

———. "Red Hat Did Not Undo Vatican Harm." *National Catholic Reporter* 31 (Sept. 8, 1995): 2.

Nichols, Aidan. "An Yves Congar Bibliography 1967–1987." *Angelicum* 66 (1989): 422–66.

———. *Yves Congar.* London: Geoffrey Chapman / Wilton, Conn.: Morehouse-Barlow, 1989.

Nissiotis, Nikos A. "Visions of the Future of Ecumenism." *Greek Orthodox Theological Review* 26 (Winter 1981): 280–304.

Oelrich, Anthony. *A Church Fully Engaged: Yves Congar's Vision of Ecclesial Authority.* Collegeville, Minn.: Liturgical Press / Michael Glazier, 2011.

O'Meara, Thomas. "Ecumenist of Our Times: Yves Congar." *Mid-Stream* 27 (Jan. 1988): 67–73.

———. "'Raid on the Dominicans': The Repression of 1954." *America* 170 (Feb. 5, 1994): 8–16.

———. "Reflections on Yves Congar and Theology in the United States." U.S. Catholic *Historian* 17 (Spring 1999): 91–105.

Pellitero, Ramiro. *La teología del laicado en la obra de Yves Congar.* Pamplona: Navarra Gráfica Ediciones, 1995.

Philibert, Paul J. "Yves Congar: Theologian, Ecumenist, and Visionary." U.S. Catholic *Historian* 17 (Spring 1999): 116–20.

Quattrochi, Pietro. "General Bibliography of Fr. Yves M-J. Congar." In *Yves Congar: Theology in the Service of God's People.* Edited by Jean-Pierre Jossua, 185–241. Chicago: The Priory Press, 1968.

Radcliffe, Timothy, OP. "*In Memoriam* Yves-Marie Congar, OP." *Doctrine and Life* 25 (Sept. 1995): 469–73.

Skira, Jaroslav Z. "Breathing with Two Lungs: The Church in Yves Congar and John Zizioulas." In *In God's Hands: Essays on the Church and Ecumenism in Honor of Michael A. Fahey, S.J.* Edited by Jaroslav Z. Skira and Michael S. Attridge, 283–306. Bibliotheca ephemeridum theologicarum Lovaniensium 199. Leuven: Peeters and Leuven University Press, 2006.

Van Vliet, Cornelis Th. M. *Communio sacramentalis: Das Kirchenverständis von Yves Congar—genetisch und systematisch betrachtet.* Mainz: Matthias-Grünewald, 1995.

Vauchez, André, ed. *Cardinal Yves Congar 1904–1995: Actes du colloque réuni à Rome les 3–4 juin 1996.* Paris: Cerf, 1999.

Vezin, Jean-Marie. "Une présentation raisonnée de la bibliographie d'Yves Congar." *Transversalités: Revue de l'Institut catholique de Paris* 98 (2006): 37–59.

Wedig, Mark, "The Fraternal Context of Congar's Achievement: The Platform for a Renewed Catholicism at Les Éditions du Cerf (1927–1954)." *U.S. Catholic Historian* 17 (Spring 1999): 106–15.

Willebrands, Cardinal Johannes. "Forum: Yves Congar, OP, Man of Unity." *Doctrine and Life* 45 (March 1995): 247.

Williams, A. N. "Congar's Theology of the Laity." In *Yves Congar: Theologian of the Church.* Edited by Gabriel Flynn, 135–59. Louvain Theological & Pastoral Monographs 32. Louvain: Peeters Press / W. B. Eerdmans, 2005.

"Yves Congar, maître en théologie." Special issue, *Transversalités: Revue de l'Institut catholique de Paris* 98 (2006).

3. Modern Sources to Which Congar Refers in the Works Translated in This Book (in addition to those listed in the bibliography at the end of Part Two)

Abert, F. P. *Das Wesen des Christentums nach Thomas von Aquin: Festrede zur Feier des dreihundert und neunzehnjährigen Bestehens der Königl. Julius-Maximilians-Universität Würzburg gehalten an 11. Mai 1901.* Würzburg: H. Stürtz, 1901.

Acerbi, A. *Due ecclesiologie: Ecclesia iuridica e ecclesiologia di communione nella "Lumen gentium."* Bologna: Editione Dehoniane, 1975.

Alberigo. G., ed. *Les églises après Vatican II: Dynamisme et prospective; Actes du colloque international de Bologne, 1980.* Théologie historique 51. Paris: Beauchesne, 1981.

Alszeghy, Z. *Nova creatura: La nozione della grazia nei commentari medievali di S. Paolo.* Analecta Gregoriana 81. Rome: apud aedes Universitatis Gregorianae, 1956.

Backes, I. *Die Christologie des hl. Thomas v. A. und die griechischen Kirchenväter.* Paderborn: Schöningh, 1931.

Barauna, G. ed. *L'Église de Vatican II.* Unam Sanctam 51b. Paris: Cerf, 1966.
Bardy, Gustave. "Dons du Saint-Esprit, 1: Chez les Pères." *DictSpir.* 3:1579–87.
Baumstark, A. *Liturgie comparée.* 3d ed. Chevetogne: Éditions de Chevetogne, 1953. ET: *Comparative Liturgy.* Revised by Bernard Botte. English edition by F. L. Cross. Westminster, Md.: Newman Press, 1958.
Bernard, P. "Communion des saints, 1: Son aspect dogmatique et historique." *DTC.* 3:429–54.
Berresheim, H. *Christus als Haupt der Kirche nach dem heilegen Bonaventura: Ein Beitrag zur Theologie der Kirche.* Bonn: Ludwig, 1939.
Blic, J. de. "Pour l'histoire de la théologie des dons avant s. Thomas." *Revue d'ascétique et de mystique* 22 (1946): 117–79.
Bobrinskoy, B. "Liturgie et ecclésiologie trinitaire de saint Basile." In *Eucharisties d'Orient et d'Occident,* 2:197–240. Lex orandi 47. Paris: Cerf, 1970.
Bolotov, V. "27 Thesen über das Filioque." *Revue internationale de théologie* 6 (1898): 681–712. French translation in *Istina* 17 (1972): 261–89.
Bori, P. C. *Koinōnia: L'idea della communione nell'ecclesiologia recente e nel Nuovo Testamento.* Brescia: Paideia, 1972.
Borne, E. "Liberté spirituelle et liberté temporelle." In *L'Église et la liberté: Semaine des intellectuels catholiques de Paris, May 4–10, 1952.* Paris: Flore, 1952.
Bosc, J. et al., *Vatican II: Points de vue de théologiens protestants,* Unam Sanctam 64, 109–27. Paris: Cerf, 1967.
Cabrol, F. "Épiclèse." *Dictionnaire d'archéologie chrétienne et de liturgie.* Vol. 5, bk. 1, *Encaustique—Feu.* Edited by Fernand Cabrol and Henri Leclercq, 142–84. Paris: Letouzey et Ané, 1922.
Cazelles, H., P. Evdokimov, and A. Greiner, *Le mystère de l'Esprit-Saint.* Tours: Mame, 1968.
Chavasse, A. "L'épiclèse eucharistique dans les anciennes liturgies orientales: Une hypothèse d'interprétation." *Mélanges de science religieuse* 3 (1946): 197–206.
Cerfaux, Lucien. *Le chrétien dans la théologie paulinienne.* Lectio divina 33. Paris: Cerf, 1962. ET: *The Christian in the Theology of St. Paul.* Translated by Lilian Soiron. New York: Herder, 1967.
Chenu, M.-D. "Les signes des temps." *Nouvelle revue théologique* 87 (1965): 29–39.
———. "La théologie de la loi ancienne selon s. Thomas." *Revue thomiste* 61 (1961): 485–97.
Chevallier, M.-A. *Souffle de Dieu: Le Saint-Esprit dans le Nouveau Testament.* Vol. 1. Paris: Beauchesne, 1978.
Clément, O. "Quelques remarques d'un Orthodoxe sur la constitution *De ecclesia.*" *Oecumenica* 1 (1966): 97–116.

D'Agostino, F. "Lex indita e lex scripta: La dottrina della legge divina positiva (lex nova) secondo s. Tommaso d'Aquino." In *Atti del Congresso internazionale di diritto canonico "La Chiesa dopo il Concilio," Roma, 14–19 gennaio, 1970*, 2: 401–15. Milan: A. Giuffrè, 1972.

De Halleux, A. "La profession de l'Esprit dans la confession de Constantinople." *Revue théologique de Louvain* 10 (1979): 5–39.

de Lubac, Henri. *Corpus mysticum: L'Eucharistie et l'Église au moyen âge.* Théologie 3. Paris: Aubier, 1944. 2d ed., 1949. ET: *Corpus mysticum: The Eucharist and the Church in the Middle Ages.* London: SCM, 2006.

———. *Les églises particulières dans l'Église universelle.* Paris: Aubier, 1971.

———. *Exégèse médiévale: Les quatre sens de l'Écriture.* 2 vols. in 4 bks. Paris: Aubier, 1961.

Dumoutet, É. *Le Christ selon la chair et la vie liturgique au moyen âge.* Paris: Beauchesne, 1932.

———. *Corpus domini: Aux sources de la piété eucharistique médiévale.* Paris: Beauchesne, 1942.

Dupont, J. *Gnōsis: La connaissance religieuse dans les épitres pauliniennes.* Paris: Gabalda / Louvain: Nauwelarts, 1949.

Ebeling, G. *Dogmatik des christlichen Glaubens.* Vol. 3, *Der Glaube an Gott den Vollender der Welt.* Tübingen: Mohr, 1979.

Elert, W. *Abendmahl und Kirchengemeinschaft in der alten Kirche, hauptsächlich des Ostens.* Berlin: Lutherisches Verlagshaus, 1954. ET: *Eucharist and Church Fellowship in the First Four Centuries.* Translated by N. E. Nagel. St. Louis, Mo.: Concordia, 1966.

Émery, Pierre-Yves. *Le Saint-Esprit présence de communion.* Taizé: Les Presses de Taizé, 1980.

Gardeil, A. "Dons du Saint-Esprit." *DTC.* Vol. 4, bk. 2, 1728–81.

———. *La structure de l'âme et l'expérience mystique.* 2d ed. Paris: Gabalda, 1927.

Geiselmann, J. R. *Die Abendmahlslehre an der Wende der christlichen Spätantike zum Frühmittelalter: Isidor von Sevilla und das Sakrament der Eucharistie.* Munich: Max Hueber, 1933.

Gillon, L. B. "L'imitation du Christ et la morale de s. Thomas." *Angelicum* 36 (1959): 263–86.

Goldammer, K. *Die eucharistische Epiklese in der mittelalterlichen abendländischen Frömmigheit.* Bottrop, Westphalia: Buch und Kunstdruckerei, 1941.

Grabmann, M. *Die Lehre des hl. Thomas von Aquin von der Kirche als Gotteswerk.* Regensberg: Manz, 1903.

Grillmeier, A. "Konzil und Rezeption: Methodische Bemerkungen zu einem Thema der ökumenischen Diskussion der Gegenwart." *Theologie und Philosophie* 45 (1970): 321–51.

Gy, P. M. "Eucharistie et 'Ecclesia' dans le premier vocabulaire de la liturgie chrétienne." *La Maison-Dieu* 130 (1977): 19-34.

Hazim, Bishop. "Address Opening the Assembly of the World Council of Churches, August 1968." *Foi et vie* (November-December 1968): 12-15 or *Irénikon* 42 (1968): 349-51.

Hamer, J. *L'Église est une communion*. Unam Sanctam 40. Paris: Cerf, 1962.

Hauck, F. "*Koinōn-* im Neuen Testament." *TWNT* 3: 804-10. ET: *TDNT* 3: 804-9.

Havet, J. "Les sacrements et le rôle du Saint-Esprit d'après Isidore de Séville." *Ephemerides theologicae Lovanienses* 16 (1939): 32-93.

Haya-Prats, G. *L'Esprit force de l'Église: Sa mesure et son activité d'après les Actes des Apôtres*. Paris: Cerf, 1973.

Héris, Ch.-V. *Le mystère du Christ*. Paris: Éditions de la Revue des Jeunes, 1927. ET: *The Mystery of Christ: Our Head, Priest and King*. Translated by Denis Fahey. Westminster, Md.: Newman Press, 1950.

Hryniewicz, W. "Der pneumatologische Aspekt der Kirche aus orthodoxer Sicht." *Catholica* 31 (1977): 122-50.

International Catholic/Methodist Commission. "Final Report: 3rd Cycle of Conversations (1977-1981)." *Service d'information* (Vatican Secretariat for Promoting Christian Unity) 46, no. 2 (1981): 87-100. ET: "The Honolulu Report." In *Growth in Agreement: Reports and Agreed Statements of Ecumenical Conversations at a World Level*. Edited by Harding Meyer and Lukas Vischer, 367-87. Ecumenical Documents 2. New York: Paulist / Geneva: World Council of Churches, 1982.

Jaschke, N.-J. *Der Heilige Geist im Bekenntnis der Kirche: Eine Studie zur Pneumatologie des Irenäus von Lyon im Ausgang vom altchrislichen Glaubensbekenntnis*. Münsterische Beiträge zur Theologie 40. Münster: Aschendorff, 1977.

John XXIII. "'Ecclesia Christi lumen gentium': Message de S. S. Jean XXIII au monde entier un mois avant l'ouverture du concile (11 Sept. 1962)." *La documentation catholique* 59, no. 1385 (October 7, 1962): 1217-22.

Jugie, M. *De forma Eucharistiae, de epiclesibus ecclesiasticis*. Rome: Officium Libri Catholici, 1943.

Jungmann, J. "Die Gnadenlehre im Apostolishen Glaubensbekentnis." *Zeitschrift für katholische Theologie* 50 (1926): 196-217.

Kasper, Walter. *Dogme et Évangile*. Tournai-Paris: Casterman, 1967.

Kasper, Walter and Gerhard Sauter. *Kirche, Ort des Geistes*. Ökumenische Forschungen: Ergänzende Abteilung; Kleine ökumenische Schriften, 8. Freiburg: Herder, 1976.

Kretchmar, G. "Le développement de la doctrine du Saint-Esprit du Nouveau Testament à Nicée." *Verbum caro* 22, no. 88 (1968): 5-55.

Kühn, U. *Via caritas: Theologie des Gesetzes bei Thomas von Aquin*. Göttingen: Vandenhoeck & Ruprecht, 1965.

LaBourdette, M.-Michel. "Dons du Saint-Esprit, 4: Saint Thomas et la théologie thomiste." *DictSpir.* 3:1610–35.

Lachaga, J.-M. *Église particulière et minorités ethniques: Jalons pour l'évangélisation des peoples minoritaires.* Paris: Centurion, 1978.

Laminski, A. "Die Entdeckung der pneumatologischen Dimension der Kirche durch das Konzil und ihre Bedeutung." In *Sapienter ordinare: Festgabe Erich Kleineidem.* Edited by Fritz Hoffman et al., 392–403. Erfurt Theologische Studien 24. Leipzig: St. Benno, 1969.

Landgraf, A. "Die Lehre vom geheimnisvollen Leib Christi in den frühen Paulinenkommentaren und der Frühscholastik." *Divus Thomas* (Fr.) 24 (1946): 217–48, 393–428; 25 (1947): 365–94; 26 (1948): 160–80, 291–323, 395–434.

Lanne, E. "L'Église locale et l'Église universelle." *Irénikon* 43 (1970): 481–511.

la Potterie, Ignace de. "L'arrière fond du thème johannique de la vérité." *Studia Evangelica: Papers Presented to the International Congress on the Four Gospels Held at Christ Church, Oxford, 1957,* 73:277–94. Berlin: Akademie-Verlag, 1959.

———. "L'onction du Christ." *Nouvelle revue théologique* 80 (1958): 225–52.

Lebreton, J. *Histoire du dogme de la Trinité.* Vol. 1. 4th ed. Paris: Beauchesne, 1919.

Lécuyer, J. *Le sacerdoce dans le mystère du Christ.* Lex orandi 24. Paris: Cerf, 1956.

Legrand, H.-M. "Inverser Babel, mission de l'Église." *Spiritus* 63 (1970): 323–46.

———. "Pour être catholique, l'Église doit être particulière." *Cahiers saint Dominique* 127 (April 1972): 346–54.

———. "La présidence de l'Eucharistie selon la tradition ancienne." *Spiritus* 69 (1977): 409–31.

———. "Le sens théologique des élections épiscopales d'après leur déroulement dans l'Église ancienne." *Concilium* 77 (1972): 41–50.

———. "Synodes et conseils de l'après-concile." *Nouvelle revue théologique* 98 (1976): 193–216.

Le Guillou, M.-J. "Église et 'communion.'" *Istina* 6 (1959): 33–82.

Lisiecki, S. "Die gratia capitis nach Alexander von Hales." *Jahrbuch für Philosophie und spekulative Theologie* 27 (1913): 343–404.

Lyonnet, S. "Liberté chrétienne et loi de l'Esprit selon S. Paul." *Christus* 4 (1954): 6–27. Reprinted in *La vie selon l'Esprit, condition du chrétien.* Paris: Cerf, 1965. 169–95. ET: *St. Paul, Liberty and Law.* Rome: Pontificio Instituto Biblico, 1962.

Manning, Henry Edward Cardinal. *The Temporal Mission of the Holy Ghost, or Reason and Revelation.* London: Longmans, Green, 1865.

Margerie, Bertrand de. *La Trinité chrétienne dans l'histoire.* Théologie historique 31. Paris: Beauchesne, 1975. ET: *The Christian Trinity in History.*

Translated by Edmund J. Fortman. Studies in Historical Theology 1. Still River, Mass.: St. Bede's Publications, 1982.

Marliangeas, B.-D. *Clés pour une théologie du ministère:* "In persona Christi," "in persona Ecclesiae." Théologie historique 51. Paris: Beauchesne, 1978.

———. "'In persona Christi,' 'in persona Ecclesiae'." In *La liturgie après Vatican II*, 283–88. Unam Sanctam 66. Paris: Cerf, 1967.

Martins, José Saraiva, ed. *Credo in Spiritum Sanctum: Atti del Congresso teologico internazionale di pneumatologia in occasione del 1600o anniversario del 1 Concilio de Constantinopoli e dei 1550o anniversario del Concilio Efeso, Roma, 22–26 marzo, 1982*. 2 vols. Teologia e filosofia 6. Città del Vaticano: Libreria ed. Vaticana, 1983.

McDonnell, Kilian. *Charismatic Renewal and the Churches*. New York: Seabury, 1976.

Merleau-Ponty, M. "Foi et bonne foi." In *Sens et non-sens*, 305–21. Paris: Nagel, 1948. ET: *Sense and Non-Sense*. Translated and with a preface by Hubert L. Dreyfus and Patricia Allen Dreyfus, 172–81. Evanston, Ill.: Northwestern University Press, 1964.

Mersch, E. *Le Corps mystique du Christ: Études de théologie historique*. 2d ed. Brussels and Paris: Desclée de Brouwer, 1936.

Michel, A. "Trinité (missions et habitation des personnes de la)." *DTC*. Vol. 15, bk. 2, 1830–55.

Möhler, J. A. *La symbolique*. 2d ed. Translated by F. Lachat. Paris: L. Vivès, 1852–53. ET: *Symbolism: Exposition of the Doctrinal Differences between Catholics and Protestants as Evidenced by Their Symbolical Writings*. Translated by James Burton Robertson. Introduction by Michael J. Himes. New York: Crossroad, 1997.

———. *L'unité*. (German edition published in 1825.) ET: *Unity in the Church or the Principle of Catholicism: Presented in the Spirit of the Church Fathers of the First Three Centuries*. Edited and translated with an introduction by Peter C. Erb. Washington, D.C.: The Catholic University of America Press, 1996.

Moeller, C., and G. Philips. *Grâce et oecuménisme*. Chevetogne: Éditions de Chevetogne, 1957.

Monneron, Jean Louis et al. *L'Église: Institution et foi*. Bruxelles: Facultés universitaires Saint-Louis, 1979.

Moretti, Roberto. "Inhabitation, 2: Réflection théologique." *DictSpir*. Vol. 7, bk. 2, 1745–57.

Mouroux, J. *Le mystère du temps*. Théologie 50. Paris: Aubier, 1962.

Mühlen, H. *Morgen wird Einheit sein: Das kommende Konzil aller Christen, Ziel der getrennten Kirchen*. Paderborn: Schöningh, 1974.

Mura, E. *Le Corps Mystique du Christ*. 2 vols. Paris: Blot, 1934.

Nautin, P. *Hippolyte, Contre les hérésies, fragment: Étude et édition critique*. Paris: Cerf, 1949.

———. *Je crois à l'Esprit dans la sainte Église pour la résurrection de la chair.* Unam Sanctam 17. Paris: Cerf, 1947.

Nissiotis, Nikos A. "The Main Ecclesiological Problem of the Second Vatican Council and the Position of the Non-Roman Churches Facing It." *Journal of Ecumenical Studies* 2 (1965): 31–62.

———. "La pneumatologie ecclésiologique au service de l'unité de l'Église." *Istina* 12 (1967): 323–40.

———. "Pneumatologie orthodoxe." In *Le Saint-Esprit*, 85–106. Geneva: Labor et fides / Paris: Librairie protestante, 1963.

Oulton, J. E. L. "The Apostles' Creed and Belief Concerning the Church." *Journal of Theological Studies* (1938): 239–43.

Orbe, A. *La unción del Verbo.* Estudios Valentinianos 3. *Analecta Gregoriana* 113. Rome: Libreria editrice dell'Università Gregoriana, 1961.

Paul VI. "Discours prononcée par S. S. Paul VI lors de l'ouverture de la deuxième session du concile." *La documentation catholique* 60, no. 1410 (Oct. 20, 1963): 1345–61. ET: "At the Opening of the Second Session of the Ecumenical Council." *The Pope Speaks* 9, no. 2 (1964): 129, 130.

———. *Marialis cultus* (February 2, 1974). *AAS* 66 (1974): 113–68. ET: "Devotion to the Virgin Mary." *The Pope Speaks* 19, no. 1 (1974/1975): 49–87.

Philips, G. "L'influence du Christ-Chef sur son corps mystique suivant saint Augustin." In *Augustinus magister: Congrès international augustinien, Paris, 21–24 septembre 1954*, 2:805–15. Paris: Études augustiniennes / Besançon: Imprimerie de l'Est, 1954.

Pius XII. *Mystici corporis. AAS* 35 (1943): 193–248. ET: *Mystici Corporis: Encyclical Letter of Pope Pius XII On the Mystical Body of Christ.* In *Selected Documents of His Holiness Pope Pius XII 1939–1958.* Washington, D.C.: National Catholic Welfare Conference, 1958.

———. *Mediator Dei. AAS* 39 (1947): 521–95. ET: *Encyclical Letter of His Holiness Pius XII on the Sacred Liturgy.* In *Selected Documents of His Holiness Pope Pius XII 1939–1958.* Washington, D.C.: National Catholic Welfare Conference, 1958.

Przywara, E. "Das Dogma von der Kirche: Eine Aufbau." *Scholastik* 19 (1944).

Rahner, K. *Dieu Trinité, fondement transcendant de l'histoire du salut.* Mysterium salutis 6. Paris: Cerf, 1971. ET: *The Trinity.* Translated by Joseph Donceel. New York: Herder and Herder, 1970.

———. *Éléments dynamiques dans l'Église.* Paris: Desclée de Brouwer, 1967. ET: *The Dynamic Element in the Church. Quaestiones disputatae* 12. Translated by W. J. O'Hara. Freiburg: Herder / Montreal: Palm, 1964.

———. "Das neue Bild der Kirche." *Schriften zur Theologie*, 8:329–54. Einsiedeln: Benziger, 1967. ET: "The New Image of the Church." In *Theological Investigations.* Vol. 10, *Writings of 1965–67, 2.* Translated by David Bourke, 3–28. London: Darton, Longman and Todd, 1973.

———. "Réflections théologiques sur l'Incarnation." *Écrits théologiques*

3:81–101. Translated by Gaëtan Daoust. Textes et études théologiques. Paris: Desclée de Brouwer, 1963; also *Sciences ecclésiastiques* 12 (1960): 5–19. ET: "On the Theology of the Incarnation." In *Theological Investigations*. Vol. 4, *More Recent Writings*. Translated by Kevin Smyth, 105–20. Baltimore: Helicon / London: Darton, Longman and Todd, 1966.

Refoulé, F. "L'Église et le Saint-Esprit chez Luther et dans la théologie catholique." *Revue des sciences philosophiques et théologiques* 48 (1964): 428–70.

Reid, J. K. S. "Le Saint Esprit et le movement oecuménique." *Lumière et vie* 13/67 (1964): 65–86.

Rodriguez, Isaias. "Lévitation." *DictSpir.* 9:738–41.

Rosato, Philip J. "Called by God in the Holy Spirit: Pneumatological Insights into Ecumenism." *The Ecumenical Review* 30 (1978): 110–26.

Rouse, R. and S. Neill. *History of the Ecumenical Movement.* Vol. 1. London: SPCK, 1958.

Salaville, S. "Épiclèse eucharistique." *DTC.* Vol. 5, bk. 1, 194–300.

Salet, G. "La loi dans nos cœurs." *Nouvelle revue théologique* 79 (1957): 449–62 and 561–78.

Schell, H. *Das Wirken des dreieinigen Gottes.* Mainz: Kirchheim, 1885.

Schlier, Heinrich. "*Parrēsia.*" *TWNT* 5: 869–84. ET: *TDNT* 5: 871–86.

Schlink, Edmund. "Die Struktur der dogmatischen Aussage als ökumenisches Problem." *Kerygma und Dogma* 3 (1957): 251–306.

Schniewind, Julius and Gerhard Friedrich. "*Epaggellō* im NT / *epaggelma* / *proepaggelomai.*" *TWNT* 2: 577–82. ET: *TDNT* 2:581–86.

Siegwalt, G. *La loi, chemin du salut: Étude sur la signification de la loi de l'Ancien Testament.* Bibliothèque théologique. Neuchâtel and Paris: Delachâux & Niestlé, 1972.

La signification et actualité du 2e concile œcuménique pour le monde chrétien d'aujourd'hui. Les études théologiques de Chambésy 2. Chambésy: Éditions du Centre orthodoxe du patriarcat œcuménique, 1982.

Šilić, R. *Christus und die Kirche: Ihr Verhältnis nach der Lehre des Heilegen Bonaventura.* Breslau: Müller und Seiffert, 1938.

Smit, G. C. "Épiclèse et théologie des sacrements." *Mélanges de science religieuse* 15 (1958): 95–136.

Stolz, A. *De Sanctissima Trinitate.* Freiburg im Briesgau: Herder, 1941.

Théophanie Series. Paris: Desclée de Brouwer, 1982–.

Thielicke, H. *Der evangelische Glaube: Grundzüge der Dogmatik.* Vol. 3, *Theologie des Geistes.* Tübingen: Mohr, 1978. ET: *Theology of the Holy Spirit.* Translated and edited by Geoffrey Bromiley. Edinburgh: T & T Clark, 1982.

Tillard, J.-M. R. *L'Eucharistie: Pâque de l'Église.* Unam Sanctam 44. Paris: Cerf, 1964. ET: *The Eucharist: Pasch of God's People.* Translated by Dennis L. Wienk. New York: Alba House, 1967.

Tromp, Sebastian. *Corpus Christi quod est Ecclesia*, Vol. 1. Romae: Aedes Universitatis Gregorianae, 1937. 2d ed. 1946.

———. "L'Esprit Saint, 4: Esprit Saint âme de l'Église." *DictSpir*. Vol. 4, bk. 2, 1296–1302.

Tschipke, T. *Die Menschheit Christi als Heilsorgan der Gottheit: Unter besonderer Berücksichtigung der Lehre des Heiligen Thomas von Aquin.* Freiburg: Herder, 1940.

Turrado, L. "El bautismo '*in Spiritu sancto et ignis*'." In *Miscellanea biblica A. Fernandes. Estudios eclesiásticos* 34, nos. 134–35 (1960): 807–18.

Tyszkiewicz, S. *La sainteté de l'Église christoconforme: Ébauche d'une ecclésiologie unioniste*. Rome: Pontificium institutum orientalium studiorum, 1945.

Useros Carretero, M. *"Statuta Ecclesiae" y "sacramenta Ecclesiae" en la eclesiología de s. Tomás de Aquino*. Analecta Gregoriana 119. Rome: Libreria editrice dell'Università Gregoriana, 1962.

Vagaggini, C. *Initiation théologique à la liturgie*. 2 vols. Bruges: Apostolat liturgique / Paris: Société liturgique, 1959–63. ET: (based on 4th Italian edition) *Theological Dimensions of the Liturgy*. Translated by Leonard J. Doyle and W. A. Jurgens. Collegeville, Minn.: Liturgical Press, 1976.

Vandenbroucke, François. "Dons du Saint-Esprit, 2: Le moyen âge." *DictSpir*. 3:1587–1603.

———. "Esprit-Saint, 3: Dans la liturgie." *DictSpir*. Vol. 4, bk. 2, 1283–96.

Vanhoye, A. *Prêtres anciens, prêtre nouveau selon le Nouveau Testament*. Paris: Éditions du Seuil, 1980. ET: *Old Testament Priests and the New Priest according to the New Testament*. Translated by J. Bernard Orchard. Petersham, Mass.: St. Bede's Publications, 1980.

Vauthier, E. "Le Saint-Esprit, principe de l'unité de l'Église d'après saint Thomas d'Aquin: Corps mystique et habitation du Saint-Esprit." *Mélanges de sciences religieuses* 5 (1948): 175–96; 6 (1949): 57–80.

Vonier, A. *L'Esprit et l'épouse*. Translated by K. Lainé and B. Limal. Unam Sanctam 16. Paris: Cerf, 1947. English original: *The Spirit and the Bride*. London: Burns, Oates and Washbourne, 1935.

4. Patristic and Medieval Sources to Which Congar Refers in the Works Translated in this Book (in addition to those listed in the bibliography at the end of Part Two)

Augustine of Hippo. *De Trinitate*. In PL 42:821–1098. ET: *The Trinity*. Translation, introduction, and notes by Edmund Hill. Edited by John A. Rotelle. The Works of St. Augustine: A Translation for the 21st Century, vol. 1, no. 5. Brooklyn, N.Y.: New City Press, 1996. First published 1991.

———. *In Ioannis Evangelium*. In PL 35:1579-1976. ET: St. Augustine. *Tractates on the Gospel of John*. Translated by John W. Rettig. Fathers of the Church 78, 79, 88, 90, 92. Washington, D.C.: The Catholic University of America Press, 1988-95.

Bonaventure. *Quaestiones disputatae de perfectione evangelica*. In *Opera omnia*. Vol. 5, *Opuscula varia theologica*, 117-98. Ad Claras Aquas (Quaracchi): Ex Typographia Collegii S. Bonaventurae, 1891.

Cabasilas, Nicolas. *Explication de la divine liturgie*. Translated by S. Salaville. SChr 4. Paris: Cerf / Lyon: L'Abeille, 1967. ET: *A Commentary on the Divine Liturgy*. Translated by J. M. Hussey and P. A. McNulty. London: SPCK, 1960.

Cyril of Alexandria. *In Joannis Evangelium*. In PG 73: 9-1056 and 74: 9-756. ET: Cyril of Alexandria. *Commentary on the Gospel according to S. John*. 2 vols. Oxford: James Parker & Co., 1874.

———. *Thesaurus de sancta et consubstantiali Trinitate*. In PG 75: 9-656.

Cyril of Jerusalem. *Catechesis 19, Mystagogica 1*. In PG 33:1065-76. ET: *Catechetical Lecture 19, First Lecture on the Mysteries*. NPNF. Second Series, 7:144-46.

———. *Catechesis 23, Mystagogica 5*. In PG 33:1109-28. ET: *Catechetical Lecture 23, Fifth Lecture on the Mysteries*. NPNF. Second Series, 7:153-57.

Ephraem of Syria. "Sermo IV In hebdomadam sanctam," alternatively named, "Sermo quarto de passione." In *Sancti Ephraem Syri. Hymni et sermons*. Vol. 1. Edited by Thomas Joseph Lamy. Mechliniæ: H. Dessain, Summi Pontificis, S. Congregationis de Propaganda Fide et Archiepiscopatus Mechliniensis Typographus, 1882.

Evagrius of Pontus. *Les leçons d'un contemplatif: Le Traité de l'oraison d'Évagre le Pontique*. Ed. I. Hausherr. Paris: Beauchesne, 1960. ET: Evagrius of Pontus. *The Praktikos; Chapters on Prayer*. Translated by John Eudes Bamberger. Spencer, Mass.: Cistercian Publications, 1970.

Gregory of Nazianzus. *Lettres théologiques*. Edited by Paul Gallay with collaboration of Maurice Jourjon. SChr 208. Paris: Cerf, 1974. ET: *Faith Gives Fullness to Reasoning: The Five Theological Orations of Gregory Nazianzen*. Introduction and commentary by Frederick Norris. Translated by Lionel Wickham and Frederick Williams. Supplements to *Vigiliae christianae* 13. Leiden / New York: E. J. Brill, 1991.

Gregory of Nyssa. *Quod non sint tres dii*. In PG 45:115-36. ET: *On "Not Three Gods."* NPNF, Second Series, 5:331-36.

Hippolytus. *Contre les heresies*. In P. Nautin, ed. *Hippolyte: Contre les hérésies, fragment; Étude et édition critique*. Études et textes pour l'histoire du dogme de la Trinité 2, 231-65. Paris: Cerf, 1949.

———. *La Tradition apostolique d'après les anciennes versions*. Translated by Bernard Botte, 2d ed. SChr 11 bis. Paris: Cerf, 1968. ET: *The Apostolic Tradition: A Commentary*, by Paul F. Bradshaw, Maxwell E. Johnson, and

L. Edward Phillips. Edited by Harold W. Attridge. Hermeneia. Minneapolis, Minn.: Fortress, 2002.

Hugh of St. Victor. *De sacramentis christianae fidei*. In PL 176:173–613.

Irenaeus of Lyon. *Adversus haereses*, 5 books. In *Sancti Irenaei episcopi Lugdunensis libros quinque adversus haereses*. Edited by W. W. Harvey. Cambridge: Cambridge University Press, 1857, and *Contre les herésies*. Edited and translated by Adelin Rousseau, Louis Doutreleau, Bertrand Hemmerdinger, and Charles Mercier. SChr 100, 152–53, 210–11, 263–64, 293–94. Paris: Cerf, 1965–82. ET: *St. Irenaeus of Lyons: Against the Heresies*. Translated and annotated by Dominic J. Unger with further revisions by John J. Dillon and, for Book 3, by M. C. Steenburg. Ancient Christian Writers. Vols. 55, 64, 65. New York: Paulist, 1992–2012.

———. *Ostensio apostolicae praedicationis*. Patrologia orientalis 12:756–801. *Démonstration de la prédication apostolique*. Translated by L. M. Froidevaux. SChr 62 Paris: Cerf, 1959; new version: Translated by Adelin Rousseau. SChr 406. Paris: Cerf, 1995. ET: *Proof of the Apostolic Preaching*. Translated by Joseph P. Smith. Ancient Christian Writers 16. Westminster, Md.: Newman Press / London: Longmans, Green and Co., 1952; and St. Irenaeus of Lyons. *On the Apostolic Preaching*. Translation and introduction by John Behr. Crestwood, N.Y.: St. Vladimir's Seminary Press, 1997.

Isidore of Seville. *De ecclesiasticis officiis*. In PL 83:737–826.

———. *Etymologiarum*. In PL 82:28–728; also *In Isidori Hispalensis episcopi Etymologiarvm sive Originvnm libri 20, recognovit breviqve adnotatione critica instrvxit W. M. Lindsay*. 2 vols. Scriptorum classicorum bibliotheca Oxoniensis. Oxford: Clarendon Press, 1911.

Jerome. *Commentariorum in Michæam prophetam*. In PL 25:1151–1230.

John Chrysostom. *De sancta Pentecoste: Homilia 1*. In PG 50:453–62.

Justin. *Apologie pour les chrétiens*. Edited and translated by Charles Munier. SChr 507. Paris: Cerf, 2006. ET: *St. Justin Martyr. The First and Second Apologies*, Translated by Leslie William Bernard. Ancient Christian Writers 56. New York: Paulist, 1967.

Maximus the Confessor. *Opuscula theologica et polemica ad Marinum*. In PG 91:9–216.

———. *Expositio orationis Dominicae*. In PG 90:871–910. ET: *Commentary on the 'Our Father'*. In *Maximus the Confessor: Selected Writings*. Translated by George C. Berthold. Classics of Western Spirituality. New York: Paulist, 1985.

Passio sanctarum Perpetuae et Felicitatis. For example, the edition of Cornelius Ioannes Maria Ioseph van Beek, Nijmegen: Dekker & Van De Vegt, 1936. ET: Thomas J. Heffernan. *The Passion of Perpetua and Felicity*. New York: Oxford University Press, 2012.

Peter Damien. *Dominus vobiscum*. In PL 145:231–52. Partial French translation in *La Maison-Dieu*, 21 (1950/51): 174–81. ET: *The Book of "The Lord Be*

With You," St. Peter Damien: Selected Writings on the Spiritual Life. Translated by Patricia McNulty, 53–81. New York: Harper and Brothers, 1961.

Peter Lombard. *Magistri Petri Lombardi sententiae in IV libris distinctae.* 3d ed. Vol. 2, bks: 3–4. Spicilegium Bonaventurianum 5. Rome: Grattaferrata, 1981; also PL 192:519–964.

Richard of St. Victor. *De Trinitate 4.* In PL 196:892–992; also *La Trinité.* Translated by Gaston Salet. SChr 63, Série des textes monastiques d'Occident 3. Paris: Cerf, 1959.

Symeon the New Theologian. "Discours 6." In *Catéchèses 6–22.* Edited by Basile Krivochéine. Translated by Joseph Paramelle. SChr 104. Paris: Cerf, 1964. ET: "Discourse 6." In *Symeon the New Theologian, The Discourses.* Translated by C. J. de Catanzaro. Classics of Western Spirituality. New York: Paulist, 1980.

Theodore of Mopsuestia. *Homélie catéchétique 15, 1re sur la messe*; *Homélie catéchétique 16, 2e sur la messe.* In *Les homélies catéchétiques: Réproduction phototypique du ms. Mingana Syr. 561 (Selly Oak Colleges' Library, Birmingham).* Edited and translated by Raymond Tonneau and Robert Devreesse. Studi e testi 145. Città del Vaticano: Biblioteca Apostolica Vaticana, 1949. ET: *Commentary on the Lord's Prayer and on the Sacraments of Baptism and the Eucharist.* Translated by A. Mingana. Woodbrooke Studies 6. Cambridge: Heffer, 1932. Reprint: Piscataway, N.J.: Gorgias Press, 2009.

Index of Biblical References

Genesis
1.2: 33
2.7: 34
3.5: 45
6.3: 34
12.1: 138

Numbers
11.25: 19

1 Samuel
10.5–6: 19

1 Kings
18.38: 170n18

Judith
16.14: 34, 105n5

Job
15.13: 105n5
27.3: 34
33.4: 34
34.14–15: 34

Psalms
2.7: 103, 104
33.6: 84, 105n5
104.28–30: 34
147.8: 105n5

Qoheleth (Ecclesiastes)
12.7: 34

Wisdom
1.7: 33, 96, 435, 257
7.22–23: 96n26
7.22–24: 96n26
9.11: 96n26
12.1: 33, 96n26

Isaiah
11.1ff.: 75–76
11.4: 105n5
32.15: 117
34.16: 105n5
40.3ff.: 84n2
44.3: 117
48.16: 19
58.6: 84n2
59.21: 117
65.17: 43n10
66.22: 43n10

Jerome
31.31ff.: 117

Ezekiel
3.12: 19
36.25ff.: 117
36.26–27: 19
37.1–14: 34
39.29: 19

Joel
2.28ff.: 117
3.1: 20, 119
3.1ff.: 117

Matthew
3.3: 84n2
10.18–20: 108t
10.19–20: 20
10.28: 62
10.40: 106n6
12.28: 118
16.18: 189
17.25–26: 41
19.28: 48
19.29: 118
28.18–20: 134, 227

Mark
1.3: 84n2
1.10–11: 103
3.13: 227
10.17: 118
13.10–12: 108t

Luke
32-35: 103
1. 35: 119, 169, 188n74
1.55: 118n7
3.4ff.: 84n2
3.22: 103
6.19: 62
9.48: 106n6
10.16: 106n6
10.21: 39
10.25: 118
18.18: 118
21.12–15: 108t
24.25-27: 250
24.33: 92
24.48–49: 139
24.49: 106n6, 118n7, 188n77, 133n2

John
1.11: 109t
1.12: 102
1.13: 104
1.16: 185
1.17: 109t
1.29-34: 105
1.33: 165n9
2.22: 80n10
3.3–8: 118
3.5: 20
3.8: 134
3.13–16: 221
3.16: 109t, 249
3.16–17: 106n6
3.19: 109t
3.21: 139
3.22: 109t
3.34: 106n6, 188n77
4.10: 63n22, 105
4.10–15: 109t
4. 12–13: 38n34
4.16: 38n4
4.23–24: 88
4.24: 56

285

John (*cont.*)
4.25: 109t
5.31ff.: 109t
5.33: 109t
5.37: 106n6
5.43: 109t
6: 172n21
6.32–35: 109t
6.57: 106n6
7.7: 109t
7.14ff.: 109t
7.16: 106n6
7.17: 109t
7.37–39: 105
7.39: 188n77
8.13ff.: 109t
8.20: 109t
8.26: 109t
8.28: 109t
8.36: 41
8.38: 109t
8.42: 106n6
9.41: 109t
10.36: 106n6, 232
10.38: 60
12.16: 80n10
12.28: 109t
12.31: 45n13
12.32: 230
12.48: 109t
12.49: 109t
13.7: 80n10
13.33: 109t
14: 92
14.6: 109t
14.10: 109t
14.16: 20, 38n4, 57, 106n6, 107, 109t
14.16ff.: 105, 109t
14.17: 109t
14.19: 109t
14.20: 109t
14.23: 38n4

14.26: 20, 57, 62, 79, 106n6, 109t, 250n16
14.26ff.: 105
15.22: 109t
15.26: 61, 62, 79, 106n6, 109t, 188n7, 211, 247
15.26–27: 79, 138
16: 92
16.7: 106n6, 109t, 188n77
16.7ff.: 105
16.7–11: 80
16.8: 109t
16.8–11: 250n16
16.11: 45n13
16.12ff.: 80n10
16.13: 20, 80, 109t, 136
16.13ff.: 109t
16.13–15: 79
16.14: 109t, 110
16.16ff.: 109t
16.25: 109t
16.28: 109t
17.1: 109t
17.4: 109t
17.18: 106n6
17.21: 60
17.26: 77
18.37: 109t
19.34: 105
20.19–23: 105
20.21: 106n6
20.22: 62
21.15–16: 189

Acts
1.4: 118n7, 126
1.4ff.: 188n7
1.4–5: 133n2

1.8: 139, 188n7
1.14: 93n17
1.15: 92, 93n16
2.1: 93n16, 93n17, 259
2.3: 93
2.17: 20, 119
2.29: 80
2.31: 118n7
2.33: 133n2, 188n77
2.38: 63n22
2.42: 94, 101
2.46: 93n17
2.47: 93n16
3.21: 43
3.25–26: 138n13
4.8: 44n11
4.13: 80
4.24: 93n17
4.27: 103
4.29: 80
4.31: 44n11, 80
5.12: 93n17
5.30–32: 188n77
8.1: 256
8.20: 63n22
10.38: 91, 103, 119
10.45: 63n22
11.16: 188n77
11.27: 81n10
13.1: 81n10
13.32–33: 104
14.3: 80
14.16: 138n13
14.22–23: 256
20.17: 256
15.25: 93n17
17.30: 138n13
18.25–26: 44n11
20.28: 135
26.6ff.: 133n2

Romans
1.4: 91, 104
2.29: 89n4
2.4: 138n13
5.1–11: 92
5.5: 77n4, 89n4, 117
6.3: 179n47
6.5–6: 24
6.9: 230
7.6: 84
8.1–30: 106
8.1: 108t
8.2: 84
8.5ff.: 84
8.9: 38n4, 62, 76, 87, 108t, 110
8.10: 108t
8.11: 38n4, 76, 116
8.12–13: 26
8.13: 84
8.14: 76, 84, 85
8.14ff.: 221n39
8.14–16: 60n19
8.14–17: 84, 102, 116
8.15: 27, 40, 89, 95, 191
8.15–17: 67
8.16: 20, 57
8.18–25: 24, 34
8.18–30: 141
8.19ff.: 43
8.21: 116n4
8.21–23: 43
8.23: 116
8.26: 21, 57, 89
8.26ff.: 221
8.26–27: 89
8.27: 57
8.28–30: 220
8.32: 249
8.38–39: 78
8.39: 108t
11.1: 38n4

11.17: 86n8
12.4–8: 216n29
12.5: 108t
12.6: 81n10
13.8–10: 155n19
13.8–12: 42
14.17: 108t
15.6: 93n17
15.13: 117, 119
15.16: 89, 108t, 182, 232
15.19: 119

1 Corinthians
1.2: 108t
1.9: 94n19
1.30: 108t
2.1-5: 119
2.13: 76
3.10ff.: 250
3.13: 30
3.16: 38n4
3.16–17: 87
3.17: 91
6.9–10, 118
6.11: 108t
6.19: 38n4, 87
10.16: 94n19
11.4–5: 81n10
11.20: 81n10
11.27: 179
11.29: 179
12.3: 40, 108t, 110, 140: 221, 250
12.4ff.: 93
12.4–7: 216, 255
12.7: 47, 96
12.8–11, 216n29
12.9: 80
12.10: 29, 81n12, 119
12.12–13: 47, 101, 106
12.13: 20, 76, 108t, 110, 179n97, 181, 221, 250
12.27–30: 216n29
12.28: 81n10
13: 50
13.4–7: 155n19
14.1–33: 29
14.26–40: 81n10
15.24–25: 45n13
15.28: 116n4
15.44–49: 43
15.45: 61, 91, 104, 110, 116
15.50: 118

2 Corinthians
1.3–7: 86n8
1.22: 24, 61, 89n4
2.17: 108t
3.7ff.: 44n11
3.12ff.: 44n11
3.14–17: 141
3.14–18: 105
3.16–18: 79
3.17: 41, 61, 84, 107, 136, 155, 188n78
5.5: 42, 61
5.21: 108t
6.16: 87
12.12–13: 47
12.13: 181
13.13: 47, 51, 57, 76, 94
13.14: 221n39

Galatians
2.9: 94
2.17: 108t
3.2: 105
3.5: 105
3.14: 105, 118n7, 133n2
3.14–18: 118n7
3.26–29: 118n7
3.27: 108t
4.4: 106n6
4.4–6: 76, 111, 221n39
4.4–7: 102
4.5: 106n6
4.6: 27, 40, 62, 67, 89, 95, 110, 116, 188n78, 191
4.6ff.: 60n19
5: 84
5.2: 118
5.13: 86
5.14: 155n19
5.16: 45, 85
5.16ff.: 84
5.18: 84, 86, 155
5.22: 21, 85, 86n8
5.22–23: 151n14
5.25: 45, 85

Ephesians
1.3–14: 220
1.3–23: 141
1.13: 105, 118n7
1.13ff.: 133n2
1.13–14: 118
1.14: 61
1.17–18: 118
1.21–22: 45n13
2.15ff.: 179n47
2.19–22: 60n19, 87
2.20: 81n12
2.21: 108t
2.21–22: 179n47
2.22: 108t
3.5: 79, 81n12
3.16: 119
3.17: 89n4
4.4: 47, 110
4.4–6: 233
4.6: 40
4.7: 216n29
4.11: 81n10
4.11–12: 216n29
4.12: 179n47, 217, 263
4.13: 101
4.15–16: 179n47
4.16: 158n25, 232
4.25: 95
4.30: 43, 57
5.5: 118
5.18: 108t
5.19: 89
6.12: 45
6.17: 105
6.18: 89

Philippians
1.5: 94n19
1.19: 44n11, 62, 188nn77–78
1.19–20: 44n11
2.1: 76, 94n19
3.1: 108t
3.3: 88
3.10: 94n19
4.7: 108t

Colossians
1.8: 108t
1.18: 105
2.10: 45n13, 108t
2.15: 45n13
2.19, 179n47
3.16: 89

1 Thessalonians
1.5: 105, 119, 256
1.5–6: 86n8
2.12: 118

1 Thessalonians	Philemon	4.10: 216n29	Jude
4.7–8: 84n3	6: 94n19	4.13–14: 116	3: 136
4.8: 63n22, 84, 105	Hebrews	2 Peter	Revelation
5.19–20: 81n10	1.5–6: 104	3.9: 138n13	1.2–3: 250n16
5.19–22: 29	1.6: 104	3.13: 43n10	1.5: 105
5.23: 89n3	4.12: 105		1.8: 136
	6.4: 63n22	1 John	4.8–6.17: 105
2 Thessalonians	7.3: 104	1.3: 94	5.6: 105
2.13: 84n3, 108t	10.19–20: 156	1.6: 94	5.9: 105
	10.25: 78n7	1.7: 94	19.10: 79, 140n19, 250n16
1 Timothy	13.8: 137	1.14: 103	
6.14: 134n4		2.1: 57	
	James	2.20: 141, 234	21.1: 43n10
2 Timothy	2.5: 118	2.27: 141, 234	21.6: 105, 136
1.7: 119		3.1–3: 102	22.1: 105
1.14: 81	1 Peter	4.1–3: 105	22.13: 136
	1.3: 104	4.1–13: 250n16	22.17: 89
Titus	1.10–12: 249, 250n16	4.3: 79	22.20: 89
2.13: 134n4	1.11–12: 79	4.8: 56	
3.4: 263	1.12: 105	4.9: 106n6	
3.5–6: 176	3.20: 138n13	4.12–13: 38n4	
3.5–7: 118	3.22: 45n13	4.16: 38n4	
		5.6: 136, 139	

General Index

Abelard, Peter, 174
Abraham: promise of Holy Spirit, 118n7; start of public revelation, 132, 138
Acerbi, Antonio, 48n17, 226–27, 238nn30–31
Acts of the Apostles, 68, 79, 112
Adam, eschatological (Jesus Christ), 43, 104, 116
Afanassieff, Nicholas, 100n39
Albert the Great, St., 148n8, 174, 191, 192n87
Alexander of Hales, 148n8, 184, 192n87, 276
"Already" and "not-yet" theme, 24, 41, 45, 49, 106, 238, 239, 249
Ambrose, bishop of Milan, St., 61, 167–68, 213
Ambrosiaster, 34
Anaphora. *See* Eucharistic Prayer
Anselm, archbishop of Canterbury, St., 56, 58, 174, 175, 192n87, 209, 210
Anselm of Laon, 175
Anthropology: deficient, 6; non-materialistic, 28; "oriented to God" (Neher), 138; oriented to the transcendent, 39; pneumatological, 5, 157; pure, 159; transcendental (Rahner), 29, 114
Anthropomorphism (of the Trinity) and latent tri-theism, 59, 210
apologetics: Congar and, 3–4; motive for Christological model of Church, 215

Aristotelianism, 145
Aristotle, 149, 152, 185, 186n67
Asceticism, 26, 41–42, 68
Asting, Ragnar, 139
Athanasius, patriarch of Alexandria, St., 53, 169n16, 180n50
Aubert, Jean-Marie, 128
Auden, W. H.: *Christmas Oratorio*, 37
Augustine, bishop of Hippo, St.: baptism, 96n25; believing, 244; bishops and people, 100, 218–19, 258–59; Christ as head of the Church, 183; Christian liberty from law, 41, 86; the Church as Trinitarian, 240; Eucharistic epiclesis, 167–68; fall of Rome, 142–43; *filioque*, 61–63, 212–13; forerunner of St. Thomas's gospel-based moral theology, 153; on God, 38–39; the Holy Spirit binds believers to Christ, 76–77; imagery for the Trinity, 56–57, 61, 209–10; Jesus' "servant form," 103; law of communion; 208; letter to Januarius, 161n28; mystery of the Spirit, 194n91; Ps 33:6 as revelation of the Spirit, 105n5; sacramental eating of Eucharist, 179; Trinitarian "persons," 57–58, 60, 209–10; unity of local Church, 256
Avicenna, 185n67

Baggio, Sebastiano, cardinal, 235n23
Banawiratma, Johannes Baptista, 206n10
Bandinelli, Robert, 175n31

289

Baptism: into Christ, 108t; effective for remission of sins, 117; entry into divine life, 73, 84, 105; epiclesis and, 168, 181n51; Hugh of St. Victor on, 183; of infants, 96, 184; institution by Jesus Christ, 134n5, 250; instrumental cause of gift of the Spirit, 106; of Jesus, 53, 103, 104–5, 169, 221; ministries based upon, 255n31; in same Spirit to form a single body, 108t, 221; St. Thomas, 176n36, 180; Trinitarian character of, 55
Barth, Karl, 64, 65
Basil, bishop of Caesarea, St., 33–34, 53, 95, 168, 206n7
Baumstark, Anton, 181n51
Beatitudes: St. Thomas on, 128, 145, 150–52
Bellarmine, Robert, St., 253
Benedict XIV, pope, 210
Berengarius of Tours, 171–72
Berger, Peter, 223
Bergson, Henri, 138, 159
Bérulle, Pierre de, 120n13
Billot, Louis, cardinal, 228
Bloch, Ernst, 138–39
Blondel, Maurice, 114, 137n11
Bobrinskoy, Boris, 95n23, 100n39, 258n39
Boethius, 58
Boff, Leonardo, 228, 233, 258n39
Bohr, Niels, 213
Bolotov, Vasilii Vasilevich, 66n26
Bonaventure, St.: Church as Body of Christ, united by the Holy Spirit, 184, 189n79, 191; imagery for Trinity, 56, 210; interpreting history, 141
Bonhoeffer, Dietrich: costly grace, 159; freedom through discipline, 26, 84
Boniface IX, pope, 195n92
Borne, Etienne, 115n2
Bosc, Jean, 113, 164n6, 195n94
Bossuet, Jacques-Bénigne, 69, 143
Bouyer, Louis: imagery for the Trinity, 56; infallibility, 98–99; pneumatology, 88, 206n10, 246n7
Bulgakov, Serge, 56

Cabasilas, Nicholas, 168n2, 170
Callistus III, pope, 195n92
Cantor, Georg, 55
Capernaism, 172n21
Cappadocians, 181
Cardijn, Joseph Leo, cardinal, 81
Celestine I, pope, 54
Cerfaux, Lucien, 85, 107n7
Cerinthus, 53
Ceres (Roman goddess), 44
Changeability: suffering of God, 32
Character: development of, 21, 38n3; sacramental, 177, 216, 231, 252
Charismatic Renewal, 4, 17, 24, 25, 27, 79, 81, 85, 89, 113, 207–8, 220, 255, 263
Chavasse, Antoine, 177
Chenu, Marie-Dominique, 72
Chevallier, Max-Alain, 79n8, 206n7
Christology, 4, 32, 88, 101, 129, 183, 195n94, 209, 219, 241, 242, 254, 264; heresies related to, 53; pneumatological, 5, 47n16, 91–92, 1032-13, 206, 221
Christomonism, 6–7, 8, 9, 65, 91, 100, 112, 126, 128–30, 162–63, 164, 194, 202n3, 227, 232, 234, 254, 264
Chrysippus, 22
Church: Christological model, 199, 214–15, 219–20, 251–54, 264; communion, 5, 6n10, 48, 51, 65, 90–100, 164, 201, 217, 219, 222, 226, 237, 241, 259; "continued incarnation" of Christ, 228; local, as subject, 50–51, 97–98, 201, 205, 217–18, 234–36, 240, 241, 256, 257–58; Mystical Body of Christ, 8, 47n16, 49, 95n22, 113, 178, 184, 185n67, 187, 189n80, 191, 195, 221, 250, 256, 261–62; paternal model of, 97, 199, 214–15, 218, 251, 259; "People of God, Body of Christ, Temple of the Holy Spirit," 87, 241; pneumatological/Trinitarian model, 97, 181, 199, 201, 205, 216–19, 221–24, 225, 251, 254, 259, 261, 264; pyramid, 50, 65, 91, 97, 215, 252; result of Trinitarian processions, 240; sacrament

290   General Index

of salvation, 191, 230, 239; *societas perfecta* (perfect society), 5, 90, 215, 226; 251; teaching and taught, 218–19, 258–59; wayfarer or pilgrim, 81, 238; whole Church, historical subject of Tradition, 80–81, 98; whole Church, subject of Liturgy, 99, 112–13, 219, 260
Cicero, 152
Clement of Rome, 80, 112
Cochran, David R., 236n25
Collegiality, 237, 262
Communion of saints, 78, 95, 146n3
Consecration (of the Eucharistic elements), 165–67, 173, 175–77, 181–82, 221
Congar, Yves: apologist, 3–4; contributions to pneumatology, 4–5; inclusive language, 12; influence of Orthodox thought, 6
"Contempt for the world," 26
Corbon, Jean, 262
Corecco, Eugenio, 161n29
Council of Constantinople: anniversary of, 198, 199, 208–9; on Holy Spirit, 53–54, 61–62, 136, 180, 192, 204–5. *See also* Creed of Nicaea-Constantinople.
Council of Ephesus: anniversary of, 198
Council of Florence, 66, 177, 213
Couturier, Paul, 56
Cracco, Giorgio, 46
Creed of Nicaea-Constantinople: "I believe," 53, 57, 146n3, 191–92, 244, 246; introduction of *filioque*, 212; normativity of, 66, 209, 214. *See also* Council of Constantinople
Creeds: literary form, 201, 243–44; pneumatologically deficient examples, 207; Trinitarian structure, 61, 117, 168, 201, 204, 245
Cullmann, Oscar, 89n6
Curé of Ars, 42
Cushing, Richard, cardinal, 160
Cyprian, bishop of Carthage, St., 208, 237, 240

Cyril, bishop of Alexandria, St., 62, 119, 168n14, 169n16, 180, 185
Cyril, bishop of Jerusalem, St., 79, 136, 168

Damasus, pope, St., 208
Delahaye, Karl, 260n44
Delebecque, Edouard, 93n16
Delhaye, Philippe, 128, 152n16
De Lubac, Henri, 30n16, 141n21, 171–72, 235n23
Descamps, Albert-L., bishop, 227n9
Diakonia, 100, 116, 216–17
Dieringer, Franz Xavier, 195n93
Dimitrios, patriarch, 66
Dionysus (Greek god), 25
Dodd, C. H., 94
Donoso Cortés, Juan, Marquis de Valdegamas, 214, 251
Dumoutet, Edouard, 175–76
Dunamis/eis (power/powers), 45; Holy Spirit as, 68, 111, 119
Dunn, J. G. D., 103n2
Dupanloup, Félix, bishop, 262
Dupont, Jacques, 25, 94

Eastern Christianity, 8, 37, 118, 164, 170, 196, 210, 212. *See also* Orthodox theology
Ebeling, Gerhard, 117, 223, 245
Ecclesiology: pneumatological, 5, 9, 91, 182, 197, 199, 205, 240. *See also* Church
Economy. *See* Salvation
Ecumenism, 1, 3, 35, 48–49, 81–82, 91, 205–6, 208–9, 222, 230, 236, 239–40, 255, 263
Elert, Werner: changeability, suffering in God, 32
Elijah, 170n18
Émery, Pierre-Yves, 29, 30n14, 34n18, 57
Enlightenment, 23, 30, 214n25
Ephraem of Syria, St., 180n50
Epiclesis: absence in Roman canon, 76; Eucharistic, 90, 167–68, 170; in ordinations, 261;

Epiclesis: (cont.)
    in post-Vatican II Eucharistic
        Prayers, 1, 3, 4, 181–82, 262; presupposed for all sacraments, 90, 112–13, 168, 261–62; Syrian, 62
Epiphanius, 62, 136
Eschatology. See History; Salvation
Eucharistic Prayer: consecration of the Eucharistic elements, 175; epiclesis in Post–Vatican II examples, 181–82, 262; Mozarabic, 256; Trinitarian structure, 40, 89n7, 168, 223–24, 250n17
Eugenikos, Marc, bishop of Ephesus, 213
Evagrius of Pontus, 118n9
Evdokomov, Paul, 100n39, 103

Fabrice (La chartreuse de Parma), 142
Fahey, Michael, 209n15
Faustus of Riez, 78
Fécamp, Jean de, 83
Felicity. See Perpetua and Felicity
Fesquet, Henri, 112n11
Filioque. See Trinity
Fink, Karl August, 46
Fleming, Richard, bishop of Lincoln, 143
"Flesh," 26, 41, 42, 45, 84, 85, 106, 151
Florovsky (Florowsky), George, 195n94
Fragoso, Antônio Batista, bishop of Crateus, 100
Frederic of Lorraine, 173
Freedom, Christian, 41–45, 84–86, 115, 146–48, 220. See also Holy Spirit
Friedrich, Gerhard, 133n2
Froidure, M., 152n16

Gandolph, 175n31
Gardeil, Ambroise, 72, 148n8
Garin, Etienne, 220n38
Gasser, Vincent, bishop, 253
Geiselmann, Johannes Rupert, 165, 170n18
Gertrude of Helfta, 60
Gilbert de la Porrée (of Poitiers), 183n58

Goldammer, Kurt, 167n11
Gore, Charles, 245–46
Grabmann, Martin, 185n67, 192n87
Grandfield, Patrick, 90n9
Grace of union, 186
Gratia capitis, 88, 91, 112, 174, 182–94
Gratia creata, 91, 184
Gratian, 172
Gregory VII, pope, 172n22
Gregory of Nazianzus, 119
Gregory of Nyssa, 62, 118n9, 168n14, 187n70, 211n20, 249n15
Grivec, František, 92n13
Grondijs, Lodewijk H., 170n17
Groppe, Elizabeth, 9n7, 16n1
Günther, Anton, 58

Hahn, Auguste, 244
Halleux, André de, 247
Hamer, Jerome, 94
Havet, J., 165n8, 166n10, 170n18
Haya-Prats, Gonzalo, 79
Hazim, Ignace, bishop of Lattakia, patriarch of Antioch, 111, 136
Hegel, Georg Wilhelm Friedrich, 30–31, 41, 110, 248
Hermann, Ingo, 107n7, 142n24
Hervé de Bourg-Dieu, 183n58
Hippolytus, 40n5, 44, 78, 181, 248–49, 255n31, 260
History: of Church, 20, 132, 237–38; definition of, 136, 138; divine plan for human, 50, 73, 75, 81, 127, 131–33, 136, 139–41, 186–87; dynamic force of the Spirit in, 30, 67, 111, 136; eschatological goal, 34, 40–43, 83–84, 114–20, 234, 264; God as subject of, 32, 64; Holy Spirit as promotor of divine plan, 139, 204–5, 222–23, 248; of humanity, 115, 132; intermingling of salvation history and secular history, 132–33, 135, 140; interpreting "signs of the times," 140–41, 144; Jesus Christ, Lord of, 140, 144; newness of, 80, 110, 136–37, 139, 220; quest for freedom/liberation 31, 41; of revelation 132, 138; sacramen-

tal time, 97, 135, 228; of salvation (*kairoi*) 32, 52, 63, 132, 137, 141–42, 168, 209n16, 242n39; of spirituality 21, 22; study of, 126–27; of the world (*chronos*) 24, 26, 31, 38, 105, 111, 132, 135, 142. *See also* Salvation

Hödl, Ludwig, 172n22

Hoffman, Fritz, 161n29

Holy Spirit: baptism and, 105–6; charisms: 29, 49–50, 80, 90, 96, 99, 112, 128, 144, 146, 156, 158n25, 163, 192, 205, 216–17, 226, 235, 237, 255, 256, 263; co-institutor of the Church, 92, 233, 250–54; communicator of divine life, 36–39, 60–61, 67, 73, 84, 94, 102, 120, 146, 169–70; consoler, 68; creator/giver of life, 119, 247–48; discernment of, 27, 29–30, 85, 127; eschatological/ultimate gift, 41, 60, 104, 116, 120, 201, 220, 223, 245; first fruits of promised salvation, 24, 61, 133, 238; first installment/pledge of promised fulfillment, 24, 61, 96–97, 106, 118, 133, 238; fruits of, 24, 84–85, 146–51; gifts of, 48, 49–51, 73, 85–86, 92, 98, 138, 145, 148–52, 200–201, 204, 216–17, 235, 239, 255–56; guarantor of sacramental efficacy and doctrinal orthodoxy, 80, 135, 204, 234; guide to truth, 20, 34, 79–80, 99, 111, 109t, 136, 139, 234; indwelling presence/presence as cause, 33; *kenōsis* of, 56–57, 134, 247, 249; "Lord", 119, 247–48; makes people children of God, 20, 34, 41, 43, 57, 60, 67, 73, 76, 84, 85, 102, 106, 114, 116, 134, 150, 220, 223; and non-Christian religions, 34–35; paraclete, 20, 33, 57, 79, 107, 111, 163, 188, 248; principle of catholicity, 96, 135–37, 234–35; promised one, 20, 60–61, 79–80, 92, 106, 117–18, 133, 190; and sanctifying effect of receiving the Eucharist, 166–67, 169, 173, 179; source of diversity of spiritual gifts, 47, 50–51, 235–36, 257; source of faithful renewal, 46, 80–81, 137, 139, 221, 233, 239; source of faithful transmission of Gospel in new circumstances, 79–81, 135–37, 220, 233; source of freedom, 41, 44, 73, 84, 106, 116, 136, 139, 141, 146–47, 155; source of interiority and communion, 38, 76–77, 92–97, 232–35, 257; spiritual aquifer, 199, 217, 262–63; testimonies about, 19–21, 75–82; universal presence, 22, 23, 48, 68; "vicar of Christ," 7, 65, 112, 126, 163; "who has spoken through the prophets," 79, 111, 117, 134, 139, 146n3, 249. *See also* Epiclesis

Honolulu Report (International Catholic/Methodist Commission) on Holy Spirit, 49n20

Hryniewicz, Waclaw, 100n39

Hugh of St. Victor, 183

Huguccio, 175n31

Humani Generis, 126n2

Humbert da Silva Candida, cardinal, 172–73

Ignatius, bishop of Antioch, St., 78, 112, 256

Innocent IV, pope, 143

Innocent XI, pope, 195n92

"In persona Christi" theme, 177, 200, 216, 231, 252–53

Irenaeus, bishop of Lyon, St.: Christ/Word and Spirit/Breath are God's two hands, 7, 25, 47, 106, 126, 220, 248; Church is where the Spirit is found, 78, 260; divinization through Son's gift of Holy Spirit, 180n50; faith is the Spirit in hearts of believers, 105; Holy Spirit anoints Jesus for his ministry, 169; Holy Spirit communicates Christ, 111; Holy Spirit perfects Christ's gifts, 60, 119; Holy Spirit renews both Church and faith, 20; Holy Spirit speaks through prophets, 79; prayer is Trinitarian, 40; Ps. *33:6* is a revelation of Holy Spirit, 105n5

Isidore of Seville: definition of an article of faith, 245; theology of the Eucharist, 165–66, 170n18, 174

Jansenism, 26, 42
Jeremias, Joachim, 40
Jesus: anointed by the Holy Spirit, 20, 67, 103–4, 169, 221; "forma servi/forma dei," 91, 103–6; instrumental causality of his divinized and divinizing humanity, 91, 116, 171n19, 179, 185–88, 190–92; as Melchizedek, 104; Sacred Heart devotion, 187; as Word, 47–48, 111, 134, 227, 231, 264
Joachim of Fiore, 30n16, 31, 110, 133, 156n22, 264
John XXIII, pope, St., 81, 126n2, 139, 229, 242
John Chrysostom, 176, 237
John of Damascus, 62, 180, 185, 187n70, 240
John of Ragusa, 143
John of St. Thomas, 150n13
John of the Cross, 77n4
Joseph of the Holy Spirit, 150n13
John Paul I, pope, 200
John Paul II, pope, St., 66, 198, 200, 205, 209
Journet, Charles, 195n93, 228
Jugie, Martin, 167n11, 170n18
Jüngel, Eberhard, 32
Jungmann, Joseph Andreas, 192n87
Justin Martyr, St., 79, 180n50

Kantor, Georg. *See* Cantor
Kasper, Walter, 63, 116n4, 136n8
Koch, L., 169n15
Koinōnia, 5, 93–95, 221
Komonchak, Joseph, 198
Kretschmar, George, 180n50
Küng, Hans: changeability, suffering in God, 32; Christianity as radical humanism, 37; Church's "un-wesen," 24; Jesus creates "conditions favorable" to appearance of Church, 228
Kwiran, Manfred, 230n14

Lachaga, José-Maria de, 235n23
Langton, Stephen, 83, 174
Lanne, Emmanuel, 234
Lauret, Bernard, 4n4
Lebbe, Frédéric-Vincent, 81
Lebreton, Jules, 107n7
Legrand, Hervé, 96n27, 97n30, 98n31, 99n35, 217n30, 218, 219n36, 253n24, 254, 256, 258
Leo the Great, pope, St., 61, 213
Leo XIII, pope, 252
Leo of Ohrid, 173
Lex orandi, lex credendi, 53–54
Lienhard, Marc, 178
Littledale, Arthur Vincent, 17n2
Liturgy of St. James, 180n50
Llamera, Marcelliano, 128
Lossky, Vladimir, 163, 188n76, 189, 193
Lottin, Odon, 148n8
Luther, Martin, 178
Lyonnet, Stanislas, 91, 152n16

Mabundu, 27
Macedonius, bishop of Constantinople, 54
Malebranche, Nicolas, 114
Manning, Henry Edward, cardinal, 204
Manzarene, M., 94
Marcel, Gabriel, 142
Marie of the Incarnation, 85
Maritain, Jacques, 21, 159
Marliangeas, Bernard-Dominique, 177n40, 252n23
Martin I, pope, St., 59
Maximus the Confessor, St., 59, 62, 77n4, 118n9, 213
Mayflower Puritans, 143
McDonnell, Killian, 27n8
Mediator Dei, 195n92, 253, 262
Merleau-Ponty, Maurice, 248
Messiaen, Olivier, 37
Middleton, Richard, 192n87
Ministeria Quaedam, 261
Ministries, 9, 49–51, 99–100, 205, 216–17, 250, 255–61, 262–63; Christ's determining of, 134–35; 227; definition of, 255

294   General Index

Moeller, Charles, 184n61, 196n95
Möhler, Johan Adam, 9, 91, 92, 195, 254, 259
Mokambi, 27
Moltmann, Jürgen: changeability, suffering in God, 32; eschatology, 223; Trinitarian theology, 64
Monda, A. M. D., 152n16
Montis, Vincent Puchol, bishop of Santander, 143
Motovilov, Nicholas, 43n9, 118n8
Mühlen, Heribert: changeability and suffering in God, 32; ecclesial status of non–Roman Catholic churches, 48n19, 239; economy of salvation, 63; pneumatology, 63n23, 164n6, 193-94, 196n95; pre-Trinitarian monotheism, 37, 205
Mury, Gilbert, 142
Mystici Corporis, 47n16, 95n22, 226, 238

Nautin, Pierre, 192n87
Neher, André, 138
Neil, Stephen, 207, 263
Nicetas of Remisiana, 78
Nicetas of Stethatos, 173
Niederwimmer, Kurt, 89n6
Nietszche, Friedrich, 25, 26, 115
Nissiotis, Nikos A., 6–8, 100n39, 157n24, 162–64

Ogorodnikov, Alexander, 222
Omnebene, 175n31
Oosterhuis, Huub, 207n13
Origen, 141
Orthodox theology, 1, 6, 8, 37, 61–62, 65-67, 81, 100, 162–64, 188–89, 199, 203–4, 207, 211, 212–14, 230, 247, 254, 262, 263. *See also* Eastern Christianity
Oulton, J. E. L., 192n87
Our Father: pneumatological reading of "thy Kingdom come," 118, 249n15

Parrēsia (assurance), 44, 80
Pascal, Blaise, 28n10, 30, 114–15
Patrick, St., 20, 76

Paul VI, pope, 49, 139–40, 200, 203, 209, 229, 242
Perichōrēsis, circumincession. *See* Trinity
Perpetua and Felicity, Sts., 44
Petau, Denis, 193
Peter Damien, St., 96
Peter Lombard, 175n31, 178, 183n58, 252
Peter of Poitiers, 175, 184
Peter of Tarantaise, 192n87
Peter the Cantor, 175, 184
Philip the Chancellor, 148n8
Philips, Gérard, 7, 88, 129, 184n59, 184n61, 196n96
Pilgram, Friedrich, 91, 97
Pitra, Jean Baptiste François, cardinal, 143
Pius II, pope, 195n92
Pius XI, pope, 42, 226n4
Pius XII, pope, 47n16, 126n2, 195n2, 226, 253, 262
Plioutch (Plyshch), Leonid, 55n3
Pneumatocentrism, 4, 100–101; no Breath without Word, 24, 101, 219–20, 264
Pneumatology, 131, 157, 165, 214, 251; since Vatican II, 205–6
Pneumatomachi, 53
Polyeutis, 35
Praepositinus, 175
Prayer: distinctly human, 39; and Holy Spirit, 20–21, 39–41, 68, 84, 88–89, 95, 221–22; Trinitarian shape of Eucharistic prayers, 40, 168; Trinitarian shape of personal prayer, 40, 57. *See also Epiclesis*
Pre-Trinitarian monotheism, 37, 97, 205, 251
Prophecy, 19, 75–76, 81–82, 111–12, 117, 127, 136, 140, 144, 204, 233, 249–50

Quas Primas, 238
Quasten, Johannes, 181n51

Rahner, Karl: bestowal of Spirit and life of grace, 88; ecclesial renewal, 46n15; economic Trinity

Rahner, Karl: (*cont.*)
    is immanent Trinity, 32, 64; God as
    Father, 246n8; God has a history
    in Jesus Christ, 32; local church,
    234, 256; "Persons" of the Trinity as
    "modes of subsistence," 59; tran-
    scendental anthropology, 29, 114
Ralph of Laon, 184n60
Reception, 98, 160, 208, 237
Refoulé, François, 4n4
Régamy, Pie-Raymond, 28
Reid, J. K. S., 162n2
Res contenta et significata vs. *res
    significata et non contenta*, 174,
    178, 239
Res tantum, 179
Richard of St. Victor, 56, 58, 21
Ricoeur, Paul, 36
Robin, Marthe, 43n9
Robinson, A. T., 37
Romero, Oscar, bishop of San Salva-
    dor, 45
Rouco-Varela, Antonio-Maria, 161n29
Rouse, Ruth, 207, 263
Roux, Hébert, 162n2
Rublev, André, 210–11

Saints, 24, 26–27, 43, 78, 84–85, 86, 117,
    137, 152, 217, 222, 238
Salaville, Sévérien, 167n11, 168n12,
    170n18
Salet, Gaston, 154n17
Salvation: Church as means of, 48,
    116, 190–91; Church as universal
    sacrament or sign of, 191, 230, 239;
    costly character of, 115; and divine
    self-communication, 32-33, 63, 114,
    247–48; human well-being and,
    83–86, 114–20; joint missions of
    Word and Spirit in the economy
    (history) of, 32, 61, 63-64, 92, 102,
    106–13, 136, 170, 220, 228; Orthodox
    view of its unfolding, 163, 190; and
    unity of Mystical Body, 256
Samonas, Melkite bishop of Gaza,
    170n17
Sartori, Luigi, 258n39

Saturn (Roman deity), 44
Schauf, Heribert, 193
Scheeben, Matthias Joseph, 193
Schelling, Friedrich Wilhelm Joseph,
    110
Schillebeeckx, Edward, 252n22
Schlier, Heinrich, 41, 44n11, 45n13
Schlink, Edmund, 54
Schmemann, Alexander, 6
Schniewind, Julius, 133n2
Seesemann, Heinrich, 6
Seneca, 22
Sequela Christi, 26, 147, 156
Seraphim of Sarov, 43n9, 118n8
Shamanism, 22
Sicard of Cremona, 175n31
Simon, Master, 175n31, 177
Sobornost, 81, 164, 262
Soehngen, Gottlieb, 152n16
Spiritual experiences: and human
    fulfillment, 38, 73; openness to the
    transcendent, 38, 73; and psycholo-
    gy, 22, 27–30, 39, 88
Stoicism, 22, 52, 145
Superman (Nietzsche), 26, 115
Symeon the New Theologian, 83, 118n8

Tarasius, Patriarch, 62
Teilhard de Chardin, Pierre, 38
Tertullian (Holy Spirit as "Vicar of
    Christ"), 7, 112, 126, 164
Theodore of Mopsuestia, 170–71
Theologal, 68, 128, 185
Theresa of Jesus (of Avila), St., 220
Theresa of the Child Jesus (of Lisieux),
    77n4
Thielicke, Helmut, 117n5, 245
Therrien, Gérard, 29n12
Thomas Aquinas, St.: appropriation
    of communion to Holy Spirit,
    192–93; beatitudes related to
    virtues and gifts of Holy Spirit,
    150–52; Christological model of
    the Church, 216; the Church as the
    Body of Christ, 185, 192; Church law,
    160–61; *cogitatio*, 36; the Eucharist,
    178–80; gifts of Holy Spirit and the

virtues, 85, 148–49, 150; grace, 88; Holy Spirit and Baptism, 176n36; Holy Spirit and communion in the Church, 47n16; images of the Trinity, 56, 209–10; *imitatio Christi/sequela Christi*, 146, 156; instrumental causality of Christ's holy humanity, 185–88; moral action, 127–28, 145–161; New Law and Christian liberty, 41, 155–56, 159–60; "Persons" of the Trinity, 58; pneumatological anthropology, 157, 159; priest acts as Christ, 177, 216, 252; sacraments, 252; salvation through Son and Spirit, 106; structure of the Creed, 245; words of institution, 175–76; unity of Mystical Body, 256

Tolstoy, Leo, 55

Trinity: appropriation to Holy Spirit of communication of divine life, 87, 146, 149, 157, 167, 185, 185n67, 190, 192–93; *filioque* controversy, 61–67, 163–64, 187–88, 194, 188–200, 204, 211–14, 263–64; imagery for, 28, 55–56, 209, 210; immanent Trinity revealed by economy of salvation, 32–33, 63–65, 114, 171, 246; *perichōrēsis*, circumincession, 60, 107n7, 211; "Persons" of Trinity, 54, 56–60, 63, 66–67, 110, 210; relationship between processions and missions, 32, 63–64; simultaneity of processions, 66–67, 210–11

Tromp, Sebastian, 92n13, 192n87, 95n92

Tschipke, Theophil, 185n64, 187n70

Tyrrell, George, 54, 258

Urban II, pope, 155
Urs von Balthasar, Hans, 82, 111, 133, 136
Useros Carretero, M., 154n18, 161n29, 185n67

Vajta, Vilmos, 162n2
Vandenbroucke, François, 148n8
Van Vliet, Cornelius, 126

Varillon, François, 32
Vatican II: Christocentric character, 226–32; Church as missionary, 227; ecclesiology of communion, 48, 50, 91, 226, 226, 228, 241; ecumenism, 48, 239; historical sense and awareness of eschatology, 233–24, 238; imperfect implementation of communion model of Church, 48, 205, 252, 254; local church, 218, 234–36, 256; ministries, 205, 216, 255–61; non-Catholic observers on, 6, 162–63, 203; non-Christian religions, 36; pneumatological ecclesiology, 113, 129, 196, 200–201, 205, 232–40, 242, 255–61; pneumatology, 48, 113, 196, 203, 233; post-conciliar Eucharistic Prayers, 181, 262; Trinitarian vision of Church, 87, 181, 225, 226, 240–42, 254, 262; Trinitarian vision of God, 205

Vauthier, E., 191n85
Vischer, W., 162n2
Vogel, Cyrille, 252n22
Volk, Hermann, cardinal, 169n15
Vonier, Anscar, 89
Von Schulte, Johann-Friedrich, 252n22

Walf, Kurt, 90n9
Waterloo, Battle of, 142
Weber, Hans Emil, 195n94
Weil, Simone, 24
Westphal, Gaston, 162n2, 203n3
William of Auxerre, 184
William of Champeaux, 175
William of St. Thierry, 77
Words of Institution, 176, 177. *See also* Consecration
World Council of Churches, 49n20, 66

Yves of Chartres, 172, 175

Zanetti, Pedro Serra, 93n16
Zapelena, Timiteo, 92n13
Zeon, 170
Zizioulas, John D., 8, 222n45

Spirit of God: Short Writings on the Holy Spirit was designed in Meta, and composed by Kachergis Book Design of Pittsboro, North Carolina. It was printed on 60-pound House Natural Smooth and bound by Sheridan Books of Chelsea, Michigan.

www.ingramcontent.com/pod-product-compliance
Lightning Source LLC
Chambersburg PA
CBHW020316010526
44107CB00054B/1859